Clouds

EAST KNOYLE, WILTS.

PARTICULARS

OF AN EXCEEDINGLY VALUABLE, HIGHLY IMPORTANT, AND WELL UNDULATED

Freehold Residential Investment

AND

SPORTING DOMAIN;

TOGETHER WITH A

WELL-TIMBERED PARK, known as "CLOUDS,"

Studded with Stately Elms, Wide-spreading Beeches, Oaks, Scotch Firs, and other fine Ornamental Forest Trees and Evergreens, affording a most

CHARMING SITE FOR A MANSION

On the remains of the present Residence.

Most desirably situate in the PARISHES of EAST KNOYLE, CHICKLADE, and PERTWOOD, on the North-east confines of the Vale of Blackmoor, and commanding, especially from Windmill and Haddon Hills, most Extensive and Panoramic Views of the Lovely and Richly-Timbered Scenery of that much-admired District, the Dorsetshire Hills being visible in the distance. Seven Miles from Warminster, Six from Shaftesbury, Seventeen from Salisbury, and Three from Semley Station on the South Western Railway, and thus within Three Hours' of London. The whole comprising, exclusive of the Commons, an Area of about

4,207 ACRES

OF HIGHLY PRODUCTIVE

Arable and Grass Lands, with Downs, Woods, and Plantations,

DIVIDED INTO

ELEVEN WELL-ARRANGED FARMS,

MOSTLY WITH

CAPITAL FARM HOUSES, HOMESTEADS, & COTTAGES.

On a portion of the Estate, on which there is excellent Clay, are

Capital Brick and Tile Works and Lime Kilns,

LIKEWISE

VALUABLE AND ALMOST EXCLUSIVE COMMON RIGHTS

Over Windmill Hill, Knoyle Hill, and other Commons, together containing about 125 Acres, and

THE ADVOWSON OF PERTWOOD.

The Hunting in this District is notoriously first-rate, the Meets of the Blackmoor Vale, East Dorset, and South Wilts Hounds being within easy reach. The Estate is bounded by the Properties of the MARCHIONESS of WESTMINSTER at Fonthill, MARQUIS of BATH, Lord HEYTESBURY, Sir HENRY HOARE, Bart., the Duchy of Cornwall, and ALFRED MORRISON, Esq.

The Property is well intersected by good hard Roads. The Woods and Plantations are well adapted for rearing a large Head of Pheasants. The Estate is well stocked with Partridges and Ground Game, and renowned for its covers, and the Shooting and Sporting, including the Coursing over the whole, is reserved from the occupations.

The upper portion of the estate abounds with Hares, and a considerable part being open Downs and Uplands, coursing may be enjoyed to any extent.

About Three-fifths of the Estate rests on the Chalk, and the remainder on the Green Sand and Kimmeridge Clay. From the Green Sand, on which Knoyle Village is placed, several inexhaustible springs of the finest water rise at an elevation sufficient to supply most of the Cottages by gravitation.

The entire Property produces a Rental, including the estimated value of the Woods and Plantations and Shooting in hand, of about

£4,624 PER ANNUM.

TO BE SOLD BY AUCTION, BY

MESSRS. DRIVER,

AT THE MART, TOKENHOUSE YARD, LOTHBURY, LONDON,

On WEDNESDAY, the 15th day of NOVEMBER, 1876,

At TWO O'CLOCK precisely, in ONE LOT, unless an acceptable Offer is previously made by Private Contract.

Mr. CRAMOND, *the Bailiff residing at East Knoyle, will show the Property.*

Printed Particulars, with Plans, may be obtained at the Grosvenor Arms Hotel, Shaftesbury; the Railway Hotel, Semley; the Bath Arms, Warminster; the White Hart, Salisbury; the Queen's, Manchester; the Great Northern, Leeds; Hen and Chickens, Birmingham; the Adelphi, Liverpool; of Mr. CRAMOND, East Knoyle; of Messrs. RAWLENCE & SQUAREY, Land Agents, Salisbury, and 22, Great George Street, Westminster; of Messrs. STILL & SON, Solicitors, 5, New Square, Lincoln's Inn, London; and of

Messrs. DRIVER, Surveyors, Land Agents, and Auctioneers, 4, Whitehall, London.

Clouds

The Biography of a Country House

Caroline Dakers

Yale University Press
New Haven and London 1993

Set in Perpetua by SX Composing Ltd., Essex
Printed and bound in Hong Kong through World Print Ltd.

Library of Congress Cataloging-in-Publication Data
Dakers, Caroline,
        Clouds : the biography of a country house by Caroline Dakers.
            p.   cm.
        Includes bibliographical references and index.
        ISBN 0–300–05776–8
        1. Clouds (East Knoyle, England) 2. Webb, Philip, 1831–
1915 —   Criticism and interpretation. 3. Wyndham family—Homes and haunts—
England—East Knoyle. 4. East Knoyle (England)—Buildings,
structures, etc. I. Webb, Philip, 1831–1915. II. Title.
        NA7333.E28D35   1993
        728.8'09423' 19—dc20   93–13472
                                                                                              CIP

A catalogue record for this book is available from the British Library.

Endpapers: Clouds hall carpet, designed and hand-knotted by Morris and Company, woven *c.*1886–9, sold by Dick Wyndham 1933, acquired by the Tennant family for Glen, sold 1986 at Sotheby's.

Frontispiece: Part of the original particulars of the Clouds estate, sold at auction by Messrs Driver, 1876.

In memory of my parents
John Albert Stewart Dakers 1909–1979
and Enid Nest Williams 1909–1989

The Clouds Family Tree

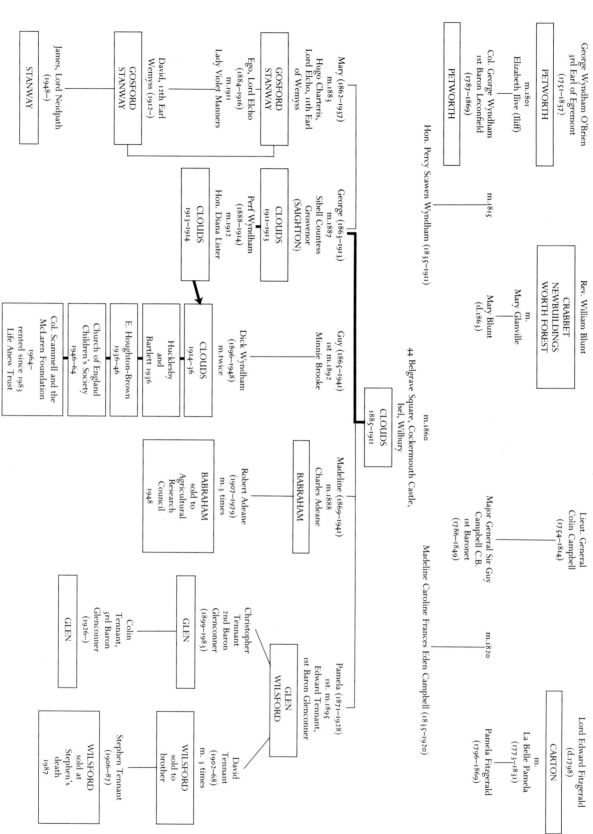

Contents

Photographic Acknowledgements

Black and White Photographic Credits

Mr James Adeane: 2, 38, 54, 55, 59, 127, 128.
Author: 3, 13, 37, 39, 56, 57, 61, 63, 73, 74, 75, 99, 101, 109, 113, 126, 129, 132, 136.
Birmingham Museums and Art Gallery: 22.
Miss Ada Blake: 26, 131, 133, 134.
Mr John Brandon-Jones: 42, 43, 45, 47, 49, 52, 76.
Building News: 19.
The Castle Howard Collection: 17.
Christie's: 41.
Country Life: 25, 28.
Courtauld Institute (Photographic Survey):   4, 5, 6, 7, 36, 68, 84, 91, 92, 103.
Mrs Angela Culme-Seymour: 119.
Lord Egremont (Petworth):   4, 5, 6, 7, 91, 92.
Mrs Hall: 40, 60, 62, 72, 93, 102.
Mrs Catherine Hesketh: 122.
The executors of the estate of the late Mr Geoffrey Houghton-Brown: 70, 100, 108, 124, 125.
Mrs Hyde: 1.
Mrs Patrick Leigh-Fermor: 118.
Duke of Leinster: 10.
Mrs Lomax: 123.
Museum of Fine Arts, Boston: 114.
Peter Nahum Ltd: 65.
National Portrait Gallery: 27.
Lord Neidpath (Stanway House):   8, 9, 11, 14, 15, 16, 18, 21, 24, 36, 44, 53, 58, 64, 66, 67, 69, 77, 79, 80, 83, 84, 85, 87, 94, 95, 103, 105, 117, 130, 136.
Private Collections: 12, 20, 23, 46, 48, 68, 81, 82, 86, 88, 96, 97, 106, 107.
RIBA Prints and Drawings Collection: 19, 29, 30, 31, 32, 33, 34, 35, 50, 51.
The Earl of Shaftesbury: 98.
Sotheby's: 78, 86.
Southampton City Arts: 104.
Mr David Tennant: 89, 90, 115.
Mr Henry Bingham Towner: 116, 121.
The Earl of Wemyss (Gosford House):   75, 99.
The Women's Institute Scrapbooks (East Knoyle):   71.
Ms Joan Wyndham: 110, 111, 112, 120.

Colour Photographic Credits

Mr Philip Adeane: Plate XXV.
Author: Plates XII-XV, XVII-VIII, XX-XXIII, XXV.
The British Library: Plate XVI.
The Castle Howard Collection: Plate III.
Christie's: Plates IV, XXVI.
The Fine Art Society, London: Plate II.
The Forbes Magazine Collection, New York: Plate VIII.
The Metropolitan Museum of Art, New York: Plate XIX.
The National Gallery of Ireland, Dublin: Plate I.
Lord Neidpath (Stanway House):   Plates IX-X.
Private Collections: Plates IV, VII, XI-XV, XVII-VIII.
RIBA Prints and Drawings Collection: Plates V-VI.
Sotheby's: Plate XI.

Introduction

When Percy and Madeline Wyndham bought part of the Seymour estate at East Knoyle near Salisbury, and commissioned Philip Webb to design their country house, they assumed the completed work, Clouds, would remain their family's rural seat for generation after generation; its unique collection of art treasures preserved intact to be enjoyed and added to by their descendants. However, in 1924, only thirteen years after Percy's death, Clouds House was let to strangers; in 1937 the estate was broken up, the parkland surrounding Clouds was divided into building plots, Clouds House was sold to a retired barrister from Wimbledon and reduced, with the help of the army and dynamite, to a more convenient size.

The story of Clouds is about the planning and creation of the major work of one of Britain's greatest architects, realised through the patronage of an unusual, aesthetically advanced aristocratic couple. It is also about the relationship between the Wyndhams and contemporary artists and designers, those whom they patronised and those who were guests at their country houses. By the end of the nineteenth century Clouds was famous for its weekend parties at which some of the most successful artists and writers hob-nobbed with beautiful society hostesses, members of the government and wealthy landowners and financiers.

There are few books which focus on an individual house, but Clouds is special. To Edward Burne-Jones, whose family were among the Wyndhams' most frequent guests, the name alone made it sound 'as if it were in Heaven'.[1] During its occupancy by Percy and Madeline Wyndham it was recognised to be 'the house of the age', unique not just in appearance and contents, 'a glorified Kate Greenaway affair, all blue and white inside, and all red and green outside',[2] but also for its atmosphere, the nature of the life lived in it. It set the style for a particular way of country house life which, over a century later, continues to be regarded as an ideal, 'perhaps one of the most agreeable ways of living that has ever been devised'.[3]

The civilised and leisured way of life of some of Percy and Madeline Wyndham's closest friends has been covered, some think 'done to death', by recent chroniclers of the Souls, the aesthetically minded aristocrats who formed a group within society in the decades before the First World War. Arthur Balfour was the acknowledged leader, three of the Wyndhams' children were active members of the group, consequently Clouds was used by the Souls for convivial weekend parties. Despite a number of books by and about the Souls, Nancy Ellenberger's unpublished doctoral thesis remains the only full scholarly treatment of their social activities and economic and political power and makes extensive use of primary sources.[4] Clouds, while in no way a history of the Souls or even of individual Souls, describes their milieu and, to some extent, reassesses their modest achievements.

Behind the façade of gracious living lurked failures, tensions and disasters: the story of Clouds has a tragic dimension. The Wyndhams' eldest son George, dubbed 'the handsomest man in England' and tipped to be a Tory Prime Minister, held cabinet

1 At Clouds House, 29 December 1908: the meet celebrates the coming-of-age of Perf, grandson of Percy and Madeline Wyndham, only son and heir of their eldest son George Wyndham.

xi

office for only five years before resigning and descending into depression and drink. He died of heart failure, aged only forty nine.

Five of Percy and Madeline's grandsons died in the First World War, including George's only son and heir. Clouds passed to his cousin Dick Wyndham, decorated in the war for bravery, but more interested in the world of 'champagne bohemia' than being a conventional English country gentleman. Social, political and economic forces had turned the palace of art into a vast white elephant; the surviving grandchildren could no longer justify the amount of privilege enjoyed by Percy and Madeline, however wonderful they were, 'because all privilege must be won at the expense of other people's deprivation. And what could justify that?'[5] Bit by bit Dick Wyndham disposed of the contents of Clouds, of single cottages, odd fields, finally the entire house and estate. He burnt quantities of letters from grateful house-guests, also documents relating to the building of the house. In August 1915, Emery Walker had written to Madeline Wyndham:

> In going through the papers of our friend the late Mr Philip Webb, to whom I am executor, with Mr S.C. Cockerell, we found a large number of documents relating to the building of Clouds – chiefly accounts, bills of quantities and such like documents. It occurred to us that these papers though of little interest perhaps now, might in the course of a hundred years or more acquire some value in connection with your beautiful house, and I write to ask, therefore, if you would care to have them . . . They might be put away in a corner of your muniment room, to rejoice the heart of an antiquary of the future.[6]

Emery Walker was right in thinking such papers might be of interest 'in the course of a hundred years or more'; unfortunately the contents of the muniment room at Clouds did not survive Dick Wyndham's residency.

This book is an attempt to bring together as much material as survives; to reveal Clouds through all its manifestations from social powerhouse to its most recent use as a refuge, retreat and treatment centre for society's waifs and strays; to show its significance within the history of architecture, art and design; its economic and political function within late nineteenth-century society; ending, eventually, in part-demolition and adaptation – some call it mutilation – to institutional use.

The design and building of Clouds has been described in some detail by W.R. Lethaby, the biographer of Webb;[7] also by John Brandon-Jones who holds the Webb archive. Their main aim has been to explain the peculiar genius of Webb through the creation of his most ambitious commission. Many other architectural historians, including Mark Girouard, Jill Franklin, Roderick Gradidge and Mark Swenarton, refer to Webb's work at Clouds within the context of Victorian and Edwardian architectural history; the changing plans of country houses; the relationship between Webb and the Society for the Preservation of Ancient Buildings, Morris and Company, the Arts and Crafts movement and the beginnings of socialism.[8] A full biography of Webb and his work has recently been completed as a doctoral thesis by Sheila Kirk.[9]

However, the contents of Clouds and its significance as a centre for the patronage of art and design in late nineteenth century Britain have not been examined fully. Design historians consistently pay tribute to the radical taste of Percy and Madeline Wyndham, bringing together Webb, Morris and Company, fine eighteenth-century furniture, blue-and-white china and the work of Edward Burne-Jones. The same few photographs of the interior are repeatedly published. Art historians and the biographers of Victorian artists (especially Burne-Jones, Watts, Sargent and Leighton) provide individual insights into the relationship between the Wyndhams and specific artists, and the acquisition of some of the paintings. The Etruscans, Valentine Prinsep, and the enamellist Alexander Fisher are only beginning to receive critical attention. By contrast, the historians of the landed aristocracy and rural economy – F.M.L. Thompson, Martin Wiener, Pamela Horn (in particular her studies of servants and labourers), David Cannadine, J.V. Beckett, L. and J.C.F. Stone – have provided the general background, the context in which to place Clouds.

Neither Percy nor Madeline Wyndham appears to have kept journals or written autobiographies. There are, however, memoirs of their family and friends which offer social and political insights on the period from their marriage in 1860 until the First World War: the detailed, occasionally incredible revelations of Percy's cousin and Madeline's lover Wilfrid Scawen Blunt; the memoirs of the Wyndhams' daughter Mary, Countess of Wemyss and their granddaughter Cynthia Asquith; the letters of their son George; the letters between Mary and her lifelong friend Balfour.[10] Recent biographies of Cynthia Asquith, George Wyndham, Wilfrid Scawen Blunt, Arthur Balfour and the Tennant family provide further material. Later Wyndhams who owned Clouds, in particular Dick Wyndham, have also been filled out by biographies of David and Stephen Tennant, Tom Driberg, the Sitwells, Wyndham Lewis and Edward Wadsworth.[11]

The buying and selling of country houses and their estates involves solicitors, estate agents and sometimes auction houses with the production of many documents, catalogues, surveys, conveyancing papers, maps. The difficulty of storing papers presents long-established professional firms with the decision of what to keep, what to destroy. Clouds has been relatively fortunate. The estate which Percy Wyndham purchased in 1876 was auctioned by Messrs Driver: the company is now Drivers Jonas Chartered Surveyors and Planning Consultants and their archive is preserved in a mighty vault off Pall Mall in London.

Dick Wyndham tried to sell the estate twice, in 1932 and again in 1936: the particulars from both attempts have survived in the archives of the estate agents Knight, Frank and Rutley, and Senior and Godwin. Further conveyancing papers have been kept by an Exeter firm of solicitors, originally Houlditch, Anstey and Thompson, now Anstey, Sargent and Probert. One of their partners is a trustee for the estate of the property developer who bought Clouds from Dick and sold it on to the Houghton-Brown family. The catalogue drawn up by Knight, Frank and Rutley of the contents sale is preserved in the National Art Library of the Victoria and Albert Museum along with relevant catalogues from Sotheby's. Records relating to Clouds's use from 1944 to 1964 as a home for unwanted babies are preserved by the Children's Society (originally the Church of England Incorporated Society for Providing Homes for Waifs and Strays). Without institutions like these keeping their records in perpetuity, and libraries dedicating space to such archives, reconstructing certain aspects of the past becomes mere speculation.

The survival of below stairs material relating to Clouds has been even more hit or miss. Indoor and outdoor staff, agricultural labourers, even tenant farmers rarely had time or inclination to create archive material or space to keep correspondence, diaries, memorabilia to be passed on to their children. Photography was a pastime for the better-off but fortunately Madeline Wyndham occasionally turned her camera towards the servants. Diary and letter writing was similarly a pleasure for those with leisure time for reflection and money to pay for illumination after dark; again Madeline herself preserved a few letters written to her by the housekeeper and butler.

2 Clouds House from the
south-west, c.1900. In an
album given by Madeline
Wyndham to her daughter
Madeline Adeane, October
1917.

There are descendants of some of the Wyndham employees, who still live in and around East Knoyle. They all have stories to tell of life at Clouds, anecdotes passed down to them by parents and grandparents. Some keep mementoes which trigger memories. The estate carpenter's granddaughter, for example, has a silver bracelet given by Madeline to her mother when a baby, for her christening present. It is evidence to her of the respect with which the Mallett family were held by their employees. She describes the visits to the Malletts' cottage by celebrities staying at Clouds; her grandmother was so affected by the family position and status that she would not allow her children to play with their neighbours in Milton village. The widow of the grandson of the head gardener, Harry Brown, occupies one of the cob cottages designed by George Wyndham and William Mallett as part of the first stage of improvements in Milton village. She carefully preserves photographs of the Wyndham family though she has no records of Harry Brown; she can explain the life of Milton village – where the blacksmith worked, the location of the shepherd's cottage – from her cottage garden.

Though these local residents have a generally rosy view of their former landlords, of a golden age in which everyone knew their place, and everyone was part of a caring, stable community, through their anecdotes they also reveal harsher experiences: difficult births, struggles to raise children, damp cottages and painful deaths. The Wyndhams are remembered most of all for their gifts, for the parties at Christmas and the treats for the village school, also for the stream of celebrities invited to Clouds House, 'all sorts of clever and notable people'[12] who appeared, to the delight of the community, at church on Sundays. Some played golf on the golf course Percy

Wyndham made on the downs. The Wyndhams put East Knoyle and its immediate environs 'on the map'.

Local pride and interest in the history of East Knoyle has encouraged the preservation of community records. A history of the local school has been published; a daughter of Canon Milford, vicar during the Wyndhams' residency, has published her memoirs; the present owner of Clouds House and of many neighbouring farms has written a history of East Knoyle parish; the Women's Institute has kept scrapbooks stuffed with invaluable material, including an interview with Harry Brown and reminiscences of the Wyndhams' parties.[13]

Though Clouds passed out of the Wyndhams' ownership in 1936, many descendants own substantial country estates. The family trees of Percy and Madeline's five children unsurprisingly include men and women who share many of their interests: the land, politics, the army, the arts. But late twentieth-century economic pressures have forced some of the landowners to actively farm their land; the art connoisseurs are also art dealers or auctioneers; the discriminating society hostesses are, by day, running strictly commercial interior design businesses. And friendships and marriages continue to be made within the same families – Wyndhams, Tennants, Charterises, Adeanes.

Many of the Wyndham descendants, both direct and indirect, are owners of artefacts once at Clouds; some have considerable collections of family letters and photographs; a few, including Madeline and Percy's eldest daughter Mary, Countess of Wemyss, have written family histories.[14] Their continuing interest in their family history ensures the preservation of archive material, but just one decision to expunge the past – Dick Wyndham's, for example – can result in that past literally going up in smoke.

Clouds House was threatened with demolition more than once but managed to survive and create for itself an independent existence as an institution. It is now a centre for the treatment of alcohol and drug dependency. It bustles with activity, the bedrooms are full, over fifty patients and almost as many staff sit down to lunch. The only items left in the house from the Wyndhams' collection are those which were too difficult to move, including Della Robbia plaques firmly cemented to the walls. In the drawing room, over 50 feet long, the furniture is institutional. But Webb's ornate plasterwork ceiling has survived intact and around the house there is still much evidence of his craftsmanship and good design: fireplaces, plasterwork on ceilings and dadoes, floor tiles, fitted cupboards, carved stone pillars and wooden banisters. A fountain trickles in the goldfish pond installed, incongruously, in the centre of the great hall, but Webb's delicate plaster wall decorations can still be seen and most of the carved stone pillars which soar up to the teak-framed lanterns.

Clouds House is still recognisable as the palace of art Webb designed for the Wyndhams. Some of the proposed building plots in the park were never developed. Though Madeline Wyndham's peacocks no longer strut along the terrace, the 'wide embrace' of England, Henry James's 'admirable picture', is still glimpsed through the drawing-room windows and from the balcony overlooking the park.

Acknowledgements

For lending me invaluable material, reading drafts of the text, and sharing their knowledge of the period, I owe especial thanks to John Brandon-Jones, Ingrid Channon, Mark Girouard, the late Geoffrey Houghton-Brown, Lord Neidpath, Pauline, Lady Rumbold, Francis Wyndham and Joan Wyndham. Many other direct descendants of Madeline and Percy Wyndham have also been most helpful: (in alphabetical order): James and Olinda Adeane, Philip Adeane, Rose Adeane, Penny Allen, Colin, Lord Glenconner, Christine Page-Blair, David Tennant and David, Earl of Wemyss. And I have received considerable assistance from Nick Barton, Director of the Life Anew Trust and all the staff at Clouds House; Miss Ada Blake, retired Matron of the Children's Society home at Clouds House; Max Egremont; Colonel Stephen Scammell; and Robert Baldock, my editor at Yale University Press.

The Twenty Seven Foundation generously provided a grant towards the collection of photographic material; the Central School of Art and Design (now Central Saint Martins College of Art and Design) provided financial assistance to enable me to carry out research into country house patronage at the Royal College of Art.

Many other members of the Wyndham family and their friends, individuals and companies now occupying houses once owned or visited by the Wyndhams, also the staff of libraries and art galleries, auction houses, estate agents and firms of solicitors, and scholars of the period have generously provided time, information and advice: Virginia, Countess of Airlie, Frances Alderson, Mark Amory, Miles d'Arcy-Irvine, Melanie Aspey (News International; the *Sunday Times* archive); Rosalind Bailey, D.W. Bamber (Governor) and the staff of HM Prison Service Hewell Grange, Nicola Beauman, Alan Bell (Rhodes House Library), Mark Bence-Jones, Barbara von Bethmann-Hollweg (née Wadsworth), Barbara Blackburne, Jennifer Booth (Tate), Kildare Bourke-Borrowes, Simon Blow, the staff of the British Library, the late Major Peter G. Brooke, Mary Burkett (Isel); T.H. Carter (secretary to the Duke of Westminster), Lt. Col. and Mrs A.V. Claydon, Michael Colborne (secretary to the Duke of Westminster), Angela Culme-Seymour; Richard, Earl of Dalkeith, Lord Eden, Julian Fane, Mrs Hilary FitzGerald (née Houghton-Brown), the Keeper of Manuscripts and staff of the Fitzwilliam Museum, Queenie Fletcher, Letitia Fowler, Christopher Frayling, Norma Fryer (Institute of Practitioners in Advertising); Conor Gallagher, Oliver Garnett, Charlotte Gere, Mrs James Giles, Mr Gowing (Knight, Frank and Rutley), Lord Gowrie, the staff of the Guildhall Library, A. Hague (Wortley Hall Labour's Home), Mary Hall, Mrs Hatfield (Eton College), Beth Humphries (Yale University Press), Mrs Hyde; The Institute of Practitioners in Advertising, Christopher Jackson (Children's Society), Elvira Kakebeeke-Mosselman, Kerry Kennedy, Sheila Kirk, Pat Knight (secretary to the Duke of Westminster), Anne Cecile Lansing, Joan Leigh-Fermor, the Duke of Leinster, Deidre Levi, Anne Lomax, Michael Luke; the Hon. Diana Makgill, Lord Margadale, Alison McCann (West Sussex records), Anthony McGreevy (A. Emms of Bath), Baron Jean Mayeur, James Mayor, Major Adrian Mertz,

Penelope Middleboe, John Myers, Lady Morrison, the staff of the National Art Library at the Victoria and Albert Museum, Alan Neil, Cathy Newberry, Rosemary Olivier, the Earl of Oxford and Asquith; Linda Parry (Victoria and Albert Museum), Mr and Mrs John Pinchas, Lord Plymouth, Jeremy and Anne Powell, Jean Pratt, Peter Quennell, John Rayner, Arthur Richards (Prudential), J.C.N. Robinson (Anstey, Sargent and Probert), Albert Russell (Scottish Record Office), Diana de Satchi, Mary Schoeser, Julian and Lavinia Seymour, Mr and Mrs Francis Sitwell, Mrs Angela Small (Royal Agricultural Society of England), Gertrude Stevenson (Weston), Serena Sutcliffe (Sotheby's wine department); Martin Taylor (Imperial War Museum), Patricia Templing (Old Wellingtonian Society), Lance Thirkell, Peter Thornton (Soane Museum), F.M.L. Thompson, Henry Bingham Towner, Francis Wheen, Mrs R. Woolstone, Elizabeth Wyndham, Mark Wyndham, Melissa Wyndham.

For help with picture research and for permission to reproduce pictures I would like to thank the late Lady Adeane; Joanna Banham and Julie Findlater of Leighton House; Martin Beisly and Jane Holland of Christie's; Hugh Brigstoke, Sara Colegrave, Nicola Gordon Duff, Alice Munro-Faure, Simon Taylor and Julia Yerrell of Sotheby's, Doreen Burke of the Metropolitan Museum of Art; Andrew Causey; Mrs Ralph Cobbold; the staff of the Courtauld Institute, Photographic Survey and Witt Library; the late Sir Brinsley Ford; Alastair Forsyth of Southampton City Arts; Jonathan Franklin of the National Portrait Gallery; Christopher Gibbs; Vivien Hamilton of the Burrell Collection; Adrian Le Harivel and Paula Wicks of the National Gallery of Ireland; Eeyan Hartley and Christopher Ridgeway of Castle Howard; Julian Hartnoll; the Hon. Simon Howard; Deborah Hunter, Julie Murphy and Julia Rolfe of the National Galleries of Scotland; Richard Jefferies and Hilary Morgan of the Watts Gallery; Margaret Kelly and Bonnie Kirschstein of the Forbes Magazine Collection; Elaine Kilmurray; Raymond Lister; Jeremy Maas; Edward Morris of the Walker Art Gallery; Peter Nahum; Christopher Newall; Richard Ormond; Simon Reynolds; Isla Robertson of the National Trust of Scotland; the staff of the Royal Institute of British Architects; Lord Shaftesbury; Kenneth Sharp of the South London Art Gallery; Peyton Skipwith of the Fine Art Society; Judy Weinland of the Museum of Fine Arts, Boston; Tim Wilcox of the Hove Museum and Art Gallery; Stephen Wildman of Birmingham Art Gallery.

For permission to publish correspondence between Dick Wyndham and Edward Marsh I would like to thank the Henry W. and Albert A. Berg Collection, the New York Public Library, Astor, Lenox and Tilden Foundations. For permission to publish material from the Wilfrid Scawen Blunt papers, I would like to thank the Syndics of the Fitzwilliam Museum, Cambridge.

Finally, I would like to thank Nigel Cross for reading many drafts of the text, and providing perspective and constructive criticism throughout the four years of research and writing.

1 Percy Wyndham and Madeline Campbell

On 24 May 1888 Madeline Wyndham began writing her daily letter to her eldest daughter Mary, Lady Elcho. It was early in the morning, the sun was streaming through the open window of the Spring Bedroom on the first floor of Clouds House. To the east she had a clear view of the gardens she had designed, the Rose Garden, the Magnolia Garden, the chalk-walled Spring Garden and beyond, the cherry-tree walk. To the south she could see the grassy slope of the park and in the distance the tree-covered hills of Fonthill.

> I must write you a line in bed as it is too early to get up but it is all so lovely . . . a sort of mad chorus going on outside – a thrush holding the audience at this moment! or rather drowning the rest of the singers, a *Cuckoo* & a perfect din of doves Tame & wild & the Peacocks screaming with Spring delight . . . Oh how I wish you were here to enjoy the spring with *us* – & see the little *Spring Garden*, walled *you never saw any thing like* the flowers in it *it is* a perfect place the 6 magnolia *trees covered with flowers* – perfect masses of tulips scarlet purple yellow with narcissus & all *kinds* of delicious blossoms – and the apple trees (cuckoo again! thrush never ceasing!) . . . *When will you see it?*

Madeline and Percy Wyndham had moved into Clouds House in September 1885. One of their earliest visitors was Henry James, who used the couple as a model for Mr and Mrs Gereth in *The Spoils of Poynton*. The Gereths spent their entire married life creating Poynton: 'the perfect accord and beautiful life together, twenty-six years of planning and seeking, a long, sunny harvest of taste and curiosity'.[1] Madeline and Percy spent the first half of their married life – twenty-five years – 'planning and seeking'. They were married in 1860 and began collecting paintings and furniture almost immediately. They bought the Clouds estate in 1876 and commissioned Philip Webb to design their 'house of the age' but it was not ready for occupation for another nine years. Clouds was, like Poynton, an ideal:

> there were places much grander and richer, but there was no such complete work of art, nothing that would appeal so to those who were really informed.[2]

Madeline Wyndham had considerable artistic talent and maintained close relationships with many of the artists and writers whom the couple patronised. Percy was a hot-tempered aristocrat, a traditional Conservative Member of Parliament, deeply in love with his wife, passionate about hunting, shooting and, later in life, golf. He provided the money for Clouds, some £200,000 to buy the estate and build the house. He also agreed to the wholly radical choice of Webb as architect. Webb was uncompromising in the standards of his professional practice, his designs were not particularly accessible, and he listened but rarely submitted to the views of his clients.

Yet he developed a close relationship with both the Wyndhams, respecting Percy's fairness and high standards and Madeline's aesthetic taste.

His clients' unconventional upbringing and family backgrounds undoubtedly provided the foundations for their unorthodox architectural taste; also their interest in contemporary art and design, which was uncommon among aristocratic families, the upper ten thousand. Percy and Madeline enjoyed being different from the majority of their peers, secure within their own exclusive circle which was defined by their perception of good taste.

Percy Scawen Wyndham was the youngest surviving son of Colonel George Wyndham of Petworth – created first Baron Leconfield in 1859 – and Mary, daughter of the Reverend William Blunt. He was born in 1835. From the age of two until his marriage to Madeline Campbell in 1860, his home was Petworth House. He grew up surrounded by priceless treasures amassed by his Wyndham and Percy ancestors. The wealth and the generosity of his grandfather, the third Earl of Egremont, were legendary; Petworth was a place of welcome and hospitality for the most noted artists and writers of the day.

The Wyndham fortune stemmed from land and came through a series of advantageous marriages. Charles Wyndham, Percy's great-grandfather, became the first very rich Wyndham when, in 1750, he inherited the earldom of Egremont, the barony of Cockermouth and part of the Percy estates in Sussex, Yorkshire and Cumberland. His inheritance descended through his mother, Catherine Seymour, sister to the Duke of Somerset – who was also Earl of Northumberland and Egremont. The Duke had no son and his property was divided after his death. A cousin inherited the ancestral Seymour estates and became the eighth Duke; his son-in-law inherited the Percy estates and the title Earl of Northumberland, elevated soon after to a dukedom. The third major beneficiary was his nephew Charles.[3]

With his new title of the second Earl of Egremont, Charles moved from his relatively modest seat at Orchard Wyndham in Somerset to Petworth, which had been in the Percy family since 1150. He used some of his fortune to lay out, with the assistance of Capability Brown, the park at Petworth; he also bought major paintings and antique sculptures, and employed Matthew Brettingham to design a gallery for his collection. In London he built himself a new house, also by Brettingham, at 94 Piccadilly. Charles Wyndham's son George succeeded to his father's title in 1763, aged only twelve; in 1774 he inherited yet more estates, this time in Ireland, from his uncle Percy Wyndham O'Brien, heir to an Irish earldom.

Under George Wyndham O'Brien, third Earl of Egremont, Petworth entered its golden age. The North Gallery was filled with paintings and sculptures by leading contemporary artists: Turner, Reynolds, Gainsborough, Wilson, Zoffany, Romney, Fuseli, Thomas Phillips, de Loutherbourg, Flaxman, Westmacott, Northcote, Rossi. Turner had his own studio above the chapel. One of Egremont's grandchildren remembered following the Earl to the studio, 'his slow, sliding step, to say nothing of the unnumerable train of dogs that always accompanied him informed the great painter of the approach of his host, and he then unbolted the door, which he always kept locked against all other visitors'.[4] When Benjamin Haydon visited Petworth in 1826 he was 'placed in one of the most magnificent bedrooms I ever saw. It speaks more for what he thinks of my talents than anything that ever happened to me'. Haydon added: 'the very animals at Petworth seemed happier than in any other spot on earth'.[5]

4 George, third Earl of Egremont,
by George Clint.

For all his wealth and power, Egremont was not at ease in society. He disliked ceremony, being painfully shy, and was well known for his unconventional manners. From 1825 he spent most of his time at Petworth: he preferred the company of artists to that of grandees. Greville summed him up: he was 'blunt without rudeness, and caustic without bitterness; shrewd, eccentric and benevolent'.[6] His friendship with artists and writers was sincere. They were not merely employed as 'useful and obedient instruments' with which to embellish Petworth; they were respected as guests.

Though the legend that Egremont sired seventy-two illegitimate children was probably an exaggeration, the Earl certainly indulged in many liaisons. Lady Melbourne is the best known of his mistresses, her son William Lamb, later Prime Minister, said to be Egremont's son. But Egremont also had a constant companion, Elizabeth Ayliffe, whom he eventually married in 1801 after the birth of all their children, one of whom was Percy's father, George. The marriage was less successful than the affair and in May 1803 a deed of separation and settlement was drawn up. Egremont acquired estates in Australia to provide for Elizabeth. As a descendant put it, the Earl had 'needed a mistress but he could not manage a wife'.[7]

Egremont's eldest son George married Mary Blunt in 1815. The couple lived at Drove, a substantial house near Chichester (where Percy was born) until inheriting Petworth on the death of the Earl in 1837. Mary was a religious fanatic and she turned the palace of Petworth into almost a fortress. Her evangelical fervour and strict observance of convention created a bulwark of defence around George as she dedicated her life to restoring a good name to the Wyndhams after the rakish misdemeanours of her father-in-law.

5 Mary, Lady Leconfield, and her surviving sons Henry and Percy by Sir Francis Grant.

When she married George, he and his brothers and sisters were legally entitled to use only the name Ayliffe. In 1838 they petitioned to be allowed to take the surname of Wyndham but their cousin, who had inherited the earldom, blocked the petition. In January 1839 the petition was finally granted: George, by now over fifty years old, could legally use his father's name. He was granted the title Baron Leconfield in 1859.

George and Mary Leconfield had ten children. Their eldest son contracted cholera and died in 1837, the year they moved to Petworth; he was twenty years old and unmarried. Henry, Percy's elder brother, became the new heir. Once installed in Petworth, neither children or servants were allowed any contact with the town beyond the estate walls.[8] Mary Leconfield never entered it except in a carriage. As neither George nor Mary encouraged visitors to Petworth, young people were invited for just six weeks of the year to provide companionship for their children. Henry and Percy were at least given the relief of boarding-school: both went to Eton. But the daughters had highly boring lives. The only conversation which animated their father concerned hunting. Their mother forbade the reading of all novels. As Percy later explained to Madeline, his sisters read 'nothing', they would always feel that 'they lost the best and most undisturbed time in their lives for reading'.[9]

In complete contrast was the Petworth of their grandfather's day. Then the vast palace was filled with people of all ages and backgrounds:

with visitors coming and going as they pleased: they were welcome without notice. There was no leave-taking either: you didn't say goodbye, you just left. Guests found themselves confronted with nurses and babies, girls exercising the pianoforte, boys exercising ponies. Nobody was ever quite sure whose children they were. There were artists all over the place, some doing original work, other copying Vandycks. In the old library you might have discovered Sir William Beechey altering the figure and background of Gainsborough's portrait of Egremont's mother. . . . Then there would be Carew, the sculptor, modelling and messing about in his bedroom, or chiselling a medallion or two downstairs.[10]

Though Lady Leconfield would have preferred that her daughters were not presented at Court, she was persuaded otherwise. She had the satisfaction, at least, of forbidding the girls from waltzing when they did attend London balls. Nor were visits to the capital undertaken lightly. Mary refused to travel on a train in the company of strangers, so all the vacant seats in her first-class compartment were occupied by the upper servants. She only once took a cab in London and on that one occasion managed to break her finger. As a result, whenever she was forced to go to London, the carriage and horses were put on the train and she waited at the station until they were ready to take her on to the family house at 4 Grosvenor Place.[11]

George Leconfield was like his father in many respects: he was shy, taciturn and solitary. On the other hand, he was neither particularly well read nor cultured: he had no interest in the arts or in politics. And he possessed a violent temper. While his wife tried to ensure strict moral standards were adhered to at Petworth, he himself engaged in vicious, petty disputes with his own younger brother Henry, a distinguished soldier who had offended society by abandoning his wife and eloping with the wife of a baronet.[12]

Egremont had earlier given both Henry and George sufficient money to establish their own separate packs of hounds: George was living at Drove so his pack hunted from the south of Petworth to the sea; Henry's home was Sladeland so he hunted to the north of Petworth in the Weald. However, when George moved into Petworth in 1837 he took his pack of hounds with him and immediately began hunting over the land used by his brother. Henry was already seething about supposed slights to his mistress, who was not accepted by Sussex society; also he failed to get selected to represent West Sussex in Parliament. He carried on hunting his pack over the same land as George. The rivalry amounted to war: local landowners were lobbied, pamphlets were published, and finally George threated to butcher all the foxes in his coverts in Sussex if Henry didn't withdraw. Fortunately Egremont had bequeathed Cockermouth Castle to Henry for life (the Cumberland estates brought him an income of £15,000 a year), so he could retire to the Lake District. But George never allowed any of his children to visit their Uncle Henry.[13]

Jealousy and ill-temper marred the relationship between Percy and his own brother, also called Henry. Their father openly demonstrated his preference for Percy, his youngest son, with whom he shared his passion for the land. Henry was to be enraged by the terms of his father's will, and the generosity shown to Percy.

Percy learnt from his father not only the duties and responsibilities pertaining to the ownership of land, but also the emotional and spiritual rewards to be found in such a

6 (left)   Colonel George Wyndham, first Lord Leconfield by Thomas Phillips.

7 (right)   General Sir Henry Wyndham by Thomas Phillips.

relationship. In trying to describe his father to Madeline, shortly before their marriage, Percy wrote that 'you would like going about the country with him & hear him talk to farmers, keepers, and labourers, his keen common sense going to the root of everything'.[14] As the owner of large estates in County Clare, George Leconfield concerned himself with the plight of the Irish during the harvest crisis of the 1840s, even helping them to emigrate to his estates in Australia.

The favouritism shown to Percy was extended to Madeline after their marriage; until his death in 1869 Leconfield made the young couple welcome at Petworth. Percy, Madeline, their growing family and personal servants stayed at Petworth for up to six months every year. Madeline painted delicate watercolours of the interior which reveal an intimate, everyday life being led within a spectacular setting.[15]

The Leconfields allowed their sons considerably more freedom than their daughters. By contrast, though Percy's own daughters were still educated at home while his sons went to Eton, he encouraged them to read widely and without restriction; he also saw nothing wrong in communicating with local villagers as well as with all the artists, writers and socialist architects and designers who came to stay. From a very young age his daughters and their nurses went abroad with their parents, while as teenagers they travelled throughout Europe with only their governess or personal maids. Like his own sisters, however, their only route out of the parental home was via marriage.

Percy's elder sisters, Fanny and Blanche, married immediately they came of age. Fanny settled down with Alfred Montgomery, who was widely believed to be the son of the Marquis of Wellesley rather than the first Baronet Montgomery and, from the security of her own home, began to write novels. Though Mary Leconfield may have disapproved of her daughter's becoming a novelist, some of the words of advice offered by Fanny in her books on the guidance and raising of children sound remarkably close to the opinions of her mother, and remarkably asinine:

The danger is in confounding works of imagination with works of passion. You might give your little girls most of the plays of Shakespeare to read with impunity, but you would incure great risk by making them intimate with Lalla Rookh and Byron.[16]

Blanche married Richard Bourke, eldest son and heir to the Earl of Mayo, owner of Palmerstown in County Kildare and almost 8,000 acres of Irish estates. The Mayos were deeply religious and consequently a suitable choice as far as Lady Leconfield was concerned; their evangelicalism instilled in their son a deep sense of duty towards society. Richard was a charismatic individual, an accomplished sportsman, and socially enlightened. Marriage to Blanche brought him introductions to the most exclusive members of the British aristocracy; when he was made Chief Secretary for Ireland in 1852 his own family's position in the Irish Ascendancy was reinforced. His official residence in Dublin and his country home at Palmerstown were significant magnets for politicians and society; it was in his home that his young brother-in-law Percy was introduced to the unattached Madeline Campbell, descendant of the Dukes of Leinster and of Richmond.

Helen, Percy's 'simple' sister, could not take the escape route of marriage. She lived at Petworth until the death of her father, walking in the grounds, sewing, take tea every day at the Rectory. On receiving the news of her father's death her only response apparently was, 'Now at last I can use the downstairs lavatory.'[17]

Percy was able to maintain a close relationship with one particular survivor of the easy going, cultured world of his grandfather. His Aunt Charlotte was Egremont's favourite child. She was herself an intellectual, widely cultured but also eccentrically forgetful. Like her father she cared little for the opinion of society. As her daughters put it, 'she had a dignified manner and an absent mind. She was very learned and read Hebrew fluently besides many profound books, so that the common things of existence were apt to be ignored by her'.[18] She married John King, who obligingly changed his name to Wyndham-King, and the couple settled in Coates Castle, close to Petworth, at the insistence of Egremont. The Wyndham-Kings and their three little girls were constant visitors at Petworth. Both Percy and Madeline visited Charlotte in London during the last ten years of her life. One of her daughters, Lilla, married the artist Roddam Spencer-Stanhope. His close links with G.F. Watts (his teacher), Philip Webb (who designed a house for him), William Morris, Edward Burne-Jones and Val Prinsep began in the 1850s. When Percy and Madeline launched themselves in the London art world a few years later, Spencer-Stanhope, their cousin-in-law, was to give them invaluable support.

Both Henry and Percy had the advantage of their sex, to go to Eton, then university, the army or both; in addition their father paid for them to travel through Europe with personal tutors. Percy went straight from school into the Coldstream Guards, the regiment of his reprobate Uncle Henry. He was seventeen years old, and ambitious. He reported to his mother that by getting into the regiment in 1852 instead of 1853 he would 'if he ever should become a General gain ten years by it'.[19]

As a young officer, living in the family house in Grosvenor Place, Percy enjoyed a privileged lifestyle. He had to attend drill at the barracks in Portman Street three times a day, at 8 a.m., 11 a.m. and 3 p.m.: it lasted one and a quarter hours each time. But otherwise he was free to enjoy being a young, wealthy bachelor in London, kitted out in his handsome Coldstream uniform. Even his mother recognised as much, commenting: 'he is now launched upon the world'.[20] There were invitations to parties in London and to country house weekends (he wasn't so keen on the shooting at Cowdray: 'sometimes they shoot a man instead of a Bird');[21] his fellow officers came from some of the most powerful and wealthiest families in the country. Contacts made at Eton were reinforced and extended through the army; the sisters of his new friends were eager to meet this eligible young man. He might not be the heir to Petworth but as the favoured younger son of a major landowner his prospects looked promising.

Unfortunately for Percy and his fellow officers in the 1st Battalion Coldstream, 1853 was not so propitious a year after all; their busy social calendar and undemanding daily drill were to be interrupted by war. Britain had been at peace since Napoleon's defeat at Waterloo. The Crimean War turned out to be an incompetent affair in which more men died through disease than fighting. It began with a confrontation squabble over the respective rights of Eastern Christians and Roman Catholics in Ottoman-controlled Jerusalem and quickly developed into a conflict between those great powers with interests in the Near East: Ottoman Turkey, Russia, Britain and France.

By March 1854 Percy was on his way to the Crimea. A brigade order issued on 10 February had called up the 1st Battalion Coldstream, the 3rd Battalion Grenadiers and the Scots Fusiliers; they were to be held in readiness to proceed on foreign service.[22] The Brigade sailed from Southampton on 22 February aboard the steamship *Orinoco*. The battalion consisted of 35 officers (Percy was a lieutenant), 919 men and 32 women. The average age of the men was twenty-nine but some of the junior officers were, like Percy, under twenty years old.

The brief stay in Malta must have been a revelation to the young soldiers, particularly those who had never left Britain before: the art, the architecture, the beautiful women. One veteran of the Crimea recalled the 'dark-eyed, olive-cheeked *signoras*', also the stately cathedral of St John in Valletta, the 'richly sculptured balconies, the ornate portals . . . so many splendid evidences of educated taste and of large public spirit',[23] created by the Knights Hospitallers. Percy was experiencing his own Grand Tour, though in unusual circumstances and with no opportunity to return with spoil to Petworth.

From Malta the battalion proceeded to Scutari: 'delicious scene! At our feet rippled the limpid waters of the Bosphorus, on the opposite [European] shore towered the airy minarets of Stamboul.'[24] For six weeks the soldiers enjoyed sport, good food and fine, but not exceedingly hot, weather. In June the holiday ended, a decision having been made to occupy Varna in Bulgaria. After steaming up the Bosphorus, the 1st Coldstream set their camp about three-quarters of a mile from the town, 'on a slimy flat, close to a large lake of stagnant water'. One of the officers later recalled their condition:

> Before a week elapsed, the intense heat, bad water, indifferent and insufficient food, and the monotony of inaction began to tell upon the men; they were afflicted with diarrhoea and other ailments, so that the health of the troops, hitherto entirely satisfactory, rapidly deteriorated.[25]

Varna itself, added another, 'should only be seen through a telescope'.

> Once within its walls, every preconceived illusion vanishes, you wade knee-deep in slush, you are nearly knocked over with ineffable stinks; those beautiful minarets which looked so poetic, whilst you paced the transports' deck, can only be approached through a maze of nasty alleys, plentifully supplied with dung-hills and

open cess-pools, and infested with droves of mangy curs. The red, yellow, and green paint, the white-wash, the sycamores, the cypresses, that lately glanched so cheerily in the sunshine, turn out, on closer acquaintance, to be the slimsy disguises of tottering, bulging, rat-eaten rottenness.[26]

The move to Aladyn on 1 July brought no relief. 'This seventh heaven of the artist is but the mahogany coffin, bedizened with brass nails and gilded hinges.' The day was divided into three parts: 'drill and exhaustion'; 'torpor and tobacco'; 'foraging and feeding'.[27]

During the month at Aladyn about one-fifth of the battalion was admitted to hospital with typhus, dysentery or ague. A move on the 27 July to Guereklek, a village about three miles away, brought a new danger: cholera. Hospital marquees were erected, each containing fifteen patients in every stage of the epidemic:

the strong man wrung with the first spasms; the doomed wretch cold, pulseless, livid, with myriads of flies swarming in and out of his open mouth, and clustering upon his fixed eye-balls; the blue swollen corpse just rid of unspeakable torment. Was there a soldier of the division that gazed unappalled on those immedicable heaps of tortured humanity – the quick gasping and screaming by the side of the stark dead? Not one – the boldest stood aghast, every heart was softened. In the midst of life we were in death! Whose turn next?[28]

A heavy torpor hung over the camp. The men were depressed and unable to eat their rations of meat. When the battalion was ordered back to Varna on 16 August the journey of 15 miles took three days to complete.

The 1st battalion Coldstream spent 75 days in Bulgaria. Twenty-eight men died from cholera and 25 from typhus, hundreds spent part of the time in hospital. When the battalion proceeded on to the Crimea it consisted of only 26 officers and 737 men. Percy Wyndham was not of the company. He had finally collapsed at Guereklek and was invalided home along with five other men. Shipped back to England, Percy retired from the Coldstream Guards on 24 November 1854. He was lucky to have survived the gruelling experience of Bulgaria and to be spared the later Crimea campaign. Twelve officers out of the original thirty-five in the 1st Battalion were killed, or died of wounds or disease.[29]

Peace terms were finally agreed on 1 February 1856. Meanwhile, having recovered from his experiences in Bulgaria, and no longer burdened with a soldier's responsibilities, Percy decided to enjoy himself. He had the run of the house in Grosvenor Place with the company of his cousin Wilfred Scawen Blunt, five years his junior, until Wilfrid obtained his first posting to Greece at the end of 1859.[30] His elder sisters Fanny and Blanche had establishments in Mayfair; Blanche could also offer the attractions of Dublin society and sport in County Kildare where her husband was Master of the Kildare Hunt.

On his twenty-first birthday in 1856 and in recognition of his interest in the land, George Leconfield purchased for Percy a sporting estate at Much Cowarne in Herefordshire: it would provide him with a useful income.[31] Percy was now in a position to consider marriage, though unless he married an heiress, any hope of obtaining a house in London and a country house (the Much Cowarne estate had no sizeable mansion) would be entirely dependent on further advances from his father and from his inheritance.

8 Wilfrid Scawen Blunt
photographed by Lady Alice
Gaisford c.1868. In an album of
photographs by Lady Alice
Gaisford.

The friendship between Percy and cousin Wilfrid lasted their lifetime, surviving
almost insuperable odds, for Wilfrid not only seduced Percy's wife Madeline, but also
his daughter Mary who, as a result of their affair, gave birth to a child. Wilfrid was an
exceptional individual, a romantic in politics and in love; he was a poet and a scholar of
Arabia; a womaniser, an adventurer and an explorer. Like Percy's Aunt Charlotte he
offered a refreshing antidote to both the evangelical atmosphere of Petworth and the
conservative masculine atmosphere of the army. He enjoyed hunting and shooting and
was deeply attached to the Sussex countryside. When his elder brother died and he
inherited the family estates, Wilfrid took on all the responsibilities of the committed
land gentleman, but still found time for philandering. And like Percy he set about
building his own country house, though he was his own architect. Such a combination
of qualities and interests undoubtedly appealed to Percy, who, throughout his life,
enjoyed the company of men whose politics, attitudes to marriage and social
background were often completely different to his own. Though Conservative in his
politics, Percy was not conservative in his friendships.

  Few of Percy's letters have survived and it is doubtful that he kept a diary.[32] His
character emerges only through the occasional comments of acquaintances, references
in letters of his wife and children, and the evidence offered by his own friendships.
One letter he wrote to his eldest son George was carefully preserved. It was to be read
by George as his regiment proceeded towards the Sudan in 1885, to a war which Percy
regarded as 'wicked and utterly purposeless'. It reveals Percy's deep love of his
children, a passion which is also present in the love letters he wrote to Madeline before
their marriage.

My own dearest dearest boy, I must say once how *deeply deeply* I love you. I cannot express how I feel that my whole being is filled with *eager tender love for you my darling*. One cannot say this speaking but I should never forgive myself if I had not told you. I know you feel all you give up in going away, but these occasions lift one up above all the *petty* accidents of Time and Space and leave Love and Duty *standing* as they *will stand for ever*. This is what I mean when I say sometimes 'after all nothing matters', the dust in front of our own door is all we are responsible for. This is a blessed thought. You know *how* I disapprove of the whole Egyptian business so I like to tell you that I send you *my own darling* away quite as willingly as for the justest and most necessary war imaginable. I like you to know that, that I dont think *for a moment* your most *precious* life thrown away, if the worst comes, for sweet Duty's sake. We suffer for the sins and mistakes of others, as others in turn (dreadful thought) suffer and will suffer for ours, but judicially we are only responsible for what we do or leave undone ourselves. I wish I could give you dear boy the best thing I have, I would part with it myself to do so, my *assurance* of the certainty of life after death, and that you *will* see your loved ones again whatever happens, and if, which God forbid you pass from this plane I should not let it alter my life but think of you as my dear George still, who I shall see again. God & all good spirits keep you *my darling*. I cannot make you know what I think of you, but I feel to have *had such a son is not to have lived in vain*.[33]

Contemporaries most often noted Percy's temper and arrogance, his conversation peppered with expletives; he was passionate in his affections towards his family but he could also be passionate in argument, sometimes losing the notorious Wyndham temper. He relished debate, frequently urging his children to argue with him. Though those who worked for him were fiercely loyal, he was known to shoot at his game keepers when he missed his target. His tenderness and affection were revealed within the privacy of his home and caught in the occasional family photograph as he cuddles a son or daughter.

Percy's interests were varied, ranging from the more conventional management of his estate and enjoyment of hunting and shooting, to a serious commitment to the preservation of ancient buildings and the support of contemporary art and design. It would appear he had no relish for a military career after his experiences in Bulgaria, and he never revealed personal ambitions as a politician beyond a local level. Yet his pride in the military and political achievements of his own sons was genuine; he was supportive and devoted as both a father and husband.

2

Towards the end of 1859 Percy was the guest of his brother-in-law Richard, Lord Naas, who, as Chief Secretary for Ireland, occupied his own lodge in Dublin's Phoenix Park. There is no way of knowing whether Percy's sister Blanche deliberately sought out a match for her eligible and handsome brother. However, at some point during the visit, Percy was introduced to one of the guests of the Viceroy, staying close by in the Vice-Regal Lodge: this was Madeline Campbell, and Percy fell instantly and passionately in love.[34]

If Percy was hoping to marry an heiress, then falling in love with Madeline Campbell was a mistake. But if he was determined to marry for love, and trusted that whoever he chose would also please his father, then Madeline was the perfect choice. She had no money, no property and no detractors. Her mother Lady Campbell nicknamed her 'the Sunny Baby' the moment Madeline was born, writing to her best friend, the novelist Emily Eden,

> I have really escaped with my life – *I ain't dead yet*, but such a big monster of a girl! – a regular Megalonia of a female, that if you happened to find a loose joint of hers you would think it must belong to an antediluvian Ox. *Je vous demande un peu* what am I to do with a seventh girl of such dimensions? . . . It is very good of Lord Auckland [Emily Eden's brother] to stand for my girl. I really believe she is harmless, for she could knock me down, but she is merciful! What shall we call her? I had some thoughts of Rhinocera. She was born the day the Rhinoceros landed, or Cuvier [French naturalist], because I was reading his life and works just before she was born, and took a passion for him. Might she not be called Eden? – Her other name is to be Madeline – her Godmother's name.[35]

Madeline Caroline Frances Eden Campbell was born on 20 June 1835 in County Armagh, where her father Sir Guy Campbell was serving as Deputy Quartermaster-General. His salary was £600 per annum and he and his wife Pamela were struggling to raise their large family (Madeline was the ninth of ten children), which also included a further daughter by Guy's first marriage. In 1841 Sir Guy was promoted Major-General in command of the Athlone district and the entire family established themselves in a house called 'The Moorings'. His final posting, at the end of 1848, was an Colonel of the 3rd West India Regiment, but he died suddenly in January 1849 at Kingstown, Dublin.[36] Pamela Campbell was left with a pension of under £600 a year. She eventually settled at Woodview, Stillorgan, a comfortable brick house close to Dublin. The few surviving photographs from the 1850s show Lady Campbell and her unmarried daughters relaxing in the Stillorgan gardens in the company of young men, shaggy dogs and caged birds.[37]

The Campbells were married for twenty-nine years and appear to have been devoted to one another, as well as to all their children. Even after the death of Sir Guy, no stultifying religious piety descended on the household; the atmosphere at Wood-view and all the many homes rented by the Campbells was always one of close family affection and loyalty. Emily Eden probably based the character of Lady Eskdale in her novel *The Semi-Attached Couple* on Pamela, with her 'loving nature' and 'gentle and caressing manner'. Lady Eskdale's chief joy in life is watching her children make happy marriages. She 'could not picture to herself life without husband and children, and had never brought herself to believe in the existence of an unhappy marriage'. She is adored by the young, including her own children, all of whom believe her 'more beautiful in her middle-age than the rest of the world in their prime'.[38]

The warmth and informal ease of the Campbell household, the open expression of affection between husband and wife, parents and children, became a model for Madeline herself in her role as wife, mother and hostess. It was a complete contrast to the atmosphere in which Percy Wyndham was raised. It was also a contrast to Pamela Campbell's own childhood.

Pamela was the eldest child born to Lord Edward Fitzgerald and his wife, 'La Belle Pamela'. Her grandparents on her Anglo-Irish side were James Fitzgerald, first Duke of Leinster and his wife Emily Lennox, one of the beautiful and cultured daughters of the third Duke of Richmond; on her French side her grandparents were presumed to be Louis-Philippe, Duc D'Orleans and the governess of his children, Madame de Genlis, the writer of popular and influential books on the education of children.[39]

Before Pamela was three years old, her father was dead. Lord Edward Fitzgerald had begun his military career conventionally enough for the younger son of a duke, joining the Sussex militia under his uncle, the Duke of Richmond. He saw action in America and Canada and became an MP. On a visit to Paris in 1792 he met, fell in love with and married Madame de Genlis's 'adopted' daughter Pamela; he also stayed with Tom Paine and under his influence became increasingly sympathetic towards the cause of the United Irishmen, the creation of an Irish republic independent of Britain. He was overheard toasting the abolition of all hereditary titles and was cashiered from the army.

Lord Edward and his wife settled in County Kildare. Three children were born: Edward in 1794, Pamela (Madeline's mother) in 1796 and Lucy in 1798. Lord Edward was becoming more and more deeply embroiled in Irish revolutionary politics. He joined the United Irishmen officially in 1796 and the following year headed a military committee whose aim was to link up with the French and lead a rising against British rule.[40] The rebellion was planned to begin on 23 May 1798 but on 11 May a reward of

9 Woodview, Stillorgan, Dublin, c.1860. Lady Campbell is seated to the right of the doorway with an unknown man: Madeline Campbell is to the left of the doorway. In the garden from left to right: an unknown man, Mary Campbell, Julia Campbell, Colonel Eardley Maitland.

£1,000 was offered for Lord Edward. He was already in hiding, paying secret visits to his wife as she gave birth to Lucy. But on 19 May he was arrested and taken to Newgate Gaol in Dublin. During his arrest he was shot in the arm and two weeks later he died in prison. 'Young, beautiful, kind, noble, highly-born, the friend of princes, the most adored of human creatures, he died in as great a loneliness as any soul ever passed to its Creator.'[41]

Ireland had a hero, but Pamela Fitzgerald lost her home and all financial security. She was ordered to leave Ireland, even though Lucy was just six weeks old, and a bill of attainder was passed against Lord Edward which deprived her of his Kilrush estate and an income. Members of the family, including the Duchess of Leinster, the Duke of Richmond and Lord Holland, appealed to the King against the attainder but lost: Lord Edward had, in effect, been found guilty of high treason.[42]

The family was forced to separate: Pamela Fitzgerald took her eldest daughter to Hamburg where a niece of Madame de Genlis was living.[43] Within a short time she had married again, no doubt hoping for some financial security, to Mr Pitcairn, the American consul. Unfortunately the marriage was not a success and the Pitcairns were separated by 1808. Madame de Genlis was by this time back in Paris. She had been forced to leave the city after the fall of the Duc d'Orleans (he had been guillotined in 1793). But with the advent of the reign of Napoleon she was back in favour; the Emperor gave her his personal protection. So Pamela, now a young girl, accompanied her mother to Paris to renew the relationship.

Her meeting with Madame de Genlis made a lasting impression on the girl:

I never met so industrious a woman besides her genius and she had the art of making one love work. She netted, embroidered, made baskets, and was always at something, was wonderfully abstemious and almost starved herself, not from religious motives but for health, living on herb soup, sorrel and roots, scarcely any meat . . . Her room was full of little tables covered with souvenirs and miniatures and albums, busts over which she threw net and lace veils to keep them from dust. She had all sorts of snuff-boxes and curiosities and a coral chaplet of praying beads which had been blessed and given her by the Pope.[44]

By the time Madame de Genlis died, her granddaughter was herself married and a mother, and passed on to her children stories of the resourcefulness and intelligence of their great-grandmother – successful authoress, mistress, handsome, witty and above all a survivor. She lived through the fall of the *Ancien Régime*, under which she had enjoyed considerable prestige, she survived the revolution and the reign of terror, she was supported by Napoleon and finally lived on into a gracious old age under the restored monarchy.

Pamela had little time to settle down in Paris. Her mother was not long in finding herself another admirer, the Duc de la Force, and settled down with him at Montauban, according to one account, dressing up as a shepherdess and making artificial flowers.[45] She approached her Fitzgerald relations to provide a more suitable education for Pamela who, in 1811, was taken under the protection of Emily, Duchess of Leinster, to be 'finished off' in the élite society made up of Ireland's Georgian ascendancy and England's great Whig families.[46]

From a childhood spent travelling around the continent with a vivacious but spendthrift mother, Pamela was thrust into a world of culture, elegance and power. The Dukes of Leinster owned 70,000 acres of County Kildare, their country seat was

Carton House and they also had property in Dublin and London. Her memories of her
father were slight but her grandmother, the Duchess of Leinster, marked his death in
prison every year:

> The 4th of June, when the guns fired for the King's birthday, was always a dark day
> in the house; poor Grandmama appeared in deeper mourning, and somehow there
> was a sort of stillness; we . . . went softly, tho' nothing was said to note it; but it was
> the anniversary of my father's death. Grandmama wore his coloured handkerchief
> next her heart, and it was put into her coffin with her.[47]

In 1820, Pamela went on a trip to Scotland and sent Emily Eden a description of her
first meeting with Sir Guy Campbell:

> Before you read thro' this letter call your maid, and get the smelling bottle, for you
> will certainly faint away with surprise and wonder, who would have thought it! I
> don't believe it myself so I cannot expect you to believe it, but I am going to be
> married perfectly true in about a months or six weeks. I am going to be married to
> Sir Guy Campbell . . . He is uncommonly right-headed, of course it follows he is
> liberal, *wide*-minded and indulgent, at the same time I see he can take violent
> dislikes.[48]

Sir Guy Campbell was a professional soldier. He had earned his military honours fighting Napoleon's army in the Peninsular War and his exploits featured in the monumental history of the war written by Pamela's cousin and close friend, Sir William Napier.[49] At the Battle of Waterloo Sir Guy commanded the 6th Regiment, he then went on half-pay and in 1817 he married Frances Burgoyne, daughter of the celebrated general and dramatist, John Burgoyne. A daughter, Fanny, was born in 1818, but Frances died the same year, leaving Sir Guy a widower at thirty-two with a tiny baby to raise on only a small army pension. In 1819 he finally retired from the active list.

Sir Guy Campbell came from a rather different background to Pamela's. Where she could offer a mixture of English, Irish and French aristocratic blood, a romantic past and exceptional good looks, the Campbells offered a more conventional approach to life. Sir Guy was the first Baronet. He was descended from a line of Scots loyal in their service to the crown, utterly reliable on the battlefield, strong leaders of men, honourable and brave. Ironically, Sir Guy's father Colin, also a professional soldier, led the 6th Regiment against the Irish rebels during the 1798 rising in which Lord Edward lost his life. For Colin, the campaign was a personal triumph. His final posting was to Gibraltar as Lieutenant-Governor. He died there in 1814 and the following year Guy was created a baronet in recognition of his father's services on the island during the Napoleonic Wars.

When Sir Guy met Pamela Fitzgerald he could offer her neither a home nor financial security, but the couple apparently fell instantly in love – and remained so all their married life. A few weeks after the wedding Pamela wrote to Emily Eden, 'I like Sir Guy more and more, he understands me so well, he knows my faults, which is a great relief, for I have no silent obliquity to smother, or no good behaviour to act up to more than is comfortable'.[50]

For the first few years of their marriage they moved from one rented house to another, a baby was born almost every other year, servants and children fell ill with scarlet fever, there never seemed sufficient money to cover expenses. Then, in 1827, Sir Guy received the welcome news of a posting to Ireland as Deputy Quarter-master-General. Pamela sent Emily Eden her impressions of Ireland; her emotional ties to the Irish people and their rights made her sceptical of the justice of British rule. On first landing at Cork she was struck by the condition of the people: 'Oh Emily, it is melancholy to see the misery and cunning and degradation of these poor people . . . sick beggars! they show us such legs! and one was driven up in a barrow, legless!'[51]

A year in Limerick and Pamela was beginning to sound like her dead father:

Is it possible that Lord Anglesey is to be our Lord-Lieutenant? Am I really to pray for him, and for the sword the King puts in his hand, every Sunday in church? Oh dear, dear! What a wretched country this is – it worries the spirit to see it.[52]

A move to Armagh in 1828 brought out her sarcasm: 'there is not that variety of dislocation among the limbs of the beggars which now and then accorded us a topic in the south'.[53]

Pamela's three sons all pursued military careers, and four of her daughters married professional soldiers. There was an understanding, within the family, of the significance and dangers of military life which continued down through the generations; if Percy chose to share his experiences in Bulgaria with Madeline (there are no written references in the family archives) she would have been able to respond appropriately. Closeness, support in times of family loss, sociability, interest in culture and politics, a passion for Ireland, personal knowledge of 'running the empire', a shared inheritance of revolution and radicalism but also a shared conviction in the duty to serve: these aspects derived from Campbells and Fitzgeralds, Napiers, Lennoxes and Foxes, the recent turbulent histories of Ireland and France all met in Madeline and her brothers and sisters.[54]

Lady Campbell's very special contribution was her love of family: Madeline extended the meaning of family to include her closest friends, lovingly welcomed into the Wyndham personal network regardless of their class or background. The atmosphere which prevaded Woodview, Stillorgan, when Percy became acquainted with Madeline, must have exercised considerable charm on the bachelor. Madeline had personal attractions as well: she was unusually beautiful, with a sensual mouth, deep-set glowing eyes with dark eyebrows (Percy called her Cobra because of her eyes) and hair growing low on her forehead. Wilfrid Blunt described her as 'royally beautiful', 'full of natural wit', a 'tall strong woman . . . no porcelain figure like the beauties of the last century, nor yet the dull classic marble our fathers loved'.[55] Women friends were never critical: she was 'charming', 'genial', always entertaining company and a contrast to her 'cultivated but crotchety' husband; she was also a talented artist.[56]

3

Percy and Madeline became engaged towards the end of the London season in July 1860. In Ireland, where their courtship began, they had visited the fishing village of Blackrock, close to Dublin. Madeline bought Percy a small blue china fish for the princely sum of sixpence. In return he sent her a gold cross but Lady Campbell, scrupulous concerning social etiquette, made Madeline return the gift. Nearly thirty years later, Madeline was rigorous in supervising the behaviour of the prospective son-in-law of her own daugher Madeline. Charles Adeane sent his gift of a bracelet to the mother, 'for you to give to yr daughter may I say with my love? It is too dear of you to say that I have acted as you would have liked.'[57]

The season in London provided a variety of opportunities for meetings, at Lady Campbell's house in Jermyn Street, the Duke of Leinster's house in Carlton House Terrace and the Leconfields' town house. A visit to a pleasure-ground had made them gratifyingly late for dinner but then Percy foolishly missed an opportunity to share a seat in a carriage with Madeline:

> I very much regret the fatal mistake I made about the seat in the carriage. That precious chance is gone for ever but one has to learn every thing by experience, who knows what we might have knocked out of one another?[58]

Just ten days later Percy's reactions were a little quicker and he was able to exchange kisses with Madeline on the Leinsters' balcony, 'very nice,' he wrote, 'I think too of those kisses.'[59]

Only Percy's letters to Madeline survive. He was deeply in love and inhibited neither by his mother's religious fanaticism, nor his father's taciturn shyness.

Dear Glory of my Life, Sweet darling, dear Cobra, dear Gull with the changing eyes,
most precious, rare, rich, Madeline, sweet Madge of the soft cheeks, God bless you
for ever you very dear darling . . . Oh! what talks we shall have about every body and
every thing. I feel so confident in your great love, that I think you would love me
through all weaknesses, & faults; past, present, and to come. I love you better than
anything in the world . . . I feel a strong, silent feeling in my heart, *a power of sticking
to you for ever*.[60]

Lady Campbell explained Madeline's financial situation to Lord Leconfield: it would be
up to him to provide the couple with an income:

I suppose you know Madeline has no fortune. I have had rather a struggling life of
many trials. I became a widow ten years ago, & have much to thank God for, in that
He enabled me to bring up my children upon less than six hundred a year, on my
death the girls will each have fifty pounds a year and that is all! So you must be
content with Madeline's good qualities as her portion.[60]

George Leconfield was indeed pleased with Madeline's 'good qualities' and thought her
a suitable wife for his favourite son. Lady Campbell was relieved:

it has made me very happy that Madeline should have been so warmly welcomed
among you all. I know you will love her for she is most loveable & I trust her in
perfect confidence to your son, whom I liked so very much from the first day of our
acquaintance . . . I do not wonder you prize him, he is so good & pleasant.[62]

The usual practice was for both sides to contribute as much as they could reasonably afford and, ideally, equal amounts, so that their children had sufficient capital to live off, at a level suitable to their position in society.[63] George Leconfield, however, was in the unusual and expensive situation of having sole responsibility for providing the capital for his son and daughter-in-law to live off. He provided Madeline with a marriage settlement of £22,500, which would give her a personal income of £900 per annum. Percy would have received a similar amount, also most of the income from the Much Cowarne estate in Herefordshire, bringing the couple a total income of between £5,000 and £6,500 a year. Leconfield also continued to increase the value of the Herefordshire property on behalf of his son, repairing farm buildings, improving drainage and purchasing additional small pieces of land. By 1863, when a resettlement document was drawn up settling Much Cowarne on Percy and, in the case of his death, on his children, the property was worth £114,000.[64]

The marriage was fixed for 16 October. But, in the middle of the wedding preparations, Percy's Uncle Henry suddenly dropped dead. The question as to which Wyndham would succeed him in the West Cumberland parliamentary seat was immediately raised. With some persuasion from his own family, from the Conservatives in the constituency and from Madeline herself, Percy reluctantly agreed to stand, though he confessed to his fiancée, 'I have never thought much of the immediate questions of the day; more of general principles'.[65]

At once he was caught up in election plotting. The agent Colonel Lowther and his brother-in-law Lord Naas (MP for Cockermouth) tried to bring forward Uncle Henry's funeral so as to 'get the writ out next Monday and to have the Election a whole week earlier, and so prevent the other party having time to concoct an opposition'.[66] George Leconfield refused to alter the date of the funeral but it hardly mattered as Percy confessed he was 'safe as a Church to get in'. He continued to serve in Parliament as Conservative MP for West Cumberland until 1885.

The unexpected turn of events meant that Percy and Madeline would begin married life facing the uncertainties and responsibilities of a parliamentary career. However they were provided by George Leconfield with a northern home, Cockermouth Castle, which Turner had painted while under the patronage of Lord Egremont: it remains a romantic site. The medieval castle lies above the River Derwent at its confluence with the River Coker, so is surrounded by water on almost three sides. The habitable part, within the outer ward, was built at different times, from the late eighteenth to mid-nineteenth centuries.

The wedding took place, as arranged, on 16 October, at Stillorgan church in Dublin. Afterwards, the couple departed for a honeymoon touring France, the first of many trips to Europe which they would make on their own and with their children, Madeline sketching and taking photographs, both visiting the studios of artists, buying paintings, sculptures and textiles with which to enrich their homes in London and the country.

2   Early Married Life and Patronage, 1860–76

I

Until the death of George Leconfield in 1869, Percy and Madeline Wyndham had an income of at least £5,000. If Percy received the total rental income from his Herefordshire estate (his father paying for maintenance and improvements) their income would have been closer to £6,500. This was not sufficient to buy or build a country house, but it provided adequate means with which to run a London house and Cockermouth Castle, to visit the country houses of friends and relatives, to take trips abroad and to begin collecting art. By the time Leconfield died, the Wyndhams not only had the beginnings of an original collection of contemporary art, they were also familiar with the work of some of the most successful and distinguished artists, designers and architects of the day, including Philip Webb, the future architect of Clouds.

Percy acquired a house in London in January 1862. He bought the remaining 62 years of the 99-year lease to 44 Belgrave Square, for £16,500. When the original lease had been drawn up in 1825 the ground rent was fixed at £10 a year.[1] All the Wyndham's five children were born at 44 Belgrave Square: as they grew up they earned a reputation for boisterous play in the exclusive gardens of the square. The monthly nurse who attended Madeline after each birth was Mrs Bowler, who had been nurse to Percy and his sister Constance when they were born at Drove.[2] An excited and also relieved Percy wrote to his sister, Fanny Montgomery immediately after the safe arrival of Mary, the first-born, on 3 August 1862:

> Madeline was safely confined of a fine daughter at [quarter] past 4 this afternoon . . . *The* pains began at about 11 this morning and lasted as I have said, till 4–15. The birth was very hard owing to the size and hardness of the child's head (for which I am afraid I am to blame) as no progress was made the birth had to be assisted, which made the last hour a very anxious one . . . The child weighs 11 lb. of course we should have liked a boy, but I am very thankful to God that matters have gone so well.

When baby George was born just over a year later on 29 August 1863, Lady Campbell wrote to Percy, 'you deserved a boy for having so graciously received the girl last year'. The arrival of a second boy, Guy, in 1865, made this junior Wyndham line doubly secure.

A similar routine was followed by the couple every year until the death of Percy's father. The winter months were spent at Petworth with some good hunting for Percy.[3] He could also reach London easily by train once Parliament reconvened in February

13   44 Belgrave Square,
London, 1992.

(Parliament sat for six months, from the end of the fox-hunting season to just before the opening of grouse-shooting). Mary Leconfield died in 1863. She suffered a heart attack after making an unprecedented visit to the Foreign Office to obtain news of her nephew, Wilfrid Blunt, who was seriously ill in Spain. Widowed, George Leconfield would allow only his immediate family to stay at Petworth.

Percy's sister Helen continued to live with her father, still apparently afflicted by bursts of unsociable temper. Madeline took on the role of intermediary between her father-in-law and Helen. On one occasion this involved issuing Helen with strict instructions as to her movements in the house: 'in the daytime you will [go] to the Marble Hall or where you like & come to the library just before dinner also sit in the library after dinner'. She added, 'the 5th Commandment tells us to honour our Father & Mother'.[4]

Percy and Madeline based themselves in London for the season, from April to July, attending the regular functions pursued by society, spending weekends at Petworth or at the country houses of friends and relations, making the required appearances in the House of Commons. Unlike many MPs, however, Percy did not neglect his constituency. He could easily reach Cumberland by train for brief visits and his entire family travelled up to Cockermouth at the end of each summer, to remain in the Lake District throughout the autumn months. The Wyndhams fell in love with the castle and the surrounding countryside. Photographs reveal the children, Mary, George and

14 (right)   Guy, Mary and George Wyndham at Cockermouth 1867.

15 (below)   Wilfrid Scawen Blunt and his sister Alice as Holofernes and Judith. Photograph taken by Lady Alice Gaisford c.1868. The boat was owned by Reginald Talbot.

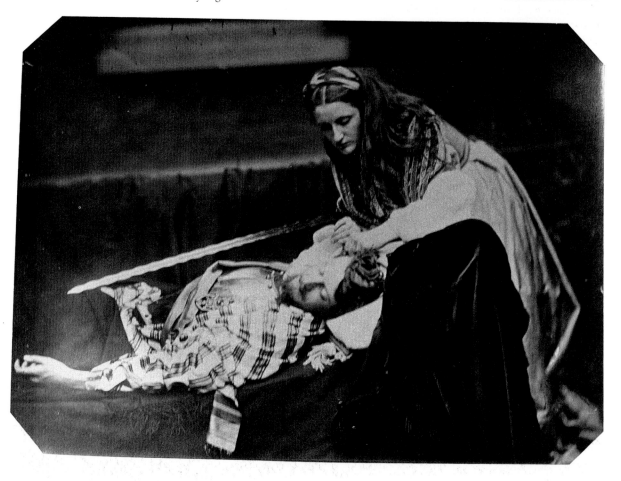

Guy, playing in the castle, peering over the battlements, looking, with their long hair and velvet outfits, like characters from the romances of Walter Scott, one of their favourite novelists. The boys were given their own suits of armour, all the children were read to from Malory's *Morte D'Arthur*.

In London, Sussex and Cumberland, at the weddings, christenings and coming-out celebrations of society, through introductions at country house weekends and shooting parties, the Wyndhams gradually acquired the circle of friends who would remain fairly constant throughout their married life. There were plenty of relations on either side from which to select a congenial few, including the Ellises at Hyères on the Mediterranean and the Spencer-Stanhopes just outside Florence. Charles Ellis, married to Madeline's sister Emily, designed his own house, La Luquette; Roddam Spencer-Stanhope acquired the Villa Nuti at Bellosguardo, overlooking Florence.

A special friend of Madeline's pre-dating her marriage, was Hugh Grosvenor, a Liberal MP until he became the third Marquess of Westminster in 1869; he was made first Duke of Westminster in 1874. He was ten years older than Madeline, married first, unhappily, to Constance Leveson-Gower, daughter of the Duke of Sutherland.[5] He quickly became a close friend of Percy's, agreeing to act as his trustee, and was closely involved in the Wyndhams' later building plans. Percy's closest female friend pre-dating his marriage to Madeline was the talented amateur photographer Lady Alice Kerr, daughter of the Marquis of Lothian. Until her marriage to Thomas Gaisford in 1870, she shared the responsibilities of hostess at the Lothians' country homes of Blickling, Newbattle and Monteviot. She also recorded the visits of friends and relatives – Wyndhams, Talbots, Cowpers, Herberts[6] – with her camera, dressing the young aristocrats in ancient costume, photographing them enacting scenes from the Bible or medieval legends. She was herself pursued for a time by Wilfrid Blunt. She photographed Wilfrid as Holofernes, with Alice Blunt, Wilfrid's sister, taking the part of Judith. Wilfrid also posed for his portrait dressed up in the unlikely role of Sir Galahad.

As certain houses are returned to again and again, a pattern is discernible in the Wyndhams' social visits from early in their marriage, and real friends become distinguishable from mere acquaintances. The significant factor in the development of their close relationships is a shared interest in the arts, especially contemporary art. Most of the Wyndhams' aristocratic friends owned or were brought up with important family collections of paintings, sculpture, furniture, porcelain, acquired, often on Grand Tours, by previous generations.

The majority restricted their support for contemporary art to the commissioning of portraits; at a time, however, when there was an extraordinary revival in the art of portrait painting and almost all the greatest painters were occasional or predominantly portraitists. Lord Cowley, for example, whose son William Wellesley was a fellow officer with Percy in the Crimea, was one of Frederic Leighton's first patrons, commissioning the artist to paint his wife and three children while living in Frankfurt in 1851. Shortly after, Francis, seventh Earl Cowper visited Leighton at his studio in Rome, then invited the artist to Wrest Park to paint portraits of himself, his mother, brother and sisters.[7]

The Marquis of Lothian invited Watts to Blickling to paint himself and his wife; Watts was then invited back by the widowed Marchioness to paint her dead husband and to design his memorial for the parish church. Lady Lothian also bought some of Watts's imaginative paintings and she commissioned his pupil, Roddam Spencer-Stanhope, to decorate her drawing room.[8]

Other friends the Wyndhams made in the early years of their marriage included the Earl and Countess of Airlie, who commissioned portraits from both Leighton and George Frederick Watts, also Blanche Airlie's younger sister Rosalind and her husband George Howard, heir, as his mother-in-law put it, to 'all the Howard honours in the direct line:[9] the earldom of Carlisle, Naworth Castle, Castle Howard and nearly 79,000 acres of land. The Howards were not typical among these cultured aristocratic families. They took art patronage beyond the commissioning of portraits, actively seeking social intercourse with their favourite artists. George Howard was himself a talented painter who regularly exhibited his work; he and Rosalind not only commissioned portraits from both Leighton and Watts, they also bought work from the Pre-Raphaelites, from the Etruscan group of painters and from Morris and Company; they commissioned Philip Webb to design their London house and Burne-Jones to paint murals (completed by Walter Crane) for the dining room. They invited artists to their London and country homes and regularly visited artists' studios in London and in Italy.[10]

The Howards were an important influence on Percy and Madeline from the mid-1860s, providing an example of aristocratic patronage of artists at a social level and on a relatively modest annual income. The couples' artistic taste was very similar. They shared an affection for Italy which they visited annually and George Howard painted, so they both acquired landscapes by the Etruscan artists such as Giovanni Costa and George Mason; they liked the dream-fantasies of Edward Burne-Jones and at one time each couple owned a version of his *Annunciation*; they bought furnishings from Morris and Company; their closest art-friends were Frederic Leighton, Valentine Prinsep and

16 (left)   Madeline Wyndham, early 1860s.

17 (right)   Madeline Wyndham by George Howard.

Edward and Georgiana Burne-Jones; they were the only aristocrats to commission houses from Philip Webb.

2

Percy wrote to Leighton in the spring of 1865 to ask whether he could paint Madeline's portrait. Leighton's paintings had been well received at the Royal Academy exhibition the previous year, the first critical triumph since his painting, 'Cimabue's celebrated Madonna is carried through the streets of Florence' was shown at the Royal Academy in 1855 and bought by the Queen for £600. Percy may have got to know Leighton before his marriage to Madeline. In his reply, Leighton calls Percy his 'old friend'; perhaps Percy visited his studio in Paris or Rome during his art tours of Europe. They were also both members of the Volunteer Movement, Leighton serving in the 38th Middlesex (Artists) Rifle Volunteers, Percy in the Sussex Regiment 6th Corps Petworth.[11]

By selecting Leighton to provide the first of their commissions, the Wyndhams unwittingly set the seal on the whole future direction of their patronage. Through Leighton and Watts they became members of one of the most effective arts circles to emerge in London. It never had an official name, but it could be called the Holland Park arts circle, for it was based in and around the homes of Watts and Leighton, and Leighton's next-door neighbour, Valentine Prinsep.

Leighton was too busy to paint Madeline; he had only just agreed to paint a portrait of Rosalind Howard.

> It would have given me real pleasure to paint a portrait of Mrs Wyndham both as the wife of an old friend and if I may say so without impertinence for her own picturesqueness – it is therefore with immense regret that I am forced to forego that pleasure – I have already 5 portraits [sic] in hand (two of them full-length) . . . for the next 12 months it will be entirely impossible to me to begin any more.[12]

Percy then wrote to Watts who, like Leighton, was hardly encouraging when he replied on 5 July 1865:

> As I have so many portraits it seems little affectation to make a show of hesitation about undertaking more but I really do want my time for work of a more poetic character. Mrs Percy Wyndham is however too good a subject to be given up without regret. At present it is certainly quite impossible for me to undertake anything new but in or after the month of December I shall be very happy to try if I can make a picture that may please you.[13]

Watts's disastrous and short-lived marriage to Ellen Terry had ended in June; he was also inundated with commissions, including portraits of both Rosalind and George Howard, and of Blanche and David Airlie. The portrait of Rosalind was completed in July. Watts's letter to Blanche suggests the Airlies were paying for it:

> Will you kindly inform me to whom the picture I have painted of Mrs Howard belongs & whether I had best send it home. I have quite finished it & have some reason to hope it is considered to be satisfactory.[14]

He was eager to break the 'bad habit of keeping so many things in my studio'; also he was anxious to resume painting Blanche. 'I shall look forward to the resumption of our (to me) pleasant sittings.'[15]

Percy meanwhile did not give up on Watts and after repeating his request, on 11 December he received a definite agreement from the artist to start the portrait, 'at the time most convenient & agreeable to Mrs Wyndham as I do not intend to paint any portraits excepting one or two already promised . . . I have no doubt I can easily make Mrs Wyndham's time fit into my engagements.'[16] The price agreed at this stage was £600. According to Watts's widow and biographer, sittings were meant to start in the summer of 1866; they were delayed, however, until the spring of 1867.[17] Watts's method of working was slow. He was not completely satisfied with his portrait of Madeline until 1874 and it was first shown in public at the opening exhibition of the Grosvenor Gallery in 1877.

Percy finally paid Watts £1,000.[18] Until the death of his father, such a figure represented almost one-fifth of Percy's total annual income. Paintings by the most successful contemporary artists were expensive. Early Renaissance paintings could be snapped up in mid-century for under £100 but works commissioned from some living artists could demand prices of over £5,000. The dealer Flatow, for example, commissioned *The Railway Station* in 1860 from William Powell Frith for £5,250; the same year Gambart commissioned *The Finding of the Saviour in the Temple* from William Holman Hunt for 5,000 guineas.[19]

It is useful to consider the incomes of some of the Wyndhams' aristocratic acquaintances in relation to the contemporary art market. It explains why many of the 'upper ten thousand' could not afford to patronise living artists even though their own lifestyles appeared comparatively luxurious. A bachelor could live comfortably on about £1,000 a year. A spacious flat in Mayfair would cost about £150 per annum; dinner at his club about 4 shillings; a suit of evening clothes from a Savile Row tailor 11 guineas and a morning suit 8 guineas; dress shirts 10sh. 6d. each. There would be little left over for a painting by a well-known contemporary artist. George and Rosalind Howard, when they first married, managed on an income of £1,400,[20] which would explain why Rosalind's sister Blanche probably paid for Watts to paint her.

The Wyndhams' friend Lord Elcho, heir to the Earl of Wemyss, managed in some style on only £2,000 per annum for the first eleven years of his marriage to Lady Anne Anson, daughter of the Earl of Lichfield:

> on this sum we had to set up, that is, find a house in London [St James's Place], furnish, get what plate we required – plus my Oxford spoons and forks, and keep house, and a family should we be blessed with one . . . Somehow we managed to get on, living comfortably, having an excellent house in London, buying pictures, and finally, in 1851, taking a share in a deer forest; all this without getting much into debt.[21]

From his undergraduate years at Oxford Lord Elcho was an avid collector of paintings but his income restricted his purchases to examples from the Renaissance, usually for less than £100 each. Even though he was a close friend of many contemporary artists including Landseer, Watts and Burne-Jones, he could not afford to commission works by them until he became tenth Earl of Wemyss, in 1883, at the age of sixty-five. Even then his portrait by John Singer Sargent was paid for by subscription, the money being raised by all his parliamentary colleagues. However, he spent some £70,000 of his

18   Francis Charteris, Lord Elcho
(later tenth Earl of Wemyss) by an
unknown artist.

inheritance on extending Gosford House in East Lothian to display his own and the
family's collection of paintings and furniture.[22]

Percy Wyndham's brother Henry was considerably wealthier, even before he became
Lord Leconfield. Unlike Percy he married an heiress, Constance Primrose,
granddaughter of the fourth Earl of Rosebery. When they married in 1867, George
Leconfield settled £35,000 on Constance, bringing in around £1,400 per annum. If,
according to normal practice, this was matched by Constance's grandfather, their
income would have been nearer £2,800, from this joint settlement of £70,000. In
addition, Henry was given the management and income of the Cumberland estates,
making a grand total of some £9,000 per annum.[23]

Henry's passions were hunting, shooting and fishing. His surviving letters to
Constance (who stayed at Petworth while he went off hunting and shooting) are filled
with details of the sport: 'I have only killed 8 fish & lost 12 that were at the point of
death. Thine, Henry. PS I enclose a fish.'[24] Constance, meanwhile, took an interest in
the arts and patronised Morris and Company for wallpapers and fabrics. When Henry
inherited Petworth he invested a considerable sum on alterations to the house to
designs by Anthony Salvin; he also commissioned Salvin to design a new London house,
completed by George Aitchison. The difference in the relative wealth of the brothers
remained constant all their lives. When one of Henry's six daughters married in 1899,
he provided her with a settlement of £25,000; the bridegroom's family had to find the
same amount.[25] Percy had only three daughters to provide for, but when Mary
Wyndham married the son and heir of their friend Lord Elcho, she received £15,000 as
her settlement.

Frederick Leighton's income in the late 1860s was about £4,000 a year, his outgoings
a mere £800. He never married and never acquired a country house and estate, so
enjoyed the complete freedom to spend his income just as he wished, on foreign travel,

entertaining lavishly at his house in Holland Park and providing generous assistance to less well-off artists. By 1880 he was earning £8,000 a year and thereafter his average earnings were some £10,000 a year; in 1892–3 his income touched £21,000. He was able to spend £4,500 on building the first part of his London house, not including the interior decorations; the Arab Hall was added later. Number 2 Holland Park Road first opened its doors to society at the end of 1866.[26]

3

The first artist's studio with which the Wyndhams became familiar and which provided their introduction to the Holland Park arts circle was not Leighton's, but Watts's, close by at Little Holland House, where Madeline went for her sittings. The hostess was Sara Monckton Prinsep and she presided over a flourishing cultural salon from 1850 until the demolition of the house in 1875.

Sara Prinsep was one of the seven 'singularly handsome' daughters (a further two daughters never reached adulthood) of James and Adeline Pattle. Her father was reputed in the family to have been an 'extravagantly wicked man and the greatest liar in India', who drank himself to death. This did not prevent Sara and her sisters from making fortunate marriages. Maria, for example, married an Anglo-Indian, Dr Jackson: their grandchildren included H.A.L. Fisher, Vanessa Bell and Virginia Woolf.[27]

Sara's forte was 'lion-hunting' and her first most important lion was George Frederick Watts.[28] Her husband Henry Thoby Prinsep was the son of John Prinsep, who had amassed a considerable fortune in India towards the end of the eighteenth century. Thoby pursued a successful career in the Indian civil service, becoming a member of the Indian Council. The Prinseps were also interested in art, as practitioners and collectors. Thoby and Sara returned to London in 1843, and while Thoby continued his work as a director of the East India Company, Sara made use of his private income to establish her salon, first at 9 Chesterfield Street, then at Little Holland House, which the Prinseps rented from Lady Holland at the suggestion of Watts himself, the favoured friend of the Hollands.

Watts was without a permanent home of his own at the time. He found the company of the Prinseps supportive and flattering, so when Sara offered him accommodation in the house, 'he came to stay three days, he stayed thirty years'.[29] The arrangement suited both hostess and tenant. Watts brought with him most of the leading artists and writers of the day: Tennyson, Browning, Ruskin, members of the Pre-Raphaelite group, Leighton, as well as every member of society who valued personal contact with the art world, including Gladstone and Disraeli. But while Watts contributed enormously to the success of the Little Holland House salon, he in return found in the Prinsep and Pattle families all the adoration he could desire: Sara's sister Sophie Dalrymple gave him his title 'Signor'.

Little Holland House was the dower house of Holland House and on the edge of the extensive Holland Park, with its stately trees and wide green spaces. On Sunday afternoons in the summer, Sara Prinsep held open house, with croquet and bowls on the lawn. In the evening, the crimson sofas and chairs which had been arranged under the shade of the trees were carried into the house: specially favoured guests were invited to remain for an impromptu dinner-party. Georgiana Burne-Jones recalled 'low, dimly lighted, richly coloured rooms' and dark passages opening into Watts's studio; the table was always spread with 'a sense of boundless welcome'.[30]

Watts only accepted two pupils, Roddam Spencer-Stanhope and Valentine Prinsep, neither of whom was to become a major artist. Their talents rested more on their good breeding and sociability; they contributed to the success of the Little Holland House salon, which widened its circle throughout the 1860s to include the homes of Prinsep himself, Leighton and Burne-Jones. The 'at-homes' and 'open days', private art shows and musical parties, formal and informal, created an effective network of contacts between artists, architects and designers and their potential patrons. This cultural circle mirrored the elaborate web of connections which operated in society itself:

> like a vast spider's web with filaments invisible yet tougher than the toughest steel, all these relationships spread and multiplied, throwing, through marriages, a network of fine glittering strands over the whole of the British Isles, enclosing society in its seemingly imperishable web.[31]

Artistic commissions, rather than marriages, created the 'network of fine glittering strands' which eventually spread throughout Britain connecting town and country houses, churches and model villages, their outward appearance and their inner contents.

The circle's success was assured right from the start. It offered a subtle combination of exclusivity and good entertainment, designed to attract a wide range of artists and designers but also aesthetically inclined members of society who liked to consider themselves a little different.

> At a time when it cannot again be too strongly emphasized, genius was treated as an eccentricity rather than courted as a divine asset, when an *artist* and a *gentleman* were terms held to be antipodean, men met there on a footing which had the attraction of novelty.[32]

Once accepted as committed members, the Airlies, Cowpers, Lothians, Ionides, Wyndhams and Howards rarely bothered to look elsewhere for any of their art requirements. Here they could find portrait and landscape painters; architects; interior designers; designers of wallpapers, carpets, upholstery and furniture; ceramicists; landscape gardeners, all of whom came with a sort of Holland Park seal of approval.

Just like society itself, the club had unwritten rules by which its members had to abide. For example, a professional artist member (male) was not expected to make love to, or even contemplate marrying an aristocratic member. Edward Burne-Jones tied himself in emotional knots when he fell in love with Frances Horner of Mells Park, but in his case the frustration and yearning probably helped to inspire yet more languishing knights at arms. However, his son Philip's passion for Percy and Madeline's daughter Mary and his inevitable disappointment when she married the heir to an earldom was to contribute to his own tragic life. On the other hand Roddam Spencer-Stanhope was perfectly free to marry Percy's cousin Lilla Wyndham-King: Spencer-Stanhope's mother Lady Elizabeth was a descendant of the Earl of Leicester. And when Valentine Prinsep married Florence Leyland, the beautiful daughter of the wealthy industrialist and patron of the arts, he was creating the sort of dynastic liaison that society itself would have supported; but rather than acquire more land through the match, he secured further links between money and the arts.

Spencer-Stanhope became a pupil of Watts in 1850, once his mother Lady Elizabeth was reassured by the surroundings of Little Holland House and the character of the teacher: 'I am very glad I have seen him [Watts] and his pictures, which *must* be the result of a highly religious mind'.[33] As Spencer-Stanhope knew the Lothians of Blickling, he may have been responsible for introducing Watts to the household and the resulting commissions.

Val Prinsep came under the influence of Watts as soon as the artist became a lodger in his parents' house. In 1856 he finally decided to give up his intention of following his father's career in the Indian civil service in order to devote his life to art. The following year, through Watts's influence, both Spencer-Stanhope and Prinsep were invited to collaborate on the Oxford Union murals, working alongside Rossetti, Morris, Burne-Jones, Arthur Hughes and J. Hungerford Pollen. The same group of artists established their own exhibiting society, the Hogarth Club, in 1858 and were soon joined by other artists disillusioned with the Royal Academy, which either refused their works or hung them badly. Watts joined, as did Leighton and Philip Webb.[34]

Webb was already a close friend of Morris and Burne-Jones. He was senior assistant in the office of the architect George Edmund Street when Morris joined as a pupil in 1856. Three years later, when Morris married Jane Burden, one of the models 'discovered' in Oxford and used for the murals in the Union, Webb was commissioned to design his first house for the couple. The Red House at Bexleyheath was also the first of Webb's houses designed specially for an artist. Fortunately for Webb, there were other members of the group of artist-friends wealthy enough to commission his services: Spencer-Stanhope and Val Prinsep. While the Red House was being completed Webb began Sandroyd near Cobham for Spencer-Stanhope, ready for occupation in 1860.[35]

Val Prinsep had to wait until 1864 for Webb to begin on his home, this time in Holland Park. It was the first of several artists' houses to be built on the Holland estate. Being so close to Little Holland House, it became a sort of show-house for Webb and helped to advertise his individual style to all the members of the Holland Park arts circle.[36] The Howards, for example, were frequent guests of Prinsep and undoubtedly decided to commission Webb to build their own house on Palace Green after getting to know 1 Holland Park Road, though Rosalind commented: 'we should not have black doors'.[37] The Wyndhams were also familiar with Prinsep's house before the Howards' was completed.

The outside of 1 Holland Park Road was, typically of Webb's design, conspicuous for an entire absence of ornament.[38] From the garden, the most noticeable features were the enormous Gothic-arched windows of the studio. Inside, the studio was the most significant room in the house, 40′ × 25′, the walls painted salmon-red. There was an adjoining room connected by big folding doors in which the artist could tackle particularly large paintings, the Delhi Durbar commission, for example. There was also a dressing room for models just off the main studio and an additional staircase for the servants, who occupied two bedrooms in the attic but carried out their chores from rooms below the ground floor. In Prinsep's house, models were permitted to come up to the studio using the main stairs: unlike some of his fellow artists, Prinsep refused to treat them as second-class citizens. Morris wallpapers covered the walls in the other rooms of the house and the woodwork was painted brown apart from in the dining room, where it was dark green. Prinsep's taste for the Orient was evident from the quantity of blue-and-white china and the use of Japanese leather-paper on door panels, for dadoes and below the handrail on the stairs; Italian tapestries hung in the dining-room and hall.

Plate 1 (facing page) Lady Pamela Fitzgerald (La Belle Pamela) and her daughter Pamela, Lady Campbell, mother of Madeline Wyndham, by J. Mallary, c.1800.

The house cost almost £3,000, paid for by Prinsep's father. Val never made a large amount of money as an artist but did have the advantage of a private income; he also married an heiress. When his father-in-law, Frederick Leyland died in 1892, Val immediately commissioned Philip Webb to virtually double the size of the house so that it almost touched the Arab Hall of Leighton's house next door.[39]

Leighton did not become President of the Royal Academy until 1878, but his architect George Aitchison designed a house which would present a backdrop magnificent enough for the future leader of the Victorian art world. The first stage was completed at the end of 1866 and almost immediately Leighton began to hold the parties which became an essential part of the London season. He realised the importance of presentation:

> When so much money was at stake it was inevitable that the art world became organised into an art market. The packaging was an important as the content, if not more so. The moneyed public who visited artists' houses expected a certain standard of taste and lavishness as a guarantee that they were on to the genuine article.[40]

Leighton was not simply a talented artist; the style in which he entertained was effective in putting his aristocratic guests at their ease. He possessed the looks, charm and talent to attract 'all the great ones of the London world'[41] to his home, so many that their carriages blocked Holland Park Road. The speed with which he made an

19   Valentine Prinsep's house, 1 Holland Park Road (now 14), illustrated in *The Building News*, October 29 1880.

Plate II (facing page, above)   Preliminary sketch for *The Evening Hymn* by George Mason. The whereabouts of the final oil painting owned by the Wyndhams is unknown.

Plate III (facing page, below)   *Women Stealing Wood* by Giovanni Costa, 1873–7, first exhibited at the Grosvenor Gallery, 1877 and titled *Evening on the Sands at Ardea*. Sold by the Wyndhams through Colnaghi to George Howard, Earl of Carlisle in 1899 for £100 plus 5 per cent commission.

impact on society is reflected by his glittering presence in Disraeli's novel *Lothair*, which was published in May 1870. Mr Phoebus is a thinly disguised Leighton, and 'the most successful, not to say the most eminent, painter of the day':

> his appearance was striking. Above the middle height, his form, athletic though lithe and symmetrical, was crowned by a countenance aquiline but delicate, and from many circumstances of a remarkable radiancy. The lustre of his complexion, the fire of his eye, and his chestnut hair in profuse curls, contributed much to this dazzling effect. A thick but small moustache did not conceal his curved lip or the scornful pride of his distended nostril, and his beard, close but not long, did not veil the singular beauty of his mouth. It was an arrogant face, daring and vivacious, yet weighted with an expression of deep and haughty thought.[42]

The studio at 2 Holland Park Road was 58' × 25' with a gallery at the east end. The walls were painted Indian red and the woodwork, as in the rest of the house, black and gold. In this house, models reached the studio by a private staircase; for society the approach was by a far grander staircase, designed to show off the aesthetically inclined visitors to maximum advantage. They included Leighton's 'old friend' Percy Wyndham and his wife, also the most famous musicians and singers of the day, persuaded by the artist to perform in his studio: the pianist and conductor Charles Hallé, founder of the Hallé concerts in Manchester; the violinist Wilma Neruda who became Hallé's second wife in 1888; the violinist Joseph Joachim and his friend the cellist Alfredo Piatti; the mezzo-soprano Pauline Viardot-Garcia and the pianist Nathalie Janotha.[43]

As well as giving financial support to less well-off artists, organising exhibitions on their behalf and commissioning works for his private collection, Leighton also found them patrons from among his acquaintances in society. He was probably responsible for introducing both the Howards and the Wyndhams to the paintings of Giovanni Costa and George Mason, members of the Etruscan School. Certainly Percy was buying work by Mason before 1868.

George Mason had become friendly with Leighton and Costa in Rome, and his painting, *Ploughing in the Campagna* was enthusiastically received at the Royal Academy in 1857. The following year Mason married, but financial difficulties and depression interrupted his painting. Only Leighton was able to persuade him to begin again in 1862. He settled in Hammersmith, where he was visited by Costa, and received financial help from both Leighton and Watts, as well as recommendations to potential patrons. Leighton himself commissioned his own version of *The Wind on the Wold* from Mason, who began exhibiting again at the Royal Academy.

Two letters survive from Mason to Percy. The first, dated simply 1 February, is a response to Percy's commissioning two paintings: neither party knows one another personally:

> Sir – I must apologise for not having answered your letter before.
> I shall be glad to do the two paintings for you which you require and feel much obliged to your consideration in leaving the choice of subject to me.
> To determine the size and importance of the pictures it only remains for me to know what price you are disposed to give for each picture.[44]

Percy must have been confident of Mason's style to offer such a free hand to the artist. But he could have seen Leighton's version of *The Wind on the Wold*, also *The Gander*, exhibited at the Royal Academy in 1865. One of the commissioned paintings was to be Mason's masterpiece, *Evening Hymn*, hung in the Royal Academy in 1868. It received enthusiastic reviews:

> [It] simply represents groups of village-girls returning homewards in their Sunday cotton prints, and relieved against a deep, rich glow of sunset deepening into twilight, which gives to their figures a spirit-like vagueness and beauty exquisitely accordant with the suggestion of the solemn stillness of the hour of nightfall being broken only by innocent harmonious voices singing their even-song of prayer and praise.[45]

The Wyndhams liked it so much they also bought a small study of the dog. Other paintings by Mason acquired at this time included *The Swans: Yarrow*, exhibited at the Royal Academy in 1866, a sketch for it, *The Gander* and two landscape studies. Madeline may also have brought Mason's work to the notice of Hugh Grosvenor, who became a patron.

Later, on a visit to Italy in 1874, the Wyndhams visited Costa's studio and bought a large oil painting, which they exhibited at the Grosvenor Gallery under the title, *Winter Evening on the Sands near Ardea, Rome*. Costa had begun the work twenty years before on his expedition into the Campagna with Leighton and Mason. It makes an interesting pair with Mason's *Evening Hymn*. When Costa's work was shown by the Fine Art Society in 1882 one critic drew links between the two artists:

> The same refined sense of beauty, the same poetic feeling, are present in the works of both. They both looked with deep sympathy on the lives of the workers and toilers around them, and have shown in their pictures how fully they realise the intimate connection that exists between the daily tasks and simple joys of the poor and the beauty of earth and sky which embraces them.[46]

Though it is not possible to identify all the paintings that can be seen in photographs of the interior of Clouds (no photographs survive of the interior of 44 Belgrave Square), many are obviously from the Etruscan School, by followers of Costa and Mason if not these specific artists. Madeline and Percy appreciated the very special response to Italy as represented by the Etruscans: 'idyllic Italy, classic Italy, known and felt in all its radiance of light, its delicacy of tint, its restful nobility of form, and purity of outline'.[47] The subjectivity of the Etruscans' approach to landscape, in England as well as in Italy, linked their artistic interpretations to the spiritual feelings about land shared by Madeline and Percy:

> they sought to describe the physical sensations of being in the open air, but for them even more important was the evocation of the spiritual associations, which may be literary, historical, political or purely personal, which attached people to those places.[48]

George Howard also painted in the Etruscan manner, and Leighton was the group's champion in Britain, all of which added to the attraction of the painters for the Wyndhams.

Social contacts between the Holland Park artists and their patrons continued throughout the London season but were maintained mostly by letter over the rest of the year: only a few artists positively enjoyed staying in country houses, though most were persuaded to make brief visits. The artists remained closely identified with the city, working in their own studio-homes: Watts and Burne-Jones were unusual in acquiring second homes in the countryside, and Watts unique in eventually settling permanently in a Surrey village. Leighton, for example, does not appear to have visited the Wyndhams in the country, though he was a frequent guest in Belgrave Square.[49] Watts also rarely stayed at country houses, however much he admired the beauty of the hostesses. He wrote to Blanche Airlie in 1872: 'Many thousand thanks for your invitation . . . [I] wish that I could come, but what should I do in the "Halls of dazzling light"?'[50] To Madeline he wrote of the pleasures of riding over the downs, but he still remained in London within the security of the Prinseps' household.

While continuing to paint in his studio, Watts wrote letters to his patrons which reveal the intricate negotiations that were conducted between artist and patron over the precise cost and size of a painting. Before Madeline's own portrait was finished she began negotiating with Watts about the price of other paintings, a version of *Orpheus and Eurydice*, also *Endymion*. Wilfrid Blunt, who accompanied Madeline to Little Holland House for some of her sittings, records that she was used by Watts as a model for Eurydice. Watts was difficult to pin down when it came to the question of money:

> I cannot find out that I really fixed any price on the picture [*Orpheus and Eurydice*]. If you have any distinct impression that I did so of course I shall abide by the arrangement.
> If I were putting a price on it now for the first time I should say to you (remembering that it was by way of being yours when it was much less finished) 200 guineas – I should ask £250 if it were mine and I could send it to the exhibition [RA]. For the Endymion I shall ask 500.
> In fixing my prices now and for the future I am and shall be guided by the market value for of course a picture is (within certain limits) worth as much as it will fetch in the market, but I trust to you to tell me exactly what you think.[51]

Madeline accepted Watts's price, 200 guineas, for *Orpheus and Eurydice* and she allowed him to exhibit the painting at the Royal Academy; William Graham bought *Endymion*. Watts continued to worry about the arrangements:

> Had your impression been that smaller sum than I thought of had been named, of course I should have felt bound to abide by it, but as it is the price will be two hundred and ten pounds (like Doctors we always work for the guineas).

The dimensions of the painting ($20.5'' \times 13''$) were also sure to disappoint:

> I don't think you will care less for your picture because the picture is not so large as you expected, no doubt it is but fair that a professional man should after hard work and anxiety be able to make a good income.[52]

He had to justify his position to his patrons, to explain why his paintings could indeed fetch such a large amount in the market-place.

Edward Burne-Jones's opinion of country house visits was expressed in a letter to Olive Maxse:

from the dawn when a bore of a man comes and empties my pockets and laughs at my underclothing and carries them away from me, and brings me unnecessary tea, right on till heavy midnight I [was] miserable – and if there is one of all the company that it would be nice to spend all the time with I can never be with her (him I mean) somebody else steps in first as at the pool of Siloam.[53]

His wife was more politic: 'by degrees Edward went more and more into Society, but compared with those to the manner born his most was not much'.[54]

The two artists who seem to have enjoyed the country house scene were Richard Doyle and Val Prinsep. Both stayed with the Wyndhams at Cockermouth Castle in the late 1860s, though Doyle could not compete with the social graces and charm of Val Prinsep, indisputably the most sociable of the Holland Park circle. His consummate charm was his most, indeed his only, enduring characteristic; his painting style changed with every passing fashion. Called a 'glorified dilettante' by some critics, assured of financial security, 'he seemed always content to bask in the reflected glory of others'.

> Striking in his looks, if not particularly handsome, warm, gentle and kind, with a boyish sense of fun, and a skilled raconteur with a great sense of humour, he was naturally extremely popular.[55]

Val Prinsep painted at least two studies of the Wyndhams' daughter Mary on his visits to Cockermouth; the full-size painting was exhibited at the Royal Academy in 1870. He painted George and Guy together at about the same time and also appears to have painted Madeline, though only a letter from Mr Speaker Denison to Percy, dated 26 April 1869, survives as evidence:

> I called on Mr Prinsep on Saturday afternoon, and after telling him what had past [sic] between us about the watercolour sketch of Mrs Percy Wyndham, I asked him if he would be so good as to sell it to me – He answered he was sorry he could not comply with my request because he considered that he had presented it to Mrs Percy Wyndham. Perhaps something could be arranged about this – If I was to present Mrs Percy Wyndham with a small pocket mirror, by looking into it, she could always see something better than the Picture. But I await anything you may please to say about it.[56]

Prinsep continued to be a country house guest of the Wyndhams until the early 1880s. In 1881 he was a guest at Wilbury in Wiltshire for two weeks, painting Mary and George, playing tennis and party tricks. There is no evidence, however, that he stayed at Clouds; Edward Poynter replaced him as the regular country house weekend artist.

4

When Henry Wyndham became the second Baron Leconfield, Percy lost the hospitality of Petworth and his northern home in Cockermouth Castle. Financially, however, Percy benefited considerably, so much so that according to family legend he and his brother had a fight 'over the port and their inheritance'[57] in the Square Room at Petworth. For some years both wives, who were the best of friends, could communicate only by letter. Constance wrote rather pathetically to Madeline not long after her husband inherited Petworth:

> After much consideration I resolved not to ask Henry about that matter we discussed on Saturday. It seemed to me that it would be disloyal to him so long as he was not on friendly terms with Percy, to ask to see Percy's wife here. I think that you will quite understand what I mean, & you know without my telling you how very very glad I should be to see you, if things were otherwise.[58]

George Leconfield had made his will on 21 August 1867,[59] shortly after the marriage of Henry to Constance Primrose. Most of Henry's inheritance was passed down to him via the settlement drawn up in Egremont's will: Leconfield had enjoyed only a life interest in the family estates. Percy's inheritance came from the property which Leconfield could dispose of independently, including the Much Cowarne estate in Herefordshire which was confirmed as his in a separate codicil and valued at £114,000.

The trustees appointed to act for Percy were his brother-in-law, Colonel Robert Nigel Fitzhardinge Kingscote, a widower – Percy's sister Caroline died in 1852 only a year after their marriage – and a Sussex clergyman. They were charged with raising an immediate £20,000 for Percy from land in Sussex over which Leconfield had a life interest according to the terms of Egremont's will. They were also to hold in trust for Percy and his heirs the land in Sussex known as the Marlborough estate (Leconfield had bought it from the Duke of Marlborough), though if Percy wanted to sell it, his brother had an option to buy. Similary they were to hold in trust for Percy and his heirs Leconfield's entire residuary estate, which comprised land in Yorkshire, Cumberland and Ireland, three life policies (valued at a total of £15,000), shares in turnpike roads and gas companies and £16,000 cash.

Henry had a three-year option to buy the land and the shares and decided to take up the offer. On 1 October 1869 the brothers agreed on a valuation: Henry would pay Percy £48,725 8sh. 10d. on or before 25 March 1875. Until then he had to pay Percy interest of £3 10sh. per cent per annum, some £1,800. Letters between Henry and his solicitors suggest he bought Percy out early, around December 1873, when the balance due was £44,072 16sh. 9d. In John Bateman's *New Domesday Survey* of 1876 Percy Wyndham no longer owned any land in Sussex so it could be assumed he also sold the Marlborough estate to his brother to round off the property surrounding Petworth. Yet in 1913, when Percy's son and heir George rationalised the family estates to provide for his own son's marriage settlement, the Wyndhams still owned some property in Sussex and Yorkshire. Bateman's survey was not infallible. Percy inherited absolutely his father's estates in South Australia. He was also left thirty oil paintings from East Lodge, Leconfield's house in Brighton, and all the gold and silver plate from the house, 'whether useful or ornamental'. In addition he acquired the Grove Plate and Grove Service and first choice of five carriage horses.

A priority in 1869 for Percy and Madeline was to find a new home in Cumberland, not just because it was Percy's constituency, but because they had grown to love the Lake District. They were fortunate: Sir Wilfrid Lawson, a local landowner, happened to have a country house to spare just a few miles to the north-east of Cockermouth. Isel Hall had been used as a dower house up until 1867, but it then became vacant. Sir Wilfrid's main residence in Cumberland was Brayton House.

Isel is a spectacular house with fine views to the south. The oldest part is the peel-tower, dating from the reign of Henry VIII, which was added to later in the sixteenth century. The hall has an enormous fireplace and linenfold panelling, and there is more sixteenth-century panelling throughout the living rooms. Again the Wyndhams had found a house rich in history, a romantic home to inspire their children's play and their own visions of the 'perfect' country house; they rented it from Sir Wilfrid until 1877. It was occupied by the whole family throughout the autumn months when Percy dealt with most of his constituency business, although he often travelled up to Cumberland by train from London at other times of the year. The children spent much of the year at Isel together with their nannies, tutors and, from 1875, their governess. Richard Doyle painted several views of the house and distant mountains and exhibited them at the Grosvenor Gallery in 1877 and 1878. By then, the Wyndhams had given up their northern home so were anxious to keep at least one of Doyle's watercolours as a memorial. Percy approached the artist, who replied from his club, the Athenaeum, on 26 May 1878:

> Although not anxious to part with that view of Isel . . . you wishing to have it is quite another matter and I am very much pleased that you should desire to become the owner – and like to think of the drawing finding a home in your house.[60]

20 The servants at Isel Hall, 1870s.

Though Percy still had to wait for the balance of his inheritance to be paid by Henry, from 1869 the Wyndhams had sufficient additional income to undertake considerable decorative work in their London home as well as commissioning further paintings. They were familiar with the effects achieved by the partnership of George Aitchison and Frederic Leighton at 2 Holland Park Road so commissioned the pair to redesign parts of the interior of 44 Belgrave Square. Aitchison's first designs, for the decorations of the main staircase hall, doorways and passages leading off, and including five paintings by Leighton to be placed high above the second-floor landing, were completed on 26 October 1869. He produced further designs for the inner hall, dated 23 July 1871.[61] When the American Moncure Daniel Conway published his *Travels in South Kensington with notes on Decorative Art and Architecture in England* in 1882 he included a brief description of the work:

> In the home of the Hon. Percy Wyndham, Belgrave Square, there is a grand staircase, which has on the wall, near one of its landings, five life-sized classical figures, by Sir Frederick [sic] Leighton, and at the top a deep frieze of cormorants, storks, and other wild birds.[62]

The colours used by Aitchison – pinks, greens, greys, powder blue – with Leighton's dancing figures set against gold backgrounds, and the delicacy of the painting of decorative borders, with flowers, birds, foliage, have a vitality and freshness not normally associated with High Victoriana. The impact of Leighton's naked or semi-clad life-sized figures, visible from every point of the grand staircase, must have been considerable.[63]

A letter to Percy from Leighton probably refers to the first stage of decorative work, although it could also be referring to Percy's portrait, which was undertaken by Leighton in about 1870.[64] Leighton thanks Percy for his 'kind note & cheque just received,' and says that he is 'sincerely pleased that the result of our joint endeavour has turned out satisfactory – Goodbye till the spring. I shall be anxious to hear your adventures.'[65] Percy was off to India for a six-month visit, beginning in October 1869. His brother-in-law Lord Naas, now Earl of Mayo, had been made Viceroy of India at the beginning of the year.

While he was away Madeline's mother, Lady Campbell, died. Madeline received the usual number of letters offering condolence, including one from Watts:

> I will not attempt to offer any condolences on your bereavement, excepting that it seems to me Death is one of the least of human misfortunes, rest in the calm of which I do not doubt, & long for very often.[66]

and another from her eldest son George, now six years old: 'We are so very sorry that dear Granny had to suffer so. you must be so unhappy poor dear Mamma. How we want to kiss and hug you and try to comfort you. We will both try to be as good to you as you were to Granny.'[67]

Percy returned from India in the spring of 1870. He was not to see his brother-in-law again. Though Mayo's advice on ruling the empire was hardly unusual for the time: 'teach your subordinates that we are all British gentlemen engaged in the magnificent work of governing an inferior race',[68] he was at the same time paternalistic. The programme of rehabilitation for Indians which he initiated in the penal settlement on the Andaman Islands included craftwork. Some of the convicts made rugs which found

21 Percy Wyndham by Frederic Leighton. At Stanway House.

their way regularly to Henry and Constance at Petworth, sent, 'with the Viceroy's compliments'.[69] In February 1872 Mayo and his wife made their first visit to the settlement. But while Blanche remained in the boat, her husband was fatally stabbed in the back: his body was carried back to her by the shocked entourage. Mayo was fifty years old.

Madeline became pregnant immediately after Percy's return from India: Pamela was born on 14 January 1871. She was their fifth and last child. Their fourth child, Madeline, had been born just after the death of Lord Leconfield. Madeline almost immediately became involved in a new artistic venture which had social and educational implications, to found a school of needlework. The planning was undertaken by the group of aristocratic friends made by the Wyndhams early in their marriage, united by their interest in the arts, in particular Lady Marion Alford, and her daughter-in-law Adelaide, Countess Brownlow, chatelaines of Ashridge and Belton. Their coup was to involve two of Queen Victoria's daughters, Helena, HRH Princess Christian of Schleswig-Holstein and HRH Princess Louise. Princess Christian agreed to be the first president, Lady Marion Alford was the vice-president, Madeline and Princess Louise were members of the inaugural committee.

The motive of these artistically inclined aristocratic women was not simply to hob-nob with royalty: they aimed to supply 'suitable employment for gentlewomen' and to restore 'ornamental needlework to the high place it once held among the decorative arts'.[70] This was at a time when middle-class women without sufficient private means could find employment only as governesses or schoolteachers: the age of the secretary had not yet dawned. Women who enrolled in the Schoool of Art Needlework, as it was first called, received wages but did not also suffer the 'lowering of social status usually involved in paid employment of gentlewomen – ladies had only to mix with their own kind within the confines of the school's studio and workshops'.[71]

The first premises were set up in a small apartment above a bonnet shop in Sloane Street. Twenty young ladies were selected to join, from the 'impoverished genteel class'. In 1875 the Queen became patron and the school moved to a temporary site in the buildings on Exhibition Road which had been erected for the 1867 International Exhibition. Three years later, the school was incorporated under the Board of Trade with a Managing and Finance Committee and a salaried manager to overlook the whole concern. At this point Percy Wyndham became officially involved as one of the seven nominal shareholders. The founding ladies of the Royal School of Art Needlework were almost all proficient at needlework and interested in design work. Madeline executed an elaborate bookcase curtain designed by William Morris. This was exhibited when the school sent work to the Philadelphia Centennial of 1876. An exhibition space was filled with representative work from the school; Princess Christian won the highest possible award of the Centennial for her embroidered screen. Her sister HRH Princess Louise was a sculptress of some ability but she also designed vast curtains for Alfred Waterhouse's Manchester Town Hall, giant sunflowers worked in appliqué and crewel woolwork. Lady Marion Alford produced an influential textbook, *Needlework as Art*, in 1884.

The school was deliberately called the Royal School of *Art* Needlework. The founding members were concerned to raise needlework once more to an art form; Madeline's personal contacts with artists were to have an enormous influence on the work of the school, but the school in turn helped to publicise to a wide circle of wealthy clients the designs of some of the leading artists and designers of the day.[72] Those involved with the school, either through teaching the students or producing designs to be worked on and copied, included Burne-Jones, William Morris, Walter Crane, Leighton and Aitchison, Val Prinsep, Edward Poynter, Alexander Fisher, Selwyn Image and G.F. Bodley.

Contacts were made use of by all members of the committee to raise funds, heighten awareness of the work of the school, and eventually to obtain permanent purpose-built premises – opened in 1903 on Exhibition Road. Madeline persuaded Watts to write a lengthy letter for publication in *Nineteenth Century* (March 1881) in praise of the work of the school. He commented that, 'an amount of perfection has been reached, for which I was by no means prepared'. The artist, however, to whom she became closest, and who was involved with the work of the school from its beginnings, was Edward Burne-Jones.

He had been involved in embroidery as early as 1860, when he made a series of figures from *Morte d'Arthur* for Morris's Red House. Early in the 1870s he produced two large designs for *portières*, 'Musica' and 'Poesis', specially for the school, each worked in outline with brown crewel on linen. They were so popular that a number of copies were carried out: the Wyndhams eventually acquired a full-size cartoon of each, enlarged by Burne-Jones's assistant Charles Fairfax Murray, then completed in full colour by the artist himself when he stayed with the Wyndhams in Wiltshire.

Madeline and her children became frequent guests (Percy less often) at the Burne-Joneses' home in Fulham. The Grange, North End Road, had once been the home of Samuel Richardson. Ford Madox Brown described Edward and Georgiana's house-warming as 'a very swell affair, the house being newly decorated in the "firm" taste, looked charming; the women looked lovely, the singing unrivalled'.[73] When

22 'Poesis' by Edward Burne-Jones (Orpheus playing his lyre before the throne of Poetry). The large cartoon was included in the Clouds' contents sale, 1933 (together with 'Musica'). Acquired by Charles Adeane of Babraham, remaining in the family until 1972 when it was sold at Christies; sold again at Sotheby's in 1981.

W. Graham Robertson visited the house some years later he was struck by the darkness of the hall and dining room, 'even more shadowy with its deep-green leaf-patterned walls'; throughout, the impression was of a 'tinted gloom through which clear spots of colour shone jewel-like'. At the end of the garden was the studio added later by the artist,

> a huge barrack of a place, like a schoolroom or a gymnasium, containing none of the usual properties and elegancies of a 'show' studio, but round the walls were ranged the studies for the Perseus and Andromeda series, paintings in *gouache* of the full size of the proposed oil pictures ... Down the whole length of the bare whitewashed wall are the scenes of the pictured story ... Many other pictures, more or less incomplete, hung on the walls or stood dustily in corners, for the artist seldom worked continuously on the same canvas, but laid one after another aside, sometimes for years, while he developed other designs.[74]

The atmosphere of the house and studio was completely different to that of the aesthetic bachelor establishments of Val Prinsep and Leighton; the artist was surrounded by an adoring but also demanding family. Favoured patrons and friends were invited to become part of the household, to join in reading in front of the fire, charades, romping in the garden; on one occasion the artist wheeled his wife round the garden in a wheelbarrow to the delight of all the children present.

Mary Wyndham was close in age to Burne-Jones's children, Philip and Margaret, and from her early teens was frequently a guest at the Grange, even staying overnight. Evenings were spent sitting in front of the fire, Phil showing off his magic lantern and Burne-Jones recounting his early days living with William Morris in Red Lion Square. In the morning Margaret joined Mary in her bed for breakfast and sisterly talk, 'yards of nonsense,' Mary called it. Meanwhile their mothers developed their own close relationship, Georgiana relying on the support of women such as Madeline and Rosalind Howard when her husband was caught up in one of his infatuations.[75]

5

On 27 June 1872 the Wyndhams were invited to dinner by George and Rosalind Howard in their new house on Palace Green, designed by Philip Webb. They had been invited over a year before, when the Howards began formal entertaining, but Madeline was still nursing Pamela.[76] The Howards' house presented them with the combined efforts of Webb, Morris and Company and Burne-Jones, an alternative to the aesthetic house envisaged by the Aitchison and Leighton partnership. Webb had responded to George Howard's artistic interests, and designed a tall, mostly red brick house of four storeys, the exterior rather severe; as Lethaby put it, 'design at once sane and ornamental . . . the interior spacious, dignified and well lighted'.[77]

There had been a struggle over the original design: Webb had to defend himself against objections raised by the Commissioners of Woods and Forests supported by a report prepared by the establishment architects Anthony Salvin and T.H. Wyatt:

> We are unable to discover what style or period of architecture Mr Webb has sought to adopt. We think the combination of square, circular and segmental forms for the windows and pointed arches for the doors and recesses, unusual and objectionable.[78]

A compromise was eventually reached, Webb giving up the idea of the house being faced entirely in red brick, and introducing some stone cornices and carvings. But he still got in a swipe at all the inferior developments going up in the area when replying to the Commissioners:

> In conclusion, I must express my great surprise that you should consider it worthwhile to hinder the creation of a building which – whatever may be its demerits – possesses some character and originality, tempered most certainly with reverential attention to the works of acknowledged masters of the art of architecture and as certainly formed with a wish to avoid adding another insult to this irreparably injured neighbourhood.[79]

Morris and Company were closely involved in the interior decorations: Morris's blue pomegranate paper covered the library walls; his green pomegranate was used in George Howard's dressing room; his daisy pattern in the nursery. The ceiling of the drawing room was painted yellow and white with a Morris textile frieze in willow pattern around the walls; the floor was covered with white china matting with a Persian rug on top. The paintings in the house included Costa's *Pinewood near Pisa* in the drawing room, a small chalk head of Rosalind drawn by D.G. Rossetti in 1870, and Edward Poynter's watercolour portrait of Georgiana Burne-Jones commissioned by Rosalind in 1869, as well as George Howard's own landscapes.[80]

The most unusual room in the house was the dining room, which eventually presented the combined decorative efforts of Morris, Burne-Jones and Walter Crane. The walls and doors were panelled in wood painted blue-green and the ceiling was coffered and decorated by Morris with flowers and foliage. All the walls were covered with Burne-Jones's frieze, twelve murals depicting scenes from the story of Cupid and Psyche; the dado below the frieze was worked in a design of gold and silver by Morris; below this were inscriptions in gold from Morris's poem 'The Story of Cupid and Psyche'.

The effect of the dining room was very different to the effect created by Aitchison at the Wyndhams' house in Belgrave Square: there, delicate designs and colours, reds, powder blues, set off carefully displayed works of art; at Palace Green the visitor was enveloped in a romantic Victorian's view of a medieval golden age, all gold and silver and painted panels. The whole house presented the Wyndhams with ideas, some to be rejected, some adapted for their own Webb house. Most significantly, Palace Green was designed for an artist who was also a member of the aristocracy, a combination of relevance to the Wyndhams. The *Studio* emphasised the evident 'good taste' but also the overall impression of modesty: there was nothing showy, nothing bragging of class and wealth:

> Even its good taste is not unduly evident, but becomes the more apparent the more closely you observe it. By thus avoiding emphasis of all kinds, the treasures it holds seem but ordinary fittings, until more curious inspections shows many of them to be unique masterpieces. The majority of these are modern – a singularly pleasing exception to the average 'palace' of to-day, which, if it holds masterpieces of any kind, is singularly careful that they shall be of goodly age, hall-marked as it were with official approval of their sterling value.[81]

The Howards' guest-list holds few surprises: a combination of relatives (Stanleys, Airlies); aristocratic but art-loving friends; northern neighbours including the Wyndhams' landlord Sir Wilfrid Lawson; the artists and writers associated with the Holland Park arts circle.

The regular guests of the Howards reassembled at the Wyndhams' house in Belgrave Square, at the Grange, Little Holland House and 1 and 2 Holland Park Road. Projects were discussed and usually became realities, for example the founding of the Royal School of Art Needlework and the Grosvenor Gallery; how to assist the widow of George Mason; support for the Society for the Protection of Ancient Buildings. All of these houses were effective advertisements for their architects and designers, for the teamwork of Leighton and Aitchison, Webb and Morris and Company. HRH Princess Louise, who married George Howard's cousin, the Marquis of Lorne in 1871, was one of the first of the Howards' guests at Palace Green. She admired the Morris wallpapers so much that she persuaded George Howard to accompany her to the firm's showrooms in Queen Square, where she chose paper for her own rooms in Kensington Palace.[82]

Though members of the circle represented different political parties – Percy Wyndham, for example, was a Conservative MP, George Howard a Liberal – their political differences were not allowed to interfere with their concern for art in all its aspects. The situation changed at the 1885 general election, when George Howard took the opposite political view to his wife, opposing Gladstone's Home Rule bill and aligning himself with the Liberal Unionists. Their twenty-year-long partnership came to an end. Rosalind established herself at Castle Howard and George at Naworth.

6

23 (left)   Percy Wyndham and his son George.

24 (right)   Madeline Wyndham and her daughter Pamela, taken at Hyères, December 1873. Wilfrid Blunt kept a copy of this photograph in his memoirs.

In January 1874 the Wyndhams left their children behind at Hyères with Madeline's sister and brother-in-law, Emily and Charles Ellis; they then went on an extended tour of Italy. The visit coincided with the final payment of Percy's inheritance by his brother; added to the 1869 legacies, this now gave the Wyndhams sufficient money to acquire and maintain their own home in the country.

Percy and Madeline never seem to have considered building on their Much Cowarne estate. No records survive of Percy even visiting. There was only a 'shooting box' on the

estate in which the family could stay; it was called Cowarne Cottage and offered five bedrooms, stabling and dog kennels. The property was primarily a 'sporting domain', boasting 'six celebrated fox covers' and fourteen farms.[83] The Wyndhams were not particularly friendly with other landowners in the area and had no ancestral connections with Herefordshire.

Some time early in 1874, the retired ambassador Sir Alexander Malet decided to sell the estate of Wilbury, near Salisbury in Wiltshire. He hoped to get £150,000 for the 3,000 acres, but was not including the eighteenth-century Wilbury Park House. According to local land agents, the value of the land was nearer £90,000 and Malet received no offers that he was prepared to accept. His attempts to sell his estate coincided with the return of the Wyndhams from their tour of Italy and France. Percy also decided the property was overpriced. However, when Malet began instead to look for a tenant for Wilbury Park House, Percy again showed an interest. On this occasion a deal was struck and by the end of the year the Wyndhams were established in their, albeit temporary, home in southern England.

Charles Warre Malet had acquired Wilbury in 1803 after a distinguished and profitable career with the East India Company. The mansion had been designed in about 1710 by William Benson, who was Surveyor of HM Works immediately after Christopher Wren. Described as one of the first 'dilettanti Palladians',[84] Benson was much influenced by Inigo Jones, and Pevsner has described Wilbury as the 'first neo-Inigo-Jones house in England'.[85] The grey stone and stuccoed house now presents a classic appearance, with nine windows along the front, four central windows on the

25 Wilbury Park, south front, 1959.

ground floor set under a four-columned portico. Behind the portico is a splendid room in which the Wyndhams would hold their parties and amateur theatricals. In the grounds, and perfect for children, were grottoes, an octagonal summer-house and an archway to play under.[86]

The Wyndhams and the Malets were well acquainted through numerous diplomatic connections. As British ambassador in Frankfurt, Sir Alexander had helped Wilfrid Blunt to obtain better postings within the diplomatic service, and to get out of embarrassing romantic entanglements. Sir Alexander had two sons: Henry was an exact contemporary of Percy's at Eton and served in the Grenadier Guards at Crimea; Edward, who was two years behind Percy at Eton, followed his father into the diplomatic service and eventually became British ambassador in Berlin. The Malets spent little time in England, a factor which may have influenced their decision to sell land or at least find tenants for Wilbury. While Percy and Madeline occupied the house, Sir Alexander and his wife made use of another property close by. Lady Malet brought her own spirit paintings for the Wyndham children to see, including a portrait of Byron which celestial forces had helped her to paint.[87]

Before moving into Wilbury, probably before signing any agreement with the Malets, the Wyndhams asked Philip Webb to draw the house. They provided him with an old engraving and for five guineas he visited the property on 6 November and drew up the required plans. Webb was already being employed by the Wyndhams for minor work at 44 Belgrave Square, including alterations to a cupboard (10 shillings) and designing a chimneypiece which had a picture fitted into it (25 March). It is apparent from these slight commissions that by 1874 Webb's relations with the Wyndhams were professional; they were relying on his advice and his practical skills in relation to their properties in London and the country. Wilbury was taken as a stop-gap, while they searched for another estate to buy. Perhaps they were already considering commissioning Webb to design their country house. If so, they would have to wait their turn. Webb was entirely occupied with other major projects, including Rounton Grange for Sir Lowthian Bell. He explained to another potential employer in July 1874: 'it will be impossible for me to enter upon any fresh work for some time to come on account of present engagements'. In the same letter Webb continued, 'Also, to avoid any possibility of misunderstanding, I will say that for some time past I have decided not to undertake to build for anyone who is not conversant with my work and able to judge of what would be the finished effect of that which I should agree to carry out.'[88]

The Wyndhams were already well acquainted with Webb's work and keen to engage his services. There is no evidence to suggest they ever considered another architect for their country house, even though Webb's reputation as a despotic taskmaster was well known. 'If clients questioned, he used persuasion; and if that failed he recommended them to try another architect.'[89] They wanted to commission a house from this singular artist, the son of an Oxford doctor and just four years older than them. Webb considered greed 'the worst rot of the age', and his income amounted to an average of only £380 per annum throughout his forty years of practice.[90]

The opportunity finally came towards the end of 1876. In June, Percy sold his estate in Herefordshire; on 15 November he bought the estate of Clouds, East Knoyle in the south-west corner of Wiltshire. Messrs. Driver handled both sales so it seems likely the Wyndhams knew the Wiltshire estate was coming on to the market when they put up their own property at Much Cowarne for auction. They had discovered the piece of England they wanted to buy, and in which to establish their family seat.

The vendor of the Clouds estate was Alfred Seymour, a distant relation of Percy's,

Plate IV (facing page)   One of a sequence of five lifesize figures comprising *The Dance of the Cymbalists*, painted by Frederic Leighton, *c.*1869, for the staircase of the Wyndhams' London house, 44 Belgrave Square. Sold by Sotheby's, 1992, now in a private collection in London.

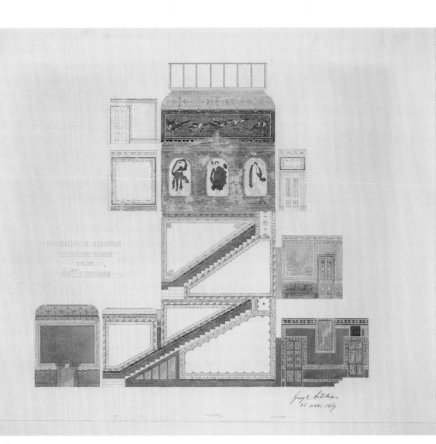

DECORATION OF STAIRCASE
44 BELGRAVE SQUARE
FOR THE
HON. P. WYNDHAM

Geo E. Aitchison
26 Oct 1869

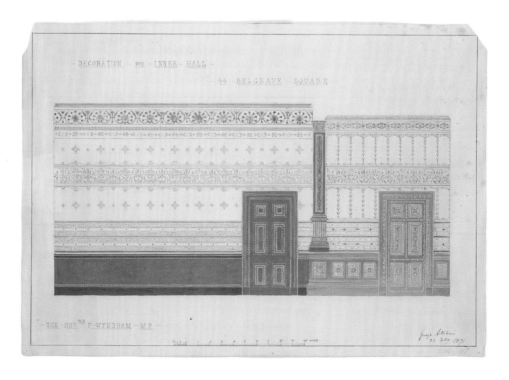

DECORATION FOR INNER HALL
44 BELGRAVE SQUARE

THE HON. P. WYNDHAM M.P.

Geo E. Aitchison
26 Oct 1871

and fellow member of the Cosmopolitan Club. The Seymour estate had been built up at East Knoyle by Alfred's father Henry, with Knoyle House, a substantial farmhouse dating from the seventeenth century, at its centre. The land which Percy bought represented about half the total estate and stretched to the north-west of Knoyle House. It already offered its own ideal site for a new mansion and Alfred Seymour, on the death of his father in 1849, was intending to build his own house, abandoning Knoyle House. He commissioned a design from Edward Blore. However, an ill-advised investment in the Somerset and Dorset Railway plunged Seymour into financial difficulties: instead of consolidating his property he was forced to sell off half his lands. Ironically, just after the sale to the Wyndhams, he inherited additional property in Northamptonshire. He tried to buy back the Wiltshire land from Percy, who refused to sell. He therefore had to content himself with substantially rebuilding and enlarging the original Knoyle House, adding a picture gallery, a central hall and circular dining-room.

Seymour was not the only local landowner known to the Wyndhams; on almost all sides there were estates owned by acquaintances, members of the aristocracy and landed gentry. The particulars drawn up by Messrs Driver carefully listed the more important neighbours and the exact distance from East Knoyle of their principal seats. Longleat (Marquis of Bath) was the furthest, 9 miles; Stourhead (Sir Henry Hoare) and Heytesbury (Baron Heytesbury) 7 miles; Motcombe House (Marchioness of Westminster) 5 miles; Wardour Castle (Earl of Arundel) 4 miles; Fonthill House (Alfred Morrison Esquire) 3 miles; Pyt House (Vere Fane Benett Stanford Esquire) and Fonthill Towers (Marchioness of Westminster) 2 miles. The local hunts had equally fine pedigrees; there were regular meets of the Blackmoor Vale, the East Dorset and the South Wiltshire Hounds.

The particulars drawn up for the Much Cowarne property had no such attractions.

26   Knoyle House, East Knoyle.

Plate v (facing page, above)   George Aitchison's design for the decoration of the staircase of 44 Belgrave Square, 1869, showing three of Leighton's Cymbalists.

Plate vi (facing page, below)   George Aitchison's design for the decoration of the inner hall of 44 Belgrave Square, 1871.

The agricultural estate George Leconfield had bought for his son was valuable only as a freehold investment and for its sporting facilities. But it did provide a higher return, rents totalling £4,980 a year from 3,140 acres; the Clouds estate rents totalled £4,624 a year from 4,207 acres.

No details have survived to reveal how much Percy had to pay for the Clouds estate or how much he obtained for Much Cowarne, but the amounts were probably similar, between £110,000 and £130,000. The Herefordshire property had been valued at £114,000 in 1867; by 1876 neither it nor the Wiltshire estate would have been seriously affected by the agricultural depression which was beginning to undermine farming in the predominantly arable eastern half of England. It would seem Percy used his inheritance to purchase the estate of his choice, rather than seek to make a profit.

The Wyndhams were still left with the rest of their Leconfield inheritance to put towards their new home, as well as sufficient funds for the interior furnishings, and Percy immediately approached Philip Webb. Rounton Grange was completed, and though Webb had just taken on the commission to design a house for Sir Lowthian's daughter Ada and her husband Major Godman, Smeaton Manor was not to be particularly large. Webb made his first visit to the estate at East Knoyle on 16 December, and on 28 December he wrote to Percy accepting the commission and setting out his terms: Clouds would turn out to be the largest and most expensive house to be undertaken by the architect.

3 Philip Webb: The Design and Building of Clouds, 1876–85

Philip Webb was the exclusive architect of an exclusive art set, who shared Ruskin's belief in the utter superiority of artistic over ordinary, conventional values.[1] His houses were all works of art in their own right, commissioned by members of the London art world or their friends and consequently designed to set off particular art collections and artistic lifestyles. His only aristocratic clients were the Howards and the Wyndhams but they also accepted the complete control of the architect. As Webb explained to Percy Wyndham: 'I do not lay myself out to do work for people who do not in any degree want what I could honestly do for them'.[2]

No recent biography of Webb has been published, and there are few articles on his work, Lethaby's study, first published in The *Builder* in 1925, and in book form ten years later, remains the fullest account.[3] Webb was consistently retiring and self-contained, and during his entire life-work of forty years only fifty to sixty complete buildings, large and small, were erected, an unusually small number. His assistant, George Jack, commented: 'had he desired he might have built many more houses, but he would never undertake more work at one time than he could personally supervise in every detail'.[4] John Brandon-Jones has suggested why a Webb building is 'more impressive than one designed by any of his contemporaries'.

> He was working at a time when the vogue was for the 'Picturesque' and many of his fellows were concerned with the appearance rather than the structure of their designs. . . . [But] every detail [of Webb's] was thought out as a thing to be made . . . The conscientious study of every minute detail of design and construction gave to Webb's finished work a feeling of reality and solidity that contrasted with the scenic effects achieved by his rivals. This quality must have been apparent even when the buildings were new. It is even more obvious now, when they have been mellowed and matured by time and weather, while so many contemporary works have become shabby or fallen to pieces.[5]

Lethaby states that Webb shared with his close friend William Morris a deep religious love of England, 'not a vague abstract love, or possessive pride and patriotism, but affection and even worship for the very earth, trees, fields, animals, ploughs, wagons, and buildings', even the weather. 'There is no bad weather, only different kinds of good weather,' claimed Webb.[6] He enjoyed anchoring a new building to something which had age and character. At Clouds this was to be a group of old farm buildings with their chalk-walled courtyard. Houses grew 'naturally' from the ground, Webb envisaging their appearance on site even before he began design work. Every commission was unique, reflecting not only the characteristics of the chosen location but also the lifestyle of the clients; perhaps this feature appealed to the Wyndhams. Webb did not provide 'comfortable conventionality' or 'exact conformity to well-known styles'; he revealed a 'real and large originality'[7] which always steered clear of

27   Philip Webb, 1873, by Charles
Fairfax Murray.

any straining after effect, and was always based on a knowledge of materials. His overall
aim was to make modern architecture in some way 'genuine'.

I

After his first visit to the estate of East Knoyle in December 1876, Webb set out his
terms in a letter written to Percy Wyndham on 28 December:

> Since my visit with you and Mrs Wyndham to Clouds Estate, I have carefully
> considered the matter, both from your point of view and my own, with regard to my
> entering upon the business of building a house for you there, if you should wish me
> to do so . . . I have thought that the suggestions I made, and the expression I gave as
> to what I should consider would be the best way of meeting the circumstances of
> the case (apart from the rude way in which I am afraid they often were given)
> seemed to meet your wishes, and therefore I should be quite willing to undertake
> the designing and superintending of the works in question if you should wish me to
> do so, subject to the following conditions. Viz. That all drawings, whether of work
> done or only proposed, should be my property. (This not to exclude my providing
> you with all the necessary plans etc. for your future use after the work has done)
> That my payment should be at the rate of 5 per cent on the cost of all works done
> under my direction, and further payment of travelling expenses for myself and
> assistants. That if plans in whole and in detail are prepared by me ready to be laid

before contractors and the works should not be carried out, 2.5 per cent on my estimated cost of the execution of the works to be paid to me. That if only preliminary sketches and plans be made, 1.25 per cent on my estimated cost be paid me for the same. I must ask you to excuse these particulars as it has been found that such care and explanation between client and architect before any work has been entered upon, tends very much to the avoidance of any dispute or awkwardness afterwards.

Percy wrote to Webb from Wilbury the following day, 'I give my adherence to all your propositions, and think your method of doing business a very satisfactory one'.

The site to which Webb was taken by Percy and Madeline was the same one chosen by Alfred Seymour for his house before financial difficulties had forced him to retrench. It was originally part of an estate which had been established in the early sixteenth century from lands in and around the hamlet of Milton. John Cloud was the first freeholder, giving his name to the estate, which was known from the mid-sixteenth century onwards as the manor of Clouds. His Clouds House was rebuilt late in the century by the new owner, Robert Goldsborough. In 1672 the manor was bought by Nathaniel Still, member of a prominent local family. For over a century the Stills acquired more land around the original manor of Clouds and some time towards the end of the eighteenth century they demolished Goldsborough's mansion and built their own modest four-bedroomed stone house. This was approached by its own carriage drive which wound through a magnificent park of just under a hundred acres, sloping down towards the village of East Knoyle. The park was carefully laid out with yews, oak, elms, beeches and Scots firs, some reputed to have been planted by William Beckford himself, for he was a friend and neighbour of the Stills.[8]

After the death of James Still in 1828, the whole estate was bought by Henry Seymour, a distant relation of the Duke of Somerset. When his son sold it to the Wyndhams in 1876, Clouds House was occupied by Mr Collins, the Seymours' gamekeeper; Mr Brockway, the estate gardener, occupied an adjoining stone cottage. There were also two other three-roomed cottages close by, originally farm buildings, with a square attached garden or yard enclosed by a wall built of blocks of chalk and roofed with thatch.

Webb agreed the site had 'exceptional advantages' for his own version of Clouds House. He later described it in a letter to Madeline as 'the most lovely place in England', and immediately began plans to make full use of the park and to preserve as many trees as possible. The old house would have to be demolished, though Webb made a careful note of parts that could be used again: oak floorboards, oak stairs, cast-iron grates and even a 'good brass knocker on N door'; a door from the cottage was reused for the luggage entrance.

Describing the way Webb worked, Lethaby commented, 'I get the impression from his country houses that it "came to him" what sort of thing he wished to build on a particular site and in its neighbourhood. This idea was worked out in the office, but the inspiration was always local.'[9] Returning to the estate in April the following year Webb climbed hills to the north, one planted with Scots firs and the other with gorse. He wrote to Percy.

From both places I could better make out the possible disposition of the parts of the new house. I felt when there that it would be well to keep as many trees as possible in the East of the present house including the two walnut trees.

In his site notebook he jotted down, almost as if the house was already built, 'there is a good view from East dining room window to the SSE catching sight of distant hills between yew & beech'. His country houses appear to grow up out of the rural landscape, not just because he used local materials and made references to the local vernacular architecture, but because he placed them in sympathetic relationship to the land. Long before his designs became realities, he was able to imagine himself inside looking out on the surrounding countryside, or outside, approaching the house through the landscape. And though he could be singularly rude if a client dared to question his designs, he was always prepared to allow Nature to dictate details: he included in the plans for the Clouds offices a courtyard to be built around a mature walnut tree.

Webb sent the Wyndhams the first rough sketch of the ground plan of Clouds on 29 January 1877. Madeline was not happy with it so Webb agreed to produce another, 'as I am not to live in the house and you and Mrs Wyndham will'. Meanwhile Percy arranged to visit Webb's Rounton Grange and Smeaton Manor. As well as being patrons of Webb, the Bell family were closely connected with the Howards. In 1873 Rosalind Howard's brother Edward Lyulph Stanley, younger brother and heir to Baron Sheffield, had married Mary Bell, daughter of the industrialist and art collector Sir Lowthian Bell; from the 1880s onwards Mary Stanley and George Howard were romantically involved with one another.[10] Percy visited Rounton Grange, near Northallerton, shortly after completion; he then called on Sir Lowthian's daughter Ada, in July, to find out how Smeaton Manor was proceeding.

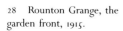

28   Rounton Grange, the garden front, 1915.

There are significant similarities and differences between Rounton and the completed Clouds. Inside Rounton, the collaboration of Morris and Burne-Jones produced an effect closer to the Gothic elaboration of the Howards' London home. Morris's wallpapers and fabrics were used throughout the house, and in the dining room Morris himself painting the ceiling. The work was so arduous that he lost his temper, explaining to his patron 'it is only that I spend my life in ministering to the swinish luxury of the rich'.[11] Round the walls hung a continuous embroidery designed by Burne-Jones and inspired by the *Romaunt of the Rose*: it took Lady Bell and her daughter Florence eight years to complete.

Such gloomy richness would not feature at Clouds, though Madeline was interested enough in the concept to obtain tracings and photographs of the embroidery to keep in one of her scrap-albums. But the external appearance of Rounton does present connections. Its high, compact design was determined in part to save some of the fine trees, also to offer magnificent views of the distant Cleveland Hills: like Clouds it rises up out of the landscape, connected to it, making use of its special features, but not afraid to offer a remarkably solid edifice. Its Yorkshire seriousness is offset by a large, square, fanciful clock tower, and the architect Alfred Powell commented 'I remember it standing up over the trees with four great chimneys and a wonderful *smile* about its front to the garden'.[12] Black-and-white photographs make it appear forbidding but its walls are of ochre-coloured sandstone from local quarries and the pantiles on the roof are orange-red. At Clouds, Webb put red tiles and red bricks on top of a house predominantly of green sandstone. Smeaton is much smaller than Rounton, built of local red bricks, but inside there are features which provide close links with Clouds. The main rooms have white-painted panelling and simpler fireplaces, altogether a lighter touch and reminiscent of the effect Webb would create in both living rooms and bedrooms at Clouds.

Members of Percy Wyndham's own family had been involved in recent building works; no doubt their experiences and the results to some extent influenced his choice of architect and provided him with forewarning of difficulties that might be encountered in the relations between architect and patron. Henry Leconfield had employed Anthony Salvin to carry out repairs and alterations to Petworth, and for all their disagreements, Percy was invited by his brother to see the completed work. Madeline wrote to her daughter Mary from Coates (where the Leconfields stayed until the work was completed), 'they have been doing a great deal & have built a new hall & entrance at the back', and she promised to send some photographs.

Salvin's speciality was castle architecture but he added to classical Petworth with notable restraint. His later work on Henry's new London house, 9 Chesterfield Gardens, did not proceed well and eventually the Wyndhams' London designer George Aitchison was called in to finish the commission and to work on the interior decorations. In the morning room he devised a delicate frieze, predominantly in pink, of boys and dolphins playing in the waves; in the hall there was a mosaic pavement, and the stairs were of marble. The Leconfields had been sufficiently impressed by Aitchison's work at 44 Belgrave Square to commission their own unique decorations; perhaps Henry had deferred to Constance's more refined aesthetic judgements.[13]

Wilfrid Blunt inherited his family estates on the death of his brother in 1872 and immediately set about rebuilding the dilapidated Tudor house of Crabbet. Rather than rely on the designs of an architect, Wilfrid and his wife Anne produced their own plans. John Pollen was their clerk of works; the builders and the raw materials were local. The result was utterly different to all the other country houses the Wyndhams would have visited: an anti-romantic, strictly William and Mary classical box. It cost Wilfrid under £5,000 and inside, as a compliment to his favourite childhood home, he copied panelling and mouldings from Petworth. when it came to architectural design, Wilfrid preferred the plain and sensible brick box, as he explained in a conversation with William Morris:

> I dawdled on talking with Morris, and trying to prove to him that he and Ruskin had done more harm than good by their attempt to make English people love beauty and decorate their architecture . . . I maintained that the old-fashioned square box style was less abominable, as were the days when it was considered bad taste to attempt any kind of prettiness.[14]

Madeline had visited Blunt in August 1873 while the panelling was being put up in the lower rooms. According to Blunt, she 'approved of the large lines we had chosen and our reversion to classical models then quite an innovation in an age of Gothic shams'.[15] Her visit to Crabbet was not simply architectural. 1873 was described in Blunt's diary as the year of Madeline, 'the occasion in our lives we took and made our own'. Their affair lasted only a few months, 'the satisfaction of a paganly aesthetic need rather than on either side a full devotion of the soul'. Madeline made sure her own relationship with Percy was unaffected: the affair 'did no worry to her domestic life which occupied another side of her large nature, was delightful to both of us while we were together, and left no string whether of remorse or insistent longing when we were parted'.[16] Unlike her friend Georgiana Sumner and her daughter Mary, Madeline did not have a child by Blunt.

Percy was given a further introduction to the profession of architecture through Webb himself. He became a founder member of the Society for the Preservation of Ancient Buildings (SPAB). The society was originally the idea of William Morris; it was founded on 22 March 1877. Webb cajoled no less than thirteen of his clients, including Percy, to join the society. There were also other old friends of Percy's on the committee, which held its first AGM on 21 June the following year. Earl Cowper was in the chair (Percy took over in 1879) and the committee members were George Howard, Richard Doyle, Eustace Balfour (architect brother of Arthur), Edward Burne-Jones, Edward Poynter, William de Morgan, William Holman Hunt, Philip Webb and Percy Wyndham.[17] Morris wrote the SPAB manifesto, which was a plea,

> to put Protection in the place of Restoration, to stave off decay by daily care, to prop a perilous wall or mend a leaky roof by such means as are obviously meant for support or covering, and show no pretence of other art, and otherwise to resist all tampering with either the fabric or ornament of the building as it stands; if it has become inconvenient for its present use, to raise another building rather than alter or enlarge the old one; in fine to treat our ancient buildings as monuments of a bygone art, created by bygone manners, that modern art cannot meddle with without destroying.[18]

The principles were eagerly adopted by Percy, who immediately interested himself in the condition of churches around his Clouds property. He took Webb in 1878 to visit St Mary's, West Knoyle, which was threatened with demolition. Percy was asked to subscribe to the fund for building a completely new church but refused, in accordance with his SPAB principles. He wrote to Webb for advice, but the architect could only reply:

you may pipe 'till you are black in the face, but you will not save that building which so much pleased us on Thursday. The list of subscribers is great enough to deface a whole country.

Only the perpendicular tower survived; the rest of the church was completely rebuilt to the design of J. Mountford Allen. Though the SPAB was unable to save West Knoyle parish church from vandalism, its later efforts to preserve the tower of East Knoyle parish church were completely successful: in the latter instance, Percy Wyndham, as the principal local landowner, was able to insist on their sensitive approach being adopted rather than demolition.

2

While Percy was being initiated into contemporary architectural practice, Madeline was involved in the opening of a new art gallery in London, which would also shake up establishment ideas and challenge the stranglehold of the Royal Academy. The Grosvenor Gallery was the idea of Charles Hallé and Sir Coutts Lindsay. Their intention was to provide a sympathetic setting in which to hang paintings, resembling, as far as possible, the atmosphere and conditions of a private home. They also hoped to persuade artists such as Burne-Jones and Rossetti to show their work publicly, bringing to an end years of self-imposed exile.[19] Suitable premises were found off Bond Street, the unoccupied warehouse of a furniture dealer, and the conversion was paid for by Sir Coutts and his wife Blanche, granddaughter of Nathan Meyer, Baron Rothschild. She eventually provided £150,000 of her own money towards the gallery and brought all her society friends to the exhibitions: the Grosvenor was the place to be seen.

The very first private view, on 30 April 1877, was ticket only; a few days later, on 9 May, a banquet was held in the ground-floor restaurant of the Grosvenor for artists and patrons. This was attended by four members of the Royal family including the Prince and Princess of Wales, and Princess Louise who was herself an exhibitor. Special Sunday afternoon receptions were held throughout the season and invitations were eagerly sought. Social snobbery was manipulated to the full by the Grosvenor committee, for the maximum benefit of the artist, although sometimes the protocol involved in handling so many royals and aristocrats proved too much for the 'bohemian' organisers. Over the arrangements for the opening banquet, Charles Hallé confessed that he and Arthur Sullivan 'spent days poring over peerages and finding out dates of creation of the various titles of nobility, so that no one should take the wrong person in to dinner or go in before his turn'.[20] W. Graham Robertson provides a glowing description of the opening day:

> The general effect of the great rooms was most beautiful and quite unlike the ordinary picture gallery. It suggested the interior of some old Venetian palace, and the pictures, hung well apart from each other against dim rich brocades and amongst fine pieces of antique furniture, showed to unusual advantage . . . One wall was iridescent with the plumage of Burne-Jones's angels, one mysteriously blue with Whistler's nocturnes, one deeply glowing with the great figures of Watts, one softly radiant with the faint, flower-tinted harmonies of Albert Moore.[21]

Madeline was already a member of the inner circle of the Grosvenor coterie and she and Percy lent a number of paintings for the opening exhibition, including their Costa and Watts's portrait of Madeline. Watts had received the final payment for the painting with his usual circumlocutory apologies.

> I have received your very kind letter & the cheque for one thousand pounds which I am unwilling to take but do not like to send back. I could not remember what the original price for the picture was to be & thought it very likely to be a smaller sum [than] the one you name. I should have taken the original price [it was £600] without a word of dissatisfaction though of course as the picture has not really been neglected but constantly worked upon for so many years the matter is a little removed from ordinary conditions.[22]

While the portrait slowly progressed, the Wyndhams had expressed interest in two further paintings by Watts, his *Daphne* (a small version was owned by Lady Lothian of Blickling) and *The Judgment of Paris*. Both paintings were sold to Louis Huth in 1872, though he almost immediately returned the *Judgment*. Watts promptly offered it to Madeline.

> With respect to the Goddess [*The Judgment of Paris*] you know I sold it, but have taken it back as its possessor who also bought Daphne finds he has too much nudity in his gallery, so I refund the money, the price is 800 guineas – I intended raising it but it may go now for that, if it remains in my studio I shall ask a larger sum.[23]

Perhaps the price was too high; the *Judgment* was bought in 1874 by Sir Alexander Henderson, first Lord Faringdon. However, the following year, Percy paid £210 for a *Nocturne* by Whistler and this painting was also loaned to the Grosvenor Gallery for their opening exhibition.

Percy Wyndham's purchase was a surprise to the artist; Whistler was not socially acquainted with the Wyndhams. Percy simply walked into the Dudley Gallery, decided he liked *Nocturne in Blue and Gold no. 3*, and bought it. Whistler explained to Alan Cole:

> You will be pleased to hear that one of my much blaguarded [sic] 'masterpieces' Nocturne in Blue & Gold has just sold itself to a total stranger (Percy Wyndham) 'for the price named in the catalogue' as the official note from the Dudley informs me – So you see this vicious art of butterfly flippancy is, in spite of the honest efforts of Tom Taylor [art critic of *The Times*], doing its poisonous work and even attacking the heart of the aristocracy as well as under-mining the working classes![24]

Whistler immediately added the Wyndhams to his own social list and invited them to his studio in Tite Street; he later borrowed the *Nocturne* for an exhibition in Paris.

The purchase of the Whistler *Nocturne* is of particular interest because it is the one known example of the Wyndhams' buying avant-garde art; otherwise the patronage of Philip Webb remains their only involvement with radical contemporary culture. The Wyndhams were unusual in their social intimacy with artists and designers, but those they chose to patronise from the early 1860s until Percy's death in 1911 are consistent in their 'Englishness' (including the American Sargent): William Morris, Watts, Burne-Jones, Rossetti, Leighton, Prinsep, Richard Doyle, Costa and Mason, Edward Poynter, later Sargent and Orpen; accessible, figurative, romantic.

By buying the notorious *Nocturne*, Percy found himself a party to one of the most celebrated clashes of taste in the history of art. Ruskin's attack on Whistler is, *inter alia*, a tribute to Percy's self-confidence as a collector:

> Sir Coutts Lindsay ought not to have admitted works into the gallery in which the ill-educated conceit of the artist so nearly approached the aspect of wilful imposture. I have seen, and heard, much of Cockney impudence before now; but never expected to hear a coxcomb ask two hundred guineas for flinging a pot of paint in the public's face.[25]

Avid readers of Ruskin, the Wyndhams found themselves caught in the middle of the row, which was finally settled in court in November 1878. Percy's purchase was introduced into the proceedings, Whistler claiming that he had been unable to get a price for his prictures comparable to that paid by Percy Wyndham since the publication of Ruskin's attack. Philip Webb stayed at Wilbury while the trial was proceeding. He and Percy discussed the case throughout dinner to the amusement of the family; Mary Wyndham thought the whole affair could have been invented by Dickens, writing in her diary 'so funny, the jury going to Westminster Palace Hotel to examine the pictures, and hearing Mr Burne-Jones, Whistler, W.M. Rossetti and all of them in the *witness* box'.

Watts's portrait of Madeline was not controversial, though Henry James's review for the *Galaxy* was far from effusive:

> 'It is what they call a "sumptuous" picture,' said my companion. 'That is, the lady looks as if she had thirty thousand a year.' It is true that she does ... The very handsome person whom the painter has depicted is dressed in a fashion which will never be wearisome; a simple yet splendid robe, in the taste of no particular period – of all periods.[26]

Watts had been characteristically self-effacing and obsequious towards Madeline about borrowing the painting for the opening of the Grosvenor:

> A thousand thanks for so liberally lending the picture, I do not know that I should have asked for it of my own suggestion, for as you know I am not fond of exhibiting at all, but the picture is certainly one of the best, and I hope it will look well for the sake of my friends more than my own. I have always regretted having finished it and sent it home for if it had still been on my hands I should most likely have seen you which now it seems to me I never do.[27]

Many critics, apart from Ruskin, were hostile towards both the gallery and the paintings. A challenge was being made to the Royal Academy and its dictatorial power; the public was being shown art which had not been automatically 'institutionalised' and made 'respectable' by the Academy's seal of approval. *Punch* summed up Burne-Jones as 'the quaint, the queer, the mystic over-much'. But Burne-Jones was himself critical of the hanging of paintings against crimson Italian silk. 'It sucks all the colour out of pictures ... I know in private houses that one's work is always destroyed by carpets and hangings, but in this Gallery, for a little time, one's colour ought to rest and tell as one meant it to.'[28] The following year the crimson silk was replaced with the 'greenery-yallery' of Gilbert and Sullivan's *Patience* fame.

The season of 1877 put Percy and Madeline at the forefront of radical cultural activity in Britain – patrons of Webb, supporters of the Grosvenor Gallery and the SPAB, owners of a Whistler *Nocturne*. After so much aesthetic activity, they went north, as usual, to Cumberland – it was to be their last autumn at Isel – and there awaited Webb's second ground plan.

3

The plan was sent up to Isel on 14 August and the Wyndhams were delighted. It had the advantage over the first of being slightly cheaper and saving more trees, also offering in Webb's words 'a perfect view of the s.e. slope of the park'. Both designs were for a house planned around an open courtyard which would be not less than 65 feet square. Webb's estimate of the costs for the house, offices and stables was approximately £62,000 if built by a local firm, and after warning Percy that a first-rate London builder might charge 20 to 25 per cent more than a country builder, he entered into negotiations with George Smith and Company of the Commercial Road, Pimlico, for a tender.

Completing work on the drawings for the house, stables and offices, then waiting for the tender from the builders, took another eighteen months. By 31 March 1879 Webb was praising Percy's 'exemplary patience' as Smiths had not yet supplied their estimate. He added that if the tender was satisfactory the stable block at least might be 'ready for housing' by June the following year: 'there would be the advantage of

29 The first design for Clouds House acceptable to the Wyndhams.

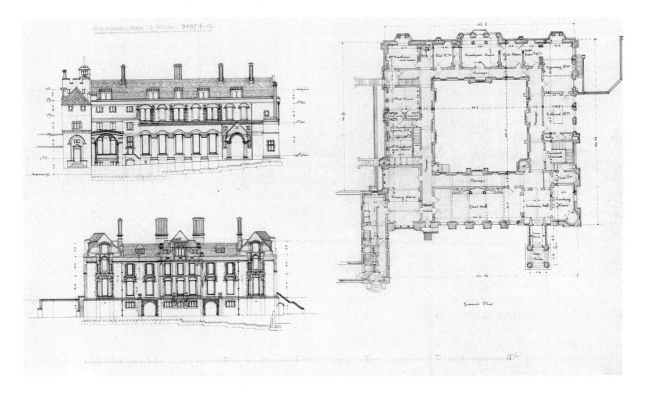

entering on the use of the stables at the warm and dry season of the year'. Smith's estimate finally arrived on 20 May 1879 but it was just over £80,000, between £5,000 and £6,000 more than Percy was prepared to pay. The building firm was unable to reduce their estimate by anything approaching £5,000 so Percy decided to defer the project for the time being. The Wyndhams were content to remain at Wilbury while their capital earned interest.

Webb was not to give up the project so easily: he went back to his drawing board and in July the same year came up with a completely new design. He wrote to Percy:

> I find, that after settling the rooms round a centre on the new scheme, and reducing their sizes considerably but in proper proportion, still, taking Smith's prices into consideration, the new design would require £75,000 for the whole of the buildings.

This time the Wyndhams were content to pay slightly more and Webb began to work on the details. The inner courtyard had gone: instead rooms were to be grouped around a central top-lit hall. After further consultations between architect and client, on 20 November Webb was able to send the Wyndhams sketches of the ground, first and second floors.

He had added oriel windows to the chief bedrooms on the south side of the first floor as Madeline had pointed out their convenience, and 'they would go very well with the general design'. She had also suggested a pair of settles to be placed either side of the large fireplace in the central hall and Webb was able to oblige her admitting 'they would be moveable, but in their places they would not interfere at all with the passage way.' Madeline's attention to detail, even at early stages in the project, suited Webb's own way of working. At the same time as he was developing the designs for the whole house, the offices and stables, he was worrying about the quality of parquet floors and considering, from the servants' point of view, the actual running of such a large house. He provided large coal bunkers on the first and second floors, as well as box rooms on each floor in which to store the considerable volume of luggage of the family and their guests. Mary Wyndham counted thirty-six boxes of luggage to be taken by train to London for the annual attendance at the season. The laundry also demanded attention from Webb; it involved lengthy correspondence with the Wyndhams and the Sheffield firm responsible for its fitting, Messrs Longden and Company of the Phoenix Foundry. When the laundry broke down at Wilbury in April 1880 Madeline asked Webb's advice. He suggested Henry Longden call at Wilbury to install new apparatus which could then be moved to Clouds.

In June 1880 Mr Goodman, the quantity surveyor, began to measure Webb's new drawings, but it was not until May 1881 that the complete bills were in the hands of George Smith and Company. When Webb received the tender on 31 May it was £4,375 above the agreed limit of £75,000. Webb offered Percy various options: he could accept the estimate from Smiths; try a country builder for a lower estimate but probably a lower class of finished work; throw out the design and go for a smaller house altogether; find another architect. The Wyndhams were adamant in sticking to their architect and his design but Madeline was tempted to try a country builder as Percy reported to Webb: 'she does not see why we should give Smith so much more than the thing can be done by another'.

Webb's response and his support for the more expensive London builder reveals much about the building trade at the time and his determination to get the very best quality of work for his client:

30–5 The final designs for Clouds House, July 1881.

30 (overleaf, above left) West elevation and east elevation.

31 (overleaf, below left) South elevation and north elevation.

32 (overleaf, above right) Plan of basement.

33 (overleaf, below right) Ground floor.

Clouds House. East Knoyle Wilts

Hon. Percy Wyndham. M.P.

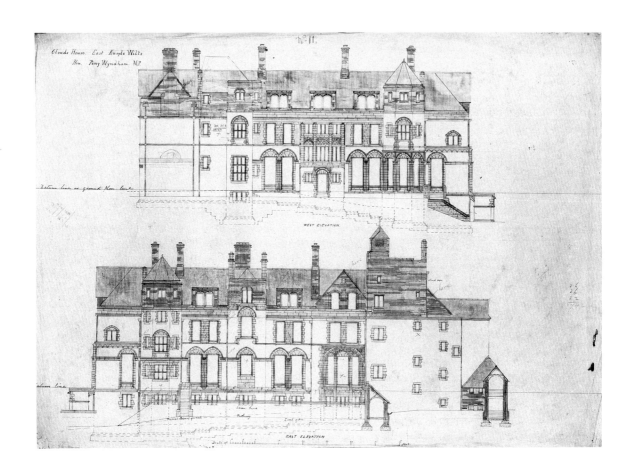

Datum line or ground floor line

WEST ELEVATION

EAST ELEVATION

Clouds House.

East Knoyle Wilts

Hon Percy Wyndham M.P.

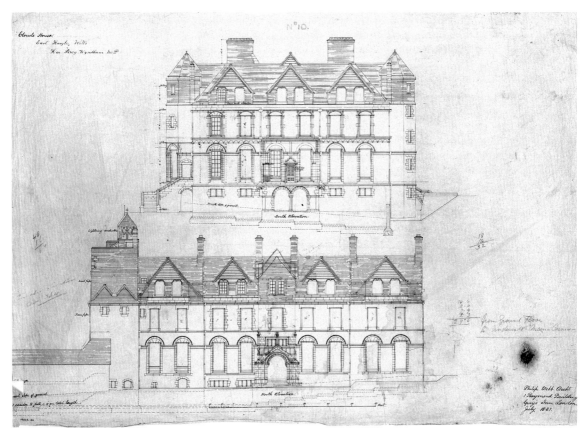

South Elevation

North Elevation

Philip Webb Archt
1 Raymond Buildings
Grays Inn London
July 1881.

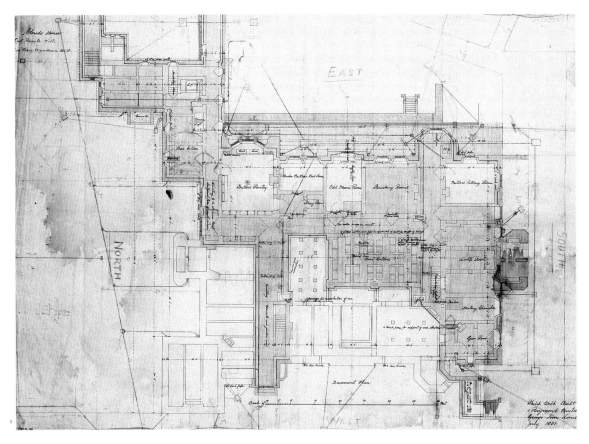

Clouds House
East Knoyle Wilts
Hon Percy Wyndham M.P.

EAST

NORTH

SOUTH

Basement Plan.

WEST

Philip Webb Archt
1 Raymond Buildings
Grays Inn London
July 1881.

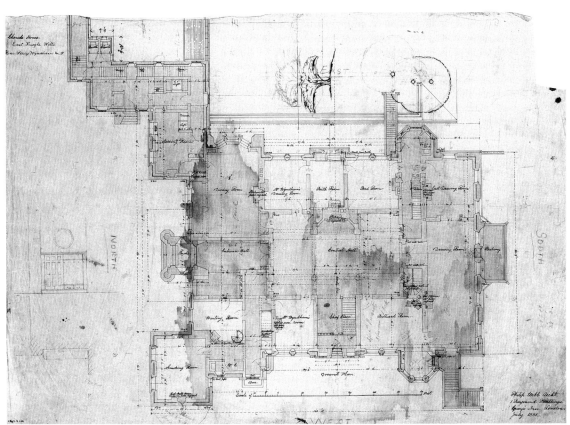

Clouds House
East Knoyle Wilts
Hon Percy Wyndham M.P.

EAST

NORTH

SOUTH

Ground Plan.

Scale of Feet

WEST

Philip Webb Archt
1 Raymond Buildings
Grays Inn London
July 1881.

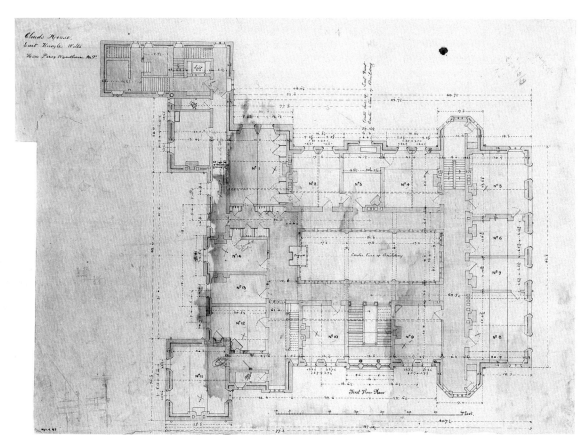

First Floor Plan

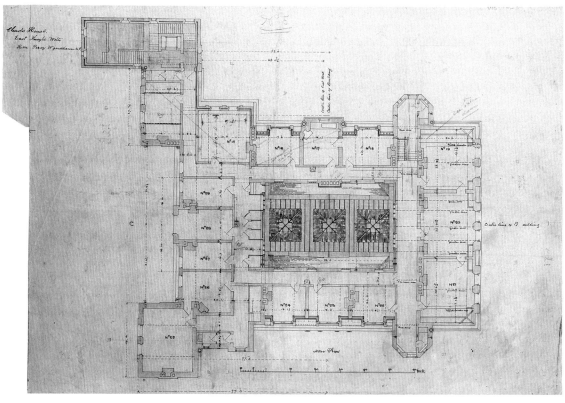

Attic Plan

As the work done by Smiths could have cost more in the doing than that of even the best country builder we should get and for these reasons among others the timbers used which have been more carefully selected, would have lain in stock for a longer time; and from there being larger quantities on hand the work men would more certainly be supplied with the best for any particular purpose. Then, as to labour; Smith's would certainly give higher wages to their men; and from working in a large way would be able to keep their best men. Also there would have been over their several trades, better educated and proved foremen. I will now take the mason's trade. One of my chief reasons for wishing, if possible, to hold to Smiths was that in the Tisbury and the local Greensandstone, they had largely used both at Longford Castle [by Salvin for the fourth Earl of Radnor, 1870–8], and the former at Lady Westminster's home at Fonthill [by William Burn for the Marquess of Westminster, 1846–52]: if I suppose we should, have Mr Cross as the foreman of masons, we should be at advantage, as he knows a great deal about the Tisbury stone, and is well aware of the custom of the quarry men of sending out from the quarry the first stone to hand without regard to its lasting character. I have no doubt that Cross's salary is as much as £300 as year, if not more: Again, as to iron work. There are to be a number of iron girders used in the house, and familiarity in their use, handling, and setting is of importance, and, practically, the same reason would run through all the trades, though not in all equal degrees.

Webb's powers of persuasion were successful: Percy agreed to accept the tender. Clouds would be completed and ready for occupation in the summer of 1884.

The agreed block plan for the house was sent to Cyrus Coombes in Tisbury for him to set out on the ground. Work began on taking up the turf, marking trees that had to be cut down and setting aside ground to be used by the builder. Webb also began the search for a clerk of works to be based in East Knoyle during the building. A bed would be provided at Slades, a substantial four-bedroomed stone house at the southern end of Clouds park; Slades was adapted to provide temporary shelter and refreshment for members of the Wyndham family and friends visiting the site for the day. The last tenant had been Captain Still, a descendant of the Stills of Clouds, and he vacated the premises on Lady Day 1877. Percy meanwhile was to find out whom his sister Lady Mayo had employed, and to approach Lord Wolverton to find out about James Simmonds, the clerk of works who had worked for Alfred Waterhouse on the building of Iwerne Minster in Dorset, not far from East Knoyle. Smiths would supply the general foreman for the work, the same man who had worked on Henry Leconfield's town house in Chesterfield Gardens.

Both Webb and the Wyndhams must have been confident at this late stage that the house they had planned for so long was at last to become a reality. However, a further complication was to delay the project. The head of the firm of George Smith and Company suddenly died. The firm was placed under legal restrictions according to the terms of George Smith's will, and after lengthy discussions with the solicitor involved, Webb advised Percy that they must withdraw from any further negotiations with the son, Henry Smith. The only option was to find a local builder, something Webb had only just managed to persuade the Wyndhams against when the tender from Smiths came in too high.

Webb set off on a tour of West Country builders, travelling to Frome, Tewkesbury, Gloucester, Blandford and Oxford. He finally selected Albert Estcourt of Gloucester, who came highly recommended after completing work for the late William Burges at

34 (above)   First floor.

35 (below)   Second floor.

Cardiff Castle. Ewan Christian also gave him a good reference. Meanwhile suitable recommendations were received from both Lord Wolverton and Alfred Waterhouse concerning James Simmonds, so he was hired in October 1881 as clerk of works at 4 guineas a week. Webb thought the salary high and told Simmonds so:

> The salary you ask, 4 guineas a week is I consider a high one for work which will extend over a space of time of between two and three years, but I shall not consider it too high if the ability, energy and honourable trustworthyness which I shall expect [from] you will be confirmed by experience. The work in question is an important one, and constant attention with aptitude, and judgment, will be necessary in you for the satisfactory carrying out of my intentions, and the contractor's responsibility.

Webb asked for his first payment (of four) from Percy on 12 August 1881:

> As, necessarily, there will be some further delay, and as my outlay on the several designs for the house has been considerable during the last four years, I shall be obliged if you can, conveniently, let me have a thousand pounds on account.

Webb received a total of £4,000 for his work on Clouds, 5 per cent of the total costs, plus travel expenses for himself and his assistants. But as he spent ten years working on designs for the house, overseeing the work and finishing off, his fee was spread thin. During the period he was most heavily involved with Clouds, between 1880 and 1888, Webb's net income was less than £320 per annum, only slightly more than the salary of a master stonemason such as Mr Cross.[29]

Albert Estcourt came up to London on 3 November to sign all the necessary papers at Webb's office, 1 Raymond Buildings, Gray's Inn. At the beginning of December, Madeline took a party of family and friends by train from Wilbury to Semley. Mary recorded the outing: 'we drove in a wagonette to Slades . . . we walked to Clouds by the approach, saw the plans & went to the windmill where the hounds were running in the valley & we had a fine sight.' Work had finally begun in earnest.

4

On 15 November Philip Webb had travelled down to East Knoyle to meet Albert Estcourt on the site and to 'set the works going'. He also met James Simmonds there, to engage him formally as clerk of works. On 29 November all three, with Estcourt's foreman Mr Hibbins, went to see the local green sandstone quarry belonging to Mr Lilly in order to select the right stone, for this project the Pinney bed. Webb was also looking into the best Portland cement to be used, eventually deciding on the cement produced by Messrs John B. White Bros. of 85 Gracechurch Street, East London, which was of the required fine ground and slow setting.

Estcourt was responsible for bringing sufficient workmen to East Knoyle, many coming from outside the immediate area. The village experienced considerable upheaval as lodgings had to be found for the outsiders. Writing to Percy on 21 January 1882, Webb reported that the work was progressing 'quite as well as I expected, and

Mr Estcourt active in pushing them along'. He was confident that the stables would be ready for occupation before 25 March 1884, according to Percy's wishes. Meanwhile he wrote to his clerk of works with precise instructions on how to get Estcourt's workmen to work to his high standards. The masons in particular were not yet able to tool the faced and moulded Chilmark stone to a 'satisfactory manner':

> from the appearance of the last piece of stone worked for me to see before I left I have no doubt that the kind of work to be done will be arrived at in a very short time. Will you be so good as far as possible to see that the masons, 'till they get their hands in, only do plain work, or work which only includes the more simple mouldings, as, the moulded work yet done would not, if continued in that manner be useable [sic]. In working all mouldings sharp tools and a light mallet will be necessary.

Madeline was kept informed of arrangements for the offices before she went with her daughter Mary to Hyères in February. Webb wrote to her on 24 January: 'I send you the engineer's re-arrangement of the cooking and other apparatuses to the kitchen-scullery, still-room etc, based, according to my directions, on the amendments and suggestions made by you on the former'. And by the end of February, the Wyndhams heard that the foundations of the main block of the house were in place, having turned out 'much better than I [Webb] expected'. Minor disagreements over design details had also been resolved, Percy agreeing to 'putting in again the ornamental drawing-room ceiling'. He also agreed to the mosaic paving to the fireplace and at the foot of the stairs in the hall (£120) and to the shafts in the hall being of Hopton Wood stone, not Chilmark.

Lengthy correspondence took place in March 1882 between Webb and Wyndham over the proposed drainage of the stables. Various authorities were consulted, including the published opinions of Colonel Sir Frederick Fitz-Wygram, who had served in the Crimea and since 1879, had been Inspector-General of the Cavalry. And a visit was made to Badminton to see the stables of the Duke of Beaufort; his son, Lord Arthur Somerset, was responsible for the stables of the Prince of Wales. After Percy had made further enquiries of his own among Wiltshire neighbours, he wrote rather apologetically to Webb, ashamed of the trouble he was causing:

> my mind has been again shaken by evidence to the effect that stables can be made without drains without any of the feared defects arising. . . . On Sunday I was at our neighbours Major Poore's at Old Lodge. I found to my astonishment he had two boxes and a stall without drains. They use saw dust. They do not clean out often at all events I could see that. The groom spoke highly of it, they use saw dust and sprinkle a little fresh over the old till a general clean out takes place.

Webb was not offended:

> It is an important question, and I am only too glad that you are taking the trouble to arrive at a reasonable decision *before* the work is done. If you do without any fall to the boxes and stalls, and dusting with clean saw dust once in the 24 hours would be a safe plan, and if possible I should advise that the stalls and boxes should be swept out with a stiff broom each day, as I believe that active decomposition sets in in about 24 hours, some clean sawdust should be sprinkled on the top of the old. The

use of saw dust would save extravagant waste of straw litter, and much prevent the staining of clothing.

There was to be a wash-house 15′ × 19′ 6″, sufficient for two horses at a time. The stalls were each 6′ 6″ wide. Both client and architect were agreed there would be no drains.

In May, Webb was turning his attention to the quality of bricks for the house. The decision had been made early in the project to employ John Howell, tenant of the brick and tile works already established on Clouds estate, to produce bricks for the new house. His 24-acre brickyard was just to the south-west of Clouds park. Webb had met Howell in June 1877 and immediately wrote to Percy, 'I am rather pleased with the appearance and speech of Howell, and should like that he should be employed'. Now, however, the bricks being produced by his brickyard were not up to Webb's standards. Webb wrote to Howell on 25 May, this time including Percy's views to support his admonishments:

I was much disappointed at not meeting you at the new house yesterday . . . The sample of handmade facing bricks shown to me by Mr Simmonds was not at all satisfactory and as the progress of the works will be seriously hindered if from your next kiln a brick more nearly approaching what is wanted is not produced I should have wished to consider with you what should be done. Mr Wyndham had often urged upon me his wish that the facing bricks should be of the character required and as I have as often told him that you had assured me you could produce bricks of the colour and quality wanted, he will be much disappointed if it should be necessary for me to apply to other brickyards for the right quality of bricks. I have directed Mr Simmonds to forward me a sample of your next kiln's burning as soon as possible and I hope they will be more to the purpose than the last.

There was a dramatic improvement in Howell's bricks, but then his roofing tiles were not ready on time. Webb reminded him on 18 August: 'you were to make some [roofing] tiles to match the old ones removed from the cottage buildings pulled down. Have you done this?' Webb was anxious because the brick-making season was coming to a close. When Howell did produce some tiles the quality was reasonable but the size was incorrect: they could only be used for the stables. There was no alternative but to approach another local brickyard, first at Donhead, then Gillingham, to find an additional supply of bricks and tiles. Eventually bricks for the top storey of the main house came from Howell's, Donhead and Gillingham, though the latter were not good enough for facing; Howell managed the tiles for the roof of the stables, offices and main block.

Other matters were also giving Webb cause for concern and on 14 July 1882 he wrote at length to James Simmonds:

I am a little disappointed at learning that I am sometimes the first to find out that things are not being done as they should be. Your time should be employed in watching each kind of work as it goes on, and *at once* correcting mistakes and directing change of proceedings, when necessary. You are aware of the kind of Chilmark stone I most want used, and, in case of doubt, as to quality, you had better go again to the quarry and find out what bed the stone comes from, which is being sent to the works. The 'Pinney' bed being the one decided on.

The main part of the house, the first and second floors, was to be built of local green sandstone so the quality was of supreme importance; Webb, however, was as particular about the materials used for filling in the cavities between the walls.

> Will you be so good as to direct that no sand of less finely ground quality than that done for me by the mill next the main block, be used for the cavity filling-in. It is of the utmost importance that this filling-in should be accurately and scientifically done the sand and cement being measured . . . Please also to agree with Mr Hibbins as to *measuring* with proper box frames, the proportions of lime and sand put into both mills. And, 'till we can decide as to the drift sand, Mr Hibbins must use the sawing grit for the cavity filling, unless he can grind some gravel to that fineness; but even then it is necessary that the quantities of sand and Portland cement should be exactly measured. I am very anxious as to the successful filling of the cavity between the two walls, and it can only succeed if the rules of materials and mixing are followed.

Just over a month later, one of Webb's assistants, Mr Buckle (to become architect of the diocese of Bath and Wells), had to report that part of the south wall of the offices had been built only 18 inches thick rather than the intended 20.5 inches. Webb wrote immediately to Simmonds: 'I hereby direct you to have this part of the walling *pulled down at once*, through its whole thickness'. On an inspection visit towards the end of August, Webb was horrified not only by the damage done to the Hopton Wood stone columns on their train journey to Wiltshire but by the inaccurate way in which the columns had been bedded: 'there is nothing to be done other than to have the work lifted and the beds of stones re-set perfectly truly, also, to have the bruises and injuries to the arrises cut away at the same time'.

Percy Wyndham was present for the August inspection. He was pleased with the work and with the progress, presumably not sharing Webb's attention to detail. When he did notice that the bedding joints in the stone columns varied in thickness, Webb quickly thought up an explanation: 'it was not finally set'. While the Wyndhams went on their annual visit to the north, Webb continued to keep his eagle eye on progress at Clouds. The setting of the Hopton Wood columns continued to be unsatisfactory: 'I had a straightedge put against the columns and found them untrue on the face to the extent, I believe, of a quarter of an inch'.

By the beginning of 1883, the Wyndham family were at last able to glimpse what their house would eventually look like. On a visit on 12 January they deliberately drove to the site by the 'approach' which wound up through the park; they tramped around in the mud and admired the stables, which were proceeding rapidly. Returning again on 21 April, they found the house itself was a solid reality. Percy wrote to Webb with his impressions:

> I was . . . very much pleased indeed with the house. It is an 'amusing' house in the French sense of the word, which cannot be conveyed by our words 'amusing' or 'interesting'. I like the down stairs passages to the offices much with the coved roof, and shape of the roof of passage at the kitchen hatch. I like the kitchen which reminds me of Berkeley & I believe the latter place influenced you a little in your design. I realized how much bigger the rooms look now the house is nearer finished.

He was not entirely happy with the stables, however. 'I cannot get over my dislike to the buff colour at the horses' heads and am determined to change them. I have given myself plenty of time and have tried to convince myself but cannot do it.' He spoke to the builder, Albert Estcourt, who was on the site and discovered that the glazed faces could be cut off the bricks and replaced with a facing of grey glazed tiles. The work would cost £175.

Webb replied at length: it was their first major disagreement and he was determined to change his patron's mind:

> I am exceedingly sorry that any of the work at Clouds should have been so contrary to your pleasure that you should have felt obliged to make up your mind to have it removed, and at great cost. It is certainly true that, if the buff glazed bricks in the stables have to be replaced by another facing, it would be better done before any other work is fixed there; but I feel that now is not a good or safe time in which to judge of the effect of the said bricks. When the boxes and stalls are made-up, the walls whitened and the rack & manger fittings in place the whole thing will have quite a different appearance.

There was a further consideration:

> As these bricks are built-in and are part of the substance and strength of the walls, if they must be removed I shall have to build up a half brick lining instead in addition to fixing the coloured tiles you are in favour of, added to which the tiles are in themselves never so secure as the solid glazed bricks.

Webb couldn't help ending his letter rather ruefully,

> I am obliged to you for the pleasant expression of approval of the great body of the work at Clouds given in the former part of your letter but I am afraid I re-read them rather as sops to Cerberus and the pleasure was somewhat qualified.

Percy was quick to mollify his architect: 'the expressions of approval were not sops to Cerberus but would have been given under any circumstances'. His son George had been to the site with Madeline and he was utterly delighted with what he saw. Also Madeline had supported Estcourt's idea of simply covering the bricks with distemper, 'then I at any time or my successor could at any time restore the present state of things'.

However, nothing was done to the bricks and nearly a year later, on 25 June 1884, Percy again expressed his antipathy to the colour, though his resolve was weakening: 'I was at Clouds yesterday and liked what I liked before as much, and disliked what I disliked before perhaps rather less.' In December he finally had to submit to Webb's choice of colour, though not without a last stand: 'I took my coachman over to Clouds the other day and he was much pleased with his quarters, and not having a sensitive eye does not mind the yellow glazed tiles.'

Percy's concern about the appearance of the stables reflected his own passion for horses. His personal ambitions on the hunting field were crowned in April 1881, while he was still living at Wilbury, when he was asked to be Master of the Tedworth Hunt. Madeline did not share his enthusiasm for riding but all their children were proficient. There are many letters from the children to their mother describing outings, usually involving accidents: this, for example, from Pamela: 'Papa went out hunting yesterday and Carbon fell down with him and he, Papa, said it served him right old pig. None was hurt as Papa would not have said that would he.'[30]

36 Wilbury, Beacon Hill in the distance, by Charles Lutyens, 1878. Included in the 1933 sale of Clouds' contents.

While Madeline collected Burne-Jones's angels, Percy's personal patronage of the arts also involved horses. Captain Charles Lutyens, father of the architect, was invited to Wilbury in August 1878 to spend just over two weeks living with the family, painting their finest horses. After much discussion on just how he would paint the horses, it was 'settled that the 8 hunters should be done in a row, a separate portrait of each horse with a whity grey (coach-house wall) background, divided from each other by partitions formed by the oak frame'. At Clouds the stables needed to accommodate the Wyndhams' twenty horses and one blind donkey, with additional space for visitors' horses. Wilfrid and Anne Blunt, for example, invariably arrived with half a dozen of their Arab horses; later, Bendor, Duke of Westminster (George Wyndham's stepson) came down from Eaton bringing half a dozen hunters and four grooms.

Though the design of the gardens was Madeline's responsibility, Percy did become involved in a minor wrangle with Webb over the design of the buttresses for the kitchen garden wall. Percy and Madeline selected the site for the kitchen garden, Throdmill Field, at the end of 1882; Madeline returned again with Webb to study the proposed site on 7 February 1883. On 28 June 1884 Webb sent his designs for the wall to Estcourt for estimates: 'the digging, concrete, walling and buttresses all round the garden will cost about £1550'. Percy had expressed a preference for 'mediaeval' buttresses rather than Webb's design. The extra cost involved was negligible, £12, so Webb had to employ additional practical and scientific arguments.

Over and above the advantage which my buttresses give for practical purposes, of casting less shade and permitting fruit trees to be trained against them, there is another. The mediaeval buttress shapes represent the appearance of counter pressure against thrust at individual points, and they would look more reasonable if there was a roof over them whereas those I would prefer merely *look* as if they were meant to steady the wall. I have designed some decent buttresses on *your* plan, but I would still much prefer to use those I had proposed.

37 The kitchen garden, 1992.

38 (facing page, above) Harry Brown in the walled garden in front of the head gardener's cottage. From Madeline Adeane's album.

39 (facing page, below) The walled garden and head gardener's cottage, 1992.

Percy was completely outmanoeuvred and replied with one of his shortest notes: 'This is to authorise you to set about building the walls. You can put up the buttresses recommended in your last.' Lethaby commented on the buttresses eventually erected, 'like the cut-waters of a bridge – a memory from Reading days of the buttresses of St Giles' Church'.[31]

Harry Brown, the Wyndhams' head gardener at Wilbury, was also consulted about the gardens from early in the project, and he eventually moved to East Knoyle with the family. The surviving old cottages in Clouds park, in between the new stable block and the domestic offices, were converted into his own 'Head Gardener's Cottage'. Webb took his height measurement (photographs reveal that he was very tall), making a note of it in his site notebook, to be taken into consideration when designing the gates in the garden walls. Such a detail was typical of Webb: he was always concerned to balance architectural considerations with the personal use of his buildings. He was also naturally democratic, making no distinction in importance between the needs of the owner of the house and those of his staff.

On 2 August 1883 Webb sent Percy a summary of progress so far along with a request for his second payment of £1,000:

I was glad to find the general works about the house advancing quickly and well. The Hall, with its lanterns, is roofed, and the timbers and dormer windows of the East and West roofs are now on, and I believe the whole of the main block of the house will be roofed and tiled in by the end of September. Most of the plastering to the offices is done, and the heating apparatus fixed and in working order in both wings of the building.

5

Throughout the project, from the first designs through to the laying of the foundations and building, the Wyndhams made frequent visits to the site, often bringing friends with them to view progress. Sometimes visits were dominated by technical details. In November 1883, for example, Madeline spent time discussing with Webb baths for the house and details about the offices including bells, speaking tubes, cupboards, the cooking apparatus and the service and luggage lifts. These were to be supplied by the Janus Works in Battersea and installed in the tower of Clouds House just below the water tank. The domestic offices were designed by Webb as a separate block so the servants had a long walk from their own domain through the basement of the main house and up flights of stairs to the bedrooms on the first and second floors. However, luggage could at least be moved up and down by lift, as could linen, trays of food and other heavy or awkward items. Webb also required instructions on the fireplaces in which to place specific tiles, including Cinderella tiles and 'canaries in cage' tiles. The latter were presumably fixed in the fireplace of the bedroom known as the 'Canary Bird Room' on the east side of the house; perhaps the Cinderella tiles were used in the 'White Dimity' bedroom.

A regular visitor to East Knoyle was the Wyndhams' close friend Hugh Grosvenor, Duke of Westminster. As early as August 1878 Madeline took the Duke to see the site with her daughter Mary as chaperon. They took the train to Tisbury, then rode to Fonthill Splendens, the house designed by Wyatt and Brandon in 1848–9 for the millionaire James Morrison, inherited by his son Alfred in 1857. Mrs Alfred Morrison was a friend of Madeline's, involved in the Royal School of Art Needlework.

The Duke passed disdainful comment on the Morrisons in a letter he wrote to Mary Wyndham immediately after the visit. He described Alfred Morrison as 'one of the sons of the Mr Morrison who from very small beginnings created a colossal fortune in trade on the principle of deriving small profits from an extensive business'. He was unimpressed by their wealth:

> Mr A is an eccentric individual with peculiar views on most things, one being never to give away a farthing in 'charity' – another to have 33 hunters valued at 300 apiece and never to ride one of them – another to rear 1000 pheasants and to shoot them all himself – another to denounce all art and artists except those of which he himself approves (and there are a queer lot).

After visiting the Morrisons, the Wyndham party rode through the extensive grounds of Fonthill, once the property of the Gothic novelist and wealthy eccentric, William Beckford. Mary appreciated the 'great broad grass rides along which we cantered, there's a beautiful piece of water and silver fir-trees and one gets views of the down country'. Beckford's Fonthill Abbey was built on the hillside away from Fonthill Splendens (which was itself constructed on the original mansion of Alderman Beckford, his father). Its astonishingly high tower had collapsed in 1825 and the Duke of Westminster's father, who later bought the estate, built a new Fonthill Abbey in the grounds.

From Fonthill, the Wyndham party rode the short distance to East Knoyle. There were frequent showers and Mary was suffering from a headache. And there wasn't very much to show the Duke apart from the site and view; Webb's workmen began levelling the ground for the house in February the following year. The visits to Clouds continued as the house neared completion. Almost every Wilbury guest was taken across the county to East Knoyle: the Burne-Jones' family, Blanche Airlie, General Napier, Lord and Lady Arthur Wellesley, dozens of nieces, nephews and cousins.

Webb stayed at Wilbury on 22 March 1884 after spending the previous day with Percy and Harry Brown at East Knoyle discussing the layout of the kitchen garden. He sent his plans for the kitchen garden to the Wyndhams on 3 April.

> The amount of ground enclosed by the walls is about 3 acres. You will see that I have marked two cisterns; one in the middle of the garden and another in the eastern boundary, and both in the line of lowest level of ground. As to the water supply, I think we may be short, therefore in building the water tower to supply the house I am putting an extra cistern in it for the service of the hot houses, as an iron pipe can readily be laid from the tower.

Another pipe was to be laid from the water tower down to Slades to supply the laundry, 'as it would be as well to give our engine at the new well as much to do as possible and save hand pumping'.

Webb's original idea for supplying water to Clouds was to use the windmill to power a pumping engine, 'as the soil in the neighbourhood must be full of springs'. He brought in a civil engineer, Richard Grantham to advise on practicalities (Grantham had lately arranged the water supply to Lord Normanton's house, Somerley in Hampshire). The Green and Trodwell springs were discovered to be the most promising for a supply of water and in October 1878 a new well was dug into the greensand stratum. Water was finally pumped by an oil-powered engine up to the water tower, which was constructed to contain a 5,000-gallon service tank. The tower was built to the west, between the main house and the windmill. Close by a covered reservoir was built, of 50,000-gallon capacity, to supply the kitchens and stables. Once the Wyndhams agreed to the kitchen garden plans, including Webb's preferred buttress design, trenches were dug and the concrete foundations laid to support the walls. The gates were fixed on 7 November 1884.

Madeline was eager to start work on the gardens nearer the main house, but Webb advised caution, even though he was forced to admit he was not a professional landscape gardener. He thought the East Garden needed delicate handling: 'doubtless you saw this in your dealing with it', so, 'would it not be well to defer fitting up the little garden house in the south wall at the bottom of garden til things are more settled? It should be a handy neat & tidy place and wd. be very convenient.' He had heard of the rather 'wild suggestion' that the garden house might be turned into a mushroom house and pointed out that the kitchen garden, where there would be a supply of proper heat, was the best position for such a building.

Madeline was anxious to erect a greenhouse for house-plants but again Webb suggested caution, 'as many things will have to be thought of with regard to it and other glass houses in Kitchen garden'. There were plenty of glasshouse manufacturers she could approach, but 'care would have to be used in dealing with them or you will be fitted with work at great cost which could ruin the appearance of the most lovely place in England'. Harry Brown was planning to live in the coachman's house in the stable block through the winter; if he was worried about his plants, Webb thought he could easily rig up some frames. At the same time Webb made sure the grates ordered

40   The water tower.

for the coachman's house would be fixed as soon as possible (September) so that Mr Brown would keep warm through the winter months.

Madeline and Harry Brown began planning the formal gardens close to the house before Clouds was ready for occupation. Actual planting was limited, however, to slow-growing yew hedges, and the chalk-walled garden was planted with bulbs and magnolia trees. Climbing plants and trees such as magnolia, vines and figs, intended to grow up the walls of the main house and the offices, could not be planted until Webb's workmen had finished.

A visit to Membland in Devon in May 1884 gave Percy a chance to experience the effects of electricity: he was not impressed and did not install it in Clouds. The large, square eighteenth-century house was the seat of Edward Baring, later created first Baron Revelstoke. George Devey had made extensions in 1877–9 and the wealth of the head of Baring Brothers was evident throughout. Percy wrote to Mary:

> Everything is very well done, signs of great wealth every where. My room & apparently all those near are filled with nice old prints in black & gold frames. The house is lit by electricity. I am not much taken with that, the light is too brilliant for ordinary times. I thought the dining room perfect till the electric light was turned on. There has been a little 'kick' in the light the engineer accounts for this by the band of one of the wheels having been too much tightened for making ice. The steam engine that generates the electricity makes the ice too.

Webb's September report on progress was satisfactory and he received his fee of £1,000:

> . . . the drying of the house much helped by this fine hot weather we have had. The

garden walls are well advanced and I am hoping that three sides of this walling will be finished by about the first week in October and the fourth side well on in that way . . . These walls are unusually well and closely built.

The carving of the capitals of the Hopton Wood stone pillars in the hall were to be done under the supervision of a London workshop run by the carver Mr MacCulloch: he sent his assistant Mr Turner with a second carver, to work to Webb's designs. Percy meanwhile organised various bits and pieces he had been acquiring for the house to be sent to the site and stored in the stables: four Istrian marble mantels; one Cippolino mantel; one large wooden mantel from Isel designed by Aitchison; one French wooden mantel; one Chippendale corner cupboard; one Dutch-looking glass; four 'fine old backs' for fires; also some inlaid panels to be used for doors.

Throughout the planning and building of Clouds Percy had been buying items specially for the new home. During the 1883 season for example, Percy added to his art collection by buying several drawings by Rossetti and a version in oils of *Beata Beatrix* painted in 1880, for £661 10sh. He or Madeline also bought two oriental black-and-gold lacquer shawl chests from Rossetti's studio sale. Percy had thought he was buying a Rossetti drawing (for £15) as early as 1878, from a dealer called Attenborough, but when he showed the work to the artist, Rossetti replied, 'I have no hesitation in saying that I

41   *Lovers Embracing*, study for the *Blessed Damozel*, by Dante Gabriel Rossetti, *c*.1876. Acquired by Percy Wyndham at Rossetti's sale 1883; sold at Christie's 1970.

never saw it before. The monogram is a tolerable imitation of mine.'[32] Enquiries were made by Percy and Rossetti, eventually exposing a woman artist who, together with a male accomplice, was busy forging the works of Rossetti, Watts and other contemporary artists.

One of the most faithful patrons of Rossetti and Burne-Jones since the mid-1860s was William Graham, also a connoisseur and collector of early Italian masters. Like the Prinseps, Graham's family had made their fortune in India and he was able to retire early with a substantial private income from the family's jute business. The Wyndhams undoubtedly knew him through his relationship with Burne-Jones; they were close friends of his daughter Frances and her (eventual) husband John Horner of Mells Park in Somerset and also acquainted with Gertrude Jekyll and her brother Herbert who married Agnes Graham in 1881. During the 1883 season they took their daughter Mary to a subscription concert at William Graham's house in Grosvenor Place where his impressive collection was hung, contemporary paintings alongside Italian masters. New hanging arrangements had been made by Graham at the end of 1877:

> We shall have poles for curtains in the big room and once they are up I think their simplicity will put the curly wurly ones . . . terrible unholsterer's gilt mouldings only fit for a cafe or dancing Hall . . . to such shame that they will go. Meantime I am thankful the red background is pleasant and calm and won't disturb the Angels with noisiness or nastiness of any kind.[33]

But the house was still brimming over with paintings, 'in every room from floor to ceiling; old and modern, sacred and profane; they stood in heaps on the floor and on the chairs and tables'.[34] Graham's interest in Rossetti may have inspired Percy. After Graham's death in 1885, his own collection was auctioned and Percy bought one of his early Italian paintings; it was given pride of place in the central hall of Clouds.

It was Webb who drew Percy's attention to the paintings at the Graham sale; Percy in turn frequently sought Webb's advice on all sorts of matters: paintings, old panelling, fireplaces, picture frames, even alarm bells. The architect appears to have enjoyed the arrangement: he never hesitated to give his opinion, however damning, on something that had caught Percy's eye. In May 1879, for example, he went off to look at some Sansovino frames for Percy but found them 'not of that excellence which would make me say "buy them" for fear of missing an opportunity which should not be lost'. He also looked at console tables, ' which would not suit the house at all', and paintings by De Witt which were 'of no value, that is, according to my lights'.

On a later occasion, in March 1882, Percy wrote to Webb, asking to meet him at Sinclair's, Marshall Street to look at oak panels, as well as some marble chimneypieces:

> There are about 844 panels of oak . . . They are worked on both sides, and would panel a small room or make a beautiful screen. He only wants 8d a foot. I think it a great chance but I should like you to see them. I had the varnish taken off one. Let me know if I shall tell him to take it off all.
>
> I went there for another purpose, to look at two Istrian marble chimney pieces. I thought they were smaller than they are. He wants £35 a piece. They are not dear but I look at it in this light if other chimney pieces would come to as much or nearly as much then I would take them but if it is an extravagance getting them then no. We have already four already besides Aitchesons [*sic*] from Isel. The oak I

think a chance if we have a room we could dado with it. It is much cheaper than the last lot I bought and much better.

Webb was unable to meet Percy but did visit Sinclair's for himself two days later.

> To speak directly, I do not myself like the panelling: It has a too large & coarse moulding, more particularly so with such small panels: added to which to put it together to panel a room, it would take a good deal of framing. The marble fireplaces were well enough, but I do not [think] them sufficiently beautiful or remarkable to advise you to buy them. We have now 4 Istrian marble f.p.s, 1 Cipolino f.p. and 2 of the Isel Hall chy.pieces, so that unless we found anything very attractive, the mantels taken in the contract would I think do well enough . . .

> P.S. If you should think differently to me, I've no doubt I could work up the panelling very well.

Webb always encouraged Percy to acquire pieces of excellent individual quality which were appropriate for Clouds. William Graham bought more works of art than he could ever adequately display in his London house; the Wyndhams' selective approach and acquisition of a large house in the country as well as in London allowed them to display their entire collection under the best conditions possible.

As well as advising on the contents of Clouds, Webb continued to undertake small commissions at Wilbury and Belgrave Square. In 1879, for example, he assisted in the framing and hanging of the Wyndhams' principal paintings up the main staircase in Belgrave Square: Leighton's five dancers at the top; below, the Mason and the Costa; Watts's portrait of Madeline; Val Prinsep's portrait of George and Guy Wyndham. Webb was less enthusiastic about joining in the Wyndhams' family and social life, though he did accompany Percy to the theatre and on one occasion gave Madeline and Mary advice on how to improve their sketches and home-made theatrical costumes. Sorting out the Wilbury mangle was a task more to his taste.

Webb left England in December 1884, touring Italy for three months. Percy wished he could go too and recalled the youthful delights of travelling without unnecessary baggage.

> I hope and believe your tour will do you a great deal of good artistically, mentally, physically and digestively. Orvietto is very good for gouty dispositions. I am afraid at our age going abroad never can be the time it used to be. I should like to have gone with you. I like to be without servants, and used to like packing and servantless condition, but I am much afraid 50 years of luxury have spoilt this and that I should hate the bore of packing etc. I am not sure though.

While Webb was still in Italy, work was carried out to convert the old cottages beside the chalk-walled garden into '(comparatively) a palazzo for Signore Brown at a cost of £200'. A greenhouse just under 100 feet long was constructed between Brown's house and the offices. Percy visited the St Pancras Ironworks with his coachman and Webb's assistant George Jack to select fittings for the stables; in March 1885 he wrote to Webb, 'I am glad you are in Venice as it will be a good opportunity to study stable fittings archaic enough to satisfy your taste'.

Back from Italy, Webb resumed his visits to Clouds and at the end of June he declared things were 'smoothing down'. The panelling was up in the entrance hall, also the high panelling in the dining room. Percy had already been thinking of a white fence for the south side of the house and Webb was in agreement, though thought it would be better round the land opposite the house and about 3′ 3″ high, the spars close enough to keep out a young rabbit. In July the position and drainage of the stablemen's latrines were resolved and William Mallett was appointed house carpenter; he was to become clerk of works for the estate until his death in 1923.

During the summer Percy arranged with Webb the insurance of the house, offices and stables. He was especially worried about fire and thought the laundry the most at risk. In May a mysterious lady had appeared at the house and prophesied that a fire would destroy the house. Wilfrid Blunt later recounted the details in his *Country Life* article about Clouds:

> a woman dressed in black, tall, and with the appearance of being a lady, came to the west door leading into the great hall. She had been noticed passing down the road from the direction of the Windmill Hill, looking about her and watching the building operations. Coming to the door, she presently began questioning the workmen, and especially one, Neil, as to the work that was being done. Then the name of the building was asked, and the name of the owner and of the architect and the builder, and she requested admittance, which was not refused her. On entering she looked round the hall, and then said suddenly, 'This house will be burnt down, and in less than three years.' With these words she went out at the door, and though followed and looked after, could not again be found, nor was anything seen or known of her from that time forth.[35]

The prophecy was correct in general: Clouds House was burnt down. The details, however, were inaccurate: Clouds caught fire in January 1889, nearly four, rather than three years after the visit of the mysterious lady in black.

6

When Clouds was virtually finished Percy sent Webb an open invitation to visit at any time; however, the architect had no desire to be transformed into a 'gentleman' and replied:

> I may have to come again on business; but as a 'gentleman', it is doubtful. Also, consider, if it takes 2 bottles of Chateau Margaux to put me in good temper when in business, I'm afraid it would take a batch if I were a guest pure and simple! Forbes [the butler at Clouds] would be inclined to draw a line instead of a cork!

While Webb preferred to stay away from the houses he had designed, except on business, his work at East Knoyle attracted the attention of some of the Wyndhams' neighbours and guests. The Wyndhams were partly responsible for obtaining three commissions for him, minor works at Rushmore, near Tisbury, Wiltshire for General Fox-Pitt-Rivers; a new house called Lapscombe (later called Willinghurst) in

Cranleigh, Surrey for the Ramsdens; and the restoration of Forthampton Court near Tewkesbury, Worcestershire, for the Yorkes.

General Fox-Pitt-Rivers had served in the Grenadier Guards in the Crimea and was one of the largest landowners in Wiltshire with an estate of almost 28,000 acres. He was a close neighbour of the Wyndhams and of Percy's niece Sybil, Marchioness of Queensberry; in 1899 his son St George married Sybil's daughter, Lady Edith Douglas. The General was the recipient of Webb's usual stubborn response to his clients after venturing to pass on a critical opinion of a fireplace designed by Webb:

> I do not see why your hall fireplace should be exempt from criticism: a good deal, however, would depend upon whether the criticisms would stand examination or not. The hasty attempt at wit with regard to the appearance of the marble and oak work in juxtaposition is not of sufficient point to disturb your peace, as it has not troubled mine.[36]

After pointing out a possible alteration, Webb concluded: 'but I should not advise you to make this change, but would recommend instead that you should read the valuable [Aesop] fable of the miller, his son, and their ass'.[37]

John Charles Ramsden was the same age as Percy Wyndham, he had fought in the Crimea and was a cousin of Lord Muncaster, the Wyndhams' close friend and neighbour when they lived in Cumberland. He and his wife visited Clouds in April 1886 and Percy reported to Webb that they were 'much pleased with the house'. By July Webb was busy with the design of Lapscombe, and wrote to Percy:

> I am afraid I cannot accept your kind call to come to Clouds and be lectured, as I have Ramsden and other bits of work to attend to: the former goes but slowly at present, and certainly has not yet advanced to that stage when he will call me 'coxcombe'. It will probably arrive at the comfortable point when I am about to send him in my bill!

Though Lapscombe was a comparatively small country house, it contained features similar to Clouds, in particular the fireplaces and plasterwork. Webb produced a beautiful carved frieze for the drawing-room mantelpiece.

John Reginald Yorke, Conservative MP, had been at Eton with Percy Wyndham, he was a close friend of Balfour and was related by marriage to the families of two of the Wyndhams' sons-in-law, the Adeanes of Babraham and the Charterises of Gosford and Stanway; his own son later married Percy's niece. In 1886 the Yorkes were guests of Mary Elcho at Stanway, only a few miles away from Forthampton Court. They were then invited to Clouds to consider whether to commission its architect to design a new house to replace their crumbling medieval home. Webb visited Forthampton Court in 1889 but, as a founder member of the Society for the Preservation of Ancient Buildings, he insisted on restoring the old house. When the work was completed the interior revealed similarities with Clouds: it was furnished with fabrics from Morris and Company and embroidery from the Royal School of Art Needlework.[38]

Recommendations from one satisfied client to the next ensured sufficient commissions for Webb. The Holland Park circle of artists and patrons provided his earlier commissions; though part of this circle, the Wyndhams were also landowners. Once completed, Clouds House introduced Webb's work to other members of the landed gentry, part of the country house network. Webb sought no other form of self-advertisement. His early design (1862) for a row of shops near Finsbury Square in London and his design for Val Prinsep's house in Holland Park were the only works he allowed to appear in contemporary architectural papers. Even after his retirement he had to be persuaded by his closest friends to allow *Country Life* to publish photographs of his houses. He was angry when Blunt's lengthy description of Clouds appeared in *Country Life* in 1904, and held the Wyndhams, as Blunt's relations, partly responsible.

> How could you & Mrs Wyndham allow my 'Squire' to *enlarge* on my professional work at Clouds? This is a breaking of a kind of tacit agreement there should be no advertisement in the public papers of your house with my name brought in; the 'careful architect' of the buildings wd. have been quite all that was necessary for the occasion. The 'blazing indiscretion' of Blunt's exceedingly skilful trumpeting made me – I assure you, blush all over; from the tip of the crown, to the bend when one sits down![39]

Blunt was Webb's landlord. On his retirement in 1900, Webb had moved into Caxtons, a cottage in Worth Forest, part of Blunt's Sussex estate. Again his friendship with landowners (however much against his socialist principles) had helped to provide for him, this time with a home rather than a commission. Webb had visited Blunt in Sussex on 26 May 1900 and explained his retirement plans, to find 'a hermitage in which to end his days'. He could afford only a low rent but Blunt promised to help: 'he has been too honest to make a fortune & talks of a £10 cottage. I shall try & find him one.'[40]

On moving into Caxtons, for the first time in a twenty-five-year-long correspondence Webb wrote to Percy Wyndham a letter which began, 'My dear Wyndham'. Previously he had stuck to 'sir' (for eight years), then 'Dear Mr Wyndham'. Percy, for his part, consistently addressed his architect by his surname only.

> My dear Wyndham,
> You see, I address you now almost as a fellow country-gentleman – (save the name), and would ask you to some shooting in the 'forest', were not my fellow trustee in the estate abroad.

As leaseholder of a country property, even if it was only a cottage Webb could afford to joke with his old patron as if they were social equals. He ended his letter with an invitation to Percy to try a turn at poaching 'on a cloudy night' in Worth Forest, 'for there is a fine chamber in the chimney bulk at Caxtons where we could stow away 50 heads or so till the cart come round'.

4 At Home

The Wyndhams moved into Clouds on 23 September 1885, even though the plasterwork was unfinished in the drawing room, the baths were not working efficiently and there were no chandeliers in the hall. The first of the family to enter the house were Percy, three of his children – Guy, Madeline and Pamela – and the governess, Fräulein Schneider. Madeline followed a day later with George, 'after the inspection [of his regiment the Coldstream Guards]'. He had just returned from the Sudan and Madeline expressed her sense of relief to her daughter Mary. 'I am only too thankful simply *brimming over* with thankfulness at being allowed to enter these walls *with the 2 boys & all well*.' The knowledge that George had been risking his life in a war to which both his parents were opposed had coloured the final months of building work and Madeline's planning of the interior decorations and arranging furniture: 'I feel sure there are mental drops of blood all over the House.'

Mary was the only member of the family not able to join in the Clouds house-warming. On 9 August 1883 she had married Hugo Charteris, Lord Elcho, eldest son and heir of the Wyndhams' old friend who had become tenth Earl of Wemyss the same year. The Elchos settled into Stanway, their country home in Gloucestershire. Mary's younger sister Madeline sent her details of the appearance of Clouds. The bedrooms looked 'scrumtious . . . what fun we are having arranging our rooms . . . the stair-case is almost the prettiest part I think'. She and Pamela were helping their mother choose carpets:

> we *think* that a few carpets are settled upon, but lately the floors have been strewn with scraps of carpet and we have stood with our heads on one side but arrived at nothing decisive. I think mine will be red, and Pamela's blue, but it is very difficult to choose from patterns.

Mary received more details about the house from Georgiana Burne-Jones, who stayed at Clouds with her daughter Margaret for ten days in November. Georgiana wrote to Mary:

> It is much larger than I thought from when we saw it unfurnished, and the hall I think is extraordinarily beautiful. I have not yet mastered all the details of the plan of the whole building, & keep discovering new rooms inside and windows outside. The Hall proves to be beautiful for music which is an additional charm, and I think your father is very much pleased at it.

Mary finally saw Clouds when she arrived for Christmas, together with her baby son Ego, Stella the chow, her canaries and 'millions of packages'. She recorded in her diary the excitement of her sisters, desperately waiting for her response: 'I was to say whether it seemed really different to what their descriptions had made me imagine.' 'Delightful' was all she could think to write.

42　Clouds House from the
south, *c*.1885. Taken by
William Weir and inscribed
'view from the south with
thumb mark storm coming
or going'.

As far as Percy was concerned, with a houseful of guests for Christmas, certain aspects of Clouds were far from delightful. The plumbing system installed by the North British Plumbing Company was causing serious and constant problems. As Percy explained to Webb, for the amount he had spent, he expected a constant supply of hot water. He gave an example of the difficulties encountered after his son George gallantly rescued a child who fell through the ice (presumably of the bathing pond, which was completed in 1885). Both were soaked.

> As it would take 20 minutes to heat the water, after he [George] had got home, after he had found a servant, after said servant had found the man to light furnace etc etc. of course no bath was possible.
>
> There is no doubt something refreshing in the idea of patrician and plebean [sic] after their common danger being relegated to the humble copper kettle of daily use but that is not what I am paying for.

All Percy required was a bath that 'any valet or ladysmaid could get ready or housemaid', but in the summer of 1886 it still needed the assistance of the house carpenter and an engineer to produce a hot bath. The circulation of the water was finally altered (at a cost of £160) and by the end of September all was working well. Percy wrote to his daughter Mary, 'the baths are right now, and you can have a common warm bath now without the assistance of 5 people. Mamma had one this morning and thus had a field-day with the sprays etc.'

At the same time, however, it was discovered that effluent from the drains was killing trees in the park, including a beech and three yews. A new sub-drainage system was dug and the yews were turned into seats. They had been expensive to acquire and troublesome to plant and Percy wanted to 'punish' them; as he explained to the tree-loving Webb, 'to fuel the eternal flames would be a lot far too good for them'. The architect was saddened by their fate: 'surely if Hell fire is not enough then perpetually being sat upon by conservative back sides is more than enough of purgatory'.

Architect and patron continued to score political points off one another in their letters for the rest of their lives but for the present Webb's work at East Knoyle was completed. To show his enormous satisfaction and pleasure with his new home, Percy wrote Webb a formal letter, thanking him 'for the way in which you have designed and built this house', with which he was 'completely satisfied'. He added:

> influential people (or donkeys as you would call them) are putting it about that this is the house of the age. I believe they are right.

I

When W.R. Lethaby described Clouds House in his biography of Philip Webb, he emphasised its social function: 'It appears to have been imagined by its gifted hostess as a palace of week-ending for our politicians.'[1] Later, John Brandon-Jones also noted the link between design and function: 'it was designed as a setting for house parties in the days when the government of England depended to a great extent upon arrangements made at these elaborately informal meetings where Cabinet decisions were anticipated and society weddings arranged'.[2]

Percy and Madeline were an individual aristocratic couple with a very particular lifestyle, which was established in the early years of their marriage and confirmed during their tenancy of Isel and Wilbury. Mark Girouard has defined it by referring to two of their most frequent guests in London and in the country:

> Balfour was a friend of the Percy Wyndhams and so was Burne-Jones. The two names give the ambience of the house: political entertaining combined with artistic discrimination. The style, sensibility and relative informality with which the two were pursued made Clouds one of the most famous country houses of its era.[3]

As the Leader of the Conservative government in the House of Commons, Balfour was the 'lion' in every country house where he was a guest. He was a friend of the Wyndhams from the mid-1870s, the putative lover of Mary Elcho and the political patron of her brother, George Wyndham. His frequent visits to Clouds ensured the significance of the house as a 'palace of weekending'. An invitation from the Wyndhams offered ambitious young members of the Conservative party the opportunity to be favourably noticed by their leader during an informal game of tennis or a stroll over the East Knoyle golf course.

The Burne-Jones family were regular guests at both Wilbury and Clouds, joining in the celebrations of Christmas and New Year, of birthdays, parties for the village schoolchildren, dances for the servants and tenants, and amateur theatrical performances. Georgiana Burne-Jones, Margaret and Philip were more frequent guests than the artist. When he could be persuaded to visit, he usually remained indoors, working on designs in his bedroom or in the drawing-room. Two days in the country were usually sufficient, as Georgiana explained:

> A visit in the house of a friend, however much he enjoyed it, was no rest to him, for it always ended in his expending his strength by entertaining his entertainers. Wherever he stayed traces of this remained behind him; there were drawings, readings, conversations, in which he poured forth the things he knew and stirred his hearers to fresh thought – all pleasure at the time, but exhaustion afterwards.[4]

He preferred to concentrate on completing his professional commitments in his London studio, relying on Georgiana to develop intimate friendships with the wives of his patrons.

Webb's challenge had been to design a house large enough to accommodate the Wyndhams' family and friends in comfort, but also to be sufficiently intimate to reflect and support their very particular way of entertaining. The Wyndhams pursued many family activities and encouraged their guests to join in, but they also enjoyed privacy, and the opportunity either to engage in more personal intercourse with one another or simply to be alone. Percy and Madeline were not interested in a 'powerhouse', a mansion which ostentatiously flaunted their wealth and social position. Though their visitors might themselves be some of the richest and most powerful men and women in the country – the Duke of Westminster, for example, was an early visitor who expressed his delight with the house though his own twelve-year rebuilding programme at Eaton had cost some £600,000, over seven times as much as Clouds – they came to the Wyndhams' country house to share their passion for the arts, for human relationships and for family life.

The Clouds visitors' books, two volumes, confirm the family orientation of the Wyndhams' entertaining. Year after year, the same relatives and friends returned to Clouds to celebrate Christmas and New Year, Easter, the birthdays of Percy, Madeline and their children. Very few guests came only once: perhaps the Wyndhams drew up a short list for Clouds from the hundreds of people who attended their more formal dinners and parties at 44 Belgrave Square. During their daughters' seasons of 'coming-out' activities, they regularly gave balls for 200. Before offering the invitation to Clouds they assessed which artist or writer would enjoy spending a Saturday-to-Monday in the country.

Clouds was very large, yet the atmosphere the Wyndhams tried to create within and around it was relaxed and informal. Their son-in-law Charles Adeane summed it up as 'the happiest and most hospitable home'.[5] Madeline was chiefly responsible. Her warmth, friendliness, genuine interest in everyone around her, from the most illustrious guests to the lowliest servant or labourer, is consistently affirmed by her friends, members of her family, acquaintances and staff. She 'would do everything for everybody else, but resisted anything being done for her own. She was a heavenly person and greatly loved by all, overflowing as she was with love and encouragement.'[6] One guest wrote to her with fervour, 'to come into your atmosphere is a boon and delight and refreshment, not only for those who belong to you but even to the stranger who feels no longer strange or outside . . . the fabric of your house may be beautiful, but the human fabric is still more beautiful'.[7] After one of many visits to Clouds, the artist Edward Clifford enthused about Madeline to her son George:

If there is a scent that is like her, it is the sweet briar – a delicious, homely fragrance. She is not (as some people have suggested) at all like a magnolia. It is much too luxurious, and overwhelming, and wealthy for her. She is never overwhelming. Her taste is perfect as to poetry, flowers, decoration, pictures, houses, garden. She is distinctly humble, and never realizes or thinks of her virtues . . . Many of us have just a touch of priggishness. She never had, not for one moment, not once in her life. She is more kind than philanthropic, more good than virtuous, more delightful than brilliant.[8]

Percy 'cultivated but crotchety' in his early thirties, was becoming a more affable host. He never prevented Madeline from pursuing her artistic enthusiasms and activities, nor did he undermine her position as hostess. His Wyndham temper still erupted, but only while shooting or playing golf. When Wilfrid Blunt visited Clouds for the first time at the end of August 1887 he commented on the change in Percy, 'who with years has grown larger minded & kinder hearted – the type now of the most excellent of English gentleman'.[9] He had left politics two years before; next to his family, his estate was the most important part of his life and he spent an increasing part of each year in Wiltshire. While Madeline stayed with Mary at Stanway or called on her artist friends in London, he remained contentedly at Clouds, driving his two youngest daughters to dog shows, to lawn tennis parties, to visit his tenant farmers.

2

When the Wyndhams' friend Walburga, Lady Paget visited Clouds she sketched its appearance, both inside and out: 'a glorified Kate Greenaway affair, all blue and white inside, and all red and green outside'. She also described the surrounding countryside, 'beautiful trees and downs all round, also windmills and adders, therefore no walking barefoot in the dew'.[10]

Wilfrid Blunt provides more detail about the 'capital' situation,

near enough to the top of the hill to have the advantage of good air & yet sheltered on all sides from the wind. There is no greater mistake than building quite on a ridge where all the winds blow for the sake alone of a view which you speedily get sick of or forget. Here you have the charm of woods all round with a peep down the valley, & three minutes walk takes you to the top.[11]

There were two approaches to Clouds for visitors in carriages. The majority rode or were driven up through the park, past the stables and domestic wing, to alight from their carriages at the main entrance on the north side of the house. Their general impression on the drive through the park would have been of varied woodland, of mature cedars, beeches and conifers, elms and limes, also clumps of rhododendrons and other shrubs, and through the trees glimpses of grassland and grazing horses.

Another approach was from Windmill Hill to the west, offering still more woodland and shrubberies, and a glimpse of Webb's water tower and the tennis lawns with their archway of roses. Tennis was a favourite pastime of the Wyndham children and many of their visitors, especially Balfour. The courts were finished in May 1886 while

Madeline was staying in Ireland. She received an enthusiastic report from her daughters: 'the courts are extra-ordinarily good. [Harry] Brown marked them out and mowed them, we had the nets mended and white tape sewn along the top, so they look all right. We had netting put up to keep the balls from rolling into the road.'[12]

Madeline planned to plant a maze between the house and the lawn tennis court. Edward Poynter was recruited in 1888 to work on designs and he went off to the South Kensington Library to research. He wrote to Madeline enclosing sketches: 'In the Encyclopaedia . . . there were plans of various sorts of mazes which were enough to shew me that ours would work out all right.'[13] In the end, however, Madeline decided there was insufficient room.

The formal gardens, designed by Madeline and Harry Brown to contrast with the more public parkland, remained hidden from view until the unsuspecting visitor was led through the great hall and into the main drawing room, with views to the south and east. The wide grass terrace along the southern side of Clouds was as high as the top of the spire of Salisbury Cathedral and offered spectacular views of the park and hills beyond. Magnolia trees were planted against the house, roses, myrtles and rosemary in the border below. Other herbaceous plants favoured by Madeline and Harry Brown included monbretias, phloxes, delphinium, peonies, gladioli, spiraeas and yuccas.[14]

The effect to the south was of openness, of the land falling away to the misty blue hills in the distance with only Webb's white-painted fence marking the end of the lawn and beginning of the park. The fence was not erected until 1886, following some discussion between Percy and his architect as to its design and the costs involved. Webb wanted it to be very well constructed,

> as permanent as possible, so that I have made it all of oak with brick and concrete base so that it should not get out of line or otherways move. Fourlegged brutes would rub against it and lively 2 legged ones would ride upon it, and it should be sufficiently rigid to withstand moderate brute force.

To the east of the house, from immediately below the east drawing room, and following the southern wall of the domestic offices all the way down to the stable block, Madeline and Harry Brown created a series of individual gardens, designed for private contemplation and conversation. Harry Brown called them 'a succession of lovely surprises'.[15] Roses were everywhere, by the turn of the century some 2,500, as well as yew trees and yew hedges, the latter clipped once a year, some in the shape of peacocks' tails in honour of the peacocks which stalked the gardens.

Vines and fig trees grew against the south wall of the offices. Against the wall of the kitchen Webb built a south-facing loggia with three oak seats, its arches clad in creepers. He cut doorways through the thatched chalk wall which survived from the original farm: inside was Madeline's spring garden planted with bulbs, cyclamens, magnolias, at its best in May when she described it in a letter to Mary, 'perfect masses of tulips scarlet purple yellow with narcissus & all kinds of delicious blossoms'.

Beyond the spring garden, a pergola garden was later created at the back (southern side) of the stable block. The architect Detmar Blow, a pupil of Webb and from 1892 a regular guest at Clouds, designed the pergola, a rough-hewn dramatic feature, and it was built by William Mallett and the estate workmen to support vines. Below were flowerbeds containing lupins and gladioli; beyond, to the south, cherry trees, more shrubs and the mature trees of the park.

43 (facing page, above) Clouds House from the north-west, *c.*1885. Taken by William Weir and inscribed 'earthquake view from the north-west'.

44 (facing page, below) Dressed for tennis: Richard Doyle, Miss Vane, Mary Wyndham, Colonel Bridgeman at Raby Castle 24 September 1880, the photograph was taken by Lady Mary Primrose, sent to Mary Wyndham and kept in her diary.

To the north-west of the house, the informal 'river walk', so called because it wound to the top of the hill, was designed to meander through a wild garden planted with bluebells and primroses, Japanese iris, azaleas, bog myrtle, Solomon's seal, myosotis, bamboos, magnolias and rhododendrons, with fine Cedar trees in the background. The 'wild' aspects of the grounds particularly appealed to Wilfrid Blunt, who would pitch his Arab tent 'in a hidden place' in the trees and entertain his favourites from among the young ladies staying in the house. He found Madeline's 'large-mindedness' truly remarkable, for though they had been lovers for a brief moment she was able to accept his seduction of her daughter Mary and her niece Dorothy Carleton. Age finally caught up with his romantic activities. On a visit to Clouds in 1901 he pitched his tent as usual and Dorothy, together with the Wyndhams' daughter Pamela Tennant, decided to spend the night in the tent. 'I lay down for an hour or two near them under a beech tree but finding it chilly came in about 1 o'clock'.[16]

At the centre of the house was the spacious top-lit hall. This was the main thoroughfare on the ground floor; all the reception rooms and Percy's own suite of rooms opened off it. The hall was also designed to be a convivial place for conversations – photographs reveal groups standing and sitting in front of the large fireplace – for parties, amateur theatricals and recitals. The Wyndhams discovered the hall's suitability for parties almost by accident. In January 1886, when they could not use the drawing room because the plastering was unfinished and the floor unlaid, they were

45 (facing page, above) Clouds House from the south-east, *c.*1885. Taken by William Weir.

46 (facing page, below) The view from Clouds House looking south-east, with the offices to the left of the photograph, the walled garden in the centre, the stables centre distance, *c.*1892.

47 A view of the hall, late 1890s (after Clouds was rebuilt). Taken as part of a series by Witcomb & Son of Salisbury and Bournemouth.

forced to use the hall for Pamela's birthday party. Percy wrote to Webb: 'the hall was highly approved of and no doubt one can give either a small or large dance with far less trouble and disarrangement than in most houses'.

Musical recitals were a feature of visits to Clouds and the grand piano in the hall was the focal point of such occasions. Sometimes the family and friends provided the music – Pamela was an accomplished guitarist – more often professional musicians were invited to play. Walburga Paget recalled the 'delicious music', often Wagner, and the playing of Mrs Arkwright and the violinist Deremberg. At 44 Belgrave Square, musicians included the pianist and composer Donald Tovey, and Isadora Duncan danced there in 1900 at the request of Balfour.

Performances of plays at Clouds were always amateur affairs though rehearsals occupied the Wyndham children, their governess, friends from Knoyle House and the Rectory for weeks on end. Madeline was usually asked to paint the scenery. The tradition had been established at Wilbury with George and Guy (home from Eton) and Margaret and Philip Burne-Jones regular members of the cast. Then the repertoire was limited to the plays of Shakespeare; at Clouds, however, restoration drama was attempted. Pamela, if acting the part of the heroine, was always supplied with a male cousin or brother to play her young lover, never one of Canon Milford's sons. Lionel Milford was apparently a good Sir Anthony Absolute in *The Rivals* and his sister Violet played Rosaline opposite Reggie Milford's Berowne in *Love's Labour's Lost*. Guy Wyndham wrote his own version of 'Little Red Riding Hood' for the family to perform.

Surviving photographs do not do justice to the hall at Clouds, and the fire destroyed the original old Italian chimneypiece. The concert grand (a Broadwood in a rosewood case) was placed in front of an exquisite Chinese painted paper screen, with eight folds each 8 feet high and 2 feet wide, covered with a continuous landscape of mountains, river scenes and pagodas. On the floor was a very large hand-knotted carpet from Morris and Company described by Madeline in a letter to Mary as, 'a lovely warm colouring . . . lovely Carnation pink with a lovely Morris pattern with green & indigo (pale) Blues & white'. It was the second of three versions of the 'Holland Park' carpet designed first of all in 1883 for the home of Alexander Ionides. The Ionides were a large and influential Greek émigré family of cotton importers. They commissioned Morris and Company in 1880 to decorate and furnish their London home, 1 Holland Park, for a total cost of £2,361 2sh. 10d.[17] Philip Webb designed additions to the house after Clouds was completed. The Holland Park carpet design combined influences of medievalism, floral realism and Eastern precision; the Wyndhams' version had a red border and indigo field.[18]

Madeline intended there to be 'very little' in the hall, 'but what is looks well'. The little included four black lacquer cabinets, richly ornamented in gilt (Madeline and Percy were fond of black lacquer furniture, which invariably formed part of the 'aesthetic interior', and collected a large quantity); woven curtains in Morris's 'Peacock and Dragon' design hung over the doors; chairs were upholstered in Morris's 'Honeysuckle' design; on the bare stone walls (a part of the hall Wilfrid Blunt disliked) hung two large tapestries. One was early Flemish, a hunting scene; the other was by Morris and Company.

William Morris first visited Clouds on 4 October 1886 to discuss designs for carpets, curtains and chair covers as well as tapestries. He produced the design for 'The Forest' tapestry, with animals by Philip Webb and foreground details by Henry Dearle. However, the proportions were not suitable for hanging in the hall and Morris accepted rejection: 'There is no mistake about the tapestry: it is true that we thought (tradesman like) that we might tempt you, but we quite understood that we were making the piece with peacock & lion at our proper risks.'[19] 'The Forest' was still woven in 1887 and sold to Alexander Ionides.

Morris's 'Orchard' tapestry was the next to be tried out: it can be seen in a faded photograph of Clouds' hall, probably taken soon after the family moved back, after the rebuilding, in 1891. Orchard was woven in 1890 from an earlier design by Morris for Jesus College Chapel, Cambridge, with background details by Dearle. Again, it appears, the Wyndhams were not completely satisfied. Morris returned to Clouds in March 1892:

> I shall be very pleased both to see Clouds House again, and to arrange about the tapestry, and am sure that it would be better to have a piece done which was made specially for the place it is to occupy.[20]

The Orchard tapestry was sold by Morris and Company to the Victoria and Albert Museum. Meanwhile the Wyndhams commissioned 'Greenery', over 15 feet long and again designed by Dearle. On this occasion the choice was right; the tapestry hung in the hall for forty years, until the contents of the house were sold by Dick Wyndham.

Morris and Company's tapestries were as expensive as portraits commissioned from some of the most successful Victorian artists. Wilfrid Blunt acquired two tapestries after he was left £1,000 by a close friend in 1896; Bendor, Duke of Westminster paid £4,600 in 1920 for the Holy Grail series of six tapestries designed by Morris and Burne-Jones for Stanmore Hall.

Apart from the hall, the drawing room was undoubtedly the most important room in Clouds: in it the Wyndhams fully displayed their taste in the fine and decorative arts appropriate for country life; they also created a room in which their guests could relax. Madeline used a table at one end for writing letters, drawing and painting. She called it her 'scrattle table'. Her grandchildren gathered round for lessons: Pamela Adeane recalled how 'she helped us to draw & paint & to trace the wonderful figures for Blake's illustrations for the Book of Job & Yonge's Night Thoughts'.[21] Her hands were always occupied, 'but her mind was free, moving among her guests, evoking and kindling'.[22]

The white plastered ceiling of the drawing room was finally completed in the summer of 1886. The design had been worked on by Webb when he was in Florence in December 1884. Madeline received a progress report from her daughters in June: 'They are making such a row in the drawing-room, the ceiling is finished and they are putting the floor down.'[23] It was Webb's second design and although Percy preferred the earlier one – 'I liked the idea of the long ceiling of one continuous pattern, as I have a great dislike to anything that divides a room into compartments' – Webb, as usual, got his way. Percy had to confess he found the finished effect 'inoffensive and light'. It was also much cheaper: 'I am quite reconciled to the drawing room ceiling on finding it will cost £300 instead of £600'.

The carpet, designed by Morris, was not, as with the tapestry for the hall, the first design he suggested to the Wyndhams. He wrote to Madeline on 30 October 1886: 'I had a kind of idea that Mr Wyndham might not like the writing, I think he must have said as much to me or Webb on some occasion. That is why I wrote about it! I must get the effect I want without it.'[24] He may have shown the Wyndhams the design he had produced for Lord Portsmouth's seat of Hurstbourne Prior near Andover.[25] This was an enormous curved carpet emblazoned with arms and mottoes, the 'writing' Percy

48 (right)   The drawing room *c.*1892, soon after the rebuilding of Clouds. Alphonse Legros's *Procession of Priests and Acolytes* is immediately to the left of the double doors (sold in 1933); Ellis Roberts's portrait of Pamela Wyndham is next to it.

49 (below)   The drawing room late 1890s. Pamela's portrait is in its new (final) position and bookcases have been built along the walls at the east end. There are two small oil paintings by Valentine Prinsep of Mary Wyndham to the right (sold 1933, whereabouts unknown) and lower right (now at Gosford House) of Pamela's portrait. The clock opposite the fireplace is an eighteenth century chiming bracket clock by Gibson of the Royal Exchange (sold in 1933). Alexander Fisher's enamel of Mary Elcho (Gosford House) is on the table below the screen. In the immediate foreground is one of a set of six Hepplewhite mahogany chairs, with shield-shaped backs and pierced vase-shaped splats, carved at the tops with wheat ears and bay leaves (sold in 1933). Photograph by Witcomb & Son.

disliked, altogether too ostentatious for the Wyndhams. The Clouds carpet has a bold arabesque floral design on a blue ground, with a grey leaf pattern border; it was the longest carpet woven by Morris and Company, 39′ × 12′3″. While it was being made, Morris lent the Wyndhams other carpets for the floor: 'we have several that we can send'.[26]

A profusion of different Morris fabrics were used throughout the house for curtains, chair covers, tablecloths and screens. Further patterned fabrics, pieces of lace, shawls and tapestry, old and contemporary, were collected by Madeline and used to cover chairs, tables and screens; she and her daughters also embroidered lengths as well as patronising the Royal School of Art Needlework. Morris patterns were mixed up in every room, just as the designer intended. He had finally perfected a limited range of vegetable dyes at Merton Abbey which created their own characteristic harmonies; in his own words, 'frank reds and blues . . . the mainstays of the colour arrangement . . . softened by the paler shades of red, outlined with black and made more tender by the addition of yellow in small quantities, mostly forming part of brightish greens'.[27] Just as Morris intended, the colours and patterns in the carpet and furnishings of the drawing room reflected the natural world beyond the windows.

Blues and reds and pinks and greens dominated throughout the house: they recur in the carpets, both those Morris designed and older rugs of Eastern origin. Madeline

50 (left) Webb's design for the frieze in the drawing room, using the Crown Imperial lily (Florence 19 December 1884).

51 (right) Webb's design, also executed in Florence, 1884, for the bird carved in the centre of the drawing room mantelpiece. The mantelpiece is now a plant container in the hall.

often remarks on these colours in letters; some woven Morris fabrics bought by the Wyndhams were produced only in limited ranges with blues and reds dominating. In the drawing room, Morris's 'Wandle' and 'Avon' textiles were used the most, the latter designed in 1887, possibly specially for Clouds; also 'Kennet'. Pieces of woven fabric, his 'Bird and Vine' and 'Tulip and Net' were used as table-covers. In the east drawing rom, which became part of the main drawing room when the white-painted double doors were opened, 'Rose' covered cushions; the Morris tapestry curtains were of a blue floral design; a Soumac rug of blue and red and a Shirvan rug of blue and green covered the floor in front of the fireplace.

Webb designed cedar bookcases for the east room and Madeline arranged her 'pink and white oriental dinner set' above them; in 1890, Webb designed bookshelves at the west and east ends of the main drawing room. There was no formal library at Clouds until George Wyndham inherited the estate. Books were such a normal part of daily life that bookshelves were provided throughout the house. A portable trolley carried reading matter from one end of the drawing room to the other and can be seen in photographs alongside the comfortable armchairs and sofas. Every surface all over the house accumulated piles of books, now an emblem of literary taste. A library would have been too formal, too much the mark of a philistine squire; the Wyndhams and their friends read constantly in private, in public, in bed, during meals (George Wyndham regularly read plays out loud to his sisters as they ate breakfast), probably in the bath. They also took and collected photographs of one another: in every room at Clouds there were photographs of family and friends, on tables, beside beds, hanging on the walls.

The majority of the books at Clouds were sold at auction in 1932. They reveal the preferred reading material of Percy and Madeline – the poetry of the English Romantics; the novels of Scott, Dickens, Hardy and Henry James; the works of Ruskin and Carlyle. They subscribed to *Country Life*, the *Studio*, the *Fortnightly* and the *Nineteenth Century*; they also collected the catalogues of exhibitions at the Burlington Fine Arts Club and possessed Crowe and Cavalcaselle's histories of Renaissance painting. Percy's enthusiasm for hunting was served by the novels of R. S. Surtees, and he possessed a history of his regiment, the Coldstream Guards; Madeline collected books by contemporary garden designers. They acquired almost all the books published by the Kelmscott Press. Balfour was a friend so they had a copy of his *A Defence of Philsophic Doubt*, as well as George Curzon's *Persia and the Persian Question* and Lord Ribblesdale's *The Queen's Hounds*. Though no philistines, their literary taste was certainly not advanced: there is no evidence, for example, that they read George Eliot, J. S. Mill, Darwin or any nineteenth-century European fiction. They preferred to watch the drawing-room demonstrations of their house-guest Sir Oliver Lodge rather than study the works of Darwin or Huxley.

Webb had been given precise instructions by Percy for the dining room at Clouds:

> We have thoroughly considered the question of the dining room, & I have got the measurements of our Isel, & London dining rooms, and think we should like a largish room, and that you may know what I mean by that it is that 35 feet in length would not be too large, & might be 40.

They were worried about the position of the fireplace. At 44 Belgrave Square the fireplace was at the side, but the room only slightly more than 19 feet wide. Whenever the Wyndhams had a dinner-party 'the fender is obliged to be taken away', also the armchairs. Webb was polite in his reply:

I am very glad that you are so carefully considering the subject [the size of rooms], and I shall not be likely to obstruct except on the score of cost. I should like to have the chief rooms 20 feet wide and this width, with *recessed* fireplaces on the sides of the rooms would give the right amount of serving way.

When completed, the dining room at Clouds was larger: 34 feet long and 28 feet wide. The original ceiling was richly decorated: Webb sent a design to the Wyndhams from Florence in November 1884. The 'enrichment' was 'done away with' when Clouds was reinstated after the fire of 1889. The fine stone chimneypiece supported on two lion columns was acquired before Clouds was completed; the table was acquired later. It was oval, of grey oak, 6 feet long and 5 feet wide. In the centre, Madeline always placed a single bowl of flowers. This was unusual for the period, when more elaborate arrangements were regarded as 'fashionable': slender glass vases dotted all over the table and connected by ropes of smilax.[28] But Madeline's flower arrangements were unusual throughout the house: she preferred tall sprays of flowers, gladioli, delphiniums, sometimes simply branches smothered in blossom, thrust into huge pots. Visitors recalled groups of flowering shrubs – orange-trees, hydrangeas and camellias – grouped together in the larger reception rooms.[29] The carpet chosen for the dining room was a large-scale version of another design from the Ionides' Holland Park house, but there used on the staircase and in the billiard room. It was not hand-knotted, but

52 The dining room, late 1890s. Taken by Witcomb & Son. The mantlepiece is now a plant container in the hall. In the 1933 sale of Clouds' contents there were eighteen oak frame dining chairs, seats and backs in brown leather with bold brass studs. Also in the sale was a Georgian mahogany circular folding-top dining table on cylindrical legs and club feet.

Plate VIII (facing page) *Orpheus and Eurydice* by George Frederic Watts, *c*.1869. There are unsubstantiated claims that Madeline Wyndham modelled for Eurydice.

53 Percy Wyndham's
bedroom on the ground
floor, 1910. D.G. Rossetti's
Study for Love (1875, acquired
by Percy Wyndham by 1899)
in *Dante's Dream at the Time
of the Death of Beatrice* is to
the right of the fireplace;
unidentified Etruscan
landscape to the left of the
bookcase; portraits of the
five Wyndham children
above.

an example of Morris's designs for the Wilton Royal Carpet Company, a 'Patent Axminster' woven on power-looms.[30] The curtains were of woven fabric, Morris's 'Bird' design.

Percy could lay claim to two separate areas on the ground floor: on the east side, his bedroom, bathroom and dressing room; on the west side his own study, the waiting room and smoking-room. Morris's 'Venetian' wallpaper covered the walls of his bedroom, 'Rose' covered the cushions in the room, as did 'Cray' and 'Medway', the latter used for a chair and the curtains.

His study could be reached directly from the central hall or could be approached along a separate passageway leading from the main entrance. Estate matters could be dealt with in private either in his study or in the waiting room situated just off the entrance hall, without interfering with or disturbing family activities or more formal receptions taking place in the central hall. This business-orientated domain on the north-west corner of Clouds also contained a smoking room. It seems that only male Wyndhams and their guests were expected to enjoy the 'pestiferous luxury' made a fashionable upper-class vice by the Prince of Wales. The billiard room, however, was for both sexes.

Webb designed the billiard room at Clouds to open off the main drawing room as well as the central hall. Before the fire, it contained a chimneypiece brought from the boudoir of Isel Hall. In 1901, though possibly not before, the walls were painted with a dark-blue wash to complement the predominantly white colour of Sargent's masterpiece, his portrait of Percy and Madeline's three daughters, which the Prince of Wales dubbed 'The Three Graces'. The painting was always intended to be hung in Clouds but this was not achieved to the satisfaction of Madeline until the architect Detmar Blow, pupil of Webb and a regular guest of the Wyndhams from 1892, came to her assistance. He stayed for a weekend in November 1901, as Madeline reported to her daughter Mary:

> Detmar Blow arrived vy last train & we have been arranging the Billiard Room all day – & I think it will look vy well – the picture looks 100 times better than it did & the room looks *larger* & the Picture *smaller*. We have put dark blue all over the walls & the Morris tapestry opposite the window & all the curtains white.

By putting the curtains '*not* over the arch but to the windows *inside*', the room was half light and half dark: 'you cannot think how well it looks'. The contrast between the dark-blue walls and the creamy, unbroken masses of the sisters' gowns, filling the lower half of the painting, which was described by Mary's brother-in-law Evan Charteris as 'a *tour de force* in characterization, drawing and the handling of white',[31] must have been dramatic.

The billiard room had a cosy recess with fitted window seats and access to the gardens. The Wyndhams enjoyed moving easily between their house and the surrounding gardens and parkland. Photographs show family and friends talking

54 The garden steps leading up to the billiard room, 1890s. From Madeline Adeane's album.

through windows, sitting on benches just outside the windows, moving around the four sides of the house, inside and out, following the sunshine or the shade. Madeline had a special cage constructed on the south terrace for her kookaburra birds, fed every morning with corn and rabbits caught on the estate. She eventually had some fifty or sixty doves, pet squirrels and thirty peacocks and peahens. Some of the birds were allowed to fly around the inside of the house over the heads of her terriers. Webb makes no comment about designing for his clients' pets.

Most of the furniture at Clouds was eighteenth-century Hepplewhite or Chippendale (original or in the style of). The Wyndhams began collecting in the 1860s and their preference for 'antique' furniture was unusual among their peers. There was very little oak because Madeline regarded it as ugly; 'keep oak out of your house,' she advised her daughter Mary when she began to furnish Stanway and her London house. She did, however, employ local craftsmen to make individual pieces of furniture. Mullins of Salisbury made her four-poster beds, Mr Escort made a sofa bed for herself and for Mary, 'about £3 *not* dear'. She ordered wooden four-poster beds against the advice of Philip Webb – 'I do not agree with Mr Webb about Brass bed steads being the *nicest*' – but Mary could have her brass bedstead if she so wished. The sofa beds were stuffed at Heals: 'I have chosen the 2nd quality Hair making them come to £10.0.0 each as a sofa is not so much used as a bed . . . if you wish to have the best *Hair* £12 write by first post to tell him to stuff *yrs* with the best'. One bed for Clouds was made from a design supplied by Blanche Airlie; it had been copied for her from the Darnley Bed at Holyrood Castle in Edinburgh.

Madeline's advice to her daughters on the contents of their new homes not only reveals the influence of one generation's taste on the next but also provides clues to further features of Clouds, in particular parts of the house which were rarely photographed. The corridor carpet for Clouds came from Maples, and Mary was sent a sample to see if it would suit her needs. The Wyndhams paid only 3sh. 11d. per yard, not 4sh. 2d., because they ordered such large quantities. Madeline also sent Mary her Morris distemper patterns used at Clouds, 'all very much you see on the same string ie different shades composed of the same colours . . . the light green was for Sibells room [Sibell Grosvenor] to go with the *blue* African marygold [Morris's 'African Marigold' textile design]'.

Her second daughter, Madeline, married Charles Adeane of Babraham near Cambridge in 1888. Their landed income was not large, as Percy explained to Mary (whose expectations were considerably greater):

> Madeline will not be *poor* some £3 or £4000 a year, but the great difference in their case is that there is nothing in the future to look to except increased expenses, and with the agricultural outlook, diminished income possibly.

The Adeanes' connections were not just with the land: members of the family have been (and are) closely connected to the court. Charles' mother Lady Elizabeth, a daughter of the Earl of Hardwicke, was Queen Victoria's 'Extra Bedchamber Woman'; his uncle Edward was a Rear-Admiral.

Babraham was a rambling Victorian-Jacobean mansion and Madeline Adeane's priority was to somehow introduce light to the rooms. Clouds was her constant reference point. In March 1889 she asked Mr Smith of Morris and Company to come to Babraham with papers and chintz: 'I think we shall paint all the upstairs, nurseries etc. white – after "Clouds" one longs for light'. A few days later she wrote to her mother: 'I have got the "Trelis [*sic*] with Birds & Roses" for the day-nursery!! & a pale blue & pale yellow for the 2 night nurseries. We have most that you have got!'[32]

Two years later she was working on two of the bedrooms at Babraham. She sent her mother all the details, seeking, as usual, her advice and approval:

> I wish you could come and *advise* about the house – we have really got a *lot* of nice furniture I think & have now a beginning to add to & collect for – I want to ask you about the big yellow room and one Sibell [her daughter] was born in the ceiling is being whitened & the doors & all the woodwork painted white. I am having the boards (going to have nothing is begun yet) stained dark oak colour a broad piece all round the room I shall put all the *prettiest* furniture into it the South of France furniture (cupboard at least) [presumably found while staying at Hyères] or what Chippendale I have got; the chintz is this yellow, how about paper?
> . . . Then the Green Vine papered bed-room & dressing room opposite are to have ceiling whitened, woodwork painted white, & boards stained round. The chintz is that broad pink & white which though not *pretty!* still is chintz & clean & is not worn out, so I thought to make that do & put a plain white paper on the walls & have all white furniture, paint the top of the bed white it has a decorated cornice thing, then *mass* all the prints in their gilt frames into this room & drawing room do you think that would do?[33]

Madeline Adeane appreciated her mother's judgement when it came to the placing of furniture and fabrics, also her unerring eye for matching colours. Artefacts were regularly dispatched from Clouds by train, always accompanied by Madeline Wyndham's precise instructions.

> I send you a bit of cheap cream damask to make a table cover for the table that you put the yellow silk on *wrong side out*. I think there might be enough of it to cut off for the long seat, but am not quite sure. I am making (or having made!) a green common silk cover for your big table and it shall be sent by post to-morrow I *hope*, but if it does not come in time, you must make a big cover of this cream damask for it, and leave the yellow silk wrong side out on the little round table. It really does not look bad. I send you a bit of red which you can use anywhere in your sitting or bedroom – a *remnant*, and also two turkish embroidered squares for *anywhere* – table-cloths, or just to put over any of the red chairs, that stand near and swear with *the greens!* I send a bit of green silk, seven yards, and some thin flannel to line it with, to cover the *long seat* if you cannot use the cream damask. You will have to join the flannel. It is all I had. *It is safest* to make up one *big* tablecloth with the cream damask, big enough for the big table one width in middle half width on each side in case the green one *does not come in time*, then you can use it on any table afterwards. Perhaps the green will not suit or match with the lovely Italian green piano cover. I fear *it will not*, and if so, *the cream will look best in the room*. Put the green *on some bed*, if it does not match in the drawing-room.[34]

Madeline Adeane was genuinely grateful: Babraham was gradually being transformed into another Clouds:

> *What* lovely silks you have sent us, Thank you *so* very much for them. The drawing room really looks *so* nice – The Green is the *exact* colour of the Piano green silk, so

the big table has got its *lovely* green cover with gold braid. Then I had a cover of the other bit of green & flannel made for round table in first window. The long seat has the cream damask *lovely* stuff & the little round table that had yellow silk inside out has got the 2 dear little Turkish embroideries, I had another *just* like them so the 3 have enveloped the table – The 2 dear little remnants I shall use in the other rooms as the pretty red of yours swears with the old maroon.[35]

Madeline and her daughter Mary corresponded at length over leather seat covers suitable for the Elchos' chairs in London. Madeline, as usual, had plenty of ideas; she was not averse to suggesting ways of achieving Morris effects but as cheaply as possible:

I think it ought to be either green or blue – *London* Brown *I do not like* as I have suffered from Brown chairs in London & hate the colour. Red I think too hot for London but that is a mere matter of taste – Green, blue, or *yellow* you might well have but then there are greens & greens, blues & blues & above all *yellows & yellows*. Morris has most beautiful colours in leather write to him & ask him for his *patterns* Some of them are *stamped* vy pretty. I do not know if they are dearer than the man in Wardour Street. Write to the man in Wardour St to send you his patterns & if they are cheaper choose the one that is nearest to the Morris *patterns*.

Madeline could be ruthless in rejecting her daughter's design preferences. Mary sent her mother samples of leather but Madeline disliked them all, especially the one to which her daughter had attached a safety-pin: 'the only safety I see in it is that you are safe not to like it & they all look so like the chairs in all the doctors & dentists waiting rooms'. She finally suggested Mary use Spanish leather, old or new. Four chairs, originally at Isel, but reinstated in the hall at Clouds, were covered with it: 'ours have jars of flowers – with a light cream coloured ground I think it better economy to have many coloured ground than a plain colour as the plain colours show every scratch & grease spot'.[36] Madeline's personal conviction was unshakeable: her aesthetic judgements were always unarguable.

The correspondence with her daughters also confirms that Madeline approached the internal arrangements of her homes with the seriousness of the professional interior designer and decorator. The consideration of colour and texture, fabrics and floral decorations occupied a large part of her time. Though there is no evidence to reveal what William Morris thought of her taste or whether he was influenced by the use she made of his designs at Clouds, other guests were sufficiently impressed to make comments on the surroundings in their 'collins' letters and to seek out the premises of Morris and Company for themselves.

3

Clouds House was staffed by about thirty men and women, many recruited from Milton, East Knoyle, and other neighbouring villages, some from the Wyndhams' own tenants' families. This compares with neighbouring Longleat, which had an indoor domestic staff of forty-three in 1900.[37] The quantity of staff had more to do with the social status and wealth of the owner than the strictly functional requirements of the house. At nearby Fonthill Abbey, for example, Lady Octavia Shaw-Stewart, sister of the Duke of Westminster, continued in her widowhood (Sir Michael Shaw-Stewart died in 1903) to employ a large number of servants, to the amazement of her niece Nellie Grosvenor:

> Every morning, from the enormous kitchen garden, there arrived in the kitchen baskets of perfectly grown vegetables, which would be perfectly cooked by a Scotch cook and her staff consisting of a head kitchenmaid, second ditto, a scullerymaid and a still-room maid. The vegetables found their wy with other dishes, six or seven courses in all, into the dining-room where my aunt Ockie and I were waited on by a butler and two footmen, Ockie nibbling perhaps at a wing of partridge. . . . Then there was the laundry with a staff of three laundrymaids, where each pillowslip was goffered by hand with a pair of tongs. Many housemaids were presided over by the housekeeper – I think the outdoor staff alone numbered seventeen. The waste of course was enormous, but the goal of perfection was achieved.[38]

Servants were by definition deferential, 'and provided a constant reminder that their master was a person of consequence'.[39]

The indoor female staff at Clouds included a housekeeper, five housemaids, cook, three kitchen maids, a still-room maid, four laundry maids and two ladies' maids; the indoor male staff included a butler, under-butler, two footmen, hall boy, and odd man (for odd jobs). There were also men employed in the gardens and the stables. The total annual wages bill was between £700 and £1000.[40] Some of the staff also worked in the Wyndhams' London house; Madeline's own maid and Percy's valet accompanied their employers wherever they travelled.

The staff occupied a separate wing, designed by Webb to appear rather like a group of cottages connecting the main house to the head gardener's cottage and, beyond, the

55   The offices from Clouds' gardens. From Madeline Adeane's album.

stable block. The only access from the offices to the main house on the ground floor was through the dinner service room, situated at the base of the tower, and into the dining room. The principle route for the servants was along the passageways that connected the lower ground floors of their offices to the lower ground floor of the main house. From there, two separate staircases led up to the ground floor, carefully tucked away beside Percy's study and behind a door in a corner of the central hall. In order to maintain the informal, easy going atmosphere it was necessary that the domestic staff should be seen as little as possible.

The offices were of a generous size, and aesthetically interesting. The kitchen, for example, was modelled on the medieval abbot's kitchen at Glastonbury, though its ventilation arrangements, as selected by Webb, were late Victorian: 'the internal or valve part is to be Boyle's patent Comyn Ching & Co. turret ventilation square'.[41] The servants' hall, some 39 feet × 16 feet, with a heavily beamed ceiling, was large enough to accommodate up to thirty for meals (Webb designed a special oak table in two parts, as well as forms) and was suitable for dances.

Though the staff at Clouds were responsible for the smooth running of the 'house of the age', little is known about their attitude to their work or to their employers – even the names of some of them are unknown. Traditional forms of address provide few clues: the female staff, apart from the housekeeper, were referred to by their Christian names, while the male staff were called by their surnames.

The Wyndhams' housekeeper at Wilbury was Mrs Peake, though she was not necessarily married – all housekeepers were traditionally addressed as 'Mrs'. She probably received a salary of £50 per annum. At Clouds, Mrs Vine took over the position, then Mrs Simnett, who was housekeeper from the turn of the century until Dick Wyndham decided to rent out Clouds after the First World War. Frank Barnes, the headmaster of the village school, was especially fond of her and regularly walked up to Clouds House to take tea in her sitting room. When she was taken ill he and Mrs Barnes took her in to live with them at Church Cottage.[42]

The housekeeper at Clouds held a position of considerable authority, second-in-command in the household after the Wyndhams. Mrs Beeton, in her *Book of Household Management*, underlined her responsibilities:

[The housekeeper] must consider herself as the immediate representative of her mistress, and bring, to the management of the household, all those qualities of honesty, industry, and vigilance, in the same degree as if she were at the head of *her own* family. Constantly on the watch to detect any wrong-doing on the part of any of the domestics, she will overlook all that goes on in the house, and will see that every department is thoroughly attended to, and that the servants are comfortable, at the same time that their various duties are properly performed.[43]

She occupied two rooms in the servants' wing, a sitting room and bedroom, both with views of the main approach to Clouds House. They were of generous size, 25 feet × 16 feet. The sitting room had a corner fireplace with blue-tiled sides, and a stone and marble mantel; it had direct access to the interconnected rooms which comprised her domain and responsibility – the china closet, the table linen room, the still room (for bread and cakes), store rooms, the larder, the game larder and the bakehouse.

The still-room maid was virtually the housekeeper's personal maid. At Clouds this was Lizzie Beaver, her name recorded by Madeline in the visitors' book because she almost died in the harsh winter of 1886. She lost her way in the snow and fog as she returned from the village to Clouds House early in the morning of 31 December, and she was not found until midday on 1 January. Illnesses, sudden death and other misfortunes that affected the staff and consequently threatened the smooth running of the Wyndhams' establishments are almost the only recorded information about individual servants. A housemaid called Lucy, for example, is mentioned in a letter written by Madeline to her daughter Mary, because she suddenly starts suffering from delusions: 'Bertha & Charlotte had to sit up with her & hold her down in bed – dont talk about this to anyone but is it not horrid?'[44] Dr Gibbons was summoned, but no further mention is made of poor Lucy.

In 1888 Dr Collins was brought in to examine Madeline's own maid, Easton: 'he says her Heart is perfectly *right* & that it is nervous shock she is suffering from'. The cause of the shock remains a mystery. Four years later Enfield, the new butler, suddenly died. Percy described the sequence of events: he 'took a chill on Friday week, and the next day . . . he was unable for rheumatic pains to wait at dinner . . . went to bed . . . inflammation of the brain came and he died in convulsions at 2.30 o'clock. His wife was in London where she had gone to be confined.'[45]

The calamities of household pets are treated in much the same way. Madeline records the vet visiting Clouds to chloroform her terrier Rose; a fox eating six of her peacocks including 'our last beautiful white Pea-Hen'; Harry Brown the gardener taking the body of Mary's dog Crack by train from Salisbury to Semley 'to bury it under the yew tree that you [Mary] planted' at Clouds. A gravestone to two of the family dogs survives close to the south-west corner of Clouds House.

Part of the housekeeper's responsibilities was supervision of the laundry. Four local girls were employed to work in the laundry, which was separate from the main house. It consisted of a washing house, an ironing room and drying room.

56 The laundry, 1992.

White linen had to be separated from muslin, coloured cottons and linens from woollens, while the coarser kitchen or greasy cloths would form a fifth pile. These greasy cloths would be put to soak in a tub filled with unslaked lime and water. Washing and rinsing would usually take up three days in each week. . . . Thursdays and Fridays were normally devoted to mangling, starching and ironing.[46]

In a house the size of Clouds, there might be a thousand table napkins a week to wash when Percy and Madeline were entertaining. Soap and soda were delivered annually by the ton and half-ton.

The regular cook was a Mrs Wilks. This was a saving. In the most affluent families, the hiring of a male cook or chef, in particular a Frenchman, was considered essential for the prestige of status-conscious aristocrats. But whereas Mrs Wilks was paid about £25 per annum, a male chef could expect a salary of over £100 per annum. Albert Gaillard was employed at Longleat in the late nineteenth century and received £130 a year; he was a friend of Monsieur Menager, the royal chef at Buckingham Palace, who received a salary of £400 a year and a living-out allowance of an extra £100.[47] At Christmas and Easter the Wyndhams indulged their sweet tooth by engaging a London chef to be responsible for the sweet course. Otherwise they were clearly not gourmets: the quality of the food served at Clouds was not significant among the attractions offered to guests.

Mrs Wilks and her predecessor at Wilbury Mrs Gladstone were skilled in making herbal medicines as well as more orthodox cooking. Before George Wyndham's wife Sibell Grosvenor gave birth to their son in 1887, Madeline sent instructions to the gardener at Clouds to pick red raspberry leaves for Mrs Wilks to dry. As she explained to Mary, Mrs Wilks 'told me how good they were for after pains'.[48] Mrs Gladstone's method of cooking truffles was passed on to Mary's cook, together with a sample, 2lb. of truffles, already cooked and 'in what Mrs Gladstone calls their liquor', dispatched by train to Stanway House.

> All Fanny . . . will have to do is to heat them, put them on the stove in their liquor & mind that she *heats* them *thro* & thro as they ought to be sent up very hot. Those that are *not* used she can put back in the liquor & keep them for 2 or 3 weeks but she must if she keeps them boil them up every now & then.[49]

The cook and her three kitchen maids were responsible for feeding the staff, family and guests. Large joints of meat were roasted in front of a fire which consumed several hundredweight of coal a day. The joints were suspended from a spit which was rotated by a hot-air engine; fat from the meat was caught in a large vat and the dripping sold to villagers for one penny per pound. At Christmas the gardeners, grooms and other outdoor staff were each given a joint of beef and a cake.

Bertha Devon is the only housemaid who is mentioned regularly by name in letters and diaries. She stayed with the Wyndhams almost all her life, first coming to work at Isel, then moving to Wilbury to work under Mrs Peake. She remained at Clouds until her retirement at the end of the First World War. Percy and Madeline's granddaughter Pamela Adeane recalled visits to Clouds as a child and being taken up to the nursery quarters by Bertha, 'a tall, tranquil person with a kind, low voice'.[50] Madeline carefully preserved one of Bertha's letters, perhaps to represent her devotion to the Wyndhams and their interests. It was sent from Clouds in January 1912 to Babraham, where Madeline was staying with the Adeanes:

thanks so much for the 5/- . . . I often talk to the Dogs . . . we had a very quiet Xmas on tuesday, all the School Children is coming up for Xmas tree. they are all looking forward to it. . . . Mr Wyndham [George] & Mr Percy is very well, they Hunt every day and Her Ladyship [Sibell] is very well, the Dogs is well & sends there Love.[51]

William Icke was butler at Clouds from 1892; at the same time, his wife was housekeeper to two spinster ladies in East Knoyle, whose house she eventually inherited. His salary was probably slightly more than the housekeeper's, about £65 per annum, in keeping with the respect which his office commanded. His bedroom was on the top floor of the offices, immediately next to rooms occupied by the footmen and visiting valets, but he also occupied a sitting room in the main house, below the east drawing room, with views of the gardens to the south and east. It was strategically positioned close to the gun room and the wine cellars. The under-butler slept in this part of the house, in a room next to the safe; the butler's pantry was directly below the dining room. It was the butler's responsibility each night to make sure the plate was carefully locked away; when the Wyndhams were absent he also locked away valuable ornaments. Madeline kept one of his letters, written to her in 1911 after the death of Percy:

57   A detail of a cupboard in the butler's pantry, 1992.

I beg to say that Lady Grosvenor [Sibell] has informed me this afternoon that Mr Wyndham [George] will be going to Clouds on Friday next and would like the servants also to go as early as possible. I should therefore be glad to know if you wish the Miniatures and Enamels to be left here [at 44 Belgrave Square] to await your arrival also if you wish me to take down the Silver Ornaments from the Drawing Room and the Lady Elcho Enamel. . . . If you wish the Enamels & Miniatures to be left, I should put them away securely in the Plate Closet before leaving.[52]

On the rung of the household ladder immediately below the housekeeper and the butler were Madeline's own maid Easton and Percy's valet Thompson (surnames only). Easton eventually retired to her own cottage in East Knoyle where she was regularly visited by all the Wyndham grandchildren. Pamela Adeane recalled such an occasion with the brutal honesty of the young visitor: 'The visit generally ended with "Kiss Eassy". This was very hazardous as she had a mole in her cheek from which protruded a stiff black hair, as sharp as a pin.'[53] Easton probably came from a more prosperous background than the other female staff at Clouds; by contrast Percy's valet Thompson, an Irishman, had worked as a whipper-in to hounds in his youth. He was an all-round sportsman and taught both George and Guy Wyndham to shoot: it was essential to employ a valet with such 'savvy' to pass on to the sons of the master. He was also, like the lady's maid, among the 'Upper Ten' of the domestic staff. Lady Violet Greville, writing towards the end of the nineteenth century, describes the attributes of a valet:

He never forgets a single portmanteau or bag or hat-box; he reads *Bradshaw* excellently; he takes the tickets, and, tipping the guard efficiently, secures a reserved railway compartment; he brings his master tea, or brandy and soda, at the stations; he engages the only fly at their destination; he has everything unpacked and ready by the time his master leisurely strolls upstairs to dress . . . He has the soul of a perfect army commissariat.[54]

Fräulein Schneider, 'Bun', occupied the traditionally unenviable in-between position of governess in the Wyndham household, not quite below or above stairs. She joined the family in 1875 to educate Mary, Madeline and Pamela (George and Guy went away to school). They learnt to speak German and French, and Mary shared Fräulein Schneider's passion for reading aloud, especially the works of Walter Scott. Most Septembers, she took the girls on seaside holidays, usually to Felixstowe; she also joined in amateur theatricals, helping to make costumes and to act. Her performance as Caliban so confused the servants in the audience that they were convinced Caliban was a woman and married to Prospero. She was skilled at embroidery, working alongside Mary on pieces designed by the Royal School of Art Needlework or copied from artists who were friends of the Wyndhams. One member of the village recalled her constantly knitting – scarlet tam-o'-shanters for the boys, blue and green for the girls, blue fisherman's jerseys for the shepherds on the estate. Like many Germans in Britain, she felt obliged to leave the family for Germany on the outbreak of the First World War, and did not return.

The outdoor staff at Clouds included Pearson the coachman, who eventually married Sarah 'the pretty 2nd housemaid', and Wareham, the under-coachman, whose daughter suffered from paralysed legs, 'the awful result, it was thought, of sitting on a cold stone when she was very hot'.[55] There was also Howard, 'the married stable-man'. He slipped over when carrying a heavy sack and injured his back soon after the

Wyndhams moved into Clouds. Madeline heard the doctor's report from her daughters: 'he is not very much injured and will get all right after he has laid quite still, isn't that a blessing?'[56] The gardeners were overseen by the head gardener Harry Brown; Thomas Hyde was head keeper, ruling over his own men, ensuring good shooting for the family and their guests. He also had to maintain staff morale when Percy lost complete control of his temper. One of Hyde's fingers was shot off when Percy swung round carelessly and pulled the trigger; a beater called Fletcher was shot in the foot by Percy for picking up the wrong pheasant. Their descendants still chuckle indulgently at the habits of the gentry – today Percy would probably face prosecution.[57] After the death of Percy, Hyde retired and took up farming, becoming tenant of Valley Farm; his son Cyril was tenant of Milton Farm.

The man who became one of the most important of the Wyndhams' employees and responsible, as clerk of works, for the maintenance of Clouds house and estate was William Mallett. He and his wife, Emma Draisey, originally came from Cheltenham in Gloucestershire. Mallett was born in 1847 and trained as a cabinetmaker; he worked for the Wyndham family first as house carpenter then as clerk of works for the estate. To begin with, in 1885, he lived at Slades House but within a few years he moved to Park Cottage (now Old Bell Cottage) in Milton, within walking distance of Clouds House, and this remained his home until his death.[58]

The Wyndhams took trouble turning Park Cottage into a suitable family home for the Malletts. Originally two cottages, it provided twice as much accommodation as was usual for a family even of nine children (two died as babies). There was a sitting room, a beamed kitchen, scullery and larder and an oak staircase leading up to four bedrooms. The wash-house was outside and the lavatory was at the bottom of the garden. Park Cottage had its own orchard, and a stable for the pony Mallett used to ride around the estate when he became clerk of works. His workshop was in the offices of Clouds and he amused visiting children by showing them the stump of the finger he cut off with a saw. He was musical and owned a piano and an organ. After church on Sundays (he was a churchwarden) members of the choir would return to Park Cottage to sing while he played. Guests of the Wyndhams were also taken to his workshop and Park Cottage. With so much attention from the Wyndhams, it was hardly surprising that Emma Mallett regarded her family as socially superior to their Milton neighbours; she apparently refused to allow her children to play with the villagers.

As the years passed Mallett became essential to the smooth running of Clouds House and estate. His personal address book included the details of the wheelbarrow makers, windmill manufacturers, picture framers, also the addresses of Wyndham children and grandchildren in London, other parts of England and abroad, including overseas postings during the First World War. In his capacity as coffin maker, he kept a record of the funerals of his employers and their family. Later, together with George Wyndham, he designed and made considerable alterations to the house and the estate.

William Mallett's descendants kept photographs of the Malletts and their family, of Mallett's workshop in Clouds House and the fire engine; they also kept his address book and some of the presents from the Wyndhams. This was unusual: 'below-stairs' rarely thought such memorabilia worth keeping. Though they may have kept a signed letter or photograph of their employers, they would cheerfully throw out their father's few jottings.

Little information survives to describe the daily round of Percy's agent, who saw to the running of the estate and was consequently one of the most significant of the Wyndhams' staff. Edward Henry Miles was from a local farming family, and after his

58 (right)   Fräulein Schneider.

59 (below)   Outside the main entrance of Clouds. From left to right: Madeline Adeane, Madeline Wyndham (holding Rhona), Lettice Adeane on Bonnie, Pearson the coachman. From Madeline Adeane's album.

death his son Hallam Miles became the agent, working for Dick Wyndham until
Clouds was sold.

The staff of Clouds regularly shared in the festivities of the family and guests, joining
in, for example, when the Wyndhams gave all the employees at Semley railway station
toast and ale at Clouds on Boxing Day. On New Year's Eve the staff ball took place in
the servants' hall; every employee was allowed to invite a friend. Carters of Salisbury
supplied the orchestra for dancing which lasted from 10 p.m. until 3 a.m. 'Sitting out'
places were provided along the passages and other rooms were arranged with tables for
cards. Many of the servants developed special talents for the occasions, especially
singing. Attending a staff party before she married, Mary Wyndham noted some of
their accomplishments: Mabel the kitchen-maid offered her version of 'Haunting
Tower', James the footman sang 'The Red Rhein Wine' and Charles the footman
finished with 'But never push a man, because he's going down the hill'. The Women's
Institute scrapbook provides a personal recollection of one such party when 'a good
time was had by all'. It was a 'red letter day', to become fixed in the memory, while
more mundane events have been erased.

It was Percy Wyndham himself who remembered the daily service provided by his
staff. At his death he left sums of money to all the domestic staff, the amounts carefully
reflecting their individual positions and their length of service. Fräulein Schneider, the
highest paid and almost a member of the family, received an annuity of £100; the agent
Edward Miles received £100 in cash. All the domestic servants who had been working

for the Wyndhams for at least fifteen years, also the coachman, the head gardener and the estate carpenter received £50; the head keeper, the head shepherd, the head carter, the head woodman, as well as stablemen and gardeners who had been at Clouds for fifteen years or more, received £15. Servants who had worked for the Wyndhams for five years or more and were over twenty-one received £2 each; servants who had worked for five years or more but who were still under twenty-one received £1. The total amount Percy left to the domestic staff was close to their annual wage bill of £1,000.

Henry James credited the English upper class with the creation and perfecting of the country house, but it flourished as a result of the considerable effort of vast numbers of servants who worked long hours but were paid a fraction of the (unearned) income of their employers.

> Of all the great things that the English have invented and made a part of the credit of the national character, the most perfect, the most characteristic, the one they have mastered most completely in all its details, so that it has become a compendious illustration of their social genius and their manners, is the well-appointed, well-administered, well-filled country house.[59]

Percy left the staff of Clouds sufficient for him not to be accused of meanness, but he was not generous.

5 The Clouds Estate and the Agricultural Community

The Wyndhams took up their responsibilities as landed proprietors as soon as they purchased the Seymours' land at East Knoyle. Though Clouds was not habitable until the end of 1885, Percy Wyndham regularly visited the estate, getting to know his tenants, seeing to the stocking of the Home Farm. He had acquired some 4,200 acres of land: of this 100 acres was taken up by Clouds park, another 125 acres was commonland, the rest was divided between eleven good-sized farms (arable and pasture), all with accommodation for their labourers. In addition there were over fifty cottages, most situated in the small village of Milton.

All the tenants were dependent on the Wyndhams for their livelihoods: Percy's job as landlord was to maintain the profitability of the estate without threatening their security. In planning to build a mansion in the middle of the property, Percy had to ensure that he could meet its running costs either from the estate itself or through external investment income. The total rents from the estate amounted to £4,624 per annum in 1876 but part of this, probably about 20 per cent, had to be spent on the unkeep of the farms, cottages, barns, walls, fences and gates, also the purchase of new machinery and stock.[1] Shooting on the estate had brought in £300 of the total rental; this would no longer be available when Percy took over the shooting for the pleasure of himself and his guests.

Percy bought his estate at the beginning of the great agricultural depression which lasted from 1873 until 1896. Though bad weather and poor harvests in the late 1870s and again in the early 1890s were partly to blame for the depression, the principal cause was the flood of imported foodstuffs, which left English agriculture 'prostrate'.[2] Imports of wheat from America, Canada, India, Australia and Argentina knocked the price of English wheat down from 56sh. a quarter in 1867–71 to 22sh. 10d. in 1894. Other grains and wool also fell in price. With the perfection of refrigerating techniques, the import of frozen and chilled meat increased from the middle of the 1880s, so meat prices also fell.

Farmers on the heaviest arable lands were the worst hit; 'sheep-and-corn' farmers were also badly affected. Stock and dairy farmers did not suffer so much, some even benefited. Cheaper bread released purchasing power for more expensive foods, in particular meat and dairy produce; cheaper grains also meant cheaper feeding stuffs for livestock producers and thus lower costs of production. The depression consequently affected individual estates to lesser or greater extents: an arable estate in Essex, for example, experienced a fall in its rents of 66 per cent whereas an estate in the North Riding of Yorkshire experienced a rise of 1 per cent. On average, from the late 1870s, agricultural rents fell by 26 per cent, stabilising in the mid-1890s.[3]

The Clouds estate was a mixture of arable and pasture. Their situation may have been similar to that of the Marquess of Bath on his Longleat estate nearby. Though his sheep and corn farming suffered severely, his dairy farms' income was stable: his total drop in rental income was some 11 per cent. By the time the Marquess reduced his

Plate X (facing page) *Mary, Lady Elcho* (née Wyndham) by Edward Poynter, first exhibited at the Grosvenor Gallery 1886.

estate expenditure, including repairs and improvements, from 23 per cent of his gross rents to 15 per cent, the agricultural depression was little more than a temporary inconvenience.[4]

Another neighbour was less fortunate. The Horners of Mells, Somerset, lived off an estate which, when they married in 1883, had a gross annual rental value of £10,000. But the agricultural depression took its toll:

> all the cottagers on the property . . . just lived on us. Their rents were a shilling or eighteenpence a week . . . as the cottages were very old there were constant repairs to be done; and none of the farms were in good order. Beef was given away at Christmas at a cost of nearly a hundred pounds. We had to roof the Park House, and lay on water. It was one long struggle against debt, which mounted slowly up.[5]

The estate had been mortgaged by Horner's father in 1865 for £55,000 to make provision for all of his ten children. Fortunes temporarily improved in 1895 when John Horner was made Commissioner of Woods and Forests by his friend Lord Rosebery, and received an annual stipend of £1,200. However, the duties that went with the post meant that the Horners had to buy a house in London: 9 Buckingham Gate. During the summer months at Mells, 'we always let it [the London house] well, because it was so near Buckingham Palace';[6] similarly Mells was let for the months spent in London. In 1900 the Horners finally gave up trying to maintain Mells Park House and moved into the considerably smaller Elizabethan manor house in the village. 'We thought that if we could manage to economise for a few years, perhaps by the time the boys were of

61   The windmill, 1992.

age we might be able to live at the Park again.'[7] Mells Park was let to the son of a wealthy Liverpool shipowner.

Lord Pembroke at Wilton had a rising burden of interest charges on improvement loans taken out in the 1860s. However, he was able to offset agricultural losses against urban gains. He chose to allow the level of estate maintenance to decline, but increased his outlay on game. He drew less and less from the estate for his personal use, until in 1896 the estate expenses exceeded the income. But his mainstay was the growing bounty of Dublin ground rents, which in 1882 had a gross annual value of £35,586.[8]

An indication of the reduction in arable farming around Clouds was the redundant windmill on the Wyndhams' estate. This had been in use not long before the estate was sold by Alfred Seymour. He had let it to a Mr Gray who ground corn for all the farmers in the district; the villagers also took their gleanings to the windmill, to be ground into flour for this own use.[9] Otherwise there are no references to the depression in surviving letters and diaries of the Wyndhams, and there are few references of any kind to the management of the estate. Evidence provided by the activities of the Wyndhams, the scale of their entertaining and art purchases, suggests that income from their investments in stocks and shares and land in Australia was more than sufficient to offset a fall in gross rents.

The Clouds estate was the recreation of a rich man, its upkeep subsidised by other more lucrative assets. As the younger son of Lord Leconfield, Percy did not inherit Petworth; however, he had sufficient personal fortune to create his own rural seat.

I

The largest farms on Percy's estate were around the edge and some had substantial farmhouses. Knoyle Down Farm, for example, to the north-east, was 737 acres in size and produced a rent of £400 a year for the landlord. The Queen Anne style farmhouse was built of brick, partly cement rendered, with stone dressings and a slate roof. It had three reception rooms, five bedrooms and was 'pleasantly situate with a Carriage Sweep'. There were eight cottages for labourers and extensive farm buildings, as the particulars of Messrs Driver detailed:

> Three-Stall Nag Stable and Harness Room, Eleven-Stall Cart Horse Stable and Loose Box, with Loft over, Gig House, Shed and Large Barn, Open Cattle Shed; Poultry House Cart and Waggon Shed, Well House, Calf Pen, and Meal House. Range of Piggeries, Cow House for Ten Beasts, Three-Stall Stable, and Implement Shed, Smiths Shop, Open Cart Shed; adjoining is a large Sheep or Lambing yard with Open Sheds around, and a spacious Waggon and Cart Shed, and Saw Pit House therein.[10]

Such a farm was self-sufficient, a community in its own right. Knoyle Down was particularly suitable for training or breeding racehorses, because it covered a large area of downland.

Pertwood Farm, just over 700 acres, on the north side of the estate, also included within its boundary a small church. St Peter's was originally medieval but had been substantially rebuilt in 1872. It was almost in the back garden of the farmhouse, which was another very large eighteenth-century residence. The living of Pertwood brought with it an income of just £94 (Percy received rent of £550 a year from the farm), regarded at the time by the vicar of East Knoyle as insufficient for the bachelor curate to support a wife, even though there was a cottage close by. Percy became very fond of the tiny church and would order his carriage to take him up to Pertwood on a Sunday instead of attending in East Knoyle; he even hoped to be buried in its graveyard, high on the downs.

Long before Clouds House was completed, Percy was taking an active part in running the Home Farm. Mary Wyndham noted in her diary for 16 September 1878:

> he bought 20 Galloways 3 yrs old at £14.14 each he will sell them again in the spring and the cost of the cake they will have eaten and their carriage from London to Knoyle is to be reckoned. He was made £184.10s by the sale of all his sheep and £146.15s by sale of wool and has now 190 lambs. His corn is in, 11 ricks of wheat, 5 of barley and six of oats.[11]

The estate did not have its own Home Farm but Percy appears to have created one for himself by breaking up Milton Farm, immediately to the north of Clouds park. It was reduced from 270 acres to 69 but retained its own substantial stone farmhouse, outbuildings and labourers' cottages. The farmhouse for the Home Farm, together with necessary outbuildings, was formed from another group of cottages originally part of Milton Farm: two semi-detached cottages dated 1716 became the six-bedroomed farmhouse. A stone and thatched cottage was turned into the model dairy with its own churn room, cooling room, butter-making room and cream room. A porch was built for church sterilising, and the floor of the dairy was made of chanelled stone pavings. Village children came up to the dairy to buy milk.

62   The village blacksmith, Milton.

The Home Farm had its own cottages for labourers, also cow houses, root and potato houses, a bacon house, four pigsties and five iron-roofed fowl houses, two calf boxes, a pig run and boiling house. Part of the land was developed as the timber yard for the estate, one field became the orchard for Clouds and another, called Throdmill Field, became the four-acre kitchen garden, enclosed by one of Webb's brick walls. All the Wyndham farms had flocks of sheep. The fat flock was kept on the Home Farm and one sheep was slaughtered each week of the year. Steer from all the farms were sent to Shaftesbury for slaughter; the local butcher kept half the meat as payment.

2

The Wyndhams' responsibilities went beyond the boundaries of their own estate. After the death of Alfred Seymour in 1888 they were expected to play a principal part in local government, local administration, in improving the environment, the health and education and general well-being of the community. This was hardly an onerous task as the population of East Knoyle and Milton in the 1880s was only about a thousand. Percy also served as a magistrate; he was elected to the County Council after the radical reorganisation of local government in 1888; he was vice-chairman for several years.

Most of the community's physical and spiritual needs were attended to on a daily basis by the vicar of St Mary's. Canon Milford, next to the Wyndhams the most influential member of the community, lived in an imposing eighteenth-century rectory, large enough to accommodate his wife, ten children, and five indoor maids. The outdoor staff consisted of the coachman, two boys, the gardener and a cowman

63 The old rectory, East Knoyle, 1992.

64   Percy Wyndham, *c.*1890.

who looked after a small herd of cows and the dairy. There was a schoolroom for the five daughters who were educated at home by a series of governesses.

The Milford daughters inevitably visited the Wyndham daughters who were still living at home, in particular Pamela who did not marry until 1895. Violet recorded her impressions in about 1886 of both Percy and Madeline:

> [Percy] squire of half the village . . . had a bald head with a fringe of white hair, and his long face had rather hooded eyes, which could twinkle with amusement, but he was decidedly alarming, with coolly critical manners, and a characteristic rather drawling way of talking. He always wore very pale homespun suits in the country, and gave an impression of scrupulous cleanliness – he was even supposed to have his coppers washed before he put them into his pockets.

To the vicar's daughter, Madeline seemed quite elderly, though she and Percy were both fifty-one in 1886.

> She had a beautiful face, and was the easiest and most sympathetic person to talk to that I have ever met . . . While she spent money lavishly [she] never seemed like an ordinary rich person, though she valued the things money could buy, pictures, lovely furniture, and garden flowers.[12]

Mrs Milford was thought by some villagers to be far too 'high and mighty': she apparently expected the village women and girls to curtsy on meeting any of her family. Men and boys were to bow and touch their forelocks. Her father was Bishop Sumner, and her sister Mary Sumner founded the Mothers' Union movement (her daughter Beatrice founded the East Knoyle branch).

St Mary's was restored in 1876 in memory of Mrs Milford's father. Arthur Blomfield, notorious for his heavy-handed 'restoration' rather than 'preservation' of English churches, was the architect who unfortunately stuck encaustic tiles on the chancel walls and floors, though he was sensitive enough to leave the unusual plaster decorations untouched. They had been devised by Dr Wren, rector of East Knoyle from 1623 and father of Christopher Wren, who was born in the village in 1632. During the Civil War Dr Wren lost his living and was put on trial: the plasterwork was used in evidence against him by his Puritan accusers, but was not finally destroyed.[13]

In 1891 the fourteenth-century tower of St Mary's was discovered to be falling down, a 'hopeless wreck', and Canon Milford approached Philip Webb for advice, undoubtedly at the suggestion of the Wyndhams. Webb was still overseeing the reinstatement of Clouds House after the fire of 1889, and he carried out a preliminary study of the tower in the summer. He recommended to the churchwardens that a careful, accurate survey be made of every part of the tower by an architectural student under his direction and Detmar Blow, who had just joined the SPAB, was appointed to the task. When a specification was finally drawn up, Albert Estcourt, the builder of Clouds House, was approached for a schedule of prices.

The approach was completely different to Arthur Blomfield's, fifteen years before, since the ideal of the SPAB was to carry out repairs in such a way that a building was hardly altered. When St Mary's tower was finally repaired, the total cost was just over £1,000; one parishioner was heard to comment he 'could not see where the money had been spent'. Webb explained to Canon Milford: 'if Mr Blow could take a body of your parishioners all over the tower, inside and out, he could not shew them more than a quarter of that which has been done'.[14] Webb was typically generous in refusing payment for his part of the project; the Wyndhams contributed £471 and also paid for the preliminary investigation and survey. The rest of the money was collected by the village through personal subscriptions and social activities, including a bazaar held on the rectory lawn, which raised £100.

For Detmar Blow the work on the tower was to provide contacts of considerable significance for his future career. He lodged in East Knoyle and spent some time with the Milfords. Violet thought him a romantic figure, good-looking with a loose homespun suit and rather long curly hair, playing his violin while her sister Mai played the piano. Neville Lytton, commenting on his attractive appearance, noted, 'there is no doubt that many of his commissions were due to the favour he found with the fair sex'.[15] In February 1893 he designed the pergola for Clouds' garden. After his work on the tower was completed he returned regularly to Clouds for country house weekends. Commissions followed, including in 1899 work for the Wyndhams in the new burial ground which was created out of a field opposite the rectory. The Wyndhams supported the work financially; Blow designed the greenstone wall which partly enclosed their own family plot.

There were two other chapels in East Knoyle in the 1880s. The Congregational Chapel was served by the ministers of the Wiltshire and East Somerset Congregational Union; the Ebenezer Chapel was founded for the primitive Methodists in the community. Education, like religion, brought together most sections of the rural community. There were no adequate facilities for a village school in East Knoyle until the Milfords came. With the passing of the 1870 Education Act, which established School Boards in every district to provide free schooling for children from five to thirteen, Canon Milford was determined to build a school in East Knoyle. He persuaded Alfred Seymour to part with some of his kitchen garden to provide a plot to build on, and to contribute towards the cost, which was £3,000. The school was large enough for 200 children; the foundation stone was laid in 1872 by Mrs Seymour and the school opened on 6 June 1873. The schoolmaster was Mr Tanswell, an awesome figure in his black tail-coat bound with braid. Miss Minns took the infants.[16]

The school building was of stone with details in the Moorish style; the designer was the same George Aitchison who worked with Leighton on the interior of the Wyndhams' London house. It is difficult to prove any connection, however; the Wyndhams did not buy their Wiltshire estate until 1876. Concerts were regularly held at the school. Alfred Seymour's daughter Jeanne was good at comic songs but Percy Wyndham lacked the 'common touch'. His recitation of Lamb's 'Essay on Roast Pig' was only politely received. On one occasion Madeline painted a woodland scene as backdrop to the school play. The scene was so realistic that a robin which had flown into the school went to perch on what it thought was the branch of a tree. It dropped to the ground stunned, and later died.

The Seymours were the first to provide the schoolchildren with annual treats, including soup in cold weather. When Alfred brought his wife back to Knoyle House for the first time there was a day's holiday. Later, Mrs Seymour and her daughter set up a boot club to help villagers save for the most essential part of their clothing. Members paid a weekly subscription of one penny; fourpence in the shilling was then added to all subscriptions over 2 sh. 6d. at the end of the year. The Wyndhams continued to give annual parties at Christmas for the children and their parents, with Punch and Judy shows and sometimes a conjuror; also parties to commemorate special

65   Miss Madeline Wyndham, drawn by Edward Burne-Jones, before her marriage to Charles Adeane; given to her mother, Christmas 1888, by Georgiana Burne-Jones and her daughter Margaret Mackail. Bequeathed by Madeline to her daughter Mrs Charles Adeane 1920; sold out of the family 1986.

occasions such as the marriage of their daughter Madeline to Charles Adeane. Canon Milford recorded the event for the parish magazine:

> On August 25th Mr and Mrs Wyndham kindly gave a treat to all the children attending the Day and Sunday School, numbering about 190.
>
> The children met at the School at 1.30 and then marched up to Clouds. As was done last year, numberless toys were provided which were lent out to the children, trumpets, whips, reins, skipping ropes, flags etc. and soon the children were playing about happily in the park. A capital game of cricket was got up for the elder boys, and lasted for most of the afternoon.
>
> The band played during the afternoon from the terrace in front of the house . . . Tea was laid for the children on long tables placed in the garden, whilst a large party of those friends who had kindly given a wedding present to Mrs Adeane, Sunday School teachers and others, were entertained at tea in the house. Whilst waiting for tea indoors, Miss Wyndham [Pamela] played and sang to her guitar.
>
> After the races, came scrambling to nuts, and apples, and then all the children . . . slowly filing past Mrs Wyndham each received a bag of sweets and a bun.[17]

The previous year the East Knoyle band gave a special performance to welcome George Wyndham and his new bride Sibell Grosvenor to Clouds. The horses were taken out of their carriage in East Knoyle, then eighty men pulled the carriage up to Clouds, the band playing all the time.

Madeline obtained the services of a London-trained parish nurse from 1887, paying the salary herself; in 1888 she paid for a warm garment to be given to every child who had attended school regularly during the year. There were probably many other instances of charity which remain unrecorded. Again, there is no way of knowing the response of the recipients. Perhaps the 'poor widows' were genuinely grateful for receiving scraps of food from Clouds collected together at the end of lunch, meat, vegetables and pudding all piled up together 'in a rich mixture' and delivered to their cottages by Fräulein Schneider and the Wyndham children and grandchildren.[18]

Some memoirs have been collected for the East Knoyle Women's Institute scrapbooks. They concentrate on parties given by the Wyndhams, presents for the children, above all the number of distinguished visitors who came to Clouds. The inhabitants of East Knoyle and Milton undoubtedly enjoyed feeling superior to their neighbours. Balfour was a regular guest of the Wyndhams and attended St Mary's on Sunday, where he could be seen by all the villagers; the Wyndhams' eldest son George, heir to Clouds, was appointed to the Cabinet as Chief Secretary for Ireland; George Curzon, Viceroy of India, was a guest, as was the famous scientist Sir Oliver Lodge. Madeline's involvement in the Royal School of Art Needlework and in enamelling brought two daughters of Queen Victoria to Clouds. When Princess Christian stayed, the older villagers were asked to tea, to be presented to her by Madeline.

Rather more patriotic than practical, at the accession of George V in 1910 Madeline presented each family with a large portrait of the King and each child with a flag and medal in honour of the coming coronation. 1910 was also the golden wedding of Madeline and Percy, and the children of East Knoyle and Milton presented them with £2 7sh. 2d. in halfpennies; this was used by the Wyndhams to buy two gold-cased stylo fountain pens. The following year the children again made a collection, this time towards a wreath for Percy, 'a great friend and benefactor to the children of this School'.[19]

3

When Percy bought the Clouds estate he was still Conservative MP for West Cumberland. He held on to his seat at the 1880 general election though the Conservatives were soundly beaten, in the countryside as well as in the towns. His letter to his electors, printed in *The Times* shortly before the election, revealed his own misplaced confidence:

> Amidst unparalleled difficulties abroad, in spite of opposition at home never surpassed in violence and vindictiveness, I claim for the Government that they have upheld the honour of England, have avoided being involved in a European war, and have largely contributed to the Berlin Settlement.[20]

His post-election analysis focused on issues closer to home: 'the members of the wage-earning class are . . . without exception, penetrated with the idea that the bad trade, want of employment, and low rate of wages during the last four or five years were entirely due to the fact that a Conservative Government was in power'.[21]

Though Percy followed an independent line to his party, for example in opposing the British occupation of Egypt, he was a high Tory when it came to reform. In 1884 Gladstone introduced his Reform Bill; this was designed to end the anomaly created by the earlier 1867 Reform Bill, whereby the labourers in the counties had been refused the vote given to their opposite numbers in the boroughs. When it was passed, 2 million new voters, practically all in the county constituencies, were added to the electorate, almost doubling the size of those eligible to vote: from 1886 a total of about 5 million. Percy did not support the bill. In a letter to his daughter Mary he referred to the 'Skunk Government'. To Philip Webb, still on holiday in Italy, he wrote: 'the delight of Labouchere and the extreme Rads is naturally very great and makes itself heard in shouts of triumph'.

The Reform Bill was accompanied by a Redistribution Bill demanded by the House of Lords. This divided up almost all the country into equal single-member districts; only the universities and a small number of large boroughs survived as two-member constituencies. West Cumberland no longer returned two members; Percy was no longer guaranteed a seat in Parliament. He never forgave Gladstone. His daughter Mary told Balfour that Percy's 'one regret on leaving the H of Commons was that he would not be able to vote against his [Gladstone] having a public funeral!'[22]

Percy's interest in national government had never been very serious. In March 1887, when his son George was about to leave the army to work for Balfour, he commented to Mary, 'George will now soon forsake the honourable profession to which he belongs to follow the low calling of the politician'. Only the sudden death of his Uncle Henry had catapulted him into a virtually safe Wyndham seat. He was not dismayed by his defeat at the general election in November 1885. It coincided with his move into Clouds; he consequently had even more time to enjoy the good life. When his daughter Madeline 'came out' in 1887 he was able to accompany her to parties and on rides through Hyde Park, now that he was not required to sit in the Commons.

Standing for Parliament was a very different experience for a candidate after the passing of the Third Reform Bill, as another aristocratic MP realised: 'Primrose League meetings, bazaars, political gatherings in schoolrooms, attended perhaps by a dozen yokels, two or three women, and a little boy . . . made life impossible'. Keeping a seat also required effort: 'the comfortable evenings at home had to give way, with distressing frequency, to the village meeting'.[23] Fighting a contested country election could also be expensive: as much as £5,000, which was more than the total rental income of the Clouds estate. Percy's son-in-law Hugo Elcho was only able to stand for Parliament when his father Lord Wemyss guaranteed to pay his expenses.

In 1890 Percy was approached by the Duke of Beaufort to see whether he could be persuaded to stand for South Wiltshire:

> I am sure you will agree with me that this country has never been threatened with such dire disaster as will befall it should Mr Gladstone get a majority in the H. of Commons at the next Election . . . Everybody who has any property & also values the integrity of the Empire & the prosperity of the country is bound to exert himself in defence of his principles.[24]

The local MP, Mr Grimshaw, had retired and the Duke was worried that South Wiltshire would be 'misrepresented by a Renegade & a Rat'. Percy would have had to persuade the Wiltshire labourers to give him their vote but his opinion of their intellectual abilities was excessively low. 'I know well how they voted here,' he wrote to Mary after the 1885 election, 'nearly all Liberal. Out of 12 illiterates 10 voted Liberal.' He considered such a result inevitable when labourers were encouraged to 'talk and think about politics' and to show 'impertinent curiosity', or, as David Cannadine has put it, 'an ominous display of non-deferential voting'.[25]

Percy still had some influence in the constituency machinery, however, and he responded to the Duke of Beaufort's approach with a practical suggestion. He recommended Lord Folkestone, eldest son of his neighbour the Earl of Radnor. The Earl had represented the constituency until 1885; Lord Folkestone was duly elected in 1892, after successfully persuading his constituents that a Conservative MP was in their best interests. He was assisted by Gladstone's attempts to bring Home Rule to Ireland: the crisis united rural communities around the Conservative (and largely landed) leadership.

As the years passed Percy became increasingly fearful of the spread of democracy. The resounding defeat of the Conservatives at the 1906 general election left him wondering, 'what will save us now? The British Constitution is quite unfitted for a legislature such as we have now.' He wrote to Mary: 'it would be better to live in Spain or Morocco than in the England of our day. The people themselves appear to be completely changed'.

4

The Radnors' seat was Longford Castle near Salisbury, one of a number of country houses and estates which dominated the surrounding landscape not just physically, but also politically, socially and economically. Once completed, Clouds joined the circle of influence which included Knoyle House, Longleat, Wilton, Motcombe, Fonthill Abbey and Fonthill House, Pyt House and Wardour Castle. Though all these country seats were economically linked to their agricultural estates, their owners' involvement in the land was in many cases only token. Michael Thompson identifies five main activities associated with life in country houses in the nineteenth century:

Life in the country houses rested on the great structure of domestic servants, but for the owners and their families it revolved round five main activities: the pleasure and interest to be derived from the gardens and park, the pleasure and excitement of country sports, the pleasure and duty of dispensing and receiving hospitality, the duty often but lightly observed of supervising the steward and agents who managed estate and household affairs, and the duty of attending to the local and county affairs of magistracy, yeomanry, churches, charities and schools.

It was a subtle blend of 'authority and obedience, freedom and restraint, leisureliness and obligation'.[26]

At Fonthill House, for example, the home of the Morrisons, private musical recitals for guests from London and a few close neighbours were balanced by annual garden parties for the immediate rural community. The Wyndhams attended both. Mabel Morrison was twelve years younger than Madeline, but they shared not only an interest in art needlework but also a passion for animals. At Fonthill there were borzois, dachshunds, chows, Afghans and poodles as well as a hundred horses in the stables. Pamela Wyndham, a potential candidate for the hand of the Morrisons' eldest son Hugh (he married Lady Mary Leveson-Gower, daughter of the Earl of Granville, in 1892) thought Mrs Morrison looked like a beautiful odalisque in a tale from the *Arabian Nights*, with her looped braids of dark hair and bright artificial colouring. Her dresses had long trains, which rolled up the priceless Persian rugs in her wake as she advanced across the parquet floor. The Morrisons' gardens were opened to the whole community for their annual children's parties; marquees were erected on the lawn, which sloped down to an artificial lake. Violet Milford remembered running races in the garden and winning gold cardboard money, 'which we then took to a gipsy caravan. The inside of the caravan was hung with presents, from which we could choose our own prize in exchange for the coin we had won.'[27]

As squire of East Knoyle Percy involved himself in village concerns when required to do so; he supported Madeline's more active charitable work for the community; like the Morrisons he opened Clouds' gardens and park for annual parties. However, his involvement in his estate was insignificant when compared to either the support by his grandfather Lord Egremont for reforms in agriculture, or the active participation by his son-in-law Charles Adeane in the improvement not only of the stock on his Babraham estate but also, in his capacity as President of the Royal Agricultural Society, of the general condition of agriculture in Britain. Percy's principal occupation after he moved to East Knoyle was enjoyment of the good life, which centred on country sports, especially shooting and golf (he built a full-sized golf course on the downs above Clouds when he was forced to give up hunting), and the pleasure of 'dispensing and receiving hospitality'.

He was probably not quite as selfish as his son-in-law Hugo Elcho who found the duties expected of him on behalf of his Gloucestershire tenants consistently onerous:

> I pumped and pumped at the frozen springs of my benevolence until an unaccustomed flow of geniality became naturally established. I have filled the house [Stanway] with poor people & myself with rich fare. I have decorated Christmas trees with tops and old ladies with red flannel petticoats. I have emptied the house of furniture and filled it with the odour of school-children. I have bored myself and entertained the neighbours and now it is all over I feel the better for it – I almost think I have enjoyed myself – time and imagination will make me sure of it.[28]

Percy's obituary in *The Times* paid tribute to his 'ready sympathy, his wise and quiet helpfulness, his courteous and upright life'. However, Clouds was designed primarily as the ideal setting for the Wyndhams' interpretation of the good life, even though its architect was a socialist; the estate and the community beyond were only the backdrop, peripheral to the main purpose of the house: the pursuit of civilised pleasures.

6   Clouds Rises

I

The implements of the little feast [afternoon tea] had been disposed upon the lawn of an old English country house in what I should call the perfect middle of a splendid summer afternoon. . . . The front of the house overlooking that portion of lawn with which we are concerned was not the entrance-front; this was in quite another quarter. Privacy here reigned supreme, and the wide carpet of turf that covered the level hill-top seemed but the extension of a luxurious interior. The great still oaks and beeches flung down a shade as dense as that of velvet curtains; and the place was furnished, like a room, with cushioned seats, with rich-coloured rugs, with the books and papers that lay upon the grass.[1]

In the opening pages of *The Portrait of a Lady* (1881) Henry James provides his idealised version of the good life available to the discerning landed classes in their country houses. The novelist was guest at one of the first parties to be held by the Wyndhams at Clouds during the first week of September 1887.

In many respects it was a typical Wyndham party: the guests were the usual mixture of family and friends, representatives of politics, the arts, the army and the land. The activities were predictable: lawn tennis, shooting, walking and riding, reading, writing, billiards and conversation. However, the political and sexual tensions between some of the guests were unusually intense. Wilfrid Blunt wrote a lengthy description of his stay at Clouds in his diary, paying special attention to Madeline's daughter Mary Elcho, 'the cleverest best & most beautiful woman in the world',[2] who was already half aware of her cousin's interest in her; Henry James was to use the visit as source material for some of his recreations of English country house life.

Percy and Madeline were together as host and hostess, and all of their children were there: Mary Elcho, expecting her third child; George, 'like a sunbeam in the house, the most delightful of young men'; Guy on leave from his regiment in Ireland; Madeline, 'like her mother, a great hearty girl', and Pamela, 'original, amusing & brim full of life'. There were two of Madeline's nieces: Pamela Campbell, 'plump, rosy, dark-haired & with violet eyes fringed with dark lashes', and Sibyl, the divorced Marchioness of Queensberry; Blunt's wife Anne and daughter Judith. A quarter of a century before, Sibyl (then Sibyl Montgomery) had been appraised for the role of Mrs Blunt:

She is now, though an interesting woman still, marked deeply with the crow's foot brought on more by trouble than time – Her husband Queensberry like all his family mad, tormented her, and, after adoring him for 20 years in vain she has at last divorced him neither more nor less by legal process to get rid of him out of her

house where he began to reappear from time to time threatening to take her children from her.[3]

She settled at Hatch House near Tisbury with her children and was a frequent guest at Clouds. Various acquaintances thought Pamela Wyndham might marry one of Sybil's sons; however, the eldest, Lord Drumlanrig and Alfred 'Bosie' Douglas, were homosexual by preference.[4]

Blunt also brought with him Godfrey Webber, one of the most regular attenders of his Crabbet Club, clerk in the House of Lords and a renowned wit. Webber privately confessed to Blunt that he found Clouds 'the largest & ugliest [house] in England'; Blunt, however, decided that it was a 'most enjoyable place . . . very practical for a large family, & on the whole I like it extremely. It has the immense advantage of standing in old grounds.'[5]

Georgiana but not Edward Burne-Jones arrived a couple of days after Blunt, followed the next day by Balfour and Henry James. Unlike Burne-Jones, James was gregarious. He relished country house visits; he enjoyed his proximity to the ruling class – an outsider with insider status – but above all the settings, the conversation, the subtle relationships between his fellow guests inspired his fiction. He was a regular guest at the Wyndhams' house in Belgrave Square and also knew Mary Elcho's Gloucestershire home of Stanway through staying in nearby Broadway with John Singer Sargent. But James's social skills immediately disappointed Blunt:

James is distinctly heavy in conversation & for a man who writes so lightly and well it is amazing how dull witted he is. This is not only that he had no talk himself but that he is slow to take in the talk of others. He tries hard, & when he does find anything to say he spoils it in the saying.[6]

But in his short story, 'The Private Life', first published in 1892, James reveals the necessity for subterfuge by the Victorian artist who is taken up by society. His public face protects his inner private world. Clare Vawnay, the character in James's story who is based on Robert Browning and 'the greatest of our literary glories', is unable to recite his latest drama to the house guests: 'he had clean forgotten every word'. But in the privacy of his own room his other self is simultaneously writing down the masterpiece. As the narrator realises, 'one goes out, the other stays at home. One's the genius, the other's the bourgeois, and it's only the bourgeois whom we personally know.'[7] James might appear dull-witted to Blunt while in public, but his private life as novelist was constantly nourished by the London season and by visits to country houses. The setting of Clouds, the political and sexual tensions between the guests would resurface in his fiction.

Percy and Madeline's eldest son George possessed many of the characteristics of the Jamesian hero, torn between the world of politics, culture and contemplation. He had married Sibell, Countess Grosvenor, the widow of Earl Grosvenor, the epileptic eldest son of the Duke of Westminster, in February 1887. In March he entered Irish politics, after being invited to become Balfour's private secretary while still on honeymoon in Rome. Though linked by marriage to the Grosvenor dynasty and soon to be talked of as a future Prime Minister, he continued to write poetry and literary essays. During Blunt's visit to Clouds in 1887 George spent part of the time reading his poetry to Blunt, who commented: 'besides several excellent sonnets he read me two longer pieces of very superior merit'; Blunt read his poem 'Esther' to George.[8] For his part, George confessed to the fear that, 'I shall get nowhere riding these two circus horses Politics and Poetry round the narrow arena of my capacity'.[9]

Nick Dormer, hero of James's novel *The Tragic Muse*, not only abandoned politics, 'it's a trade like another, and a method of making one's way which society certainly condones', for the life of the artist, the 'side of beauty', 'something better'[10] but in so doing he also gave up the chance to marry a wealthy and beautiful widow. George Wyndham, however, was convinced that devotion to such a prize as Sibell Grosvenor would offer him some hope of doing good in the world. Possibly the opposition of both the Duke of Westminster and his father, who feared George would spend his life 'as an appendage to the Duchy of Westminster,'[11] fuelled his determination to win Sibell. She was eight years older than him with three young children to raise, but George wrote to his mother: 'I feel sure there is no necessity to marry a girl for her youth and breed fools to be as uncomfortable and useless as oneself.'[12]

Unfortunately, according to some contemporaries, as well as being beautiful, Sibell was also a bore.[13] Flawed, like the most interesting Jamesian heroes and heroines, George soon transferred his devotion from his wife to Gay Windsor-Clive, Countess of Plymouth. Blunt had foretold as much on hearing of the marriage: 'these marriages with widows are a mistake for young men who are made slaves of & only regain their freedom when it is too late'.[14]

Unlike George, Balfour never married; his closest, lifelong female friend was George's sister Mary, unhappily married to Hugo Elcho. Members of the family and friends all knew of Mary's 'tendresse', as Blunt described it, for Balfour:

Balfour is here under particularly favourable [circumstances] as he is in love with Mary Elcho, to whom he makes himself of course charming, but, possibly for the same reason, I do not like him much. . . . He has a grande passion for Mary – that is quite clear – and it is equally clear that she has a tendresse for him. But what their

68 (left) Arthur James
Balfour, by John Singer
Sargent.

69 (right) Mary, Lady
Elcho, taken by Kingsbury
Notcutt 1887.

exact relations may be I cannot determine. Perhaps it is better not to be too wise, and as all the house accepts the position as the most natural in the world, there let us leave it.[15]

It was during the 1887 visit to Clouds that Blunt turned his attentions to Mary (his liaison with her mother Madeline had taken place fourteen years before). He recognised in her 'just that touch of human sympathy which brings her to the level of our sins'.[16] However, he remained at a distance for eight more years until Mary brought her children to his Egyptian home for a romantic holiday in the desert. Their brief affair resulted in the birth of a daughter.

As a detached guest, Henry James would have found various levels of intimate, implicit and explicit sexual communication (Madeline and Wilfrid Blunt; Mary and Balfour; Blunt and Mary) combined with political intrigue. Walks through the wild gardens offered privacy for lovers (James frequently sent his characters off for walks in the grounds of country houses, out of sight of their partners),[17] while competitive games of tennis, the pursuit of wild birds and rounds of golf diffused or exacerbated political differences.

As a fervent Irish nationalist, Blunt had fierce arguments with Balfour about government policy towards Ireland, in relation in particular to the Criminal Law Amendment (Ireland) Act. Guy Wyndham was involved in enforcing the act in Ireland, preventing proclaimed meetings from taking place. Blunt was characteristically delighted when he and George played lawn tennis against Balfour and Guy and gave them, 'I am glad to say, a thorough good beating, for the honour of Home Rule. Balfour is really I fancy the best player of us but he was out of form & we won 3 sets to love – one a love set.' Blunt could not help thinking the situation absurd, 'my being here playing tennis with the chief secretary on the very day of the Ballywreen meeting where he evidently expects bloodshed'. He made a careful note of Balfour's more careless remarks about some of the protagonists:

> 'I am sorry for Dillon', he [Balfour] said at dinner, 'as if he gets into prison it is likely to kill him. He will have hard labour & it will be quite a different thing from Forster's ridiculous imprisonment at Kilmainham. There is something almost interesting abt Dillon, but it is a pity he lies so. He is afraid of prison & he is right as it will probably kill him.'[18]

Perhaps Blunt's vehemence only convinced Balfour of his disruptive influence: not long after the Clouds party, in October 1887, Blunt was imprisoned for two months under Balfour's new legislation which had been brought in to keep the peace. Just before sentence was passed Balfour wrote to Mary Elcho from Dublin:

> We are trying to get your cousin in gaol. I have not heard whether we have succeeded – I hope so for I am sure Blunt would be horribly disappointed at any other consummation – thought I should be sorry for Ly [Lady] Anne who may not hold the same views about political martyrdom as her husband. He is [a] goodish poet & [a] goodish lawn tennis player & a goodish fellow.[19]

From prison Blunt sent a statement to the *Freeman's Journal* repeating the comments about Ireland made by Balfour during the Clouds visit. He was encouraged by Gladstone to repeat his statement in *The Times* in March 1888. Percy was so angry he almost vowed never to speak to his cousin again. Blunt commented, 'they [Madeline and Percy] think the thing a breach of social etiquette'. He had betrayed the confidentiality which was also a feature of the Wyndhams' style of country house hospitality. The acceptance of such confidentiality by all parties allowed open debate between guests who might represent totally opposite political parties, debate which sometimes led to radical political reform (for example the influence at Stanway of Sidney and Beatrice Webb on Balfour's education policy) and always provided fuel for the novelist.

2

Henry James's skill was to include sufficient details of country house visits to flatter his hosts but never to reveal precise locations or make explicit the sources of his characters. During the visit to Clouds, all of the guests were given tours of the house and grounds; they were also taken on visits to neighbouring 'sites', including Wardour Castle. James was given his tour in the company of Madeline and a local architect. His interest in the country house lay not so much in its individual appearance as in the way of life it revealed: the combination of appearance, setting, form and content. The activities pursued in the houses and their grounds are more important that the actual surroundings; and the style in which those activities are pursued become the final arbiter of taste and sensibility.

James regarded as of special significance what owners of country houses did with their houses and possession. In *The Spoils of Poynton* (1897) he contrasts the perfection of Poynton, the 'complete work of art', with the hideous tastelessness of Waterbath, home of the Brigstocks:

> The house [Waterbath] might have passed if they had only let it alone . . . they had smothered it with trumpery ornament and scrapbook art, with strange excrescences and bunchy draperies, with gimcracks that might have been keepsakes for maid-servants and nondescript conveniences that might have been prizes for the blind.[20]

Though Poynton is early Jacobean, social historians have commented on its similarities to Clouds,[21] not least in James's description of its owners, the Gereths, 'their perfect accord and beautiful life together, twenty-six years of planning and seeking, a long, sunny harvest of taste and curiosity'.[22] The young heroine of *The Spoils of Poynton* is given a tour, like James at Clouds, of the Gereths' 'complete work of art':

> Wandering through clear chambers where the general effect made preferences almost as impossible as if they had been shocks, pausing at open doors where vistas were long and bland, she would, even if she had not already known, have discovered for herself that Poynton was the record of a life. It was written in great syllables of colour and form, the tongues of other countries and the hands of rare artists. It was all France and Italy, with their ages composed to rest. For England you looked out of old windows – it was England that was the wide embrace. . . . There were not many pictures – the panels and the stuffs were themselves the picture, and in all the great wainscoted house there was not an inch of pasted paper.[23]

Wandering through the rooms of Webb's house, James's impression would in some respects have been similar: certainly the 'wide embrace' of England through the many windows, also the clear white plastered walls in the central hall (above oak panelling) and drawing room, showing off paintings, tapestries, carpets and everywhere 'stuffs', fabrics designed by Morris and Company. On the ground floor pasted paper was limited to Percy's bedroom, though there was more on the upper floors.

The treasures of Poynton were of high quality, but it was Mrs Gereth's personality that created the 'exquisite' effect, her relationship towards the objects as she made them 'worthy of each other and the house, watched them, loved them, lived with them'. Forced to move out of Poynton to a modest country house called Ricks, Mrs Gereth, without realising what she is doing, is able to achieve the same magic with less prestigious effects, 'little worn, bleached stuffs and sweet spindle-legs' belonging to a maiden aunt. It is Flora, again, who tours the house observing the effect:

> It's not the great chorus of Poynton. . . . This is a voice so gentle, so human, so feminine – a faint, far-away voice with the little quaver of a heart-break. You've listened to it unawares; for the arrangement and effect of everything – when I compare them with what we found the first day we came down – shows, even if mechanically and disdainfully exercised, your admirable, infallible hand. It's your extraordinary genius; you make things 'compose' in spite of yourself.[24]

Clouds contained only a few exceptional individual works of art. Its effect was achieved by just this sort of personal touch, the ability of Madeline to make things 'compose', to create a home, not a museum or a show-palace: 'There were places much grander and richer, but there was no complete work of art, nothing that would appeal so to those who were really informed'.[25]

3

At the end of *The Spoils of Poynton*, James sets fire to his 'complete work of art', utterly destroying the house and all its contents. Fire was a constant threat to property, especially to large houses set in their private parks, not easily accessible for fire engines. Clouds went up in flames during the early hours of 6 January 1889, sixteen months after James's visit. The house-guests included Mary Elcho and her three young children, Ego, Guy and Cynthia (the latter born at Clouds in 1887); also Dorothy Carleton, a niece of Madeline's and permanent resident of Clouds since the death of her parents.

The fire started on the upper floor: a nameless maid had left a lighted candle in a cupboard. Everyone was asleep and the fire quickly spread, the wind drawing volumes of suffocating smoke right through the house. Miraculously no one in the house was hurt; all escaped before the house was engulfed in flames. Mary, sleeping on the first floor, was woken up by the housemaid Bertha Devon, carrying Ego in her arms: 'Oh, Miss Mary, you must leave the house, the house is on fire.' Fräulein Schneider and Mrs Fry, the nursery nurse, rescued Guy and Cynthia from the nursery on the top floor, carrying them down the stairs wrapped in dampened blankets with wet sponges in their mouths.[26]

Most of the contents of the rooms on the ground floor were saved through the efforts of the servants, William Mallett and other villagers from Milton. Even some furniture and personal belongings from the first floor were rescued; only the guests and servants sleeping at the top of the house lost all their clothes and possessions. Madeline had time to rush across the hall in her nightgown, climb on a chair and lift down the Baldovinetti painting bought by Percy at William Graham's sale, nearly killing herself in the process: the painting was far heavier than she expected, and she fell off the chair with the massive picture on top of her. The bruise on her thigh took three months to fade but the painting was saved.[27]

Burne-Jones's cartoon of the Ascension ('the figure of Christ blessing those on Earth from above surrounded by the Arch-Angels') which hung over the main staircase was not so fortunate: only a faded photograph survives to offer some impression of the original. It was hung at Clouds in December 1887, after Burne-Jones had worked on his original cartoon for a stained-glass window. He had painted in the corners, made the top square, then 'painted in all the figures in raw umber gilding all the Halos & repainting the faces & hands with his own hand & lovely it was'.[28]

While the treasures of Clouds were piled ever higher on the lawn, the Wyndhams watched as Webb's house was reduced to a virtual ruin. Pamela stood wringing her hands and crying, 'Oh, my Bible, and oh, my canaries!' Another witness recalled Madeline standing a little way off with a 'rapt look on her face . . . she had thrown a rough homespun coat over the nightgown, and the lace frills escaped beneath the tweed sleeves and fell over her hands which were flung out in an unconscious gesture of wonder at the sight. She was entranced by its beauty and terror.'[29]

Fire engines were summoned from Mere, Wilton and Salisbury but the horses had to be caught, then icy roads negotiated. Between Wilton and Clouds, a distance of 18 miles, the horses pulling the fire engines fell down three times on the slopes and were too badly hurt to continue. Fresh horses were borrowed from nearby farms. By the time the fire engines reached Clouds they could only prevent any fresh outbreaks of fire and make sure the domestic offices were safe. It was so cold that the captain of the Wilton brigade, directing a water hose from the roof of Clouds, was frozen to the side of the ladder up which he had climbed.[30] At the same time residents of the East Knoyle and Milton began to arrive in increasing numbers: 'they sat in wagonettes, eating egg sandwiches, and hugely enjoying themselves; the scene looked like Frith's picture of Derby Day.'[31]

Pamela and Dorothy stayed in the vicarage at East Knoyle with Canon Milford's family. They were lent clothes and Mrs Milford gave Pamela half a crown so she could tip the parlourmaid.[32] Madeline, her daughter Mary and grandchildren went down to Knoyle House to rest. Since the death of Alfred Seymour in 1888, the house had been periodically let. One of the first tenants was Baron Stalbridge, younger brother of the Duke of Westminster.[33] Mary's children joined the Stalbridge children in their nursery. Nellie Grosvenor, then aged four, later recalled the excitement of the night, watching the 'glorious progress of several local fire-engines . . . enormous galloping horses . . . engines all red and gold, bells tolling, and brave helmeted men hanging on at all angles'.[34] She was not so thrilled by the arrival of the Elcho children in '*our* nursery. . . . We were told to welcome them; we did not . . . Cynthia . . . made a bee-line for my rocking-horse. I hit her, and disliked her ever afterwards.'[35]

The first survey of the damage to Clouds revealed that the interior was all but

70 Clouds House immediately after the fire.

completely gutted. Subsequently the surviving woodwork had to be cleared out, joists and all, as rot set in. The walls, however, being three feet thick and built of green sandstone, were still intact. Webb's reaction on first hearing of the devastation is not recorded, though William Morris saw him on 9 January and wrote to his daughter May of the 'bad business'; Webb 'made light of it, as he would be likely to do'.[36] The architect visited the ruin for the first time on 15 January.

Madeline spent the day after the fire sending telegrams assuring family and friends that no lives had been lost. George Wyndham wrote back to his mother immediately from Dublin: 'we will undo the bad and build up the beauty of Clouds again . . . if you are all well, all is well. The form is the reality, not the substance, and Clouds shall be again.' He wrote again the next day. The fire had made him realise how much he had grown to love the house: 'I can't cease from moving through the passages and looking out of the windows at the views we loved. How much memory is. For I never knew till now how I loved and knew every nook in Clouds. We must make it again at once.'[37] His sister Pamela described the bravery and patience of their parents: 'it makes me wonder why it should have happened to them, except that Clouds was too ideal to live, and "who the gods love die young"'.[38]

Balfour wrote to Mary from Dublin Castle: 'I did not think, when I wondered in my letter of Saturday whether it would reach you at Clouds, that before it left Salisbury Clouds would be in ashes!' He added that George was determined to see the house raised 'anew from its ashes. His chief concern is that two years of a life already too short for all he means to put into it will be wasted in the process'. Mary replied from Stanway:

I feel as if everything had been wiped out of my brain with a clean sponge or *burnt* out *not* the recollection of my friends, heaven forbid but *all* power of writing to them, of speaking or thinking or doing anything. One feels quite nerveless and listless after a shock of that description and the flat dreary feeling is bad to bear after the elation of excitation has died away. . . . Pamela, all of them were very brave and behaved splendidly (for nobody can realize what a terrible thing a real bad *quick* fire is unless they have seen it and lived through it). But I do grieve *so* for Papa and Mama I've aches and aches for them and I have not suffered half enough. I wish I could lighten their load – it's too hard; all their love and labour lost, when one *did* so want them to enjoy the well-earned fruits of all their pains – this time the house looked more perfect than ever and a lot had been done. Papa is broken hearted and cannot share George's sanguine views – at 25 and 55 [one] sees thro' very different coloured spectacles.[39]

George offered Saighton, his Cheshire home, as a temporary refuge, but Percy and Madeline had already decided to start rebuilding Clouds as quickly as possible.

The plan to rebuild depended on the insurance companies paying up: without that, as Percy told Burne-Jones, only a reduced house could be built, and 'George must furnish it afterwards'. By the beginning of March Percy had heard that the Sun Insurance Company would pay the whole of his claim: 'if the Royal do the same my money loss will amount to £3000'.[40] Webb noted that the Royal eventually paid £28,345 12sh.; The Sun Insurance Company paid £27,000, paying up 'like their namesake the great luminary'.[41] The estimate for rebuilding was £26,741 17sh. 3d. Webb's fee was £900. Clouds could be totally rebuilt and refurnished: George would inherit not only the house but many of its treasures.

James Simmonds was re-employed on 19 June as clerk of works for the 're-instating' of Clouds House; his work was completed at the end of September 1891 just after the Wyndhams moved back again. Albert Estcourt was engaged to carry out the building works and he used the same workforce responsible for the original house, even giving some of the men the same tasks as before. Webb designed few visible changes to Clouds; his 'distinct improvements' included fire-proof flooring and additional tin-lined upper pipes to carry the hot and cold water supply. Percy also got a new boot cupboard in his dressing room.

Advice on fire precautions were supplied in part by Captain Shaw of the Southwark fire brigade, who was regularly approached by members of the landed gentry after fires destroyed their properties. Percy contacted him in May 1890 and he replied immediately:

I am not at all surprised at hearing from you – I only wonder why it should have been so long delayed. When Warwick Castle was burned, Lord Warwick wrote to me within a week – When Inverary was partly burned the Duke of Argyll wrote & telegraphed. . . . I shall be charmed to see you. . . . It is painful to watch the loss of really valuable property in England, which cannot be replaced by any expenditure of money, & all for want of the simplest precautions.[42]

From their temporary lodgings at Knoyle House, Percy and Madeline spent days sifting through the remains of Clouds, looking in the outbuildings to see what had been recovered. Percy searched obsessively for his writing table: two of its drawers had been found but not the ones containing important family papers. Madeline was more fortunate in finding some bookcases, which she then had removed to the servants' hall. Many of the books from the house had been saved by the servants and were piled up in dog baskets. Madeline, Pamela and Dorothy Carleton and 'the four burnt-out housemaids' spent some contented hours putting them back on to shelves, trying to turn the offices into a second home. As Madeline explained to her daughter Mary, 'we have an object to work for'.

The cellar of Clouds was still hot for a week after the fire, but Madeline 'could kiss the ashes' when she found a whole variety of souvenirs, Mary's paintbrushes and silver scissors, the nails from the billiard table (the table had been saved by the villagers, who regarded it as particularly valuable), a selection of Percy's shirt collars and handkerchiefs, even 'Mrs White's little green bead trimming pinned on a bit of paper!' One evening she and Fräulein Schneider decided to play piquet and after a search discovered the box with all its contents just as it was left when they played the last time, the night before the fire. 'Sultan died that evening, and they sat up playing very late, you [Mary] watching them. There was the score book you gave them with the last score entered and the date Jan.5th.'

Friends of the Wyndhams exchanged information about the cause of the fire and extent of the damage. Georgiana Burne-Jones expressed her horror to Mary Elcho: 'it seems so utterly impossible that that beautiful monument of loving and successful labour should have disappeared'. Edward Burne-Jones wrote at length to Frances Horner who had paid her first visit to Clouds with her husband in 1888.

> I saw Percy on Sunday last night and no stoic could show less sign of dismay, though the blow has fallen most heavily on him . . . the great hall was like a funnel for the flames – and the whole house was ablaze in a little time – none had time to dress – only to escape in their night things and watch the havoc . . . a brief life the poor house had, but Mrs Wyndham could say in a day or two that at least death had never entered it – which was pretty & like her to say.[43]

He did not seem to mind the destruction of his own creations.

The painter Giovanni Costa heard of the fire in Rome and wrote to Percy, anxious for news of his painting:

> I have still all the studies of it & feeling that in that picture I did not say my last word, I should like for my own delectation to repaint it for myself, of course should you still possess it I shall not repaint it, I do not like even to ask your leave to do so.[44]

The Costa was not destroyed: it was most likely still hanging in Belgrave Square along with Mason's *Evening Hymn*, the portraits by Watts and Leighton of Madeline and Percy, Watts's *Orpheus and Eurydice* and Val Prinsep's portrait of George and Guy.

The quantity of objects saved from Clouds, and the size of some of them, is remarkable. Webb's placing of the majority of the servants in virtually separate accommodation was undoubtedly the major factor; once fully awake it was easy for them to rush over to the main house and use the generous number of doors giving access to rooms on the principal floor. Even large rugs and carpets were rescued, including a pretty white and coloured Indian carpet from Mary's bedroom and, most extraordinarily, Morris's enormous carpet from the main drawing room.

One consequence of the fire at Clouds was the establishing of a fire brigade at East Knoyle with its own fire engine, probably with the advice of the authorive Captain Shaw. William Mallett was made captain, with some twelve trained men under him, all of whom worked on the Wyndhams' estate. The engine was kept at Clouds and the fire bell was fixed to the wall of a house in Milton. Once the bell was rung it took about ten minutes for the horses to be harnessed and the engine manned; if the fire was too far away from the bell, the fire brigade was summoned by sending a telegram to Clouds. The headquarters of the fire brigade was William Mallett's workshop at Clouds: he kept his uniform, boots and axe in a special cupboard.[45]

72   The Clouds estate fire engine. William Mallett is to the front, with moustache.

The Wyndhams established a temporary home in the domestic offices of Clouds during the two years it took to rebuild their house. This was no discomfort, as Madeline observed: 'It is a good thing that our architect was a socialist, because we find ourselves just as comfortable in the servants' quarters as we were in our own.'[46] Only close family and friends came to stay, including Georgiana Burne-Jones and her daughter Margaret Mackail, also John and Frances Horner from Mells. Philip Webb was persuaded to stay overnight for one of his site inspections but this was unusual; even on business he rarely stayed longer than a day at Clouds.

4

The new Clouds, the 'Beautiful Phoenix', was entered for a second time on 29 August 1891; Percy and Madeline's children sent letters, 'to wish *Good Luck*'.[47] Only a few days

73 In the offices during the rebuilding of Clouds, 1889–91. From Madeline Adeane's album.

later, Percy went up to Scotland to see the newly completed alterations and extensions to Gosford, the home of his old friend and Mary's father-in-law the tenth Earl of Wemyss. Though the Wyndhams and the Earl of Wemyss were art patrons and collectors, and personally involved in a variety of artistic activities, and though the building costs incurred at Clouds and Gosford were comparable, the appearance, the atmosphere and the lifestyle associated with the two houses were totally different.

Unlike Percy and Madeline Wyndham, Lord Wemyss wrote and printed his memoirs, analysing a long life which he regarded as successful and fulfilled: 'I am not vain, I am self-confident, self-reliant'. His son Evan Charteris summed up his personal conviction: 'If he ever had doubts he never showed them, if he saw any force in his opponent's arguments he never admitted it.'[48] His passion for art was the 'gilding' of his life: 'Art that has ever been inherent in my nature. I was, I feel, born an artist and my true feeling and love for it may be seen in the contents of the family nest.'[49] When he inherited the earldom in 1883 he immediately set about planning to rebuild and eventually move into Gosford. The house had been designed by Robert Adam and completed in 1803 but was never occupied by the family. Lord Wemyss's grandfather demolished the wings, and his father contemplated demolishing all that was left, but was dissuaded. Making the surviving Adam centre habitable and adding two wings cost some £70,000. The northern 'Elcho' wing was designed specially for Hugo and Mary; the southern wing was for Lord Wemyss and his wife, and to create extra space in which to display his art treasures.

The architect was William Young; his relationship with his patron appears to have been the opposite of the relationship between Webb and the Wyndhams: he may have designed the extensions to Gosford but Lord Wemyss *planned*. The emphasis was on solid grandeur, a quality which epitomises Young's other major designs: the Glasgow City Chambers and the War Office in Whitehall. A new entrance was made in the southern wing, leading into a vast marble hall with columns and facings of alabaster, the plasterwork a baroque treatment of leaves, swags of fruit and swans (part of the family arms).

Though there is no record of Percy's first impressions, the comments of other visitors have survived. Edwin Lutyens called on Lord Wemyss a few years later when he was working on Grey Walls for Alfred Lyttleton and he wrote to his wife, 'I feel I could have done *so* much better'.[50] He compared the house to a rendition of 'God Save the King' but sung flat. George Wyndham's friend Gay Windsor-Clive thought the marble hall would be satisfactory if in Italy, 'and were it connected to a house in the same style'. She was frozen to death both in and outside the house, 'though Lord and Lady Wemyss, both past seventy, were always hot'.[51] The Elchos' daughter Cynthia recalled her childhood impressions: 'the house seemed so bleak – so without atmosphere, like a handsome person without charm. The rooms were airless and except with the aid of a long hooked pole, it was impossible to open or shut any of the heavy windows.'[52] Mark

74   The south wing and main entrance to Gosford House, designed by William Young for the tenth Earl of Wemyss.

75 *Venus* by Frank Charteris, tenth
Earl of Wemyss.

Girouard has commented, 'Adam would not have liked what Young did to his own
Gosford'.[53]

The evidence of Lord Wemyss's personal interest in art was the only aesthetic link
between Gosford and Clouds. Like Madeline, he hung his own watercolours all over
the house. He also wrote poetry and towards the end of the century he took up
sculpture (Madeline took up enamelling). He shocked his family by using his second,
young, rather pretty wife as the model for his life-sized naked statue of Venus. The
completed work, 'a five feet eight woman with no approach to clothing save an arrow
for her hair and a looking-glass in hand',[54] was finally exhibited at the New Gallery
before taking its place at Gosford.

Back at Clouds, Percy and Madeline received John and Frances Horner, the first
guests in the rebuilt house. Clouds 'risen' was to attract a new wave of attention from
architects and critics. An 'American globetrotter' called Mr Ellicott called at Clouds
soon after the Wyndhams moved back in, to see 'the masterpiece of modern English
Domestic Architecture'. Only Fräulein Schneider was available to show him round but
she made a profound impression, as Philip Webb reported to Percy:

Mr Ellicott wrote appreciatively of the kind attention paid to him at Clouds by 'a
young lady called Fraulein'! Who knows but, if he visits enough country houses in
England, France, Germany, Italy, and perhaps the principality of Monaco, he may
carry back to – say – Chicago, a titled lady, to ornament the profession of

76   Clouds House from the
south-west, late 1890s.
Taken by Witcomb & Son.

arch[itect]re in a strange land? We reverse the practice, and from America we gild our titles!

Webb's advice to Mr Ellicott was that 'modern architecture was not worth running about for to see'. However he was more sympathetic towards architects new to the profession, 'suckling architects',[55] who might benefit from looking at Clouds, 'so as to learn what to avoid'.

Architectural journalists were much worse than architects. Incensed by one article, Webb wrote to Percy,

I think all journalists and such like might profitably be swept into 'Jonayes belly' [sic], who would write about modern buildings. I think you would wisely stick a warning inscribed board on your Clouds gate post, that no more of such cattle will be admitted to graze there.[56]

The visit of the Horners to Clouds was followed by the first visit to the rebuilt house of its future owner, George Wyndham, his wife Sibell, and their young son Percy. George and Sibell had only one child, probably because the birth of Percy almost killed his mother. In July 1896 Wilfrid Blunt refers to Sibell expecting another baby: if true, she must have suffered a miscarriage.

Sibell had given Madeline cause for concern throughout her earlier pregnancy,

77 Sibell Countess Grosvenor
and Perf Wyndham, *c.*1889.

apparently not gaining sufficient weight. Venus, the morning star, 'presided at his birth
shining straight through the window', but less than an hour after the baby boy was
delivered, on 5 December 1887, Sibell suffered a haemorrhage. George wrote to his
mother: 'she got weaker & weaker, it was quite terrible. But by battling for nearly 3
hours we got her round.' Madeline commented to Mary, 'Oh what it would have been
& might have been too terrible to think of.'

    Young Percy, known to the family as Perf, also Perfoo and Perks, appeared to be the
guarantee to the Wyndham line at Clouds, the eventual heir to the house reborn. In
1892 George wrote a poem to celebrate the rebuilding of Clouds House. He called it
'The Ballad of Mr Rook':

Clouds House! Clouds House! Stands tall and fair
New-risen from the ground.
Good meal and corn I trow may there
For any rook be found.[57]

He also wrote a poem about his son the same year to celebrate his fifth birthday:

Heart's Delight is five years old
His face is fresh and sunny
His English hair just touched with gold

Amidst a browner honey
And English eyes of deepest blue
Whose courage looks you through and through.[58]

Perf's courage was tested when he went to France with the Coldstream Guards (his father's and grandfather's regiment) at the beginning of the First World War. By then both his grandfather and father were dead; he was twenty-six years old, a married man and the owner of Clouds.

7 The Wyndham Circle: Country House Patronage at Clouds, Stanway and Wilsford

The rebuilding of Clouds House coincided with a considerable increase in the influence of the Wyndham family in politics as well as culture. Madeline consolidated her position as one of the more original and most attractive hostesses of the period, and was also a competent artist. Percy continued to commission artists to produce work for Clouds and for the homes of his children. From the late 1880s until the First World War many parties at Clouds were dominated by members of the Souls, the social group within the 'upper ten thousand' which centred on three families: the Wyndhams, the Charterises of Gosford and Stanway (the children of the Earl of Wemyss) and the Tennants of Glen. Mary and Hugo Elcho were leading members, also George Wyndham and his close friend Gay Windsor-Clive (though not his wife Sibell). Balfour was regarded as their intellectual and political leader.[1]

The Souls were predominantly conservative, aristocratic and cultured: their preferred social activities were more intellectual than the gaming and womanising of the Prince of Wales's 'Marlborough House set'. They enjoyed golf, tennis and bicycle rides; scrabble in French and German; the paintings of Burne-Jones and his followers and the latest novel by Henry James. They met throughout the London season, but country weekends spent in their own country houses or their parents' homes offered them informal, unscrutinised pleasures. They reacted against the philistinism of their peers rather than against their parents' generation: Percy and Madeline Wyndham, the Cowpers, Brownlows and Pembrokes were regarded as 'honorary' members. And through the Souls, the tastes of Percy and Madeline influenced another generation of artists, writers and architects.

The 'networking' process was not confined to the arts: in September 1898, Guy Wyndham was at home on leave from the 16th Lancers stationed in India, to attend Staff College. His visit coincided with a weekend at Clouds devoted to the defence of the nation. Percy and Madeline were host to 2900 soldiers who camped in Clouds Park while engaged in manoeuvres on Salisbury Plain. Members of the government, two generals and two daughters of Queen Victoria joined the Wyndham family at Clouds. Two weeks later, George Wyndham was promoted to Under-Secretary at the War Office and Guy was selected to be Deputy-Assistant Adjutant-General in Natal by Lord Wolseley, who reassured George that 'he should have selected Guy in *any case* on his Staff College reports'.[2]

Though it would be false to imply that weekends of successful military and political manoeuvres in and around Clouds House brought promotion to the Wyndham sons and their friends, the hospitality offered by Percy and Madeline and the careful choice of guests, repeated at other country houses, undoubtedly contributed to the selection process.

I

For the artists and architects who visited the country houses of the Wyndhams and their circle, the hospitality brought with it the possibility of future work; inevitably, writers found material for fiction and drama as well as appreciative readers. Those who enjoyed such hospitality and fulfilled the expectations of their hosts could find themselves spending almost every weekend of the year in country houses, but for professionals leisure time was hard to find.

Some of their hosts spent almost every weekend, except during the three months of the London season, dispensing hospitality in their own properties or receiving it while staying at the country houses of their friends. Those with homes close to London also provided country hospitality during the season. Consequently few of the owners of country houses shared or understood the demands being made on some of their guests: publishers' commissions, openings of exhibitions, impatient clients and creditors.

Among the correspondence sent to the Wyndhams and their children by artists and writers there are as many excuses for not coming to stay as there are acceptances. Wells, a regular guest at Stanway, would prevail upon his wife to make his apologies for him: 'he sees his duty as a series of uninterrupted weeks given to a new novel that he is just beginning to write, & he sees a visit to you as a self indulgence conflicting with that little scheme'. Sometimes he explained the problem himself:

> I wish I wasn't a book writing person and given to having fits of nerves about my work. I ought to have been a peer. I am modest & public spirited & everyone would have liked me as a peer. But instead I have to keep on & on writing books, I have to, and you cant imagine what it is. Do you know that I must have written & sold about a million & a half words.

None of the important late Victorian painters – Whistler, Burne-Jones, Watts, Rossetti, Leighton, Sargent – were enthusiastic about staying at country houses, though all made use of the London season to cultivate rich and aristocratic patrons. Their first commitment was to their work. The artists who were regular country house guests, who obviously enjoyed the company and the games, were all in the second or third rank: Valentine Prinsep, Dicky Doyle, William Blake Richmond, Edward Poynter, Edward Clifford, Ellis Roberts. The most successful artists, then and now, commanded high prices for their work and expected patrons to come to their studios. Their earned incomes were, in many cases, higher than the unearned incomes of their patrons.

Watts, for example, though frequently invited, never stayed with the Wyndhams in the country. However, he continued to receive their commissions. He had painted George Wyndham in 1884, shortly before George's regiment was sent to the Sudan; he painted a similar rapid sketch portrait of Guy in 1890 just before his regiment was sent out to India.

Burne-Jones was notorious for turning down country house invitations, often sending his wife or children in his stead. He made his one and only visit to Clouds in October 1892 but stayed only one night; he was breaking his journey to Mells Park House in Somerset, the home of Frances Horner, with whom he had been infatuated since she was in her teens. The visit to Clouds and Mells was immediately preceded by a crisis in his relationship with Frances. In London during the early summer months

Pieces from Clouds House:
Plate XII (facing page, above left)   Part of a dinner service, marked 'Rousseac'.

Plate XIII (facing page, above right)   Part of a dinner service, marked 'made in France for F. Crook 12 Motcomb St Belgrave Sq'.

Plate XIV (facing page, below left)   China dog from Clouds' drawing room.

Plate XV (facing page, below right)   Child's chair upholstered with Morris and Company woven textile *Peacock and Dragon*.

78 Frances Horner by Edward
Burne-Jones, 1879. Sold at Sotheby's
1975.

there had been many emotional meetings. Perhaps he had made some physical
advance: he describes in a letter his mingled feelings of 'awe and worship and
wantonness', and he promised 'never to be bad again . . . if our hands have to loosen
our souls never shall – never'.[3]

His preparations for the visit were extensive. He stayed indoors to avoid the slightest
chance of catching a cold; 'my heart thumps already – what will you do if it thumps
itself out of the bars and drops on your carpet?' He was still writing to Frances as the
train left Waterloo for Tisbury, the railway station for Clouds.

> I'm travelling to Clouds & in a minute comes the Guildford tunnel . . . it is so
> strange – and I vowed so long & loud I would never go to you. But there seems to be
> no Guildford tunnel . . . I shall be dumb I know – I shall never know what to say to
> you. Will you lead me about by the hand? . . . may I sleep on the mat outside your
> door?
>
> England looks boring this evening – but my eyes are fixed on a spot where I have
> settled it that Mells is. . . . That's Wilton on the right – I can only see trees – the
> chief interest in Wilton is that you sometimes go there – I hope that is put in the
> Guide books – And now this is Tisbury.[4]

Madeline kept no record of the visit apart from the artist's name in the visitors' book;
it is impossible to know how distracted he may have seemed. She gave him a letter
which had arrived from Frances and he was relieved to be able to take it up to his
bedroom at the end of the evening. He replied, even though he would see Frances the

next day: 'The moon is too beautiful tonight & I have shut the shutters – not to look at it & be harrowed . . . I am alone at night always – always . . . if I could turn now to you & touch do you think I should have sad thoughts? I should never know any sadness if I might live with you.'[5]

His only comment on the appearance of Clouds was that he thought he liked it; however, it was too dark to see clearly. He was sleeping in a bedroom with a view eastwards over the formal gardens and domestic offices; in the morning he was able to see the 'pretty' outbuildings but worried, 'what if I should like them better than the house – I had better not say so, thats all'. He was also anxious about the Wyndhams' servants: 'I hate a man to come & fidget over my things & empty my pockets and read my letters. I wish I had locked the door last night.'[6]

Edward Poynter was much more suited to country house weekends than Watts or Burne-Jones. The first Professor of the Slade in 1871, and Director of Art at South Kensington in 1875, his own art took second place to his public role. He first met the Wyndhams early in the 1870s – his wife Agnes Macdonald was the sister of Georgiana Burne-Jones – and he proved himself adept both at fitting into the demands of the London season and performing successfully during visits to country houses. On a visit to Wilbury in 1875 he brought his elderly father, the architect Ambrose Poynter. Agnes played lawn tennis, he indulged sixteen-year-old Mary Wyndham by drawing with one eye shut. There were walks and drives, a family performance of *The Tempest*, table-turning and seances. Every evening sixteen sat down to dinner.

He was also encountered at other country houses, in particular Wortley, the seat of Lord Wharncliffe, who commissioned him to decorate the billiard room, beginning in 1871. There, he was able to further the career of the younger, less well-known artist Walter Crane, by proposing he work on additional decorations to the billiard room. But Crane found it difficult to reconcile the expression of his own creative sensibilities inside the house with the pursuit of wild animals for sport in the grounds outside: 'there are few sounds more heart-rending than the scream of a wounded hare: then the rows of slain laid out in the stable yard at the end of the day'.[7]

Madeline and Percy took their daughter Mary to Wortley in the autumn of 1880, part of the preparations for her coming-out the following season. Fellow guests included Charles Kingsley and the Poynters. Poynter amused the party by providing sketches for picture games, and also did a rapid sketch of Mary. The following summer the Wyndhams commissioned him to paint her portrait; they commissioned him again after her marriage to Hugo. Both paintings were exhibited at the Grosvenor Gallery (in 1882 and 1886). In her diary Mary recorded the visit to see the second gouache portrait: 'We went on to Grosvenor Gallery Private View. Very hot and crowded. Mr B.J.'s blue Virgin beautiful – liked Phils [Burne-Jones] "Unfinished Masterpiece" very much. Mr Poynters yellow sketch of me we liked.' It depicts Mary reclining in a setting created by the artist to suggest her contemporary aesthetic taste; bamboo furniture, Chinese blue-and-white and lustreware 'art pottery', a Japanese screen, a goldfish bowl emphasising the japonaiserie theme.

Poynter found Mary a sympathetic subject: a further drawing is referred to by Mary, completed in July 1887, and a medallion was exhibited at the New Gallery in 1888. Both were probably paid for by Percy. The Elchos did not have sufficient income to commission work by leading Victorian artists, so after the medallion was completed, Poynter, keen to paint another full-length portrait, offered to complete the work without payment.

I hope you will not let any matter of money or payment stand in the way of having it done if you have no other reason. ... The pleasure of doing it will be quite sufficient for me, & I am sure I can make a lovely picture. It is after all only an hour or two now & then, which I can well afford to give & you really need think nothing about paying me. Or, if you do not like the idea of my doing a picture of you for nothing, you can pay me any such sum, at any time you like, as will cover my loss of time. What I want is to do the portrait *now* while you are at your best.

Poynter sent Mary gold fabric, hoping she could be persuaded to pose in it, 'it was meant for you always', also, as a joke, sketches of the different styles he could adopt. 'I think no 3 [the Intellectual] will perhaps convey to future generations the most faithful impression of the general appearance of ladies in modern society.' The portrait, however, was not completed.

Poynter continued to visit Clouds even though he received no further significant commissions from the family, and he may have been responsible for introducing the Wyndhams to his sister-in-law Alice (Macdonald), and her husband John Lockwood Kipling. After Kipling's retirement from his position as Curator of the Museum at Lahore in India, he and Alice settled at Tisbury. From the mid-1890s they became regular guests of the Wyndhams, also of the Morrisons at Fonthill. Though Rudyard

79 (left) and 80 (right) Letters to Madeline Wyndham illustrated by John Lockwood Kipling.

Kipling was critical of the Wyndhams' political views, attacking Balfour and the Souls in 'Beyond the Mill Dam', he was grateful to Percy and Madeline for befriending his parents. Alice Kipling died in 1910 in their windswept cottage above Tisbury; Lockwood died the following year of a heart attack while staying at Clouds. At Madeline's own death in 1920, Rudyard Kipling wrote to the family of her kindness to his parents; his poem 'The Glory of the Garden' is supposed to have been inspired by the gardens of Clouds House.

2

From the mid-1890s Madeline concentrated on the art of enamelling. Lockwood Kipling, Edward Poynter, Philip Webb and Detmar Blow, all provided her with ideas for her art work. She was closely associated with the enamellist Alexander Fisher and became one of his most talented pupils; she also used her influence and contacts to further his career.

Fisher is widely acknowledged as the master of the revived jewel-like 'Limoges' technique of enamelling which he learnt from the French enameller Dalpeyrat who lectured at the South Kensington Museum in 1885. Fisher set up his own workshop in the mid-1880s. In 1896 he became head of the enamel workshop at the newly founded Central School of Arts and Crafts (W.R. Lethaby and George Frampton were the joint principals), and in 1904 he established his own enamelling school in his Kensington studio. He also wrote about enamelling: *The Art of Enamelling upon Metal* was published in 1906 with a dedication to one of his most talented and supportive pupils, Madeline Wyndham.

> To the Honble. Mrs Percy Wyndham in token of deep regard for her great friendship and unfailing kindness, and for her patronage and help in reviving the Art of Enamelling.[8]

The type of enamelling practised by Fisher and his pupils was well suited to the amateur as it is relatively easy in the initial stages. It is expensive, however, so it appealed more to aristocratic women, some of whom installed small furnaces in their country houses and held enamelling parties. Fisher's own description of the ideal enamels appeared to encourage the gifted amateur:

> enamels should never be copies of anything in nature nor of any other process of painting in art. They should be creations. They are· for the representation and embodiment of thoughts, ideas, imaginings, and for those parts of a world which exist only in our minds.[9]

Still, much second-rate enamel work was produced at the turn of the century, relying too much on attractive but accidental effects rather than sound technical principles. Madeline, however, was proficient: in 1898 her enamel of 'St Francis receiving the Stigmata' was exhibited at the Royal Academy; another piece was reproduced in the *Studio* magazine to illustrate a series of articles by Fisher on enamelling. She took lessons from Fisher throughout the late 1890s, then practised at home in London.

Wilfrid Blunt called in 1896 and was taken to see the enamelwork 'she is learning to do at the studio of one Fisher, and I was shown all the process of mixing the colours, ground glass with water, and arranging them on a silver plate and burning them on a small oven.[10]

Blunt particularly liked a piece by Madeline depicting two peacocks. Madeline herself was probably not satisfied, because she asked Philip Webb to help her with another peacock enamel. He wrote back protesting his lack of practice, that he was getting old, was busy with other matters and above all knew little about enamelling; yet he still enclosed a sketch for her to use and provided her with lengthy analysis of her proposed subject-matter.

Being so much out of practice of doing such things as Peacocks and other creatures for decorative work, I am quite unhandy with brain and fingers, let alone old age at the very door, and knocking.

It is all very well your asking me to do a slight thing right off, but I must think the scheme right out, whatever it may be; and how was I to do that having no knowledge of the modern processes of enamelling? Added to which, I am all behind hand with my work, with importunate customers, and had to do the drawing I send you between-whiles; subject to the breaking-in of callers and other demands.

You rightly said, enamelling should be 'precious' – but in the Peacock case, if the thing was very small, the lovely blue eyes would be impossible. Again, if only a few

81 Webb's peacock designs for Madeline Wyndham. In an album of Madeline Wyndham's.

eyes were put, there is much difficulty in finishing the outer fringed edge of the expanded tail.

You will see that I have kept a medium size of plate, between the smallest and largest you gave me as your bounds, and yet there must be a good many eyes, or the filling in between them becomes an impossibility, but I have simplified them to the utmost.

Then, in your letter, you shewed a suggestion of background, the something here – to keep the thing from baldness, is surely necessary – so that I have put a kind of one to suit the bird, and give him scale – also to mask – more or less, the outer edge of his tail, giving a kind of halo round it, which makes the thing decorative and rich.

I have made a tracing of the contours of the bird, and set it side by side with the drawing, so that the mere outline may be quite clear to you in its parts and proportions, and you can add any background which your processes will allow.[11]

Webb may have claimed to have no knowledge of enamelling but he was able to give Madeline precise and appropriate advice for her chosen form of self-expression, which he considered 'one of the most difficult of crafts, requiring dexterity and infinite patience, with time as being of no importance'.[12]

In 1901 Madeline acquired a new oil stove from Paris, specially ordered for her by Fisher and to become the centre of rather unusual weekends at Clouds. She first tried it out at Hyères, in the home of her sister Emily Ellis, entertaining the other guests, who included the young Duke of Leinster and his brother Gerald. On the same visit, Madeline produced one of her quick watercolour sketches to record a mirror crashing to the floor in Percy's bedroom. All the guests in the house rushed to Percy's aid, only to find him calmly washing his feet, surrounded by broken glass.[13]

Alexander Fisher was invited as guest of honour to two enamelling parties at Clouds, otherwise Madeline was the instructress, sharing her knowledge with friends who included Frances Horner and her daughter Katherine, Arthur Paget and Sybil Queensberry. Walburga, Lady Paget was also an enthusiast and established a rival furnace at St Fagan's Castle, the home of her daughter Gay and son-in-law Robert Windsor-Clive. She was discovered still in her enamelling costume, by the painter Charles Gere: 'a strange priestess sort of figure in straight garments and goggles over her eyes, and curious shiny things in her hands'.[14]

Madeline took her work seriously, though her social responsibilities in London and at Clouds sometimes conflicted with her art. In 1901 she made a locket for her daughter Mary to give Muriel Paget, but it was produced in difficult circumstances:

not a good one, but the best *I could do* in two days, with a house full of people. Luckily Princess Louise [grand-daughter of Queen Victoria and an enthusiastic enameller] likes doing it *so* we sat together! & worked.

The design consisted of 'a little holy dove blessing a happy Blake-like child'. Wilfrid Blunt, one of the guests, was unkind about the Wyndhams' entertaining a member of the Royal family whom he found extremely tedious: 'It shows the extreme servility of our aristocracy that Madeline & Percy with their artistic & social instincts shd choose to be bored for a week with such a woman for the mere reason that she is "royalty".'[15]

The same year Madeline also produced an enamel picture of the Madonna and Child taken from a seventh-century design. This was followed by an 'angel of Praise' for Mary, with 'little flames all over the back ground', designed to celebrate peace in South

82 Guy Wyndham's photograph of horses being shot for food during the siege of Ladysmith.

Africa. Since the declaration of war in October 1899, the Wyndhams had been concerned for the safety of Guy, trapped in Ladysmith during its long seige. 'I often wonder what Guy with his such darling tender Heart feels,' wrote Madeline to her daughter Mary, 'when he has to dash over all those wretched Boers, & above all when he sees his own men & army killed by *hundreds* all around him it makes me so *sick*.'

Madeline did not enamel for a living and all her pieces were designed to be given away. However, she perfectly understood the necessity for the professional artist to find clients; she was Fisher's most useful and faithful patron and her own demonstrations of enamelling at Clouds encouraged her discerning friends to commission work from her teacher. Her own patronage of Fisher began in London. In 1898, towards the end of the season, the Wyndhams allowed Fisher to hold an exhibition of his work at 44 Belgrave Square. A total of 660 visitors came to the house during the three-day exhibition, nearly all invited personally by Madeline and including the Princess of Wales, Princess Victoria of Wales, the Grand Duchess of Sparta and a 'Crown-Princess of Something'. Madeline gave her daughter Mary the details:

I have been absolutely swallowed up in the exhibition of Mr Fishers Enamels which has been *most successful*. We cleared the front on Saturday 16th & arranged more or less . . . on Sunday 17th Mr Fisher worked from eleven o'clock till one o'clock placing them in the cases then people came in Lady Airlie & after lunch a *lot* of people Lady Paget Gay Windsor, Poynters Fredy & Emy Campbell, Ld Carlisle, in fact a *lot* for private view . . . then Monday Tuesday & yesterday from 11 till 7 the House streaming with people.

Balfour consequently commissioned from Fisher his grandest and most elaborate piece of work, an enormous ornate mantelpiece for the dining room of Whittingehame. It is a triptych, designed in the form of a temple, 3′1″ high, 1′2″ deep and 5′7″ wide, made of bronze, silver, enamel and semiprecious stones and with ivory figures of Faith, Hope, Charity, Inspiration and Poetry.[16]

Madeline had commissioned work from Fisher before the exhibition in Belgrave Square, including a portrait of her daughter Mary,[17] a travelling icon of Christ kept in the hall at Clouds,[18] and a panel of the Crucifixion, a gift for her youngest daughter Pamela to commemorate two years' marriage to Edward Tennant.[19] The same year she gave her daughter Madeline her own enamel of 'The Litany of the Holy Grail', set in a silver frame designed by Fisher. Fisher also designed a cover of blue, red and white enamel for Madeline's prayer book.[20] The front, set with four emeralds, one in each corner, depicted the Annunciation; the back, set with four rubies, one in each corner, depicted a kneeling winged angel. In 1914 the book was sent to be exhibited in Paris but the outbreak of war prevented its return: it was kept 'in a place of safety' until 1918.[21] Shortly before the First World, Madeline and her children combined to commission a jewelled and enamelled cross, three feet high, from Fisher. It was presented to George and Sibell on their silver wedding anniversary and placed in the chapel at Clouds which George created after Percy's death.

Much lucrative work for Fisher came from memorials to the dead. To commemorate those from the Wiltshire regiments killed in the Boer War he produced a large bronze plaque for Salisbury Cathedral. Madeline attended the unveiling before inviting Fisher back to Clouds for the weekend; she was undoubtedly involved in obtaining him the commission. He was also involved in designing the Wyndhams' own gravestones for their family plot in the East Knoyle cemetery: Percy and Madeline's were simple crosses, for George Wyndham he designed a 'fence' of angels, for Guy Wyndham's wife, Minnie a full-length angel. Further work came from the Wyndhams, their children and their friends during and after the First World War: memorials to individual soldiers and members of village communities.

Most of Fisher's commissions for Madeline had religious motifs. Her own work was similar: it closely reflected her personally absorbing religious belief, which she tried to pass on to her children. After every family tragedy she poured out her feelings in letters, and marked her own bound copy of her favourite sections of the Bible: the Book of Job, the Psalms, Isaiah, St John and Revelations. She believed she was caught up in a 'wheel', which was constantly turning, bringing first grief then joy then grief, and so on.

The work of her favourite artists offered her a way through to her spiritual world. She approached Burne-Jones's paintings with 'reverence', honouring the artist's soul as well as his hand.[22] At the auction of his work immediately after his death, she thought the sale rooms at Christie's were 'transformed into Temples of Sacred Wonder & Praise'. She and Percy continued to acquire examples of his work in the 1890s, including a cartoon of an angel for a stained-glass window at Hawarden and a large painting of an angel playing a flageolet; she carefully copied his Annunciation and Visitation from the triptych commissioned by the Dalziel Brothers and bought by Edward Clifford in 1886; she also made several copies of his design for metalwork in which the figure of Hope looks out from behind prison bars with an extended hand.

The wording is significant: 'If Hope were not, Heart should Break.'[23] Between 1892 and her own death in 1920 Madeline experienced the loss of a husband, son, daughter-in-law and five grandsons.

3

Mary Elcho inherited her mother's delight in sharing her country home with a variety of artists and writers, but she was especially skilful at perfecting patronage 'on the cheap'. Like many of the Souls, she and Hugo lacked the spending power of their parents; Hugo had to wait until he was fifty-seven years old before inheriting Lord Wemyss's title, property and wealth. The Elchos were unusual, however, in possessing their own country house, Stanway in Gloucestershire. Mary's patronage was based on hospitality and providing useful introductions rather than actual commissions.

Stanway was mostly built between 1580 and 1640. It stood, and stands, cheek by jowl with a twelfth-century church, a fourteenth-century tithe barn, an elaborately decorated Italianate gatehouse once attributed to Inigo Jones, a seventeenth-century vicarage and picturesque cottages, all in that most literary of building materials, mellow, golden, Cotswold stone. It became part of the property of the Earls of Wemyss early in the nineteenth-century but was little used until it became the home of Hugo and Mary. The ninth Earl of Wemyss (Hugo's grandfather) spent a few weeks at Stanway each year for the 'excellent' shooting and commissioned William Burn to enlarge the domestic quarters. Otherwise the house was left to 'caretakers and the tender mercies of rats, bats, moths, cockroaches, and ghosts, who roamed at will through the deserted rooms'. Mary, attuned to the aesthetic taste of her parents, thought it was just as well: 'Stanway probably suffered less through neglect than it would have, had it been continuously lived in during that dangerous period when old-fashioned things were despised and swept away'.[24]

The ninth Earl carried out some alterations. He had the old oak panelling removed from the hall; the minstrel's gallery was made into a bedroom supported by stuccoed pillars and the old Cotswold chimneypiece was taken out, to be replaced by an ugly piece of white stone. Nevertheless, Stanway reminded Mary of 'adored' Isel, her home in the Lake District as a young girl; she remained in love with the place for the rest of her life.

The Elchos took up residence in Stanway at Whitsun 1884. In March, Madeline Wyndham was already writing to Mary with suggestions about furniture:

> If you can get a realy nice table for Hugo in the big room – & a round table for tea & business in the Center rather to one side you will have all that heart can desire. Morris has lovely tables or get Mr Benson to make a green tressel table for Hugo . . . it will be cheaper than Morris.

To begin with, Madeline exercised considerable influence over her eldest daughter's homes in Gloucestershire and London. In August she stayed at Stanway for the first time, together with Percy and all Mary's sisters and brothers, also Madeline's brother Freddie Campbell and his son Jack. Hugo's father, the tenth Earl of Wemyss, was also staying, together with his other surviving sons Alan and Evan Charteris. While the men indulged in shooting, Madeline and her daughters went to work making Stanway a home in the Wilbury and Clouds tradition.

They arranged books on shelves and rummaged in the attics for relics from the past, including Chippendale chairs, 'safely stowed away . . . plush, gold nails and fringe, gilt chairs and woolwork reigned in their stead'.[25] Embroidered curtains had been cut up into valances for the attic beds so Madeline and Mary patched them together again to make curtains for the sitting room. Stanway was gradually filled with a similar Clouds mixture of antique and contemporary furniture, Morris fabrics and old embroideries, paintings of Hugo's ancestors and a few by the favourite artists of the Souls circle. And it teemed with children and dogs. Whereas Madeline had favoured terriers, Mary preferred exotic chows. Madeline not only advised her daughter on what to put into Stanway, she helped Mary with her responsibilities as the 'lady of the manor', organising village school feasts, Christmas parties, charity bazaars. Life in Stanway was in many ways a copy of life in Isel, Wilbury and Clouds.

Financial constraints meant that Mary could only occasionally patronise artists. In 1896 she shared her frustration with Balfour over not being able to afford either his brother Eustace or Philip Webb to restore the parish church of St Peter's, Stanway: 'Oh the awful feeling of helplessness and responsibility.' Instead, Lord Wemyss employed Sir Arthur Blomfield to perform a heavy-handed job, 'cruelly scraping' the interior.[26] Nevertheless, Burne-Jones's son Philip was commissioned to paint Hugo's portrait (exhibited at the Royal Academy in 1898), though it is possible Lord Wemyss paid his fees too. He was introduced by Mary and her parents to the Morrisons of Fonthill and George Wyndham's wife Sibell, and stayed at Saighton to paint Sibell, her son Perf and the gardens. In 1892 he was a guest at Fonthill while painting a portrait of

83 School Feast at Stanway House.

Alfred Morrison and immediately after confided in Mary his private views on Morrison's taste:

> Their gallery of pictures was the most depressing thing of all. I had never quite realized what unlimited wealth – combined with bad taste – could achieve. Do you remember that vast canvas, of life-size cows coming full tilt at one, with a thunderstorm raging in the background? It got on my nerves – & I wondered whether my portrait wd look like the Cow picture when it was done. But they were kind & hospitable – & everyone needn't have good taste, need they?

Mary's contemporary art collection was mostly acquired as gifts from the artists who were her friends: a gouache sketch from Edward Burne-Jones of his peacock memorial for Laura Lyttelton; another Burne-Jones drawing of his daughter Margaret given to Mary by Philip; paintings, sketches and illustrated letters from Philip himself.

Balfour played an important role in supporting the distinctive salon which Mary developed at Stanway from about 1900, dominated not by artists, like Madeline's circle of influence, but by writers. George Wyndham provided introductions to his literary friends. Her 'lions' included Max Beerbohm, Edith Wharton, H.G. Wells, J.M. Barrie and L.P. Hartley. During a prolonged visit in 1922, Barrie confessed in a letter to Pamela, Countess of Lytton:

84   Gouache sketch by Edward Burne-Jones for the peacock memorial to Laura Lyttelton. Burne-Jones to Mary Elcho, 1888: 'If you put the little peacock anywhere, prythee let it be in some remote room your own innermost bower'.

As for Stanway I think every one in it is writing a book except myself. I hear therefore lots of literary talk & pick up information about how the thing is done. So long as all are together, I fear not, but I become shy if left alone with one, having all my life had a dread lest authors should read their works to me.

L.P. Hartley, however, could only be grateful: 'everything was arranged to make even *writing* a pleasure'.

Balfour was a writer himself, and sensitive to the needs of the profession. He was responsible for obtaining Civil List pensions for W.E. Henley, editor of the Conservative *National Observer* and a friend of George Wyndham, as well as for the popular novelist Rhoda Broughton, friend of the Wyndhams and the Horners, In 1905 he provided Joseph Conrad with £500 from the Royal Bounty Fund after carrying out his own research: he 'went off to Scotland, taking with him half a dozen of Conrad's books which so impressed him, that he arranged for a substantial sum to be put at Conrad's disposal'.[27]

While staying at Stanway in 1902 Balfour was introduced by Mary to Sidney and Beatrice Webb, who were on holiday in the Cotswolds: 'the countryside is beautiful . . . latterly we have seen something of Lady Elcho, a fascinating and kindly woman married to a card-playing and cynical aristocrat, living in the most delightful old house'.[28] Back in London, the Webbs invited Mary to dinner, 'to acknowledge her kindness to us in Gloucestershire and her introduction to Balfour, an introduction which may have good results'.[29] Sidney Webb, member of the London County Council since 1892, was working on the reform of education in London and, through his social contact with Balfour, who became a regular visitor to the Webbs' home in Grosvenor Road, influenced the content of Balfour's Education Acts of 1902 and 1903. The Webbs in turn introduced Mary Elcho to H.G. Wells, who was then invited to Stanway for the first of many visits.

Two consecutive weekends in April 1908, taken at random from the Stanway visitors' book and amplified by Mary Elcho's own daily diary, reveal the typical mix of guests and activities organised for their pleasure. On Friday 3 April Mary gave dinner for six: herself, her chaperon Grace, Countess of Wemyss (her father-in-law's second wife), Balfour, H.G. Wells and his wife Catherine, and Percy Grainger. Dale and Forty in Cheltenham supplied a piano for Grainger, who entertained the party with folk songs. On both Saturday and Sunday Mary arranged for Grainger to visit elderly villagers with a folk repertoire. H.G. Wells was left alone in the 'peaceful scholarly atmosphere' of the Old Library while his wife was driven around the Cotswolds in Balfour's motor car.

The party increased in size on Saturday: Alfred and Edith Lyttelton arrived, also John Singer Sargent and Mary's friend and neighbour Eliza Wedgwood. In the afternoon the golfers (Balfour, Lyttelton and Grace Wemyss) disappeared to the golf course on Cleeve Hill while Mary took everyone else, Wells included, to visit two Cotswold churches. Balfour was 'very cross' when the sightseers arrived home late after their transport had broken down three times on the steep hills. Fourteen sat down to dinner, including the vicar Mr Worne. A visit to the local workhouse on Sunday morning was followed by 'a very long lunch' then country walks and tea at Eliza Wedgwood's cottage in the neighbouring village of Stanton. She arranged for three old men to sing for Grainger; in the evening the composer again played to the company after dinner.

The following weekend the literary celebrity was Max Beerbohm, who thoroughly enjoyed his success with the Souls. He lunched regularly in London '*chez* Lady Elcho –

sat between her and Arthur Balfour – George Wyndham on her other side. Altogether I felt quite the gentleman. It is funny that with really distinguished people I do not feel at all shy, though I feel shy with everyone else. My one difficulty is to keep myself in check. As it was, I distinctly patronized Balfour, drawing him out about the ventilating arrangements in The House, and so forth.[30]

At Stanway Beerbohm joined George Wyndham and Sibell Grosvenor, Harry and Nina Cust, Sir Walter Raleigh, Professor of English at Oxford, Sophie Countess de Benckendorff, wife of the Russian Ambassador and Sir Jasper Ridley, Chairman of Coutts and the National Provincial Bank (who was shortly to marry the Benckendorffs' daughter). The mixture of conversation – 'symposing' with a pot of daffodils ('the person who wanted to speak took a daffodil') – and country walks, visits to the poor and local churches, was disrupted by a double tragedy: the death of Billy, the lawnmower pony, and Mrs Worne, wife of the vicar. Mary discovered Prew, the Stanway odd-job man, tolling the church bell for Mrs Worne as he wept for the loss of Billy.

At Clouds, Madeline and Percy could hang the work of their guests on the walls or sit on the fabrics they designed. Mary received autographed copies of books part-written at Stanway: Maurice Hewlett, for example, wrote that 'Macmillan is to send to you, at Stanway, a copy of The Queen's Quair, as to which remarkable work you were kind enough to be interested nearly three years ago'. She also received hundreds of effusive letters and occasionally insights into the pleasures and pain of authorship. Francis Brett Young wrote to her as he began his bestselling *Far Forest*:

This is *dies irae*. I mean I am beginning my new book which has got no farther by 11.30 a.m. (when I cast it away to write to you) than two words, the title: FAR FOREST and an awful muddle of notes. At the moment I would rather do anything in the world than write. It is dreadful to contemplate the absolute creation of thirty or forty people about whom I know nothing at all except that I have got, somehow or other, to make them live. And to make them live, I have to pour into them all – *all*, every vestige of my own vitality, for the next 4 or 5 months.

Mary in turn exercised her powers of influence in 1917 to help a struggling author: she wrote to the Royal Literary Fund in support of a grant for the poet Katherine Tynan.[31]

In the end, her patronage and support has to be measured in the happiness, comfort and pleasure she offered her guests. William Rothenstein wrote to her after missing her when he called:

Stanway without you is a colourless Stanway – not, indeed, to me Stanway at all. The outsides of houses – yes I can take infinite pleasure in these; they can be noble, intimate, lyrical and dramatic in their setting. Inside, unless in some way connected with their intimate life, I never want to stop. They are bodies without souls.

Barrie liked Stanway so much that he entered into a financial arrangement with Mary and Hugo, paying some 200 guineas to rent Stanway from them for six weeks every summer from 1921 until 1932. The income probably helped to ensure Stanway's survival as a family home; Hugo was constantly threatening to close up or even sell part of his Wemyss property. Barrie also paid for a new cricket pavilion for Stanway and employed Mary's daughter Cynthia Asquith as his secretary on a salary of £500 per annum; at his death he left her £30,000 and all rights to his plays and books, apart from *Peter Pan*.[32]

Edward Marsh, private secretary to Winston Churchill and patron of artists and writers, was grateful to Mary when she invited to Stanway his young friend, the writer Christopher Hassall. She also brought together Francis Brett Young and Christopher's sister Joan, who illustrated Brett Young's book, *Portrait of a Village*. Marsh included the poetry of Mary's son-in-law Herbert Asquith in his anthology *Georgian Poetry*, though the choice forced Edmund Gosse, himself a devotee of country house visits, to protest:

> I read him forward and I read him backward and I see nothing. . . . If he were a Herbert Snooks . . . no-one would ever have looked at his verses. And people say that the 'age of privilege' is passed![33]

Marsh also patronised Mary's nephew Dick Wyndham, buying his paintings for his own collection and on behalf of the Contemporary Art Society.[34]

Angela Thirkell, the novelist granddaughter of Burne-Jones, was a frequent guest at Stanway. Her expression of gratitude was not so well received: she wrote a bestselling novel, *Wild Strawberries*, in 1934, based closely on Stanway and its occupants. All Mary's endearing idiosyncrasies were amplified. Angela at first protested her innocence: 'I have been perfectly *horrified* to hear from Papa that you felt a character in my last book to be a kind of caricature of you'. She wrote again a few days later:

> Since I have taken up being a female author I have been amused and worried by the number of people (I don't mean *you*) who insist on seeing likenesses where none were meant. . . . How much I wish one could live and die in complete obscurity,

with a kind sheltering husband. But husbands go bad in my hands . . . my star . . . makes me have to write, which at once exposes one to the glare of publicity and everything is exaggerated by the number of thousand copies one sells. I sometimes wish I had taken an alias, when one could have had a lot of the fun without the *hateful* limelight.'

Henry James had been more skilful at avoiding such a situation: houses and characters in his novels can rarely be identified with any certainty. Edith Wharton, who was introduced to the Souls circle by James, first visited Stanway in 1908. Her last unfinished novel *The Buccaneers* (1938) is set in a house which is identifiable as Stanway. In this instance the picture is wholly complimentary. Honourslove, in the Cotswolds, is 'exquisitely intimate. The stones of the house, the bricks of the walls, the very flags of the terrace, were so full of captured sunshine that in the darkest days they must keep an inner brightness.'[35] Wharton, like James an American novelist, imagines the strength of feeling of the owner of Honourslove towards his property, a feeling Mary successfully conveyed to her literary guests:

> Guy wandered out again, drawn back to the soil of Honourslove as a sailor is drawn to the sea. He himself, yard by yard, inch by inch, filling his eyes with the soft slumbrous beauty, his hands with the feel of wrinkled tree-boles, the roughness of sodden autumnal turf, his nostrils with the wine-like smell of dead leaves. The place was swathed in folds of funereal mist shot with watery sunshine, and he thought of all the quiet women who had paced the stones of the terrace on autumn days, worked over the simple garden and among the roses, or sat in the oak parlour at their accounts or their needle-work.[36]

Wharton's romantic view of the English country house echoes Mary Elcho's own description of Stanway and Clouds in her *Family Record*; also the reverential treatment given Stanway by *Country Life*, first in 1899: 'a perfect example of a charming type of the English country seat . . . lying at the foot of the steep in the midst of a lovely sylvan landscape'.[37] The magazine returned in 1916.

> It would be more difficult in England to find any landscape more attractive than this surrounding Stanway on a July morning, with veils of what the Arabs call 'woven air and sunshine' poured over the mounded woodlands that here clothe the Cotswolds, out of a pale, almost Italian sky, and below these, over the fields that are turning gold, and the grassy sides of the road, where the yellow hammer pipes above faery-kingdomes of blue crane's-bill and silvery meadowsweet.[38]

But the reality of life at Stanway for Mary was far from the ideal conveyed by the media. She and Hugo did not have an easy marriage. Balfour summed up Hugo as 'too self-indulgent to succeed and too clever to be content with failure'.[39] He was easily bored, reckless with money and consistently unfaithful. Mary meanwhile derived her emotional support from Balfour, 'indulging Hugo's passions to the extent of entertaining his amours at Stanway, and berating him in variably shrill and humorous tones for his neglect of finances, profession, and plans involving the family'.[40] Her mother-in-law, the Countess of Wemyss, was forced to admire her tolerance: 'you must have reached heights of charity and self-effacement of which *I* should have been incapable of even dreaming'.

Plate XVI (facing page, above) Winter landscape with Clouds House and windmill, one of a series of illustrations by Madeline Wyndham from George Wyndham, *The Ballad of Mr Rook* (London, 1901).

Plate XVII (facing page, below left) Enamel by Madeline Wyndham, 1901. The Madonna and Child was taken from a seventh-century design, the written part designed and arranged by Madeline. 'Behold the Lord the ruler is come a Kingdom is in his hand and power and dominion behold him the name of whose Kingdom is eternity. Dominus dixit ad me filius meustu.'

Plate XVIII (facing page, below right) Enamel by Alexander Fisher (Madeline's teacher), 1897. Commissioned by Madeline for the second wedding anniversary of Pamela and Edward Tennant. Inscribed 'This Shrine was made for Edward and Pamela Tennant and is held by them in memory of their marriage, 11th July 1897 – Alex Fisher made it 1897'. Sold by Sotheby's at the Wilsford sale to a great-granddaughter of Percy and Madeline.

4

Percy and Madeline established for themselves a loving, mutually supportive relationship: the planning of Clouds, the decision to rebuild after the fire, were shared activities. Three of their children, Mary, Pamela and George, were less fortunate in their marriages. For them and many of their closest friends among the Souls, the country house network provided opportunities to find emotional and sometimes physical fulfilment with their preferred rather than their married partners.

Constance, Lady Battersea describes the special role of the country house: 'a splendid place either for arresting or for developing friendships, its close proximities revealing so much that would remain otherwise hidden or only guessed at'.[41]

The novelist Elinor Glyn, who was installed in Montacute by her admirer George Curzon, was more explicit when she described weekends spent with the Souls and their friends: 'the good-looking unattached men had a wonderful time . . . while many husbands were the lovers of their friends' wives'. She went on to define the relationships between the sexes:

> Love affairs at this time were sentimental and refined. However ephemeral, they always contained an element of romance. They were never undertaken either for money, or out of sheer lust. A cloak of glamour surrounded the whole matter, perhaps rendering temptation all the more irresistible on that account, but nevertheless removing all element of commercial traffic or bestiality. Nothing was allowed to appear crude and blatant, and what were essentially ugly facts were made to seem beautiful and even admirable.[42]

Writing in his diary in July 1896, Wilfrid Blunt used the relationship of Mary Elcho and Balfour to define the personal relationships of all the Souls. He dismissed the possibility of Balfour being the father of Mary's sixth child, Yvo (Blunt was the father of her fifth):

> Anyhow he [Balfour] spends the whole of his spare time with her, with Hugo's entire approval. I fancy the truth of it is they have some conventional line of love making they do not overstep. It was the first law of the 'Souls' that 'every woman shd have her man, but no man shd have his woman'. All things were permissible except just the making of children.[43]

For a romantic like George Wyndham, the success of a love affair depended in part on the setting. He had a brief relationship with Ettie Grenfell of Taplow Court but his passion was reserved for Gay Windsor-Clive, Countess of Plymouth. Their affair flourished at St Fagan's, her husband's castle in Wales. Gay's mother Walburga, Lady Paget wrote that George 'was enamoured of this Arthurian country, and believed himself to be a knight of the round table'.[44] George himself described St Fagan's as 'this enchanted land of Arthurian romance'. It was built within the enceinte of a Norman fortress, with its 'pleasaunce and terraces and fishponds, and mazes of cut yews'.[45] Wilfrid Blunt was also attracted to Gay, but when he entertained the couple at Newbuildings, his seventeenth-century house in Sussex, he magnanimously sent them out into the park alone together to read poetry.

Not all of the Souls' affairs were conducted in so civilised a manner as George's with

Plate XIX (facing page) *The Wyndham Sisters* by John Singer Sargent, first exhibited at the Royal Academy 1900, sold by Dick Wyndham in 1927 through Knoedler to the Metropolitan Museum of Art, New York.

Gay or Mary's with Balfour. Harry Cust, the most charming and active womaniser of the Souls, carried on several affairs at once, in country houses scattered across Britain, but he was eventually caught out by the very un-Bohemian double standards with which the Souls pursued their extra-marital relations. He began by playing by the accepted rules of society, having affairs with only married women: Violet Manners, married to the heir of the Duke of Rutland and Lucy Graham Smith, a daughter of Sir Charles Tennant.

In 1892 Cust submitted a poem entitled 'Marriage' to the all-male Crabbet Club held by Blunt:

> Various vigorous virgins may have panted,
> Willing widows wilted in the dust: −
> To no female has the great God granted
> Grace sufficient to be Mrs Cust.[46]

But the same year Cust decided to break the conventions: he turned his attentions to two unmarried girls, Nina Welby-Gregory, granddaughter of the Duke of Rutland and Percy, and Madeline's youngest daughter Pamela. The sad story developed in various country houses. At Clouds, Cust became increasingly fond of Pamela: his suit was supported by George Wyndham and Sibell.

Pamela was regarded as the most beautiful of the Wyndhams' daughters, although surviving photographs of her are rarely as flattering as artists' portraits. In 1888 Percy wrote to his daughter Mary from Abbey Leix in Ireland, where he, Madeline and Pamela were staying with the Vescis: 'Pamela was very much admired . . . I am very much impressed with Pamela's beauty it is so refined, and delicate & perfect in finish.' By way of an afterthought he added, 'the older I get the more I think of beauty'.[47] Walburga, Lady Paget regarded her as the exception to the rule, 'pretty, good *and* intellectual',[48] but she was also spoilt and constantly sought attention.

In 1892, to commemorate her twenty-first birthday, Ellis Roberts was commissioned to paint her portrait. A member of the Royal Society of Portrait Painters, Roberts was invited to Clouds in April, perhaps to advise on the hanging of the picture in the rebuilt drawing room. He joined a party consisting of Balfour, the Elchos, George Wyndham and Sibell Grosvenor. The following year Roberts was commissioned to paint the portrait of Hermione, Duchess of Leinster. He produced one version for the Leinsters; another became the property of Hermione's lover, Hugo Elcho.[49]

Harry Cust was invited to Clouds for the first time in August 1892, in the company of Lionel and Victoria Sackville-West. The Wyndhams were not impressed by his behaviour towards their youngest daughter but, presumably for her sake, asked him to Clouds again the following summer. This time Madeline was less censorious. She wrote to Mary at Stanway: 'he does not flirt in the coarse way he did but is deferential & attentive & vy pleasant to evry one. He & George have endless arguments on Poetry'.

At Ashridge, however, Cust slept with Nina on several occasions, as he confided to Wilfrid Blunt, '& she became or thought she was with child'.

> He was now in love with Pamela more than his cousin Nina & owing to the threat of scandal in family and his whole set pressure was put on him to play the honourable part. Appeal was made to George & through him to Arthur Balfour as head of the Souls' society & intimate with them all & he decided in Miss Welby's favour, & added his political to their social insistence, & under a threat of a double ostracism thus

86   Pamela Wyndham by Ellis
Roberts, 1892. Sold in the contents
sale of Clouds, 1933, and acquired
by Stephen Tennant of Wilsford;
sold by Sotheby's at the Wilsford
sale, 1987; now in private collection
of great-grandson of Percy and
Madeline Wyndham.

applied Harry was over-powered and yielded. His half engagement to Pamela was broken off to her sorrow & followed by marriage to Nina in a London registry office.[50]

Pamela went to Saighton to recover but continued to communicate with Cust. Percy discovered that letters were being sent, and gifts were also being exchanged. He was in Bournemouth with Madeline, who had collapsed under the strain. and wrote to his daughter Mary:

> *How long is the writing to continue?* In my judgment the things seems *very far indeed from over* with the chains, rings, and copies of Brownings poems! I feel they are all so sunk in fatuity that no words can save them . . . I am thinking of writing to Pamela to say that letters from him after his marriage which would have been harmless under ordinary circumstances ceased to be so after what has passed between them.

In December Pamela was sent on an extended trip to India with her sister, Madeline Adeane. Friends of the Wyndhams meanwhile wrote letters offering their sympathy, almost as if there had been a tragic death in the family. Burne-Jones, for example, wrote to Madeline, though after some delay: 'I had shirked it, as one shirks a visit to a stricken house'. In the New Year he was visited by Nina, now Mrs Harry Cust, who asked, 'you do like my man, don't you?' He answered 'yes', but to himself added, 'may the Almighty forgive me'.[51]

Nina remained trapped for the rest of her life in an unhappy marriage, virtually deserted by her husband who returned to his philandering habits, until worn down by

87 Clouds family party in the hall, September 1894. From left to right: Percy Wyndham, Dorothy Carleton, Madeline Wyndham (seated, holding Rhona?), Madeline Adeane, George Wyndham, Pamela Wyndham, Lady Edith Douglas (seated on a cushion), Charles Adeane, Fräulein Schneider, Jill the terrier.

ill-health and drink. He lived all his life in the expectation of inheriting Belton and Ashridge from his cousin Lord Brownlow but in the end he predeceased him, dying of heart failure in 1917 at the age of fifty-five. 'Honour' had been placed before love and the gilded country house world of the Souls suddenly looked tawdry and shabby.[52]

Meanwhile, broken-hearted Pamela was without a suitable husband and the routine of country house visits was resumed by her parents, this time in search of a more reliable son-in-law. In October 1894 Percy, Madeline and Pamela visited Muncaster Castle in the Lake District, Glen in Peebleshire, Whittingehame and Gosford in East Lothian. Glen was the country house of the Liberal, self-made millionaire Sir Charles Tennant. His aesthetic taste had little in common with that of the Wyndhams. Glen was built in the Scottish baronial style and the inside looked 'as if Morris were not – nor had been'.[53] He collected the work of eighteenth- and early nineteenth-century English painters rather than the work of contemporary artists, and his daughter Margot thought his judgement 'was warped by constantly comparing his own things with other people's'.[54]

Percy, Madeline and Pamela had stayed at Glen before.[55] They visited the Tennants in October 1889 when Pamela was eighteen years old. Her sister Madeline was eighteen when she had married Charles Adeane the previous year so the earlier visit to Glen could have been planned as an introduction for Pamela to the Tennant sons, all of whom expected to inherit considerable fortunes. Eddy, the eldest, was twelve years older than Pamela; Frank and Jack were ten and six years older. However, it would appear neither Pamela nor the eligible Tennants were attracted to one another. Eddy was already the staid and respectable individual he remained throughout his life, devoted to Glen and only content when hunting, fishing or shooting. His sister Margot Asquith summed him up with just three words: 'Eddy lacks drive.'[56]

The visit to Glen in 1894 was more productive. Eddy was the only son still unmarried and by the following spring his sisters Margot and Charlotte (married to Lord Ribblesdale) were hoping he would pluck up the courage to propose to Pamela.[57] In Florence, Pamela, her parents and Eddy were all the guests of Walburga, Lady Paget. There was thick snow over the city and apparently the young couple reached an understanding on her moonlit terrace.[58] Mary heard the news of the engagement and wrote to Balfour: 'my *extraordinary* sister has telegraphed to me *at last*! She seems happy now she has made up her mind.' Madeline was simply relieved: 'How can I tell you how Thankful I am about Pamela!' she wrote to Mary. 'It is all *like a miracle* . . . he is vy vy nice. Percy likes him immensely.'

They were married in July 1895. The union of the land and industry, Conservative and Liberal politics, French, English and Scottish blood, was celebrated soon after by a gathering of Wyndhams and Tennants at Clouds for another weekend. The party was repeated a few days later at Gosford: Lord Wemyss brought together Wyndhams, Tennants and Asquiths. Though political convictions might separate the families in both Houses of Parliament, in their country houses politics were of minor importance when compared to matters such as sport, the land and the successful arrangement of marriages.

5

The Wyndhams' three daughters were brought together in February 1899 in the drawing room of 44 Belgrave Square for the first of many sittings for John Singer Sargent. The previous year Percy had commissioned Sargent to paint one large portrait of the girls. The fee negotiated was about £2,000. Sargent wrote to Percy on 20 December:

> I have received your letter, and assure you that I am looking forward with the greatest interest to painting your three daughters, and that I shall allow nothing to interfere with it on my part. Will you please let me know when you arrive in March [in London for the beginning of the season] or, at any rate when my three sitters will get together.[59]

Percy may have decided to approach Sargent after hearing about his visit two years before to the Horners at Mells Park who were considering commissioning portraits of their children. Frances had liked the artist and described him to a jealous Burne-Jones: 'he was very nice & simple, & he was very shy & not the least like an American & he wasn't very like an artist either! . . . he hated discussing all his great friends . . . & talking about his pictures'.[60]

Percy had met Sargent himself at Stanway House. Though Sargent was not a devotee of country house weekends, he did enjoy spending summers in the English countryside with his artist friends, Edwin Austin Abbey, Alfred Parsons, Frederick Barnard and Frank Millet, as well as Henry James. From 1885 onwards the group occupied houses at Broadway, a small Cotswold town close to Stanway.[61] The newcomers were immediately notice by the rural community. Mary Elcho was one of the first of their local visitors and though she could not afford to commission work from them, she invited them back to Stanway for tea and tennis year after year. They also received invitations from her parents to Clouds and Alfred Parsons gave Madeline advice on the gardens.

It was unusual for Sargent to paint the Wyndham sisters in their own home, as most commissions were executed in his studio. He included in the background of the painting Watts's portrait of Madeline which hung in the drawing room. He worked on a canvas nearly 10′ × 7′ a job which demanded as much physical labour as art, and when Wilfrid Blunt met him on the doorstep after one morning's sitting, Blunt took him 'to be a superior mechanic'.[62]

A year later he was still struggling with the faces of Pamela and Madeline. Pamela wrote to her father, who was paying the bill, to ask for permission to attend further sittings:

> I sat beside Mr Sargent last night at the Ribblesdales. He is very anxious for some more sittings from me, & enquired my plans most pertinaciously. I said I was quite ready to sit but that I should have to write & tell you – & he acquiesced saying he . . . felt *sure* you would not mean it to be as it is. Mrs Adeane [Madeline] in particular he said must be changed. Then in parenthesis 'and now I see you oh it must be worked on' – squirming & writhing in his evening suit – 'no finish – no finish' – he got quite excited. So at present it stands (as I am up in London till Thursday or Friday & he thinks the weather will hold good) that I am to turn up at his studio (where it seems he has had the picture removed to) on Sat at 2.30 *unless I hear from you to the contrary*.[63]

Pamela's next letter to her father reveals something of the experience of sitting to Sargent and is worth quoting at length.

> My sittings are over now – and he has not repainted the face. He worked on little corners of it and has much improved it I think. He has done the modelling of my nose, and taken a little of the colour out of my cheeks, this improves it – and has strengthened the lines of my hair. That is, where it was all fluffy and rather trivial looking before in the picture he has put in the sweep of hair turned back. This has strengthened it, and made it *more* like my head really. Then he has found out that the straight line of my blue 'plastron' was disturbing to the *scheme*. And much as I regret my pretty blue front I *quite* see it was rather proclusive of other things in the picture as a whole. For instance both sisters seem to *gain* by its removal – one's eye is not checked & held by it. It was too distinct a feature in itself to compose well with other parts. He has not eliminated it wholly – but has disguised it as if I had drawn the lace veil of my dress across it. My face also seems to gain significance by its removal.
>
> He is very keen that Madeline shd. sit to him again – and I hope you will use your influence if Charlie [Adeane] is against it – that she should give him a week. It is a very short time – and *then* he says he could get it done for the Acad. this year. It seems a pity if it is so near it shouldn't be managed; as we shall all be old and haggard before the public sees it! . . . about Mary says he wishes to get a more 'dreamy' expression in her eyes. He asked me if I liked it first & I *could* say honestly I liked it, but did not think it 'contemplative' enough in expression for her. . . . No

sooner had I said the word 'contemplative' than he caught at it. 'Dreamy – I must make it a *little* more dreamy!' and this he says he can do by touching the *lids*. As Mary's eyelids are a most characteristic feature of her face, I think he is right, but of course he will not do it till she sits to him.[64]

Madeline Adeane was able to 'give him a week'. The painting was finished in time for the Royal Academy exhibition in 1900.

The Times hailed the painting as 'the greatest picture which has appeared for many years on the walls of the Royal Academy', the Prince of Wales dubbed it 'The Three Graces', and further commissions followed from the Wyndhams' circle, including the portrait of Sir Charles Tennant and his son-in-law Lord Ribblesdale. Sir Charles probably paid for both pictures: Ribblesdale had little money of his own when he married Charlotte Tennant in 1877 but Sir Charles paid off the £20,000 mortgage on the Ribblesdale estate at Gisburne, bought the couple a house in Mayfair and appointed his son-in-law director of one of his companies, Nobel-Dynamite.[65]

One of Sargent's last commissioned portraits was a full-length painting of the Earl of Wemyss. Though he had virtually given up portrait painting, he was persuaded to tackle the Earl, probably by his son Evan Charteris who became a friend and biographer of the artist. The full-length portrait was paid for by a subscription collected by the Earl's friends and colleagues from both Houses of Parliament; the painting was presented to Lord Wemyss in April 1909 to celebrate his ninetieth birthday.[66]

Though Sargent's portrait of the Wyndham sisters was intended to hang in the billiard room at Clouds House, it continued to be regarded as one of his finest group portraits and it was in constant demand for exhibitions. The Wyndhams rarely refused such requests. Their own discernment and judgement as patrons and connoisseurs was exhibited on each occasion along with their paintings. In the case of the Sargent portrait, the elegance of their own three daughters and the beauty of Pamela in particular was also being displayed. Poynter persuaded them to send it to the Franco-British Exhibition in 1908: 'There is a Committee consisting of Waterhouse, Dicksee, & several other leading artists of which I am President . . . & everything is most carefully looked after.' It had only just been seen at the 'Exhibition of Fair Women' held by the New Gallery. Madeline wrote in the visitors' book for 10 October 1908:

> Sargent's picture returned today [to Clouds] unhurt save two slight injuries to the frame. What it has seen and heard if it could only speak! What variety of nations, of people, what private conversations, and what comments on itself and the Exhibition generally! The picture left Clouds on February 18th to go to the Exhibition of Fair Women at the New Gallery. There was a considerable interval of time between the closing of the Exhibition and the reception of pictures at the Franco British. It was out of the question to have it down here, and its size precluded its being taken in at 44 Belgrave Square. Eventually it was housed in Mr Sargent's Studio at Fulham till the Franco British was sufficiently finished to receive it.[67]

The Wyndhams were less fortunate when they lent their Whistler *Nocturne* to an exhibition in the Palais Luxembourg in Paris in 1892. Whistler wrote to Percy to explain the situation: 'the offending Nocturne . . . was painfully damaged – a most determined enemy, as I supposed, of course! – Mr Richards did what he could – for the moment – but there is a . . . spot left, that one of these days, I must try and cover again for you'.[68]

6

According to her descendants, Pamela always despised the Tennants' 'new money'. She asked Eddy to remove the hoardings at Glasgow Central Station advertising 'Charles Tennant & Co., Chemical Manufacturers'.[69] Glen was not her ideal country house. Although its setting is spectacular, approached by a private drive over a mile long, set deep in a secluded valley surrounded by rolling moorland and forest, Pamela disliked its cold, rather forbidding appearance. At once she planned to introduce changes to make the inside, at least, look as much like Clouds as possible:

> In my little sitting room I am going to get the Clouds drawing room chintz – and a pattern of an armchair at home – and in time get Mamma's sketches on the walls of this room.[70]

However, she soon realised she could make little impression on the internal appearance of Glen until after the death of Sir Charles.

Instead she persuaded Eddy to take a lease on Stockton, an old manor house in the Wylye Valley, just a few miles from Clouds. While her husband enjoyed the fishing and fulfilled his largely ceremonial duties within the Tennant empire, she established her unique role as indulgent mother (her five children were born between 1896 and 1906), amateur poet and essayist, host to writers and artists who shared her love of the English countryside. A regular guest at Stockton was the architect Detmar Blow; early in the 1900s he was asked to design a new country house for the Tennants.

Blow's work for the SPAB in 1892–3 on the tower of St Mary's, East Knoyle had led to a number of commissions from local Wiltshire families as well as from the Wyndhams and their friends. The experience of the work at East Knoyle also taught Blow the craft of the master builder and he began to assemble a team of itinerant craftsmen, some of whom were to stay with him for the next fifteen or twenty years. Three regular craftsmen came from the village, including his foreman-mason; in 1899 he took on the son of Oliver Lodge (a regular guest of the Wyndhams at Clouds, President of the Physical Society and from 1900 Principal of Birmingham University) as a trainee, on Madeline's recommendation. The boy wrote from Clare in Suffolk to express his appreciation:

> I have begun to learn stone carving this week, I have levelled some surfaces & am now copying a 13th century dripstone moulding with a row of dog-teeth in it . . . I have struck Architecture here, at last, & it is my calling . . . I meet lots of real people here, & Detmar Blow is very nearly an ideal person.[71]

Between 1895 and 1914 Blow had one of the largest country house practices in Britain, earning him over £250,000. Though he was the son of a shellac, tea and coffee merchant in Mincing Lane, in 1910 he married Winifred Tollemache, granddaughter of Lord Tollemache of Helmingham Hall, and bought an estate in Gloucestershire of some 1,000 acres on which to build his own country house, Hilles. His brother Sydney, an actor and playwright, wrote unkindly, 'Detmar always had rigid ideas for raising the family up! Up! UP!'[72]

Pamela got to know Blow at Clouds, where he was a regular and popular guest in the years immediately before her marriage to Eddy Tennant. After he designed the

the most wonderful hanger

STATION SALISBURY
TELEGRAMS MIDDLE WOODFORD

WILSFORD HOUSE
SALISBURY

slop

low garden

water to take

by Delmar Blow

88   Sketch of Wilsford
House by Detmar Blow.

pergola for the gardens, he advised Madeline on the internal decorations of rooms at
Clouds and sent her drawings for her enamelling. In 1898 he renovated Lake House in
the Wylye Valley with advice from Webb.[73] The house was similar to Stockton,
sixteenth century with the distinctive chequerboard pattern of flints and stone typical
of the area. In 1900 Eddy Tennant acquired the estate of Wilsford-cum-Lake, about
2,000 acres, which included Lake House and Normanton farm. There was another old
farmhouse on the site. This was carefully dismantled early in 1904 and two years later,
just before the birth of Stephen, the Tennants moved in. George sent good wishes to
his sister: 'April, Avril the month of Aphrodite, is my favourite out of all the pomp. . . .
I long to see the House whilst it is still self-conscious and appreciative of attention'.[74]
He was not disappointed. He was deeply sympathetic to Blow's efforts to create a house
which embodied all his utopian fantasies of the good life:

> Wilsford was delicious. That bit, or slip, of the river-valley and down, and the
> wideness of sky and earth it commands, is a bit, or slip, of my larger dream-life. It
> plucks at my own heart-strings! A sudden intimate aspect of loose hedge-rows, a
> keen, known, smell of chalk-dust and sheep, the little triangle of grass and trees
> where we branch from Amesbury to Wilsford . . . all these are eternal to me.[75]

Philip Webb had intended Clouds to look as if it grew up out of the landscape, but
he did not pretend it was anything other than Victorian: Wilsford looks as if it was
built at least 400 years ago, not in the first few years of the twentieth century. Blow
achieved the same effect at Little Ridge, the house he designed for Hugh and Lady
Mary Morrison in 1904. The house was partly constructed from the roofless and
derelict remains of the sixteenth-century manor house of Berwick St Leonard,

89 Dick Wyndham (Guy and Minnie's younger son) at Wilsford House, 1906, standing in front of the nursery wing.

transported to a new site on the Fonthill estate. Shortly after, he extended Hatch House near Tisbury, creating a house which appears to be part sixteenth and early seventeenth century, part eighteenth century.

Blow's architecture revealed an unquestioning reverence for tradition; at Hilles he tried to live his own Arcadian dream of the 'simple life'. His attitude to the farm that was part of his estate and visible from the front door of Hilles was unashamedly romantic: 'Having had a terrible struggle to acquire his own small fortune' he was 'determined that those who live by the land and on the land should have no other enemies but fickle nature and still more fickle politics'. Clive Aslet adds that Blow 'consequently only charged his farmer a peppercorn rent'.[76]

Pamela Tennant, living in her 'homespun haven' at Wilsford, shared many of Blow's romantic ideals, so much so that one biographer of the Tennants has suggested they were lovers. She employed few servants in the house: no butler or footmen, only a few live-in maids and a cook. The gardens, however, required sixteen men to maintain the yew hedges and tumbling borders. Blow omitted any steps leading up to the front door, 'it being considered undignified to climb steps as if in homage';[77] inside, some of the rooms were left unfinished so that Pamela and Eddy could decide on their own decorations.[78] The Tennant children slept in a cottage-like nursery wing, thatched and low-built. Adjoining it was a tiny, round two-storey children's playhouse, complete with a staircase leading up to a first-floor hideaway and a conical thatched roof.

Wilsford was Pamela's fantasy kingdom: she even had a caravan to take her children through the Wiltshire countryside, away from the 'daily routine' that 'clamps us'.[79] The Tennant fortune which she chose to despise supported a life of excessive ease. She floated to and fro between Wilsford and the Glen, appreciating their different beauties, and so well buttressed by wealth that she never had to catch a bus or think about the price of fish.

When Sir Charles Tennant died in 1906 he left his two younger sons £1 million each; Eddy received Glen and the rest of his estate and was thus able to continue Sir Charles's generous financial support of his son-in-law H.H. Asquith. In return, in 1911 Eddy was made Lord High Commissioner of Scotland and a peer of the realm. At Eddy's own death in 1920, his unsettled property was valued at £819,479 gross. Glen went to his eldest surviving son, Christopher; Wilsford and their London properties in trust to Pamela; large lump sums to his other children Clare, David and Stephen; Lake House and Dryburgh Abbey to Stephen. By comparison Percy's estate was valued at £241,162 at his death in 1911. Eddy had been able to give his daughter Clare a marriage settlement in 1915 of £100,000; Percy provided his daughters with settlements of around £15,000.

Fire had badly damaged Glen in 1905. Pamela, Eddy and the children were all staying in the house at the time. Pamela struggled backwards and forwards across the courtyard 'with my dress filled with books, my long underskirts (for we were in tea-gowns) swishing heavy with wet and mud, in a melancholy way round my ankles'.[80] Robert Lorimer, experienced at working in the baronial style, was commissioned to rebuild the house, which took two years.

Pamela was at last able to influence the design of the interior and, to some extent, the exterior. There is a carving at the top of one flight of stairs of a pelican plucking its breast to feed its young, said to represent Pamela's self-sacrifice for her own five children.[81] The artist could have been Blow; Madeline carefully preserved several of his sketches of pelicans in one of her portfolios. There are also chairs at Glen covered with Morris's fabrics; Morris wallpapers hung on some of the walls, and there are examples of Pamela's own crewelwork and pieces from the Royal School of Art Needlework. In the garden carved lettering marks 'Pamela's seat'. But Glen remained Edward's preferred home and retreat, never Pamela's. She wrote to her brother, George Wyndham, shortly after the building work was completed: 'We are enjoying ourselves here – the children *are* so happy that it compensates for the (always to me) excruciating wrench of leaving Wilsford.'[82]

In her Wiltshire home Pamela tried to create an 'earthly paradise' for her children. Eddy remained in the background, often away in London or Glen. Madeline was close by at Clouds and after the death of Percy, she frequently visited Wilsford. Pamela's closest male friend, whom she came to rely on increasingly, was Sir Edward Grey (Lord Grey of Fallodon) with whom she shared a passion for wild birds. His first marriage was never consummated (Dorothy Grey died in a riding accident in 1906),[83] and his close relationship with Pamela, which began before he was widowed, appears not to have concerned Eddy Tennant. Again Grey is cited as one of Pamela's possible lovers and perhaps the father of one of her children; they were married in 1922.

All of Pamela's children were encouraged to be sensitive and artistic, with no time for the humdrum and the ordinary. Stephen Tennant, the youngest, revealed the most artistic talent though there was probably some family string-pulling when he obtained his place at the Slade School of Art in 1922.[84] His close friend Rex Whistler became the first of a new generation of artists and writers who visited Wilsford, though he was, according to his brother Laurence, 'pulled a little off-course by that alluring friendship'.[85]

For Detmar Blow, the patronage of the Tennants was munificent. After Wilsford was completed he was commissioned to add a new wing to their London house,

90   Pamela Tennant with Stephen, 1907.

34 Queen Anne's Gate. This included a picture gallery which Eddy opened to the public. From 1902 Blow was a regular guest of Pamela's sister Mary Elcho at Stanway. In 1911 he was commissioned to design a new wing and to advise on necessary repairs to the main part of the house. Mary recalled that 'the beams supporting the stone-tiled roof were rotten, and the heavy weight of the roof was thrusting out the oriel window, whose mullions were cracking'.[86] Her eldest son Ego was not completely convinced by Blow's restoration methods:

> Blow made a descent yesterday & began knocking holes in the ceilings & walls. Raymond [Asquith] had been terrified by a large crack which appeared above his bed in the churchyard dressing-room and rained plaster on his dress-clothes. Blow investigating there discovered a prolongation of the oak ceiling in the hall, and was so excited that he ripped the plaster off. Mrs Haslam [the housekeeper] was not soothed by his explanations.[87]

After the deaths of Mary and Hugo, Blow was commissioned to design a Memorial Hall at Stanway: it survives, though its foundations are weak, close to the village war memorial.

Blow's relationship with the Wyndhams and their friends flourished until after the First World War. At Clouds he was commissioned by George Wyndham to design a library and chapel. He continued to visit Stanway until shortly before his own death in 1939. One of his last commissions was to restore a house in Painswick (close to Hilles) for George Wyndham's friend Gay Windsor-Clive, Dowager Countess Plymouth (he had designed the Plymouths' chapel at Hewell Grange). His son Richard Blow married Pamela Tennant's granddaughter Diana Bethell.

Diana is buried in the churchyard at Wilsford, her headstone designed by Roderick

Gradidge. Close by is Pamela's grave, with a headstone designed by Rex Whistler. Inside the church is a memorial designed by Eric Gill to a daughter-in-law of Sir Oliver Lodge, who made Lake House his retirement home from 1919. Like East Knoyle and Stanway, at Wilsford the Wyndham patronage of artists continued to the grave.

Blow's last years were not successful: the aristocratic patronage he had enjoyed from members of the Wyndham family and their friends since the early 1890s went disastrously wrong. At Clouds, Stockton, Wilsford and Saighton he frequently met George Wyndham's stepson Bendor Grosvenor, who became Duke of Westminster in 1899 and one of the richest men in Europe. Before the First World War, Blow worked on various commissions for Bendor, including a hunting lodge in France and the gardens at Eaton; he also designed a yacht *Flying Cloud* to resemble an eighteenth-century country house. By 1917, however, Blow was, according to Edwin Lutyens, 'doing no work except for a house for himself [Hilles] and living with Westminster, running his house, a sort of bailiff and maitre d'hotel, as far as I can make out'.[88]

After the war, few architects could survive by designing country houses: Blow took on more and more work for Bendor, eventually becoming manager of the Grosvenor estate in London and Bendor's private secretary, on a salary of £2,000 a year, 'the trusted minister in the court of an autocratic, pleasure-loving monarch'.[89] As Clive Aslet has commented, 'only an innocent could have failed to foresee the consequences. Westminster had the charm of an aristocrat and a millionaire, but he was self-indulgent, and could be both changeable and cruel.'[90] His third wife took exception to Blow. Accusations were made over the architect's assigning of leases; in 1933 Blow was ignominiously dismissed. He suffered a nervous collapse and retired to Hilles. According to his grandson he never recovered his stability but remained 'still haunted by Bendor's terrible act of desertion'.[91]

Wilsford remains the greatest surviving example of his domestic architecture, home to Pamela and Eddy's youngest child, the increasingly eccentric and reclusive Stephen Tennant until his death in 1987. Stephen spent his last years almost permanently in bed, regarded by some as nothing more than 'an old aesthete of dubious distinction'. He had replaced Pamela's worthy arts and crafts furnishings with 'white & gold & silver luxury', hand-printed wallpapers of dusky pink with gold stars, rococo sugar-candy glass mirrors, bearskins and brocade cushions, rainbow-coloured fishnets draped over screens. A young American scholar, Patricia Lee Yongue, who visited him regularly in the 1970s, wrote of him.

> I don't think he had the slightest real feeling for any of us, none that he acknowledged or even recognized. . . . I do not feel trifled with; I just felt odd that I spent so much time in Stephen's house and in his presence and had not the slightest sense that he cared in any remotely human way for me. . . . Stephen's whole approach to me was performance.[92]

V.S. Naipaul rented a cottage close to the manor house. He wrote of the slowly decaying estate in his novel *The Enigma of Arrival*; also of Stephen Tennant's 'privilege – his house, his staff, his income, the acres he could look out at every day and knew to be his'. However, it was privilege which pressed him down 'into himself, into non-doing and nullity'.[93]

8   Death Comes to Clouds, 1910–14

I

Watts and Leighton had painted Madeline and Percy early in their marriage. As the couple approached their golden wedding, Percy again decided to commission portraits of himself and his wife, but this time by William Orpen. Orpen was obviously excited by the prospect, writing to a friend, 'Is old Percy W. going to be painted this winter? It's strange how much I want to paint him. I expect he would be very difficult to manage when it came to the point.'[1] He began work during the 1904 season, painting two portraits of Madeline, seated in her own sitting-room in Belgrave Square; and one portrait of Percy, seated in his study, also in Belgrave Square.[2]

Madeline recorded some details in the visitors' book:

I sat to Mr Orpen all thro the Summer & he did two Pictures of me . . . when finished Percy took the first one, sitting at writing table in my sitting room – looking out of window – (this was exhibited in 1905) & one sitting in chair opposite fireplace reading. This Pamela got.[3]

Orpen was still painting Madeline in February the following year. She spent one morning in the Belgrave Square house, busy 'with one thing & another . . . dressed like a fool in evening dress!' waiting for Orpen to arrive. When she returned to Clouds later in the day she found her beloved pet squirrel had died. 'I have tended & loved him since 1894. 11 *years* & he was so darling & funny & tame.'

The paintings are interesting in that they show Percy and Madeline in their own rooms in London, presumably surrounded by some of their favourite pictures and pieces of furniture. Percy is seated in almost exactly the same position as his grandfather the Earl of Egremont in a painting by George Clint at Petworth. Behind him are portraits of his grandfather and another Wyndham ancestor. Madeline has paintings from the Italian Renaissance hanging on the green-covered walls of her sitting room, all of religious subject-matter. There is a magnificent lacquer cabinet and a *portière* curtain embroidered with an all-over floral design, possibly her own work or from the Royal School of Art Needlework. The version by Orpen in which she is seated reading now hangs in Stanway on a wall covered with Morris's 'Willow' pattern wallpaper (family legend claims that Morris himself hung some of the paper in the house); below are photographs of her son George and grandson Dick Wyndham, both future owners of Clouds.

Percy and Madeline's fiftieth wedding anniversary was celebrated at Clouds on 16 October 1910. There were special teas for all the Wyndham staff and tenants and for the children attending the village school. Percy and Madeline were presented by the tenants with a massive silver gilt Tudor rose bowl; the schoolchildren saved their

91 (far right, above)   Percy Wyndham by William Orpen. The portrait of Percy's grandfather, the third Earl of Egremont hanging on the wall above Percy, is now in the collection of Mrs Paul Channon, great-granddaughter of Percy and Madeline.

92 (far right, below) Madeline Wyndham by William Orpen. The oil painting of the *Madonna and Child with Saint Mary Magdalene and Saint Joseph* (attributed in 1933 to Pordenone) on the wall above Madeline was included in the 1933 Clouds' contents sale.

93 One of a series of
photographs taken of Percy
and Madeline Wyndham for
their golden wedding
anniversary, 16 October 1910.

halfpennies to buy a pair of fountain pens. The five Wyndham children gave their
parents a specially inscribed solid silver bowl. A photographer took portraits of the
couple in the main entrance to Clouds, and seated in the gardens. They were both
seventy-five years old, their line at Clouds appeared secure, their family close-knit and
affectionate; between them they owned or were heirs to a sizeable part of the British
countryside and nearly a dozen beautiful country houses. George, heir to the estates of
Percy and Madeline, had celebrated the coming of age of his only child Perf at Clouds
in 1908.

Mary Elcho was to become Countess of Wemyss in 1914 when Hugo inherited the
considerable estates of the Earl of Wemyss. Her eldest son Ego Charteris had
completed his degree at Trinity College Oxford, joined the Gloucestershire Yeomanry
and spent two years in Washington as honorary attaché at the Embassy. At the end of
1910 he announced his engagement to Letty Manners, daughter of the Duke of
Rutland; he was also reading for the bar and intended standing as a Conservative
candidate for Parliament. Cynthia Charteris had married Beb Asquith, second son of
the Prime Minister, in July 1910.

Madeline Adeane shared with her husband Charles the responsibilities of their
estate at Babraham. They had six children, all daughters except for the youngest,
Robert, born in 1905. Pamela Tennant was established at Wilsford; her husband Eddy
spent more time in London and Glen. She was the richest of the Wyndhams even
before Sir Charles Tennant's death in 1906, though she raised her five children in
ostentatious simplicity. Bim, the eldest, was still at preparatory school in 1910 but was
already revealing the artistic temperament fostered by his mother – writing poems in
praise of her beauty.

Guy Wyndham was the only member of the family without a permanent home or an estate in the English countryside. He was committed to his army career and spent most of his professional life abroad. He had insufficient capital (if any) to buy a property, and his wife Minnie, though a granddaughter of the Marquess of Headfort (whose London house was 46 Belgrave Square, next door to the Wyndhams), was not wealthy. They had married in 1892 and had three children: George Hereman, Guy Richard (known as Dick) and Olivia. Minnie also had three children, Madge, Geoffrey and Walter, by her previous marriage to Johnnie Brooke.

The golden wedding was a moment of thanksgiving for the family but Percy was already seriously ill. In the summer of 1910 he wrote to Philip Webb, 'I have had various ailments. Some serious, others only painful or troublesome. I have two nurses. This describes my state without going into particulars.' He was worrying that Clouds might be burnt down again and required information about the cost of its reinstatement in 1889–91. He wrote to Webb again a few weeks later:

> I am glad you are so well at your great age. [Webb was four years his senior] I shall be 76 next January. Neither the precepts of philosophy nor the consolations of religion can render growing old a pleasant process or age a pleasant state, though I admit with thankfulness that religion can allay the terrors of death.

According to his obituary he was well enough to take up his responsibilities as local magistrate and enjoy his golden wedding celebrations, but in December he wrote again to Webb, 'I suffer from various distressing infirmities . . . happiness and peace of mind is to me impossible'.

Percy died at Clouds on 13 March 1911. He was photographed lying in his bedroom on the ground floor of the house, surrounded by favourite photographs, paintings and

94   Percy Wyndham laid out in his bedroom at Clouds, 1911. One of a series of photographs taken by Alberts & Janis.

drawings of his children; a sketch by Watts of his wife; drawings by Rossetti and Burne-Jones. An early Italian Renaissance Crucifixion hung above his bed. He was cremated at Woking and his ashes returned for burial in East Knoyle graveyard. They were contained in an oak coffer made from trees grown on the Clouds estate. At his funeral the coffer was covered with a single wreath of bay leaves, laced with gold ribbon.

A memorial service was held at St Margaret's, Westminster at the same time as the funeral service at East Knoyle. For guests attending the Wiltshire service, a special train ran from Salisbury to Semley station. His family attended, also staff and tenants from the Clouds estate. Local landowners were present, including the Duke of Somerset, the Earl of Pembroke and Hugh Morrison, as were politicians including Balfour; artists and writers including Detmar Blow, Charles Gatty, Hilaire Belloc, Henry Newbolt and Edward Burne-Jones's son Philip.

Philip Burne-Jones expressed his sorrow in a letter to Mary Elcho: 'when I think of your father I am a child again – with the sun pouring down upon the lawn at Wilbury – and all the magic of youth & impossible hopes in the air – all life bathed in the light of Dawn for me, at all events, destined never to rise'. His unreciprocated love for Mary had been only one of many disappointments in an unhappy life lived under the shadow of his father and which ended with his suicide.

Madeline was relieved that Percy's suffering had ended. She spent her seventy-sixth birthday at Clouds, 'a Heavenly day almost too Hot with a Peacock with head turned up to heaven piercing the air with his Cries'. She continued her letter to Mary:

> Glad to be here (& not in London) *I rather love* that the 1st Birthday should be kept *quite differently* from the last . . . do you [Mary] remember 1909 the 1st year that he was *so ill* . . . the feeling that He *has left us*, never makes me *unhappy*, not half as unhappy as seeing Him suffering & *miserable Here* – that was *wretchedness*.

Percy had made his last will and testament in 1906 but he added two codicils in June 1910. His entire estate was valued at £241,162 gross. Madeline was left a lifetime interest in 44 Belgrave Square, a lump sum of £1,000 and an annuity of £3,100 to be added to their marriage settlement (which had provided an annual income of £900). Guy received £5,000 and an annuity of £850 as long as Madeline was alive but Percy's three daughters received no further provision, 'as I consider that they are sufficiently provided for by the Settlements made by me on the occasion of their respective marriages'. He originally intended to leave Madeline's niece Dorothy Carleton an annuity of £300 but cancelled this as she was to be provided for by Wilfrid Blunt with whom she was living.[4]

Apart from small legacies to Fräulein Schneider and staff at Clouds, Percy left the rest of his real estate, 'of every tenure in England the Australian colonies and elsewhere and also my residuary personal estate . . . unto and to the use of my son George Wyndham'. In the event of George predeceasing him, he left his estate to George's son, his grandson Percy Lyulph Wyndham. He had transferred his securities to George in 1906 to reduce his liability to income tax and his heir's liability for death duties. As George wisely commented, 'unless the Landed Gentry treat their personal estates on the lines of men in business [taxes] must dissipate any fortune in the course of three generations'.[5]

2

George did not delay taking up his inheritance. By the autumn of 1911 he was settled at Clouds with Sibell and Perf. His eight hunters quickly adapted to their new stables:

> They love being visited. When they hear my steps, out comes a long row of long faces on long necks over the bars of loose-boxes. Then they rub me with their noses and think in their dear, slow, puzzled way about hunting; remembering dimly that there is something else in life more glorious than eating.[6]

A typical day was spent cub hunting with Perf before breakfast; discussing plans for changes at Clouds with William Mallett, dictating letters to his secretary and talking over estate matters with the agent before lunch, 'and then household business; and then two hours' sleep. And then Lawn Tennis. And then old memories at dinner' with his mother Madeline.[7] George was contented, perhaps for the first time in his life. He had made the greatest contribution of the Wyndhams in politics but taken the greatest fall.

George was forty-seven when he inherited Clouds. His successful period in politics lasted only seven years, between 1898 when he was made Under-Secretary of War until 1905 when he resigned as Irish Secretary. During the Boer War he revealed an ability to answer the daily fire of questions in Parliament and make official statements in debates. His personal triumph came during the debate of 1 February 1900 on the Front Opposition Bench Address which deplored 'the want of knowledge, foresight and judgment of Her Majesty's Ministers in preparations for the war now proceeding'.[8] Balfour considered that George 'covered himself with glory. He has just made a speech of an hour and a half, than which I have *never* heard anything better in my long experience of the House. . . . All the best and severest judges would agree that my praise is not exaggerated.'[9] The soldiers fighting in South Africa were also impressed, as Guy discovered when he visited the cavalry camps of the force which relieved Ladysmith:

> On my asking for news I was surrounded by the officers who could speak of nothing but my brother's speech. They said it was more than any of the recent successes, for now they felt that instead of only criticism and quarrels the whole country would be behind them, and the necessary reinforcements and support ensured.[10]

After the 'Khaki' election of 1900 George was rewarded with a place in the Cabinet as Irish Secretary. He was already being tipped to become Prime Minister. His Fitzgerald (rather than Campbell) ancestry made him welcome in Ireland and he had a more sympathetic understanding of the Irish than most English politicians. His achievement in office was the passing of the Irish Land Bill. This extended the arrangements already set up by Balfour's 1892 Land Purchase Act: it made sales more profitable to the landlords without increasing the immediate payments by the tenant-purchasers. The result was an immense extension of sales.[11] At the time George appeared to his friends a contented and ambitious minister, 'sure in the belief of himself'.[12]

The following year George failed to establish university education for Irish

Catholics. Then, without his knowledge but with the approval of the Earl of Dudley, Lord-Lieutenant of Ireland, his permanent under-secretary Sir Anthony MacDonnell (an Irish Catholic) and the Irish Reform Association brought forward a devolution scheme for Ireland. Although George denounced the plan, he was held responsible, attacked by the Unionists for betrayal of their principles and forced to resign. His brother Guy commented: 'he had always been over-engined for his hull; and he allowed himself to be distracted by a multiplicity of interests'.[13] Max Egremont (also a Wyndham), wrote in his biography of George, 'full of grand proposals for the future of Ireland and passing one of that country's greatest ever measures of reform, [but he] failed to read properly the everyday reports sent to him by his Under-Secretary':

> he took too broad a view. Like most romantics he was moved more by the overall conception of a task, by its significance against the vast background of history, than by the technicalities of accomplishment. Those who served with him in Ireland could be enthused by his visionary exhortations, yet confounded by his inattention to the details that might make this vision a reality.[14]

Balfour wrote to Madeline suggesting that the best of George's career was still to come, but George was sick of politics. He held on to his Dover seat at the general election but found the electioneering process 'blatant and barbaric'.[15] He continued to support the Conservative party and later, during the House of Lords crisis of 1911, he was ferocious in his opposition to the Parliament Act. However, he devoted an increasing amount of time and energy to his other passions: literature, hunting and the army.

His most productive period as a writer and editor had been while the Conservative party was in opposition, before he became Under-Secretary at the War Office. He began contributing to W.E. Henley's paper the *National Observer* in the early 1890s; he was a director of Henley's *New Review*; he edited the poetry of Shakespeare and North's

Plutarch for the Tudor Translations; several of his studies were collected after his death as *Essays in Romantic Literature*. He also wrote, but did not publish, his own poetry. When his son Perf revealed an interest in poetry, he was delighted. He explained to his sister Pamela, herself eager to be a writer and to whom he offered much useful criticism, the overwhelming superiority of poetry, the 'fantastic':

> Perf . . . is just beginning to love Poetry. Imagine my delight at recognizing another aspect of eternity in heritage. We have pretty well gutted Keats to-day, all the Odes and 'St.Agnes Eve', with a plenty of soldiering talk, and riding talk, and political talk, thrown in, to throw up the supremacy of the fantastic.
>
> That is the river of life; the surface that reflects Heaven and derives from far sources in the hills, and goes out at last to sea, to forgather again and reflect Heaven once more. The drudgery of turning the mill, the party-political mill, of hatred, malice and all uncharitableness is but an incident.[16]

The army was also significant. While Perf pursued his career in the Coldstream Guards, George enjoyed training with the Cheshire Yeomanry; sometimes father and son were together for manoeuvres. He visited his parents at Clouds and Pamela at Wilsford when he was taking part in mock battles on Salisbury Plain. In Gloucestershire he stayed with Mary at Stanway. In September 1909, for example, he wrote to his wife from Stanway with infectious enthusiasm:

> It has, of course, been impossible for me to write during manoeuvres. But I got your letters. I never had so much joy and interest and pleasure. To you I can say that the great point for me was to be in Percy's life for four days. . . . On Tuesday – our hardest day – I went into the attack with the old battalion . . . we were out-numbered by 3 to 1. We were crushed back into a village called Deadfield. We scraped up three companies of Grenadiers and shoved them in at the critical moment. But we were almost surrounded. Billy [Lambton, the commanding officer] asked me to take a message to Sutton who had four companies further back. I nearly got shot by one of our own guns! Such was the pandemonium. But I got back, dismounted of course, borrowed a bicycle for some way, and then by running and boring through the fences, got the message through.[17]

After all the excitement, George slept in an orchard on the ground next to his son, 'and watched the stars and slept and woke feeling twenty years younger'.

Love of the army life was inextricably linked to a love of Britain and its countryside. The literature George preferred was English, patriotic, expressing a passion for the land – Chaucer, Shakespeare, Keats, William Morris and, most recent, Hilaire Belloc and G.K. Chesterton, both of whom became personal friends and were guests at Clouds from 1911:

> it is impossible to explain my pleasure [in the manoeuvres] without inflicting a lecture on strategy and tactics etc., etc. And beside all that – there were the dawns and sunsets, the lovely English land, the old churches, the hedge-row elms, the stubble fields, Kelmscott, the country-folk – and through all that mellow peace – the humming maze of men, and horses, and bicycles, and guns and field-telegraphs and heliographs and signalling, and the healthy scent of sweat and energy directed by cool intellect.[18]

John Gross, in *The Rise and Fall of the Man of Letters*, pays tribute to his scholarship; he also can't help believing George Wyndham was the invention of an (unspecified) Edwardian novelist – Henry James would do: 'The family estate with the improbable name ("Clouds"); the subaltern in barracks teaching himself Italian; the best-dressed man in the House of Commons – it all seems a little too good to be true. And what adds to the air of unreality, as Eliot remarks in his note on Wyndham in *The Sacred Wood*, is that "his literature and his politics and his country life were one and the same thing".[19]

Apart from literature, George was not especially interested in the arts: 'Art belongs to no particular date or place. A little of it is very good, eternal and universal. The rest is unimportant.'[20] Edward Clifford, William Blake Richmond and Philip Burne-Jones visited Saighton and were commissioned to paint Sibell, Perf and the house and gardens but not, apparently George. Their fees were probably paid by the Duke of Westminster or Percy Wyndham. Sibell had an allowance of £5,700 and George slightly less, but his political expenses were high (especially when he was in Ireland) and they had to rent out their London house in Park Lane towards the end of the century.[21]

Clifford painted Sibell the year before she married George; he was a frequent guest at Saighton and formed a close friendship with Sibell. They were united by a mutual interest in spiritual matters. Sibell eventually became an Anglo-Catholic, while Clifford was a member of the Church Army made up of 'godly working men' trained to preach to the poor. Edward Burne-Jones's granddaughter Angela Thirkell was less than kind to Clifford in her memoirs, *Three Houses*, referring to his 'funny affected voice' and 'romantic snobbism'. He 'so astonishingly united a deep and active feeling of religion, a passion for duchesses, and a marvellous gift of water-colour painting'.[22] His commissions included portraits of Katrine Cowper and Earl Beauchamp of Madresfield (Sibell Grosvenor's son-in-law). Sibell used his painting of the gardens at Saighton for a personal card.

Clifford also drew Madeline Wyndham and was a guest at Clouds; in 1889 he stayed at Babraham. Madeline Adeane wrote to her mother describing the experience of being drawn by him. Her husband Charles Adeane assisted as hairdresser:

> It was very amusing he is so kind about people watching – Charlie watched and Edith & Violet. Darling Charlie did my hair! and *so* well, he really got the knot we have been trying for, scraped my hair up and kept the front & side tidy then he did the twist – he is very pleased with the drawing & so is Mr Clifford. . . . Mr Clifford discovered a likeness to you in me, which I am *very* glad of.[23]

William Blake Richmond was not a religious fanatic like Clifford. His father, George Richmond, was a successful society portraitist; Madeline Wyndham's mother Lady Campbell was one of his subjects.[24] Richmond inherited a genuine appreciation of country house life and the proximity to status, power and wealth. While painting Sibell at Saighton in 1888, he wrote to his father:

> George Wyndham, with whom I am staying, is the enthusiastic secretary of Arthur Balfour; he is a clever young fellow, and quite out of the common run of young men, full of information and not without merit as a poet. His wife, 'Lady Grosvenor' (so-called), has great charm, and she should make a charming picture. We have converted a conservatory into a studio, and most pleasant the light is, no shadows,

all colours. We work till four, then ride over delightful meadows in a headlong fashion on old hunters. The evenings are spent in reading aloud and talk.

To-day we go to tea with the Duke [of Westminster, Lady Grosvenor's father-in-law] at Eaton. Watts' statue of Hugh Lupus opposite the house, with a free sky background, look superb. With all the labour he gave to it, all the changes he made, the work has the charm of a sketch for its spontaneity of intention.[25]

96 (left)   Madeline Wyndham by Edward Clifford, 1875.

97 (right)   Madeline Adeane by Edward Clifford, 1889.

Richmond was perfectly attuned to the needs of his patrons, which included horse riding and precise instructions concerning the style of paintings. George Wyndham wrote to his father at the time of the artist's visit: 'Richmond is painting away at Sibell. It ought to be a good picture. It is being done the way I like, the very opposite of Realism, a round window behind oleanders, myrtles and cypress trees.'[26]

George chose not to be painted but he did allow Rodin to sculpt his bust. He met Rodin in London in 1902 at a banquet at the Café Royal, held to celebrate the unveiling of the bronze Saint Jean-Baptiste at the Victoria and Albert Museum. George was the principal speaker at the banquet, and Rodin's host at the Arts Club, where 'the flow of wine and wit really began and we had in succession a series of *after supper* irresponsible speeches'.[27] George was involved in commissioning Rodin to sculpt a memorial of Henley and a monument to Whistler (Gwen John was the model).

For his own bust, he spent a pleasurable ten days in Paris over Whitsuntide 1904:

I desire to keep touch with letters and sculpture during these divine days of spring leaves and sunshine and so keep an escape way open from the dustiness and fustiness of politics.

He declared Rodin to be 'a very great man . . . I stand for quarter hour and then talk for ten minutes. We have run over the whole Universe lightly, but deeply.'[28] When he inherited Clouds the bust was placed in the entrance hall below large studies by Burne-Jones of St George, War and Peace.

George's taste, formed by his parents, was even less adventurous. On moving into Saighton he was delighted to receive gifts from his mother of Frederic Hollyer's reproductions of Burne-Jones's pictures. In 1901 he visited the Burlington exhibition of the 'British School' and wrote to Madeline in praise of the Fred Walkers, George Masons, early Millais and Burne-Joneses:

> But the Masons and Walkers sing out – 'Non moriar sed vivam et narrabo opera Domini'. 'I shall not die, but live, and I will declare the works of the Lord.' That is the artist's profession of immortality.[29]

For the descendant of the man who patronised Turner, his artistic judgement was weak indeed. As the new tenant for life of Clouds House he was surrounded by familiar works of art which he had no desire to rehang or replace.

George was, however, eager to learn as much as possible about the estate for which he was responsible and which his son would inherit, 'to do my duty by the little stretch of England for which I am responsible'.

> Some people inherit an estate and go on as if nothing had happened. I can't do that. My father never told me anything about this place. I lived and worked in Cheshire and Ireland. Suddenly I find myself responsible for farming 2400 acres and for paying sums that stagger me by way of weekly wages and repairs. So I ask myself 'what are

you going to do?' I mean to use all my imagination and energy to get something done that shall last and remain.[30]

This included making changes to the internal appearance of the house, building a library for himself and a chapel for Sibell.

He approached Detmar Blow to design the library and chapel. As Webb's pupil, Blow was an obvious choice and he was well known to the Wyndham family. The library was constructed along the south side of the second floor. The dividing walls between the nursery bedrooms were removed to create a space which measured 76′ 6″ × 19′. Blow provided designs for the panelling, bookcases and architectural fittings, all to be made from oak grown on the estate. But he lacked the authority of his master, Philip Webb, and George was soon making modifications. He explained to Madeline:

All the 'ways' of life show me that Eternity is true, and not time, and that other 'times' – however good – are manifestly false. Blow, who lived in 1220, now lives in 1690. But we live for ever and must say so in what we make. I shall, therefore, to come back to the library, do it in my own way and not in Blow's 'period'.[31]

George received advice from the estate carpenter William Mallett, who drew up alternative plans – he would be responsible for the final construction of the library.

We had to change Blow's design as it would have cut down the windows outside and spoilt the face of the house. So this gave me a good excuse for changing his plan inside too . . . Blow left [one and a half] feet between the book-cases and the beam in the ceiling with an ornament squashed by the beams. Mallett and I are carrying the cases up to support the beams. It will look safe and I believe be safer.[32]

Together, George and Mallett studied Webb's effects in the house, in particular his panelling and the various shapes of the windows, so that their work would all be 'in close harmony' with the original. The completed library had ten bays formed by oak open bookcases, there were six desks, 'for people who mean business'. Guy Wyndham recalled the view from the new window at the east end (designed to harmonise with Webb's windows in the kitchen range): 'one looked straight along the line of the old Roman or pre-Roman road that, pointing straight for Stonehenge, ran up by the Great Ridge Wood and dipped over the horizon'.[33] George was convinced Webb would approve.

Most of the contents of the library were sold by George's nephew Dick Wyndham in 1932 and 1933. Certain books are identifiable as George's: Henley's *Views and Reviews* signed by the author, 'to G.W. 27/4/1902'; *Fifty Years of Sport* (1913) by A.C.M. Croome and Lord Desborough (husband of George's friend Ettie Grenfell); a facsimile of the First Folio edition of the works of Shakespeare given by J.M. Barrie to Henley on his silver wedding and by Henley to George; a number of Aldine press editions of the classics; fifteenth- and sixteenth-century editions of Plutarch.

The idea for creating a chapel at Clouds for Sibell was originally Perf's. Electricity was installed in the house by George soon after he moved in (a generator was erected in a brick and tiled engine house immediately adjoining the laundry) so the lamp room in the basement was redundant. Blow's designs for the chapel were again virtually ignored by George and Mallett. George bought 100 feet of old Italian panelling with 39 pilasters. It was a chance purchase, but he discovered that the panelling was exactly the

100   The library at Clouds. The photograph was taken for the sale of the house and contents, 1932–3.

101   The chapel at Clouds, 1992.

right height for the lamp room. Working on site together, George and Mallett planned how to make the best use of the panelling without detracting from the proportions of the room. They were again struck by Webb's genius for detail, and by the quality of his workmanship. The basement rooms were as well designed as more public spaces. Sibell joked with her husband: 'the wine-cellar – if properly treated – might challenge the forest of pillars at Cordova';[34] George suggested they look for Cordova's Lion-Court in the brush room.

By working on alterations to Clouds, George discovered for himself the delight of designing. His letters frequently refer to the thrill of craftwork: 'It is great fun. I am doing it with my carpenter.' 'I am enthralled in the task of making the Lamp-room a counterpart to the underground church at Assissi'. 'We . . . are just at the ecstatic moment of deciding the size and shape of a band of mullioned windows West and East of the roof.' 'It is exhilarating to make things for yourself.' Responsibility for Clouds – the house and estate, staff and tenants – brought George more personal satisfaction than any previous experience. He wrote to a friend, 'public life is very useful as an education for private enterprise'. He planned to retire from Parliament in 1914: 'because then I shall have worked as long as Papa did. I don't want to leave off before that, but after two more years I shall feel free to live at Clouds.' To another friend he wrote:

> I cannot desert with honour during this bout of opposition, but after the next General Election and twenty-five years in the House of Commons I shall feel that I have finished that part of my duty, and at a good age [fifty-one] for beginning ten or twenty years of new work *in novitate vitae*.[35]

Meanwhile he began a series of improvements to the estate under the guidance of the agent, Miles. The disused windmill was roofed in with a stone-slate roof, 'like the shell of a tortoise' and four dormer windows 'from which it will be possible to enjoy the landscape of the South-West in any weather and ensure complete seclusion in an upper chamber, approached by a staircase winding in a spiral up the interior walls of the old building'.[36] At Pertwood Farm a new cowshed was constructed (designed by George and Mallett), large enough to hold thirty-six cows; George also started a stud for hunters. At the village of Milton, George and his agent studied every cottage and tree: their conclusions were wide-ranging and long-term, as George explained to his mother:

> I will *not* spoil that village. But I will – without spoiling it – rebuild every house, that gets no sun, on the opposite slope. That is to say I am making a plan which can be followed – if Percy cares to follow – in 10 or 20 or 30 years, as money may, or may *not*, be available.
> My plan is to fulfil three objects.
> (1) The people must have good houses.
> (2) Their houses must be the sort of houses which my neighbours can build.
> (3) Milton, in 30 years' time, must be a Wiltshire village, built of stone and chalk; and more beautiful than it is now, because its owner will have cared to think of every home, and family, and of 'old England' made new as it was in the days of 'John Ball'.
> The real distinction is not between old things and new things but between good things and bad things.

Do not, for one moment, suppose that I am careless about money. I realise that I *must* do my part, in my generation. I cannot have a stink in Milton if £150 will get rid of the stink. And the stink is there: and it must go.[37]

Building work began in Milton in 1912. George and Mallett drew up plans for the first terrace of three cottages, now numbered 51, 52 and 53. They were built of traditional cob, a mixture of clay (marl or chalk), gravel and straw, which had the advantage of keeping the interior warm in winter, cool in summer. Each cottage had three rooms upstairs, a large living room, pantry and sink room downstairs. The gardens were substantial, containing a piggery and outside lavatory. Mrs Brown, widow of the Clouds gardener Harry Brown, occupied no.53 with her daughter Fanny; the blacksmith lived in no.51 with his smithy immediately across the lane.

George combined his pleasure in sport with playing the part of squire. Five intensive days' fox hunting immediately before Christmas 1911 gave him detailed knowledge of the land surrounding Clouds, an area 30 by 20 miles, as well as introductions to his neighbours who were rich enough to hunt. Hare coursing was an even more effective method of meeting the local farmers, and also provided George with an opportunity to introduce some literary references in a letter to Hilaire Belloc:

Now, to-day, just because my boy Percy and I asked forty Farmers to course hares here twice, farmer after farmer found me out and begged me to ride over their land. The coursing of Hares – stigmatized by the Pundit of Fox-hunting as 'mad for a minute and melancholy for an hour' – is the oldest sport. And now that – Alas! – fewer farmers can afford to hunt the Fox – it is what they love. They breed the greyhounds and have, as a rule, only two outlets for their skill and keenness. They read the halfpenny Press about the Waterloo Cup and have one rotten, betting-bedevilled-meeting. But when you welcome them all on to the land and have a lunch of sandwiches in a barn and a bottle or so of vintage port, why then you feel that in the South Country we have not been Jew-ed out [George the imperialist was not averse to making anti-Semitic remarks] of the England of Shakespeare and Chaucer (before him) and Michael Drayton who in Poly-Olbion has a great passage about coursing hares.[38]

George had not inherited his father's hot temper; his relations with his staff, employees and neighbours appear to have been genuinely warm. One Saturday he was surprised to discover Mallett working on the panelling in the chapel. On being told all his employees worked a six-day week he granted everyone on the estate ten days' paid holiday a year.[39]

Confidence in his son and heir added to George's sense of personal fulfilment. In 1911 Perf was made aide-de-camp to General Rawlinson commanding the 3rd Division Salisbury Plain. He was based at Cholderton near Salisbury, close enough for his father to visit without interrupting his duties as a local landowner. He described one such occasion in September 1912 to his cousin, Wilfrid Blunt:

We have looked at what should have been the harvest; wondered if enough partridges have survived the deluge, sold 550 sheep at Wilton for just over 40/- apiece, exhibited 2 hunters at the Shaftesbury Show, and ridden over the plain 4 days to observe the final training and inspection of what I call 'Percy's Division,' because he is ADC to the General.

He added, 'manoeuvres these days are realistic'.[40] It was just two years before the outbreak of the First World War.

On Christmas Eve 1912 George wrote to his mother with news of the library, nearly finished, and the chapel. He had bought crimson material covered in doves and flames for Sibell to put behind the altar. He had been thinking of his father and his son:

> I . . . feel that he [Papa] is pleased with Perkins [Perf] & knows that all the farmers & everyone love him. I went round the Park with Miles & Perkins yesterday looking at each tree & setting where to put some limes that have grown too big for the nursery garden.[41]

George was consciously involving Perf in the estate he would one day inherit – something his own father had failed to do.

In February 1913 George was startled to receive a letter from his son explaining that he had fallen in love with Diana Lister, daughter of Lord Ribblesdale, and hoped to get married as soon as possible. Perf was twenty-five years old, Diana twenty. Perf confessed to his father that he had been a 'Blighter', but now 'I *know* I am doing right'. He was probably referring to his affair with his cousin Leila Milbanke, eleven years his senior and the wife of Sir John Peniston Milbanke. Leila had stayed at Clouds the previous summer.[42]

Perf saw Diana for the first time out hunting near Melton Mowbray on 24 January. Less than three weeks later he had proposed and been accepted. George and Sibell knew Diana's parents – her mother Charlotte, daughter of Sir Charles Tennant, had died in 1911 – but not Diana. George was relieved to discover she was an accomplished horsewoman, and 'I told him [Perf] *not* to marry an American, or a Jewess, or an heiress, but just an English young lady. So he has conformed.' He hoped Diana would support Perf's army career and become attached to Clouds.

George felt he had been denied the opportunity to 'take root' at Clouds. He had married Sibell less than two years after his parents moved into the completed house, then he was living at Saighton, in Ireland or London; only a guest at Clouds. He wrote to Perf,

> if you and she can, of your own free will, get to know this place, and help this little bit of England for which we are responsible, and '*belong*' here – then you will crown my life and I shall sing '*Nunc dimittis*' – 'my task is done'.[43]

The little that has survived concerning Perf's character suggests that he would not disappoint his father. On his engagement to Diana he wrote to Madeline, his grandmother, describing his fiancée as 'a Queen among women'. He also recalled seeing his grandfather at Clouds, shortly before his death:

> I am so glad I got to Clouds & saw darling Grandpapa, & saw what a great fight he made and how splendid and dear he was. It made me so proud, to think I had some of his blood in me, & I was proud to have yours too darling. I hope to Goodness it comes out in me!

The staff at Clouds House were delighted with the engagement. William Icke, the butler, and William Mallett both made speeches; Bertha Devon the housemaid burst into tears; the agent 'suggested that we had better postpone rebuilding the village

[Milton]'.[44] Mrs Simnet, the housekeeper, was especially thrilled: unlike her employees she had seen a photograph of Diana, supplied by a maid of Mary Elcho's.

Though George stated that he was relieved Diana was not an heiress, he had to make arrangements for the couple's marriage settlement. Before the announcement of Perf's engagement, he had been concerned that after his own death the death duties demanded from his estate would cripple Perf. He had redistributed his capital, converting investments into an insurance policy, as he explained to his mother:

> I liked your little hint about Death Duties and Insurance. But I have done it already. Papa used to say – and I quite agreed *then* – that people with an income from investments ought to save and not insure. Now all is changed owing to the heavy death duties. If I died before I can save, Percy could not live at Clouds, so I have insured my life and my saving must consist in paying the premiums. With that Perf could find the rest without having to let the place.[45]

With the 'stiff proposition' of 'launching Percy into matrimony with a young lady who requires 4 hunters', he again reviewed his property and found some 'dead wood': Terwick Mill in Sussex; head-rents in Yorkshire; 'a property nobody knows anything about in Australia'. By selling off these 'eccentricities; he was confident he could pay off Perf's debts (probably army expenses; there is no reference to Perf being a gambler), and give Diana a necklace, 'without endangering the property'. From Perf's own will it would appear Diana was provided with an income of £1,000 a year, collected from the Clouds rents; Perf presumably received the same amount.

Perf and Diana were married on 17 April 1913. George's sister Mary Elcho recalled

102   Perf Wyndham and Diana Lister, *c*.1913.

the scene in her memoirs: 'The sun shone and the sevenfold Amen was lovely. I never saw anything more radiant than George's happy face that day.' She hoped the presence of the young couple at Clouds would bring new life and happiness back to the house. 'You know how *awful* it is at Clouds now,' she wrote to Balfour,

> haunted as it is by vivid memories, presences you may almost say, of Papa and Mama, myself! you! my children, Madeline, Pamela, Guy and *all*. George feels it a bare and empty nest (with echoing rafters) for 2 old birds, and it is sad to see Mamma and Sibell sitting side by side with angel hearts but neither of them doing a single thing to make things go – or to make a warm and living centre. . . . Let the young people in I say and give them their heads, make them responsible while they are young, think how happy George will be in his library in the roof (riding when he likes) and Sibell in her chapel in the cellar![46]

George was fondly criticised by some of his friends for converting nurseries at Clouds into a library, but he regarded his action as a 'successful challenge to Fortune'. He would keep the library, 'but I hope that all the rest of the house will resound with children. I hope too that they will always play in the library when I am pretending to work. It is a long room well suited to Red Indians, or imitations of a railway train.'[47]

After the wedding, George took part in strenuous manoeuvres with the Cheshire Yeomanry – he was their commander – in Wales: 'it rained in deluges and the winds roared. We were exposed to the elements; drowned out; obliged to change horse-lines and shift tents.'[48] This was followed by a weekend party at Clouds. The guests included his sister Mary and Balfour, L.P. Jacks, lecturer in philosophy at Manchester College, Oxford, and Hugh Cecil, son of Lord Salisbury. George took his guests up to Windmill Hill for views of the surrounding countryside. Mary recalled: 'he told us of his many plans for the future – all that he meant to do for his tenants and for the advancement of agriculture in general: wonderful schemes sketched out with his peculiar gift of vivid speech and imagination'.[49] He had been invited to Paris for a few days by his stepson Bendor but delayed travelling until after the weekend.

In Paris, George indulged in book-hunting on the Quais, riding through the Forest of Fontainebleau, dining 'under a sapphire sky by an old willow tree, a fountain and a nymph in bronze' in the Champs-Elysées. His companions were Bendor, Gay, Countess of Plymouth and her daughter Phyllis Windsor-Clive. George had fallen in love with Gay only a few years after his marriage to Sibell. He confessed to Wilfrid Blunt: 'as a rule people do not know how to love; as an exception they love now here, now there, as a rarity almighty lovers find each other after both are married'.[50] Apparently Sibell, all-forgiving, did not falter in her affection for Gay and the relationship between George and Gay continued without scandal until his death. From Paris in 1913, George wrote to Sibell of receiving her 'dear letter . . . quite entering into the spirit of my "outing"'. In other correspondence he called her a 'saint'.[51]

George's last few days have been described by his brother Guy and Jack Mackail in their edition of his letters; Gay also sent an account to George's mother. Different versions continue to circulate within and outside the family; Wilfrid Blunt was convinced at the time that energetic love-making was the true cause of death.[52] More than one member of the family affirms that George did not die in the arms of Gay, but in a Paris brothel, a fact which led to much diplomatic covering up. The official version describes how, on Friday 6 June, George was unusually tired and complained of a pain in his chest. On Saturday he felt recovered and made arrangements, as planned, to return to England the following day. He was selling some of his hunters at Tattersall's on Monday, and meant to attend the second reading of the Government of Ireland Bill in the Commons.

The chest pains returned on Sunday morning, and a doctor advised he postpone his journey and rest. By the evening George was still in pain and a nurse gave a slight inject-ion of morphia. Gay had spent all day with him but returned to her own hotel (Blunt discovered their hotels were literally back to back, part of the same block and intercon-nected). Between nine and ten in the evening George died, the cause of death the passage of a clot of blood through his heart. He would have been fifty years old on 29 August.

Asquith, as Prime Minister, gave the first public tribute in the Commons on the Monday, before moving the second reading of the Government of Ireland Bill. Balfour then rose to express his grief:

> Naturally and inevitably I feel the tragedy more personally and more acutely than he [Asquith] or perhaps any other man in this House can be expected to feel it. I perhaps from my longer and more intimate knowledge of My Wyndham feel myself justified in speaking with greater confidence than any other man in this House as to the width of his accomplishments, as to the great literary and imaginative powers which never received, I think, their full expansion and their full meed of praise, and perhaps their full theatre in which to show themselves.[53]

Max Egremont provides an analysis of George Wyndham's temperament: 'acute sensitivity and an unbalanced reaction to life's circumstances – inclined one moment to euphoria, the next to depression'.[54] This explained George's failure to build on his early political career, full of 'glitter and promise'; his middle age was characterised by 'grey introspective communings of melancholia and despair'. T.S. Eliot analysed George's contribution to literature and concluded that

> We can criticize his writings only as the expression of this peculiar English type, the aristocrat, the Imperialist, the Romantic, riding to hounds across his prose, looking with wonder upon the world as upon a fairyland.[55]

Beb Asquith, who married George's niece Cynthia Charteris, knew him well and recalled how unlike a professional politician he seemed, in both appearance and outlook on life. He could not specialise: 'the artist in him was in frequent revolt against the routine of the statesman'. Chivalrous and generous, he seemed 'to have leapt suddenly, armed with sword and pen, out of the mists of the Middle Ages'.[56]

He doted on his mother and shared her confidence in a spiritual life after death: 'we are immortal, and can still live and help each other without bodies or presence in the flesh'. In all his plans for the future of Clouds he was trying to deepen her structural imprint, 'so that nobody can alter it'.[57] Compared to his father, his achievements were considerable, as soldier, politician and author. Though born into a powerful and self-confident class, 'free of doubt or pressure', he 'set out not to rest in the ease which this power and confidence could provide'.[58] In the few years that he lived at Clouds he put forward more plans for the improvement of the estate and of the conditions of its tenants than Percy in the previous quarter of a century.

His funeral took place on Friday 13 June, a close heavy day, though the sun shone over the simple internment. Perf had travelled to Paris to supervise the return of the body and wrote to Sibell from the Hotel Lotti:

It is an unfathomable callamity [*sic*] – But callamities must be borne and endured – and we must bear this – God help us – The majesty of death is so wonderful, when one is with him one cannot cry or moan he looks too much a conqueror. His soul must be right high in the Heavens now and his beautiful Body just looking as if he had won.

Guy commented: 'perhaps in his case there was more than usual occasion for thankfulness to be mingled with grief and regret. . . . He did not survive to be a childless father. He died happy. His life was complete.'[59]

3

George Wyndham left £5,000 to his brother Guy, and to Sibell he left any of his personal effects – jewellery, pictures, books – she chose to select. He left the rest of his personal and real estate to Perf. The estate was valued for probate at £205,584; death duties were £24,500. Perf also inherited most of the death duties still due from his grandfather's estate, probably around £20,000. However, according to Wilfrid Blunt, George had insured his life for £30,000, 'so the estate will not be crippled with death duties'.[60]

George had been responsible for Clouds for just over two years. Perf and Diana moved into the house in the autumn of 1913 and immediately began to plan changes they would make, though always keeping Madeline fully briefed. The young couple were interested in improving the gardens, which had been neglected by 'dear old Lampard' (who had been promoted head gardener on the death of Harry Brown). They commissioned Mr England to restore order and Perf reassured Madeline, 'he understands the whole spirit of the place so well, & is such a worker. And he gets such work out of others, & he gets it the right way, by *doing* a super human amount *himself*.'

In October 1913 Detmar Blow was invited to design a new garden between the stables and the chalk-walled garden of the head gardener's cottage, 'an idea which darling Pups [George] formulated & talked of a lot to me, & he was going to do it'. It was to be 'all ponds & rivers & bridges'. Madeline sent Perf the names of suitable plants already growing at Clouds and he replied: 'England says they want to have their feet near water & their heads out, so we will have them adjacent to one of the ponds or rivers. At present of course it looks rather chaotic, but it will soon take shape.'

On his return from Paris, George had intended sitting to Harold Speed. The commission was confirmed by Perf but as a memorial: the portrait was to be placed in Maison Dieu Hall, Dover, in honour of the town's long-serving Member of Parliament. Perf supplied the artist with his father's St Patrick's robes and court dress, worn by George at the coronation of George V; Madeline gave Speed a number of photographs of her son in various poses. The family kept a sketch, 80″ × 60″, which Perf hung in the drawing room at Clouds. When Dick Wyndham sold the contents of the house in 1933, the sketch was included among the family items acquired by Mary Elcho: it now hangs at Stanway House.

Another memorial to George was a stained-glass window, designed by J.N. Comper for St Mary's, East Knoyle. Balfour wrote the wording: 'In affectionate memory of George Wyndham, Statesman, Orator, Man of Letters, Soldier; this window is dedicated by friends in both Houses of Parliament.'

103 George Wyndham by Harold Speed.
Included in the sale of the contents of
Clouds, 1933; now at Stanway House.

George had time to agree to Alexander Fisher's design for a cross on his father's
grave at East Knoyle, also to begin constructing the central cross 'with green sandstone
about it' designed by his mother. The general design of the plot had originally been
Blow's but as usual George and Mallett overruled the architect. Perf chose the wording
for both Percy and George's individual memorial stones, set in the wall surrounding
the Wyndham plot. He remembered to send flowers to elderly relatives, 'as in former
years', and at Christmas 1913 he laid on the special teas, as usual, for the tenants and
schoolchildren. Diana described the scene to Madeline: 'I think they enjoyed
themselves, and it was a joy for Perks and me to get to know them all'. Perf felt his
father was watching over them and confessed to his grandmother 'I love keeping up all
these sorts of things'.

On the day England declared war on Germany, 4 August 1914, an expeditionary force of
six infantry divisions and a cavalry division were already beginning to mobilise. Perf's
Aunt Mary, in London to see her daughter Cynthia and new grandson, heard up-to-
date news of the war from Balfour. On her way back to Stanway she met Sibell
Grosvenor at Paddington station. Sibell was ashen-faced; all she could say was, 'Percy
[Perf] is getting ready.' As a professional soldier in the Coldstream Guards he was one
of the first to be sent to France to join in efforts to stop the German advance.[61]
Perf wrote to his grandmother from Grosvenor House on 5 August. The letter is
similar to many written in the early months of the war by officers ignorant of the
western front:

Well it has come, and I feel good in the end will come of it . . . the words 'German Empire' must be *for ever* wiped off the map of Europe. It has been a menace to peace, the haunting fear of all Wives & Mothers. All is going well here, & the spirit of the people is the right spirit. Quiet confidence. All our arrangements so far are working with the utmost smoothness. It is our custom however to make several bloomers before we really get going, so I suppose they will come, but we will recover, & carry this through to the *very end. Final.* No Germany. Blast them.

He wrote again to Madeline on 27 August from France, still confident even though the deaths were mounting among his fellow officers: 'Poor little Archer Windsor Clive was very badly wounded & I am afraid since dead. . . . Poor little Hawarden I am afraid is dead too. . . . But we absolutely slaughtered the Germans, so thats all right.'

On 14 September Perf was killed at Soissons, during the battle of the Aisne. He was twenty-six years old. His cousin Bim Tennant wrote a poem in his memory – before he too was killed during the Battle of the Somme and buried close by Raymond Asquith:

Father and son have not been long asunder,
And joy in heaven leaves mortals sad and wan,
His death salute was the artillery thunder,
Praise be to God for such an Englishman.

Letters exchanged by the family constantly refer to the double loss, of Perf and his father George, within two years. Sibell grieved at Saighton, supported by her ardent Christian beliefs mixed up with images from the *Morte D'Arthur*:

We give George back his very 'Heart's delight' – our beautiful Percy . . . Percy's last letter was so happy, rested after the Mons awful conflicts saying he was in a 'heavenly land' 'very fit & well' – & truly it is into *the* heavenly land he must now have entered – a shining Knight.

But she felt unable to visit Clouds: 'it would break my *heart* . . . I think of *Clouds* & all my little short heaven there'.

Madeline Adeane was amazed by her mother's strength and wrote to Mary: 'she goes out & is quite natural & unstrained she feels he [Perf] is with George & so many – Papa – George – Percy – her *three* . . . have sped their way to the other side'. Madeline, like her sister-in-law Sibell, found comfort in the familiar images, in being reassured that Perf's death was somehow 'glorious'.

Darling Percy was shot *dead* through the head as he was leading his men (how *glorious* the death is) out of a wood – *no* suffering no *knowing* he must die . . . Perfoo – gay debonair Fortune's Darling is *dead* – he only had one sorrow – that was his Father's Death.

Diana immediately immersed herself in war work, and in October she was in France nursing. She had been married to Perf for only seventeen months. Guy Wyndham's wife Minnie wrote to Mary Wemyss: 'Sib and your Mother feel that darling George has got his beloved son with him but this can not comfort Diana'. She added, not yet knowing the contents of Perf's will, 'Oh if *only* she had got a child God help us all.'

9 The Impact of the First World War on Clouds: Dick Wyndham Inherits, 1914–20

Perf Wyndham had made his will on 29 October 1913 in the Cavendish Hotel. It was an unusual document. The bequests to Diana were straightforward enough: £5,000 cash, the annuity of £1,000 agreed in their marriage settlement (to be charged upon the East Knoyle estate) and a further annuity of £1,000 if no son survived him. Perf's jewellery, trinkets and other personal effects were to be divided, however, between Diana and another woman, Amelia, Lady Milbanke, known to Perf as Leila. Leila also received the sum of £10,000. When *The Times* reported the contents of Perf's will in 25 November 1914 the bequest to Leila was omitted: Perf's generosity towards his mistress remained private to his family. The surviving letters that passed between members of Perf's family after the will was read do not refer to Leila. His will contained even more of a surprise.

Perf left his entire property, apart from the bequests to Diana and Leila, to his trustees, George Henry Drummond (his best man) and Edward Scawen Wyndham (first cousin and son of Henry and Constance Leconfield), in trust for any son of his 'who shall first attain the age of twenty one years'. If he should have no such son, which he did not, then everything was to pass in trust to his cousin Dick, the younger son of Guy and Minnie Wyndham. All his 'plate furniture pictures books prints china glass and other effects' in Clouds, all the 'live and dead stock implements of husbandry and agricultural effects' were in trust for his cousin 'absolutely'. His real estate in England went in trust to Dick and all the residue of his real and personal estate was to be converted by his trustees into money and invested in trust for Dick. The East Knoyle estate was left to the trustees in trust, 'to the use of my cousin the said Guy Richard Charles Wyndham during his life with remainder to the use of his first and other sons successively according to seniority in tail male'.

Perf made his will shortly after the death of his father. His grandfather had died only two years before. Undoubtedly Perf's intention was to ensure that a young male Wyndham line would inherit Clouds if he should die before having a son. Madeline realised this: the will was made 'on a *miscalculation* common to youth, of building on, & arranging for the Future on the foundation of *Time & Life*'. He chose his favourite cousin Dick, nine years his junior, as heir. If Dick produced sons the Wyndhams might still carry on Percy and Madeline's line at Clouds. Percy and Madeline's daughters, however, were horrified.

Madeline Adeane immediately wrote to her sister Mary.

I could not *believe* it and it has just put the last crushing sadness on the death of Darling Papa & the untimely deaths of Darling George & Percy – and of course it is a mistake & absolutely contrary to the spirit of Papa's & George's Wills & in direct opposition to their wishes – failing George & Percy we know Papa would have wished *Guy* & then his Boys.

Madeline could see that Perf was assuming that his Uncle Guy, if made the heir, would inherit as a middle-aged or perhaps an elderly man. He might occupy Clouds for only a few years and his death would leave his heirs (his sons George and Dick) with further intolerable death duties. But why did Perf leave everything to Guy's younger son, 'Dirty Dick', cutting Dick's brother, 'Grubby George', out completely? She continued:

> He just happened to prefer Dick of the cousins & feeling certain no doubt he would have children & that this Will would never act he just left out of account the elder generation *Guy* & chose the cousin he preferred out of his own generation in the event of he Percy having no children.

Guy was neither executor nor trustee. But as 'Head of the Family' Madeline Adeane felt he was the rightful heir. He would have inherited Clouds if Perf had made no will or simply been less specific. Perf no doubt considered all this on the outbreak of war. But he did not change his will: Dick was indeed preferred over Uncle Guy.

However much Madeline protested, it seems Guy really didn't want Clouds. Certainly his son Francis (by his second marriage to Violet Leverson) is convinced Guy had no such ambitions. His sisters were constantly championing his cause, trying to exert influence to further his military career. Now they felt Guy's 'proper place' was at Clouds, but as he explained in a letter to Mary:

> I really do not mind a bit about myself. . . . Of course I would have been very unhappy if Perf had done it for any feeling about me. Since darling George's death the love that Perf has shown me has been wonderful. It was quite surprising in its perfect consideration knowing this it does not matter a pin what outsiders may say or think. Any other difficulties of the situation that might upset other families will not upset *ours*.

Guy was perceptive. His sister were undoubtedly more concerned about what others would think, in particular that their brother had been cut out in favour of his younger son, a boy of eighteen. Minnie had to explain the news to her eldest son:

> I told him last night – he has taken it as I knew he would but of course is very much surprised as he thought Percy was very fond of him but I think I quite showed him that it was *absolutely* a thoughtless mistake & that Percy never thought it [would] come into force but I quite realize the difficulty of making everyone else think the same.

Dick received the news from his parents and was deeply shocked. Perf's unsettled property had a gross value of £179,003. Perf might have made his will with the best intentions for the future of Clouds but he had failed to share his plans with the possible heir. Dick wondered whether he could share the inheritance with his brother, but this would only be possible if his father had been given Clouds for life. And Dick could not do this until he was twenty-one. There were other difficulties with the succession. Dick's life had now taken on extra value but the trustees had no power to insure his life; yet he was about to go to the western front to take his chance with the other young officers, who included his brother George, most of his male cousins and the trustees of the Wyndham estate.

The death duties due to be paid by the trustees were particularly onerous because Dick was not a direct descendant. Madeline Adeane's husband Charles led a campaign in the press and in Parliament for landowners and their heirs serving in the forces to be exempt from death duties. A special Death Duties (Killed in War) Act was passed at the end of 1914, reducing and postponing duties on estates which passed to wives or lineal descendants. This did not protect Clouds, and writing in the *Field*, Adeane used the estate as an example to plead for exemption from death duties for anyone killed in the service of their country:

> . . . a well-known estate in the South of England, long enjoyed by a public-spirited gentleman who died only three or four years ago [Percy]. It passed to his son [George], one of the most brilliant and best-loved Cabinet Ministers of his day. He in turn died suddenly a year before the war, and was succeeded by his son [Perf], a gallant young soldier who has since been killed in France, leaving only a collateral to bear the unreduced charges on an estate already crippled.[1]

There were £24,500 of duties still to be paid on George's estate and some £20,000 on Percy's. Guy was optimistic, however, about Dick being able to look after his inheritance: 'I of course would be very unhappy if Dick were to make a mess of things but he is a dear boy and he *wont*'. If, of course, he survived the war.

Dick, the subject of so much concern and correspondence, had rather more immediate things on his mind at the end of 1914 than Clouds. He was commissioned 2nd Lieutenant in the King's Royal Rifle Corps (KRRC) on 23 December 1914. In April the following year he was posted to the 3rd Battalion, just in time for the second Battle of Ypres. The 3rd and 4th Battalions, KRRC, had been in India when war broke out. After a brief spell in England, on 6 January 1915 the 3rd Battalion took over the French line of trenches in the Ypres area. Trenches suggests some sort of order and security but these were waterlogged ditches criss-crossing a wasteland of mud in which soldiers were frequently lost and drowned. When Dick joined the battalion in April they were in reserve near Poperinghe, but on 20 April he and the battalion went back into the mud and blood of the Ypres Salient.[2]

For years afterwards Dick was haunted by the experiences of the following three weeks. Day after day the battalion was subjected to bombardment as their trenches disintegrated around them. Casualties were heavy and on 10 May Dick was promoted temporary Lieutenant. A few days later he was wounded at the dam of Bellewaarde Lake. He described the incident to his family in a characteristically light-hearted letter written from the hospital in Boulogne:

> When first the eight-inch shell came over I was talking to my men. Without *any* exaggeration it landed within two feet of me. I heard it coming along, but thought it would go over like the others. But the whistling grew into a screech, I felt it was coming 'bang' on top of me. I bent down. There was a deafening explosion, a large blaze of fire, and I picked myself up about six yards away. Nearly every man in the group I had been talking to had been hit. You will never guess where I was hit a few minutes later. It was on the tip of my nose, but it barely cut the skin and made everyone roar with laughter. I was just having my after-lunch Benson and Hedges cigarette, when they attacked again. This time it was more serious. They had broken

through somewhere and we were in imminent danger of being cut off. We fell in hurriedly and received our instructions as to what manner we should retreat in if it was necessary. A Scotch regiment was advancing in open order across a field to support us. They were under heavy fire. It was a magnificent sight. Then we were told to line the top of the dam and open rapid fire. I had just got up there when I was hit. The next thing I remember was the Adjutant telling me it was no use me trying to stop, I should only get taken prisoner, and that I'd better take my servant and try and make my way back towards Ypres. Luckily my skull proved too hard a nut to crack, so the bullet only cut the scalp and knocked me out. My asphyxiating gas-pad and my hat also protected me, for the bullet came through both.[3]

His family found the letter 'thrilling' but the account hid the pain and fear which remained with Dick all his life. In 1925 he deliberately returned to the Ypres Salient to try to get rid of the constant nightmares.

> I argued that if I drove down the Menin Road in a Rolls Royce, and smoked a cigarette on the dam of Belvarde [sic] Lake, in the evening sun, with cattle munching the long grass and the sound of a reaper mowing, then how could I continue to dream of it as mud and stench?[4]

But in 1935, twenty years after the battle, Dick was still haunted by the noise and the suffering. On a visit to the Dinka country of Southern Sudan he found it impossible to sleep wherever he heard the ripe fruit falling from the Dom palms:

104 *The Menin Road* by Percy Wyndham Lewis, acquired by Dick Wyndham in 1927 from John Quin. Purchased from the Redfern Galleries (Smith Bequest), 1952, by Southampton City Arts.

They would first strike the metallic leaves with a clang, then the ground with a heavy thud. The interval was the same as between a high-velocity gun and its bursting shell. When at last I fell asleep, I dreamed of the war. . . . The battalion is waiting beside a long road; we have been called back into the line. It is not yet light and the battle for the moment is silent. I pray that it is over. Everything is completely silent. Then the first breeze of dawn sighs in the grass and moves the naked poplars that line the road. It is bitterly cold. . . . *Fall in!* We trudge slowly along the long road. I am waiting for the scream. It comes from the head of the column: 'Oh, God, my face, my face!' – and I try to close my ears to the indignity of unbearable pain. We trudge on, left-right-left-left-left-nearer and nearer to the voice. The horror of this dream is the knowledge that soon I shall have to *see*. For the voice that is screaming is my own.[5]

On 18 November 1915, fully recovered from his wounds, Dick embarked with the 3rd Battalion at Marseilles: their destination Salonika. There would be no further major battle for the battalion. Until November 1917 they kept to a line along the River Struma, facing Bulgar troops and later the Turks across a no man's land which was two and a half miles deep. The country was rich in ancient history and classical myth: between the armies lay the ruins of the ancient city of Amphipolis; behind the enemy rose a mountain of over 6,000 feet, called Pangaion by the Greeks and Pilau Tepe by the Turks. It was the home of Orpheus. While digging trenches Dick discovered an

105   Dick Wyndham in Salonika, 1917.

ancient Graeco-Roman gold signet ring, set with a cornelian, which he kept as a memento.[6]

There was little fighting, only occasional skirmishes out on patrol. The real killer was malaria, later Spanish flu, so that by the end of the war the battalion was reduced to a fighting strength of 130 rank and file. Later their Lieutenant-Colonel, W.J. Long, explained the difference between the western front and the war in Macedonia:

> In France trench conditions are in most places far more strenuous: a Battalion may perhaps be in the trenches only a forty-eight hours' tour, and in that time may have had fighting and many casualties, and yet once out they get a rest, and perhaps many of them get leave, and all get letters from home. Out in Macedonia leave for men and for regimental officers is very rare, owing to scarcity of ships and to the distance. We have longer tours in the trenches, and less to look forward to after, and our mails are slow and somewhat erratic. Also, though we have fewer casualties from shells and bullets than our comrades in France, we get many casualties from malarial fever. . . . Probably few, if any, soldiers in the ranks would choose to stop in the Salonika Army if they were offered the choice of transferring to a Battalion of the Regiment in France.[7]

Dick was experiencing both, and his actions out in Salonika earned him the Military Cross. He had been made full Lieutenant in June 1916, then he was promoted to Acting Captain in October and Acting Adjutant in November. The chance for him to show his bravery – or foolhardiness – came on 28 May 1917. A platoon of A Company, including Captain Thurburn, had gone out to reconnoitre Amphipolis plateau. Unfortunately the enemy had occupied a bank about half a mile in front of the British outposts, and shots were exchanged. Captain Thurburn, who had apparently gone out entirely on his own initiative, was shot and fell in the long grass. Dick went out to look for him. It was difficult to locate Thurburn in the rough terrain and Dick had to struggle within 80 yards of the crest which the enemy were still holding. However, he found Thurburn and brought him in. The unfortunate captain died later that night, but Dick was awarded the MC.

Shortly after, the battalion took up their final position on the north-west side of Lake Tahinos. Dick was fortunate to get a spell of leave early in 1918 and visited Clouds in March. In September 1918 the Bulgarians began to retreat. By then the 3rd Battalion was so depleted that they could only support the Allies by consolidating new lines of communication. They sailed for Constantinople on 2 March 1919, and arrived in Aldershot on 6 June.

2

Dick returned to a house in mourning. His grandmother, Madeline, nearly eight-five years old, was desperately trying to make sense of the sacrifices made by her family. The deaths of her husband, and almost immediately after that her eldest son George, had been painful enough. But since the beginning of the war George's only son Perf had been killed, also Guy's eldest son George, two of Mary's three sons, Ego and Yvo Charteris, and Pamela's eldest son Edward 'Bim' Tennant. Mary was staying at Clouds

106 (left) Guy and Minnie's eldest son George Hereman Wyndham, killed 1915.

107 (right) Mary and Hugo's eldest son Ego Charteris, killed 1916. In a scrapbook belonging to Madeline Wyndham devoted to World War One memorabilia.

in July 1916 when the death of her eldest son was finally confirmed after months of uncertainty. Bim was killed in September. One of the last letters Pamela received from him described a lengthy conversation with a corporal in his battalion:

I had occasion to walk a few hundred yards with Corporal Jukes, one day, and he told me that his father was keeper at Clouds, and he remembered your wedding and has a photy of it at home. He knows Willson as 'Ernie' and remembers when Icke was footman! he is *such* a charming man. What is more, he has a sister, Polly Jukes (such a nice name), who was housemaid to Glen – Grandpapa at Glen.[8]

Madeline's closest friends also suffered terrible losses: the Horners had only just recovered from the news that Mells Park House had burnt down (they had continued to live in the manor house for economic reasons) when they heard that their only surviving son Edward had been killed; the Asquith's eldest son Raymond, married to Katharine Horner, was killed at the Battle of the Somme; the Desboroughs' sons Julian and Billy Grenfell and Lord Ribblesdale's only surviving son Charles Lister were all killed.

Madeline copied into her bible a poem by J. Taylor called 'Job':

No loss of sons and daughters, goods and all
Can make this man with impatience fall
Assailing Satan, tempting wife, false friends,
With perfect patience he all woes defends
'I' naked came (quoth he) into this world

And naked hence again I shall be hurl'd
God gives and takes, according to his word
And blessed ever be the living Lord.[9]

Madeline responded to personal pain and loss with her own private mystical language. Throughout the war she poured out her beliefs in letters sent to her grieving children, trying to give them a part of her strength. After Perf's death she wrote to Mary, somehow finding a way of merging all their losses, past and present, into one triumphant hymn:

> I feel very proud of all my children of their *Bravery* in Life. Papa was very very Brave & no one in this World bore an illness like His more *Bravely* & *you* & Madeline are wonderful & Pamela also wonderful & Brave Mothers – & George & Guy most wonderful *as men* in every way both in *politics* & *soldiering* & in all the big things & little things of Life – & what would this world be without Bravery. . . . I remember our darling *Brother Edward*. . . . Brother Guy died so far away from us all . . . darling sister Pamela . . . 3 old ones left Emily [Ellis] self & Freddy [Campbell] . . . & *now Perf* the 3rd generation – so, so, so sad before the bleeding wound of Darling George's Passing not heeded even by God's Mercy! which *I can see* now that it was mercy to George – going when he did.

She could, indeed, 'bear *all* things'. Perf's widow Diana, nursing in France, wrote to Madeline in a similar language: 'I know he's [Perf] close to us, but oh how I long to see him and hug him, and touch him, and speak to him. When will the veil lift, and I shall be allowed to see him in his radiant beauty.' Her father, Lord Ribblesdale, described his son Charles's response to the war: 'the Call had come upon him as the Holy Ghost came down upon the apostles – as a sudden great sound in the likeness of fiery tongues'.[10]

After hearing of the death of Guy's eldest son, George Hereman Wyndham, Madeline wrote again to Mary:

> I cannot in this world as it is now look upon death as a terror but as the *angel of release* from pain & wounds & Life – & *that* darling Boy was so ready to go, & *so loving*, & *simple* & trusting that I do not feel as if He could ever have had a very *happy life?* He had such *high ideas* for the *world* for Fraternity & *love* & Equality & Friendship that he would have had more pain & disappointment than *joy* in *life*.

Her duty was to pass her inner strength on to her children, particularly to Mary after the loss of two more sons in the war:

> you have *the joy* which is beyond all joys the faith & *knowledge* that you have safely *lodged* & *landed in Heaven two* of the most Beautiful, darling & loving Souls that were ever born into this world!

But Mary, writing in her diary on Armistice Day 1918, was less confident: 'this is the Greatest Victory – it is also the *saddest* peace . . . the hardest part is now beginning – we miss our shining Victors in the hour of Victory'. Her niece Helena Adeane wrote in her memoirs: 'the lamp is shattered. Dust appears everywhere. . . . There are no gentle flowers to be seen now. Only the blood-red poppies.'[11]

3

When Dick first went overseas, his parents were still living at Charford Manor, Downton, near Salisbury. Guy had rented the 36-roomed mansion house in 1911 while still based in St Petersburg as military attaché. There was a fire, however, at Charford in 1915. Guy was in the house at the time but unable to lift the fire extinguishers, they were so heavy. He and Minnie had to leave and settled at Clouds, trying to keep the house and gardens in some order ('darling Minnie,' Madeline observed, 'weeding & planting all day').

During the last years of the war Clouds was a convalescent home and its lofty proportions and fine parkland provided a therapeutic environment, helping to rebuild the lives of wounded soldiers. Dick's sister Olivia, 'Bunch', was a VAD and lent a hand with the patients; she also worked with her cousin Cynthia Asquith at the Winchcombe VAD hospital near Stanway House. Minnie's children by her first marriage made regular visits when home on leave. Their own children brought laughter and games back to Clouds. Minnie's granddaughter Letitia, the daughter of Madge Brooke and John Fowler, a small child of seven or eight, helped to steer the blinded soldiers around the gardens, pointing out the flowers Madeline had lovingly planted, but the soldiers could only appreciate their scents. She recalls that 'every nook and cranny in the house was stuffed with soldiers'.[12] Once or twice a week villagers from East Knoyle and Milton would come up to the house to help roll bandages using a special machine clamped to the kitchen table. Rationing was in force. Bertha Devon, promoted to the position of housekeeper, formidable in her starched white cap, weighed out the butter in the still room once a week. It was delivered from the Home Farm. All members of the family, the servants and the convalescent soldiers were given their correct allowance according to the government rules.

Minnie's grandson Peter Brooke found security at Clouds in the war years and immediately after. His parents were separated, Geoffrey serving overseas and his mother living in London, later France. He loved the house with its 'strange charm'; he was able to ride the pony Alice when she wasn't required as a lawnmower. Every morning Guy Wyndham was at Clouds he took prayers in the chapel, 'spooky' to the little boy. Peter's task was to find everyone's places in the prayer books. His father kept a couple of steeplechasers in the stables which were run by the stud groom Mr Wareham and his son. Mr Smith the chauffeur also looked after the electricity generator: Peter spent hours watching the machinery whirring away in the special 'electric light and battery house'.[13]

Guy commuted between Clouds and the War Office where he was employed in the recruiting drive. His more reliable war news was passed round the house and then the neighbourhood. Information also came via Madeline's daughters Mary and Pamela: Balfour and Edward Grey were members of Asquith's War Committee. A similar situation had existed during the Boer War: while Guy Wyndham was besieged in Ladysmith, his eldest brother George, as Under-Secretary of War, kept the family at Clouds reliably informed of events in South Africa.

Though there was activity in the house during the war years, the Clouds visitors' book remained empty. There were no entries between Madeline's June visit in 1915 and Dick's return on 8 June 1919. Madeline still had 44 Belgrave Square as her home, according to Percy's will. She called the house her 'tabernacle' where her children were all 'born and bred' and where George lived 'at the *last*'. When she stayed at Clouds she occupied Percy's old suite of rooms off the hall; she slept in the bed in which he died. She spent much of the war years reliving her past. To Mary she wrote: 'I dream [of] living again through those six months in the Soudan! . . . those two years of prolonged agony in the South African war – & now has come our fullest dread – European War'.

But she also travelled, to Saighton, Babraham and Stanway, where she could offer her comfort to Sibell Grosvenor, Madeline Adeane and Mary Wemyss; also to Ireland, as the guest of the Vescis, and to Sussex. At Petworth she dropped back into her early married years, when her three eldest children occupied the nurseries and were spoilt by her father-in-law, George Leconfield. She visited Newbuildings to see her old admirer Wilfrid Blunt, now being lovingly tended by her niece Dorothy Carleton.

Staying in Clouds in June 1917 she found herself sitting in the library George had created, remembering the room as the nursery, 'all this Place . . . so full of you'. She sent flowers to Mary, roses for love and columbine for peace, 'picked off darling darling little Colin's [Mary's son, who died of scarlet fever aged three] white painted crib. . . . His little darling soul & spirit was the *first* that ever flitted from the New built Clouds.' Mary herself visited Clouds in June the following year. She found the house quiet and sad, but 'not horridly haunted, only peaceful & fragrant with memories of happy days & sweet with the atmosphere of love'.

Madeline was continuing to commission work and to recommend artists to her family and friends, but even here the past was the inspiration: memorials to the dead provided reasonable livings for a large number of artists and craftsmen during the war years and immediately after. Alexander Fisher designed a triptych for her of bronze and enamelwork with the Greek inscription: 'the brave receive deathless praise'. He also designed a memorial to all the dead of the First World War from East Knoyle for the inside of St Mary's. His cross, designed for the centre of the Wyndham plot, had been consecrated by the Bishop of Salisbury on 8 May 1915. The sun shone, bluebells were in bloom on the hillside as the Wyndhams assembled to remember their dead, 'the inscriptions on slabs on the wall, alive & moving – 4 in 4 years'. At Clouds itself the Bishop consecrated the chapel which George had created for Sibell: 'when filled with pontiff, clergy and choir, [it] made a tiny medieval scene, illumined by a lovely sunset crimson glow'. There was only a skeleton staff living in the house. Guy brought some servants over from Charford, and the Wyndhams picnicked in the gardens.

Fisher was an obvious choice for Madeline's daughter Mary when it came to Stanway's village war memorial. He was commissioned in 1919, the money coming from church collections and donations by Mary, Hugo and Ego's widow Letty. He drew up a specification for the village 'shewing a group of St George & the Dragon in bronze supported on a column and base and steps in North Cotswold stone supplied from the Jackdaw Quarry on the Stanway Estate. The height of the whole monument to be 16 feet. The approximate cost to be £300 (minimum).' The final bill came to £699 10sh. Mary chose another artist, Eric Gill, to design a memorial inscription for the embrasure of the chancel window in Stanway's parish church, again for the men of Stanway who did not return from the war. Gill also did the lettering on Fisher's memorial.

At Saighton, Sibell Grosvenor presented a shrine to the village in memory of Perf and the other young men killed: the Dean of Chester led the service of dedication. Babraham's war memorial was unveiled in November 1921 by a cousin of the Adeanes. The inscription read: 'Live thou for England; we for England died.' Madeline and Charles's son-in-law Edward Kay Shuttleworth was one of the names honoured on the memorial; he had married Sibell in December 1914. Another son-in-law Denis Wigan, home on leave, was crippled for life in a motorcycle accident. Charles Adeane unveiled the war memorial at nearby Trumpington; the lettering was by Eric Gill.

At Mells, the Horners commissioned Alfred Munnings to sculpt their son Edward on horseback, the massive bronze to be placed in the Horner chapel of St Mary's on a plinth designed by Lutyens. The architect also designed the war memorial for the village after spending a weekend at Mells looking for the perfect site: 'my weekend was as a spring day, fun and tears. All their young men are killed.'[14]

4

Dick returned to take up his inheritance, still a young man in years (he was twenty-three on 29 August 1919), but carrying the memories of over four years of war. He was immediately faced with formidable financial difficulties. Death duties had accumulated in quick succession, on the deaths of his grandfather, uncle and cousin. Far worse than the death duties were the annuities arising from those deaths, and chargeable to the Wyndham estate. Dick's grandmother had to be paid an annuity of £3,100 which, with the income from her marriage settlement, gave her a total income of £4,000. Dick's father received an annuity of £850 during Madeline's lifetime; Perf's widow Diana

108   Clouds House, *c.*1920; Milton village to the north.

received an annuity of £1,000 from her marriage settlement, plus a further annuity of £1,000.

The Clouds estate which Percy had bought in 1876 then brought in a rent of around £4,624 per annum with land tax and other outgoings amounting to only £165. Since then rents had fallen slightly and outgoings had risen. Before 1914 the average estate might be paying 9 per cent of its gross rents in income tax, land tax and rates; in 1919 it would be paying out 30 per cent. Total estate expenditure before the war was on average 35 per cent of gross rents; after the war this rose to over 60 per cent;[15] at Clouds it had to be heavily subsidised by income from other investments, though these already been reduced in size by George.

Accounts for the Stanway estate of Mary and Hugo Wemyss for 1922 reveal a state of affairs similar to Clouds. Though the Gloucestershire estate was larger, 6,000 acres, with a gross rental income from farms, woods and game of over £7,000, expenditure amounted to just under £7,000. Property tax swallowed up £1,221; the poor and highway rates £474; the maintenance of buildings, fencing and walling and drainage £1,200; the management of the woods and game £1,556. There was little profit to be made from owning land. Stanway was subsidised with an annual payment of around £7,000 from the larger family estates in Scotland.

Dick and Guy Wyndham decided immediately to sell four of the outlying farms: Pertwood, Friars Haye, Moors and Lugmarsh, a total of 1,202 acres. The capital value of the estate was thus reduced by a quarter (at the same time reducing future death duties) and much-needed capital was released to pay death duties, to use on maintenance or perhaps to invest at a higher rate than land to provide the income for all the annuities.

The Clouds estate sales were just a tiny fraction of the avalanche of sales that took place in 1919. By the end of the year over a million acres were sold. The price of agricultural land increased dramatically during and immediately after the war. With the prospect of increased taxation (and in the Budget of 1919 death duties were raised to 40 per cent on estates valued at £2 million and over) many landowners decided to sell. By about 1921 about a quarter of England was sold. *The Times* (May 1920) caught the mood perfectly.

> England is changing hands. . . . Will a profiteer buy it? Will it be turned into a school or an institution? Has the mansion house electric light and modern drainage? . . . For the most part the sacrifices are made in silence. . . . The sons are perhaps lying in far away graves; the daughters secretly mourning some one dearer than a brother, have taken up some definite work away from home, seeking thus to still their aching hearts, and the old people, knowing there is no son or near relative left to keep up the old traditions, or so crippled by necessary taxation that they know the boy will never be able to carry on when they are gone, take the irrevocable step.

In Dick's case, no doubt with the guidance of his father and the estate manger, it made good sense. Financial worries were temporarily arrested. By the end of 1921 the boom was over; the government repealed the Corn Production Act in June 1921 and agricultural prices collapsed.

Sir John Horner delayed selling a large part of his estate at Mells in Somerset until August 1923 and suffered the consequences: his profit was sufficient to pay off his father's crippling mortgage but would have been considerably larger three or four years earlier. He also parted with the mineral rights; since then several enormous limestone

109 Alexander Fisher's memorial to Minnie Wyndham, East Knoyle.

Plate XX (facing page, above) The Dairy and Manor House Farm (the Home Farm), Milton, Wiltshire.

Plate XXI (facing page, below) Shepherd's Cottage, Milton.

deposits have been found under some of the farms which were sold. As his descendants now admit, while listening to the sound of dynamite blasting at the local quarries, ownership of those mineral rights 'could have made us very rich indeed'.[16]

Dick was still attached to the King's Royal Rifle Corps and could only stay for brief periods at Clouds. His mother suddenly contracted Spanish influenza. On 4 October 1919 Olivia, on her own at Clouds with Minnie, roared off to the doctor's on her motorbike: by the time they returned, however, her mother was dead. She was just fifty-nine years old. At her funeral boy scouts lined the path from the church to the Wyndham plot. Peter Brooke remembered one of the scouts fainting, overcome by the proceedings. Her coffin was made from oak grown on the Clouds estate, and her grave in the churchyard is covered by the finest memorial Fisher designed for the Wyndhams, a full-sized guardian angel.

Minnie Wyndham left all the pictures, china and furniture bequeathed to her by her first husband to her Brooke children and Guy spent a sad time at Clouds in November going through her belongings with Olivia for company. Particular jewellery given by Madeline and Percy to Minnie on her marriage to Guy was now passed on to Olivia. The first Christmas party at Clouds after the war was a mixture of rejoicing at the safe return of Dick, his Brooke stepbrothers and John Fowler, and sadness at the deaths of Dick's elder brother George Hereman and now Minnie. On Christmas Eve Guy wrote to his sister Mary: 'it is a glorious bright sunshiny day & we are going

out hunting – But at this time thoughts, thoughts, thoughts go round and round in one's brain.' Guy and Mary were together reading through the letters of their brother George in preparation for their publication. Mary found the ironies almost unbearable:

> after long years of exile he wanted you to start a home of yr own – & he so *wanted* you & Minnie to live at Clouds – I am so very glad from every point of view for all the days that you are able to be at Clouds but what *can* be more pathetic than his letters from the earthly point of view – 'I want no shadow cast on the autumn of Mama's life' – & Mamma has had nothing but blows!!! – 'no shadow on the spring of Percy's life; – Perf just *nipped off*! 'I want Guy & Minnie to live at Clouds' – Darling Perf himself with his unfortunate hasty blunder so complicated that – and darling Minnie has flown has left you & her earthly home!

She ended her letter to Guy, 'I hope you & Dick will still in some sort be able to take root in that part of Wiltshire [our parents] made "us" responsible for'.

Dick had been unable to help his father settle Minnie's estate. On 6 October the 3rd Battalion KRRC was sent to Mhow, near Indore. The non-regular soldiers, including Dick, were given other postings. In November he was still at Victoria Barracks, Plymouth. Then he was posted ADC to Field-Marshal Sir John French, Viceroy of Ireland, and established himself in Dublin, a city resonant with Wyndham, Fitzgerald and Campbell history. Since Lord French had been made Viceroy the political situation in Ireland had rapidly disintegrated into war between the IRA and the British. From 1919 onward, the IRA waged war against both on- and off-duty police; raids were constantly being made on country houses and some houses were burnt down. Bloody assassinations and equally savage reprisals were commonplace.[17] Dick's own relatives were affected: at Carton raiders stole the revolver belonging to the young Duke of Leinster's brother Desmond Fitzgerald, sent back from France after his death;[18] Lord Mayo's house at Palmerstown was burnt down.

There was an assassination attempt on the Viceroy in December 1919 and the Vice-Regal Lodge was on a wartime footing, 'with the ADCs in khaki and elaborate security measures'. Yet a semblance of Ascendancy social life still survived, with hunting, dinners, dances and even good-quality champagne: 'of course one must have good champagne,'[19] insisted Lord French. Unfortunately the Viceroy was better at his social duties than governing the country.

As a member of the Viceroy's personal staff Dick could enjoy to the full the parties, visits to Ascendancy houses and rural sports. Lord French had left his family in England because of the dangerous situation but had his mistress Mrs Winifred Bennett for company. Winifred's husband Andrew had pursued a diplomatic career in Bucharest, Vienna, Rome, Athens and New York and, since 1919, had been British Minister to the Republic of Panama. The Bennetts' daughter Iris was staying with her mother in Dublin. Young, unmarried, very beautiful with unusual violet eyes, she and Dick fell instantly in love.

Early in 1920 Madeline was staying with the Adeanes at Babraham. She wrote a letter to her daughter Mary: her usual reminiscing.

> I remember all all . . . & I have so much *time now to remember in!* . . . it makes me feel that *nothing is ever rubbed out or forgotten rather an awful thought* but it has its *good side* for if *nothing* is forgotten all is more or less *explained* in life.

Plate XXII (facing page, above) Nos. 51, 52 and 53 Milton: the row of cob cottages built by George Wyndham and William Mallett.

Plate XXIII (facing page, below) George Wyndham's grave, East Knoyle, designed by Alexander Fisher.

110 Iris Bennett by T. Michael Anderson.

She was wrong about the time left to her. This was to be her last surviving letter: she died at Babraham on 8 March. Like Percy she was cremated, though at Golders Green crematorium. Her ashes were brought to East Knoyle for burial in the family plot.

Madeline's funeral at East Knoyle on 12 March 1920 marks the end of an epoch of gracious living, of optimism in the future of her family and her class. Her extensive family attended the funeral, as did many of the artists and writers still living who had become friends: Detmar Blow, Alexander Fisher, Jack Mackail. She was the last Wyndham to be buried in the churchyard, the last with a memorial designed by Fisher.

Dick's appointment in Ireland was brief. He was promoted Captain in June, just after holding a house party at Clouds for Iris and her mother. Young Peter Brooke had been at Clouds for the party and fallen hopelessly in love with Iris. He showed her all round the house and estate, even taking her up on the roof to survey the extent of her future property. In July Dick was demobbed on to the Reserve Officers list. His leave began in August and marriage to Iris was fixed for October.

Guy went over to Dublin shortly before Dick's leave began to discuss financial matters. Madeline's death relieved the estate of her annuity, also of Guy's, which lasted only as long as Madeline was alive (Guy also received income from his marriage settlement, his army pension and the £10,000 capital sum left him by his father and brother). But the estate bills and other costs still greatly exceeded the income: Guy had advised Dick to set money aside in a special fund to cover this deficit, otherwise Clouds would have to be let. The decision was taken to sell the remaining four-year lease of 44 Belgrave Square (Dick and Iris could make use of Guy's London house). Harry Shaw of Haversham Manor in Buckinghamshire paid £2,000 for it. Perf's widow Diana had offered to give up her annuity (she had remarried). The savings would help to boost the special fund; Dick and Iris would have a home in Wiltshire after all. And Dick was leaving Ireland just before the escalation of the cycle of atrocities and reprisals: Lord French resigned on 30 April 1921 and the partition of Ireland followed.

10   Clouds Abandoned

I

Dick Wyndham married Iris Bennett on 20 October 1920. Their early married life had the appearance of normality. Iris continued the Clouds visitors' book, entering the names of guests, notices of gymkhanas and point-to-points. Hunting was taken up again. And after hunting, tea was served in front of the fire in the great hall. Woods, the butler, carried it in from the distant kitchen where his wife was cook.

If Peter Brooke was staying at Clouds he invariably begged Dick to play 'fox and hounds' with him. Woods, grumbling and mumbling 'that bloody boy', was sent to turn off all the lights in the house. In the chaos that ensued Dick, as the fox, rushed off to hide; Peter, trying to sound like a pack of baying hounds, was soon in hot pursuit. To Peter, Dick was a wonderful uncle; even more so when he bought the boy his first air rifle.[1] At the point-to-points Dick earned a reputation for killing his horses. Iris noted in the Clouds visitors' book for 21 April 1922: 'Poor Patsy broke her leg at the Crawley & Horsham Point to Point. Dick was riding her. This makes the third horse killed at the end of three consecutive seasons.'[2]

The newly-weds indulged in some alterations to the house. One of the bedrooms was converted into four bathrooms. Partitions were erected but they did not reach right up to the ceiling: visiting children enjoyed throwing wet sponges over the top to give unsuspecting grown-ups an unpleasant surprise. There was some house decorating: 'we had an eastern evening to celebrate the opening of the newly decorated Barrel Room',[3] and a new tennis court was built close to the water tower.

Iris took charge of the village brownies: 'My Brownies acted their little play called the *Enchanted Wood* & made £4 for the nursing association.'[4] Mary Forward, the granddaughter of the estate's clerk of works William Mallett, used to go up to the nursery to play with Iris and Dick's baby. Mary was five years old and more interested in the Wyndhams' rocking-horse than in baby Joan.[5] Iris also made friends with Guendolen Wilkinson, granddaughter of the Dowager Countess of Pembroke who had been renting Knoyle House since 1914. Lady Pembroke moved to East Knoyle when her son inherited Wilton House. There were other visitors to Clouds: Bendor, Duke of Westminster, divorced from Dick's Aunt Connie; Mrs Patrick Campbell (Geoffrey Brooke hit her with a cricket ball) and Lionel Tennyson, the second husband of Dick's cousin Clare Tennant and Captain of England against Australia in 1921. In June 1922 Mary Wemyss brought Balfour over from Stanway: Dick and Olivia taught the elder statesman how to play poker. And in October there was a special house-party to celebrate Joan's first birthday. However, the party was the last entry made in the visitors' book.

Although the marriage was without public incident, within three years Dick and Iris no longer lived together; in 1924 they were divorced, Iris and her baby daughter moved

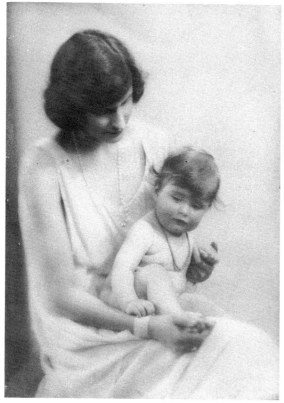

111 (above)   Dick and Iris Wyndham at Clouds House.

112 (left)   Iris Wyndham with Joan.

to London, and Dick let Clouds House. He was committed neither to the marriage nor to the maintaining of his grandparents' Wiltshire home and estate.

The marriage had begun badly. Both Dick and Iris were young and very inexperienced when they married; their honeymoon was not a success and the couple had to seek medical advice before the marriage could be consummated. Dick was still 'half-crazy' after his wartime experiences; 'war nerves and a war bride . . . he had got the two all mixed-up'.[6] When Dick's friend Peter Quennell visited Clouds in 1935 he was taken on a tour of the house, which was by then stripped of its contents, and 'as we passed a vacant bedroom, he [Dick] remarked quickly and bitterly, "This is where I spent my honeymoon."'[7] The humiliating experience was never forgotten.

According to the settlement made on Perf's marriage to Diana Lister, which was referred to in Perf's will, Clouds had to pass through the male line: it was left 'to the use' of Dick 'during his life with remainder to the use of his first and other sons successively according to seniority in tail male'. Dick had to produce a son to ensure his branch of the Wyndhams inherited the family property, otherwise Clouds passed to male Leconfields and their sons. The birth of a daughter seemed to hasten events. Only weeks after her birth, Dick was discovered by his wife kissing Irene, Marchioness of Queensberry, behind the Clouds Christmas tree. Iris began divorce proceedings and named Irene as correspondent.

Dick enjoyed the company of beautiful women throughout his adult life but his closest friendships were with men or the women he did not sleep with. His physical relationships with women were rarely satisfactory; he required the assistance of whips, handcuffs and ropes to restrain his partners – 'I do not like them to struggle' – and earned his nickname of the 'amateur flagellant' from his sometime friend, Wyndham Lewis. In his semi-autobiographical novel *Painter's Progress* he describes women as 'the killers . . . they'd been after him ever since he had become a man. Trying to hurt him – to own his body, and lay hands on his soul.'[8]

His women friends did not seem to be overly upset: while he might insist on the occasional beating, Dick was also a generous host, cultured and witty. One girlfriend had genuine difficulty choosing between a proposal of marriage (from someone else) and a summer spent motoring through France with Dick, enjoying good food, fine wine, amusing conversation and only the occasional whipping. Another was happy to tighten the ropes when she noticed the knots coming undone, lest Dick's enjoyment be spoilt.

The experiences on the western front undoubtedly contributed to his disturbed personality. But his childhood had also been a time of unhappiness and loss. His parents were abroad almost all the time from their marriage in 1892 until 1913, in Ireland, India, South Africa and Russia. Dick moved between boarding-school and grandparents, with his brother and sister his most constant companions. At Wellington College his behaviour caused the headmaster and his family concern. A letter refers to him growing out of 'this', he's good 'really', but he only stayed one year.[9] At Sandhurst he was constantly in trouble:

> his uniform was ill-fitting, an occasional button was left undone, and the intricacies of puttee-winding were quite beyond his powers. . . . Whilst I [Jack Poole] rose to the rank of sergeant, Dick I think remained a Gentleman Cadet.[10]

He found companionship and some fulfilment in the world Wyndham Lewis dubbed 'champagne bohemia', among fellow eccentrics such as the Sitwells, who shared his aristocratic background; Tom Driberg; the writers Cyril Connolly and Peter Quennell; Freddy Mayor of the Mayor Gallery; the composers Constant Lambert and William Walton; A.J.A. Symons, the artist Edward Wadsworth and his cousins David Tennant and Ann Charteris – who married Lord O'Neill, Lord Rothermere and Ian Fleming.[11] His half-brother Francis Wyndham summed up Dick's position in one of his short stories:

> now he was doggedly determined to have a *good* time at last. His money was spent on racing cars, aeroplanes, a famous wine cellar, a collection of 'modern' pictures and a series of difficult, exquisite girls. He enjoyed among his contemporaries a comfortable reputation for privileged Bohemianism, scandalising some by his 'arty' inclinations, but avoiding the kind of unpopularity that might threaten his status as a proud member of White's Club.[12]

Capable of being serious only about wine and art, he was a discerning and imaginative collector of contemporary art and a committed amateur artist of some talent.

Percy and Madeline Wyndham had drawn the line at their daughter Mary marrying Philip Burne-Jones; their sons chose military careers. Percy's cousin Roddam Spencer-Stanhope, however, had been accepted by his family as a professional artist and the Wyndhams' close friend George Howard, Earl of Carlisle, was taken seriously as a painter by aristocrats and fellow artists. But his painting did not interfere with the smooth running of his extensive family estates: there was no question of giving up one for the other.

Guy Wyndham encouraged Dick's painting when father and son managed to spend time together at Charford Manor, shortly before the war. Guy's final experience of fighting had been with the 16th Lancers during the Boer War: in 1904 he was promoted to Lieutenant-Colonel; from 1907 to 1911 he was military attaché at St Petersburg (and promoted to Colonel in 1908); in November 1913 he became Assistant Adjutant-General at the War Office. Dick movingly recalled an instance from his childhood in *Painter's Progress*:

> the heron ... standing among sedge and willow herb; and beyond, the silvered Avon, and the blue needle of the cathedral spire. He could smell the dank scent of water meadows – soft meadows trembling under an August sun. A lanky boy licking his brushes: 'Daddy, I can't get it right'.
>
> The old man would lay down his brushes and sketchbook, and come across ... they both had infinite faith.[13]

After moving into Clouds, Dick took lessons from Harold Speed, who had been commissioned to paint the posthumous portrait of George Wyndham. They made a sketching tour of Yorkshire in August 1921. The following summer Speed was a guest of the Wyndhams at Clouds with Mary Wemyss and Balfour.

A visit to Venice in October/November 1922 provided Dick with the experience of the life he would adopt in place of Clouds. The party, which included Osbert and Sacheverell Sitwell, William Walton and Hugo Rumbold, stayed with Nancy Cunard in her husband's palazzo. Wyndham Lewis was also at the palazzo, alternately painting Nancy and making love to her. Dick already knew the Sitwells, both of whom had served in the Grenadier Guards, the same regiment as Dick's cousins Yvo Charteris and Bim Tennant.

Iris remained behind in England. Villagers remember how sad she always looked, a contrast to her husband who, when he was around, always had a laugh and a wave for his neighbours as he roared through East Knoyle in his Rolls-Royce. Within a short time, however, the residents of East Knoyle and Milton were muttering about the money being wasted by Dick on champagne. Stories circulated of entire baths filled to the brim, while nothing was done to maintain Clouds and the estate.[14]

In 1922 Dick and Iris were still on friendly terms – Dick wrote an enthusiastic letter about Venice and the Sitwells:

It is an incredibly beautiful place – too good for humanity it ought to be the capital of heaven. . . . Hugo is here and a lot of annoying film producers and stars – they give hilarious parties every evening which I have to go to as I don't want to be alone, until I find my feet here – but they are not exactly the atmosphere for Venice. The producers and backers, who are most kind and well meaning people – mostly come from Manchester, and I hope they soon go back.

The only redeeming feature other than Hugo, is Wyndham Lewis, who is here drawing . . . he is purely a Bolshevick painter . . . quite amusing.[15]

Lewis, always quick to spot a possible patron, offered to help Dick with his drawing: 'I taught him how to sketch Venetian palaces, the fingers of one hand grasping the pencil and the fingers of the other grasping the nose, as all the best palaces are washed by cess-pools'.[16] He instantly recognised Dick as the descendant of 'the famous Lord Egremont, who was the patron of Turner, and a great name in the world of painting'.

What I liked about Dick Wyndham was the attractive candour and absence of vulgarity which made him seem almost like a nice workman among all these 'clever' people.[17]

Lewis assumed Dick was very well off and this was confirmed when Dick bought some of Lewis's drawings. A relationship was established which somehow managed to survive even prolonged periods of mutual animosity, until Dick's death in 1948. Lewis sketched a Venetian palace and dedicated the drawing to Dick. He drew Dick and the picture was reproduced in the *Sketch*. He also introduced Dick to Edward Wadsworth, who was to become another of his closest friends; Wadsworth in turn introduced Dick to Edward Marsh, private secretary to Winston Churchill, editor of *Georgian Poetry*, and one of the most discerning patrons of artists and writers of his day.

Dick had become part of a network reminiscent of the Holland Park circle in which Percy and Madeline Wyndham found themselves sixty years before, though none of the artists could afford to live in houses like Leighton's or Valentine Prinsep's; the incomes of the patrons were also considerably less than those of their Victorian predecessors and those with landed estates were more likely to face financial ruin than economic security.

Edward Marsh was the first known purchaser of one of Dick's pictures. He visited Dick's studio, 77 Bedford Gardens, Kensington, and bought one picture for himself, one for the Contemporary Art Society. Marsh had been made buyer of the year by the society (he would eventually become chairman), an acknowledgement of his discernment as a collector and patron of contemporary art.[18] He had begun collecting in the 1890s, concentrating on the English School *c.*1780–1830. In 1911 he made his first purchase of the work of a young artist, Duncan Grant's *Parrot Tulips* from the Carfax

Gallery. This was the beginning of a new interest in contemporary art and he rapidly acquired the reputation for recognising talent in creative artists at the outset of their careers.

After his purchase, Dick sent another drawing, as a present:

I should like to make you a present of it as a 'souvenir' of our 'deal'. I wouldn't presume to do this, if you hadn't shown a liking for some of my work, as nothing is more annoying than being *given* a drawing you don't want – But it is a good drawing and I think you will like it, but if you don't you can always bury it in that small dark alcove, which I imagine is your chamber of art horrors.[19]

Marsh's collection was crammed into his rooms in Raymond Buildings, Gray's Inn.

In the summer of 1923 Dick was off abroad again with the Sitwells, to Spain, Sicily, Naples and Amalfi. Sacheverell was researching for *Southern Baroque Art*; Dick was hard at work too. He wrote to his 'master' Lewis:

I have done three more of those ink drawings and I think they are pretty good – better perhaps than the last set. I am using a little stronger colour in places which makes them more interesting – such as in flags, or an earthen wear [*sic*] pot – or a piece of mosaic ornament. I am still only just tinting the buildings – but adding therefore stronger notes of colour here and there on the page.[20]

113 From *The Book of Towers*, Dick Wyndham, 1928.

Dick was learning how to handle the sensitive, jealous Lewis.

> Now the moment has arrived to cut the ground from under your feet, and inform
> you that the Sitwell family are here, and I sit at the same table with them, and I
> sometimes go for walks with them – *and* we talk about you some of the time, in fact
> often. But I have never heard anything but *very* great praise, admiration and a really
> genuine affection for you. Of course you will say – 'Oh – yes, they know you are a
> friend of mine, so they are careful of what they say'. But I think in a week one can
> find what a person's real feelings are about someone. And I do really think that they
> are very fond of you and I *know* that they really admire your work more than any
> other English artist.[21]

Christmas 1924 was spent at Rapallo. Dick's group made an impression on the young
Tom Driberg, who was staying at the Hotel Bristol with his mother. They consisted of
Dick, Sacheverell and Osbert, William Walton, Ada Leverson (Oscar Wilde's 'Sphinx' –
her daughter Violet had married Dick's father Guy the previous year) and the wealthy
art patron Peggy Guggenheim. Dick, complete with open-topped grey Rolls-Royce,
was making drawings of the campanile for his *Book of Towers*.

Cyril Connolly first saw Dick and the Sitwells the following Easter, staying on
holiday in Granada, together with Constant Lambert and William Walton. 'They were
really quite alarming – alarming rather than forbidding. All of them were wearing black
capes and black Andalusian hats and looked magnificent.'[22] By this time Dick had
established himself in his London studio, Iris had taken from Clouds a few favourite
pieces of furniture, some pictures and the visitors' books; the house was let.

2

The first tenant of Clouds House was Bendor, Duke of Westminster, who probably
took the house for a year from 1924 to 1925 as a favour to Dick. He and his sisters had
regularly visited Clouds as children after their mother Sibell married George Wyndham
in 1887. He had been married to Constance Cornwallis-West, first cousin of Dick,
between 1901 and 1919, and used to visit Clouds bringing his entourage of grooms and
horses with him.

While tenant of Clouds he hardly ever slept at the house, but the local community
enjoyed his occasional patronage. He took an interest in the village school and paid for
some of their outings, including a trip to the cinema in Shaftesbury to see Charlie
Chaplin. He supplied a large Christmas tree for the village hall and gave parcels to the
older residents. He was still helping the school in 1932, sending donations, probably via
the headmaster. The village held special celebrations to mark the 300th anniversary of
the birth of Sir Christopher Wren at Haslam Gardens, East Knoyle; Bendor paid for
twenty-six children to go to London to visit the sites.[23]

After Bendor, Dick found a more permanent tenant. From October 1925 until April
1932 he let Clouds House, together with the shooting, for £500 a year, to Adriaan
Willem Mosselman and his wife Nancy, who were Dutch, Adriaan Mosselman was in
the Dutch Diplomatic Service, his last post Counsellor of the Legation in Rome. He
was Nancy's second husband. They were lavish, by English standards, with their

money. Clouds House came to life again: there were hunt balls in the winter and lamp-lit parties in the grounds in the summer. Villagers with long memories still recall the extravagant entertainments. Adriaan Mosselman was keen on hunting, shooting and polo and was often away at Deauville and at Biarritz with his polo ponies. Nancy remained at Clouds with her children (four of the nine were born there). The house and gardens overflowed with children, dogs and staff.[24]

The Mosselmans kept a housekeeper, five housemaids, a butler, two footmen and four or five kitchen staff including the French chef. In the nursery there was a trained nurse responsible for the newborn baby, a head nurse, two assistant nannies, two nursery nursemaids and a nurse specially trained to tend the eldest child, who suffered from infantile paralysis. The garden was overrun by borzois, terriers, pointers and springers but there were still six gardeners to trim the hedges. Adriaan Mosselman's valet was German; the governess was Dutch. Two of the village girls, Winifred Stephens and Lucy Forward, worked in the nursery and were supplied with smart brown uniforms.

Every morning the nursery staff took all the children to Nancy Mosselman's bedroom. The staff waited outside while the children greeted their mother breakfasting in bed. During the day Nancy always spent time with the housekeeper, the head nurse, the butler and the gardener, to discuss menus, the number of guests, the progress of the children and the condition of the gardens.

The nurseries occupied the rooms on the east side of the principal floor, including Percy Wyndham's dressing room and the bedroom in which he died. All the children's prams were kept in the chapel, which caused some embarrassment when a cleric came to visit. The east drawing room was the day nursery. A small dark-room was constructed within the nursery complex; Nancy enjoyed developing her photographs close to the children. She spent time every day in the nurseries.

The children were always expensively and immaculately dressed, usually in silk or satin. Staff from Marshall and Snelgrove and Selfridges came down regularly with samples of their latest fashions, and displayed the clothes in the drawing room in front of the household. Before Christmas all the staff were invited to write lists of what they wanted as presents: Nancy bought everything on the lists. She went up to London for a week before Christmas, taking a suite in Claridges, and did all the shopping herself. Each year a different member of the staff was allowed to accompany her.

Village memories of the Mosselmans are fond: their wealth and their generosity meant they were the ideal tenants of Clouds. They offered employment, they brought a touch of the exotic, they invited the local community to their parties, they were colourful and shared some of their colour with a village which had missed Balfour in church. However, the Mosselmans never owned Clouds and its estates. They had no responsibilities as landowners; the burden of repairs was not theirs. When their tenancy expired they moved on to Rousham Park near Oxford, another ancestral home available for let.

Clouds's absentee landlord was establishing himself in London as an artist. He spent months at a time abroad, sketching and writing, and from 1927 he was the owner of Tickerage Mill, according to Peter Quennell a 'deliberately unpretentious' red-brick converted miller's cottage in Sussex.[25] He apparently never visited Clouds during the Mosselmans' occupation. Most friends had no idea he was responsible for a country house and estate in Wiltshire, or even that he was helping (not much) to support his ex-wife and daughter.

3

Under Dick's ownership, Tickerage Mill became another Clouds. It was on a smaller scale, half a dozen bedrooms, one housekeeper and one personal servant (called Squib), but the visitors' book contains the same Clouds mixture of family and friends; fewer soldiers and politicians but still landowners, businessmen, artists and designers, writers and architects, as well as journalists and art dealers. The food and drink was far superior to anything Percy and Madeline offered their guests. As a leading member of the Wine and Food Society which André Simon and A.J.A. Symons launched in 1933,[26] Dick offered hospitality that none of the participants have ever forgotten. He locked up his wine cellar when away from Tickerage, putting out only house wine for casual lodgers. There was no scented soap in the house, and he disliked women wearing perfume – it spoilt the wine.

Dick had discovered Tickerage Mill during a visit to Edward Wadsworth, who had moved from London to the Dairy House, Maresfield Park, Sussex in 1926.

> I happened to turn down a steep lane of great troughs of Sussex clay. In a wooded valley lay a mill pool – silver among silver reeds, and bulrushes just bursting in white cotton cascade. Mallard and wild duck rose vertically from the marsh; a heron flopped from the great oak to perch ridiculously on top of the purple wood. The mill house was empty, and almost lost among unpruned apple trees, and gooseberry bushes run wild; a simple tile-hung cottage that for four hundred years had refused to fall down.[27]

It cost about £2,000 and Dick probably found the money by disposing of some of the contents of Clouds; he later admitted to a cousin that he supported his self-indulgent lifestyle by selling off a painting every year. He also lived off the Mosselmans' rent for Clouds, rents from the Wyndham estate in South Australia and interest from his portfolio of stocks and shares.

Rossetti's *Beata Beatrix* was sold some time before 1928 to A.E. Anderson, who presented it to the National Gallery of Scotland. The Wyndhams' other Rossetti drawings were also disposed of: *Troy Town* eventually turned up at Colnaghi's in 1958 and was bought by the Museum of Fine Arts in Boston. The early Italian Renaissance painting ascribed to Baldovinetti which Percy bought at the William Graham sale had passed into the collection of Baron von Thyssen-Bornemisza by 1930 with a new attribution.

Dick's most spectacular picture sale was in 1927. He sold Sargent's portrait of his aunts, *The Wyndham Sisters*, to the Metropolitan Museum of Art in New York, for £20,000. Dick first lent the painting to the Royal Academy in 1926 for an exhibition of works by Sargent; probably with advice from Freddy Mayor he then placed it with Knoedler's from October. In December it sailed to New York and in March 1927 a deal was struck with the Metropolitan. Osbert Sitwell, who sailed to New York with Dick and the painting, commented, 'the sum given for it proves the folly of fashion'. He found the painting no more than 'a pleasant and competent record of three lovely women'.[28]

Dick protested that his decision to sell the Sargent was not for his own benefit. He said that he wanted to provide his father with an annuity. Guy was not well off. His army pension and the interest from the £10,000 capital left him by his father and

114 *Troy Town* by Dante Gabriel Rossetti, 1870. Acquired by Percy Wyndham at Rossetti's sale 1883; acquired by the Museum of Fine Arts, Boston, 1958.

brother were sufficient for a quiet retired life. However, he had married again in 1923, Violet Leverson. Dick's sister Olivia and Violet had become friends as VADs in the war and soon after gave a few private ballroom dancing lessons at 1 Lowndes Street, Olivia's London home. Guy probably met Violet for the first time during one of the lessons. In 1928 they bought Parliament Piece in Ramsbury, Berkshire, the 'house of our dreams', but at around £4,000, rather an expensive dream. Olivia was still financially dependent on Guy, whose family responsibilities were to increase rather than diminish, in his old age, with the birth of two sons, Francis and Hugh. Dick wrote to his Aunt Mary Wemyss in 1926.

> I look upon this painting [the Sargent] as really belonging to you and Aunt Madeline & Pamela, so would do nothing without your consent. Personally I feel very strongly that it ought to be sold and the interest on the money given to Father for his lifetime. These are my reasons – the picture has now an entirely artificial value over and above what Grandpapa payed for it – and *over* what it will be in 5 years time. At this moment I could probably get £20,000 for it – This invested would mean £1200 a year for Father which would absolutely remove all anxiety about educating his new family, and getting a new home when Lowndes St lease ends. The alternative is keeping a picture in a house, where neither I nor any heirs will ever be able to live. I feel sure that Grandpapa would have been the first to chuckle at his good buy – the painting is 'sentiment' and I feel that Father's income is a more practical sentiment, particularly as none of the family get any advantage from the picture.

Dick's justification for selling the Sargent painting was not unreasonable, but there is no proof within the family that he actually ever did help with the education or living expenses of Francis, Hugh or his sister Olivia. She eventually settled in New York after a brief marriage to an American, Howland Spencer. She was the fourth of Spencer's five wives and they divorced in 1931. Olivia established her own unique version of 'little England' in New York's Harlem, spending the rest of her life with the black actress Edna Thomas and serving visitors with Earl Grey tea, cucumber sandwiches and Gentleman's Relish.[29]

The very first visitors to Tickerage Mill, in 1927, included Olivia, the art dealer Freddy Mayor and art patron Edward Marsh, as well as Dick's current girlfriend Enid Firminger.[30] Wyndham Lewis was never invited to Tickerage or to Clouds even though he was a significant influence on Dick's development as an artist and his work formed the beginnings of Dick's considerable art collection. The artist and his pupil-patron had fallen out long before Dick acquired Tickerage: their relationship provides an interesting case study of the conflicts and misunderstandings that could develop between the patron and the patronised.

Lewis's poverty was a major factor. His financial situation became seriously straitened after John Quinn, his principal patron, stopped buying his work in 1921. Friends helped intermittently until in December 1923 Dick, the Wadsworths, Raymond Drey the art critic and his wife Anne Estelle Rice, the Fauvist painter, set up a private fund which paid Lewis £16 a month. It was a difficult, embarrassing arrangement. Payments were made monthly until February 1924. Then Lewis asked for an advance on the March payment of £6, followed by an advance on the April payment of £14. He was due no more money until 1 May but on 1 April he sent a note to Fanny Wadsworth, the unfortunate person dealing with the payments, which, according to one biographer, read, 'Where's the fucking stipend?'.[31]

Fanny sent him his next instalment, £13, on 30 April and asked him 'to put aside all personal quarrels or misunderstandings and keep to your part of the agreement by continuing to receive what has been subscribed'. He wrote back on 1 May explaining that he would accept the money, 'because I am so hard up that if the devil himself offered me anything from half a crown upwards I should have to accept it', but he wanted nothing more.[32]

So far Dick had kept out of the row. He had his first exhibition at a major London gallery, the Goupil, in April 1924 and offered to pay Lewis half of his profits: 'this might be (with luck) as much as £60 or £70'.[33] Lewis not surprisingly described Dick at this stage as 'a person who has shown the greatest interest in my work, and has given me the most generous help, of whom I am fond and whose work I have in a sense watched over'.[34] Dick sold twelve of the twenty-nine drawings in the exhibition, mostly to friends, including Wadsworth, Marsh, Sidney Schiff, Mrs A.P. Herbert (a friend of Wadsworth) and his own cousin, Lady Mary Strickland. Sacheverell Sitwell wrote in a eulogistic introduction to his catalogue: 'he has a strongly marked ability for rendering architecture, but these are no leaves from an architect's sketch book, for they have a pictorial, almost theatrical sense'.[35] His own family shared in his success: Guy wrote to his sister Mary Wemyss: 'in case you missed the notices of Dick's exhibition, I send you a good one from the *Morning Post*, which pleased him'.

Dick's success marked a turning point in his relations with Wyndham Lewis: their friendship deteriorated throughout the year as Dick finally divorced Iris and let Clouds House. Lewis was bitterly jealous of Dick's wealth and his ability to travel wherever he wished, always in comfort: in the summer Dick was in Marseilles with Wadsworth, sketching in the same steep narrow streets. Later, Dick made an extended tour of Europe, ending in Venice where

> I took an apartment for two months on the top floor of the Pallazzo [*sic*] Mala, engaged a cook house-keeper and lived on macaroni and vegetable soup. The first few weeks were slightly social and then I was quite alone; very happy and undisturbed in my own house. I did a lot of painting.[36]

Lewis's outbursts made Dick wonder whether he was liked only for his supposed wealth:

> Why I am so anxious to keep you as a friend, I don't know. I sometimes wonder whether, if you were not such a great artist, I should still have the same admiration for you as a man. As I also wonder whether you, in the event of my being penniless, would still include me in your extremely exclusive set of friends.
>
> You with your extensive knowledge of 'Behaviour' must realize that your 'grand gesture' on the one hand (your renouncing the Joint Fund) is somewhat marred on the other by your request for £30 from me. Sometimes you inspire me with a feeling that I am dealing with a very lovable and very great genius – sometimes (though still recognizing the genius) I feel that I am being duped by an adventurer.[37]

Lewis disliked the way Dick used abstractions such as 'great artist . . . it is as often used *against* a person . . . as *for* him'. He continued:

> you say you wonder if I should be your friend if you were penniless. I daresay I should find it easier to be your friend if that were so, because at least one cause of distrust would be removed on your side. I can only say that I don't think you would find me different. But let us put it another way and suppose *I* were rich, & you poor: what would happen then? Suppose I had helped you when you needed it: you would regard it as natural, you would not like me any better or any less: it would, surely, be just the same. When a liking exists, and common interests, money should be . . . taken as a matter of course. If I do not therefore appear over grateful in an obvious and demonstrative way for your help, you should not misunderstand it. If you like a person, and accept him as a true artist, from that moment conventions can be dispensed with, I should only be surprised if you *didn't* help me.[38]

Though Dick was far from a conventional member of the landed gentry, he was not a professional artist; his lifestyle was supported by a private income. As a member of 'champagne bohemia' he still expected Lewis to call on him at fixed times in the day, also to sympathise with his own difficulties concerning his marriage and inheritance. Lewis's response was reasonable: 'if you are worried, I have had far more cause to worry than you'.[39]

In 1927, when Dick bought twenty-six of Lewis's works at the New York sale of John Quinn's collection, Lewis called it 'parasitic profiteering'. The prices were ridiculously low. Two of Lewis's finest Vorticist paintings, *Kermesse* and *Plan of War*, were picked up by Dick for $15 each, less than a case of champagne. They had been bought from Lewis by Quinn during the war for £100.

Lewis finally took his revenge on Dick and the other 'gossip-mad, vulgar, pseudo-artists, *good-timers*' in *The Apes of God*, published in 1930. He attacked Bloomsbury, the

Sitwells, the Wadsworths and Dick, just about everyone who had tried to help him when he was chronically poor. Wadsworth he described as the 'rich mountebank marine-painter', with a 'bank-balance-ballast of hard-fisted Halifax bullion', a reference to his family inheritance; Fanny Wadsworth was 'a small fat half-blind ex-cook'.

Dick became Richard Whittingdon, 6′2″ tall, clumsy, often farting, ex-Sandhurst. He left the army to take up his inheritance March Park and marry; realised he was an artist of 'genius' so divorced his wife and let March to 'rich Jews', settling in his Kensington studio. Whittingdon dressed the part of the Bohemian artist when entertaining in his studio: 'in a paint-dappled smock with black-rimmed Mandarin spectacles for painting . . . chewing the cane tube of an underslung chimney-pot briar'. However, his food is delivered from Fortnum and Masons and although he occupies only one studio himself, he rents the entire block, which 'must prevent *ten* geniuses from having a roof over their genius, and must keep them in small ill-lit rooms while he sat on all these valuable workshops in solitary egotistic state'. Whittingdon is also an 'amateur flagellant'. In his studio is a 'great black cupboard' full of whips, 'a perfect hedge of birches, drover's whips, bamboos and martinets'.[40]

Lewis's attack on Dick Wyndham was uncomfortably accurate: as Lewis saw it, 'it is impossible to devise anything sufficiently cruel . . . for the invulnerable conceit of a full stomach and fat purse'.[41] Dick retaliated. He placed an advertisement in *The Times* on 2 September 1930 offering two of Lewis's paintings for sale, by the square foot, at an insultingly low price.

Percy Wyndham Lewis – Two paintings for sale, 9ft × 7ft, and 7ft × 4ft, £20 and £15; inspection – Capt. Wyndham, Bedford Gardens.[42]

Lewis gave Dick lessons and encouragement and introduced him to fellow artists and patrons. Many of Dick's drawings of buildings are similar to Lewis's; Lewis had reason to feel he had been 'had'. Dick was also beginning to make some money from his own dealings in contemporary art. Between the wars he was consistently active in the London art market, adding to his own collection but also buying and selling for profit. Art dealers who knew him recall his remarkably discerning eye. Many of his dealings were through the Mayor Gallery.

Freddy Mayor was one of his closest friends, a frequent guest at Tickerage and, together with Wadsworth, executor of his estate. Freddy extended the art education Dick had already been receiving from Wyndham Lewis, Wadsworth and the Sitwells. His parents, Fred and Hannah Mayor, had both been artists, and he became 'an astute, sensitive and respected dealer'. He knew everybody, 'not only in the artistic world but also among the young socialites of the day, and was a highly amusing adjunct to any house party in any circle'. He admitted to two main weaknesses, cocktails and 'a total lack of musicality. He only knew when the National Anthem was being played because everyone present stood up.' He was also addicted to gambling at the racecourse, casinos and clubs. If visitors to the gallery could not be persuaded to buy a Rouault or a Dali they might be given 'a hot tip for the three-thirty'.[43]

The Mayor Gallery opened in January 1925 at 18 Cork Street with an exhibition of Post-Impressionists. In March Freddy Mayor showed the work of English painters: Paul Nash, Mark Gertler, William Roberts. By the end of the year he had acquired additional premises at 37 Sackville Street. An exhibition of 'Advanced French Art' (Severini, Metzinger, Gris) in January 1926 was attacked by *The Times*: 'the advance is

Plate XXIV (facing page, above) *Babraham*, artist unknown, mid-nineteenth century.

Plate XXV (facing page, below) Babraham, 1990.

towards the bathroom – You think of washable distemper and sanitary tiles.' In April 1926 an exhibition of paintings by Matthew Smith and Michael Sevier was also given harsh treatment by establishment critics. Dick himself wrote an account of the exhibition:

> Matthew Smith was present at his private view . . . but few bothered to hush their voices when expressing their disgust at the pictures on the wall. For who could have recognised the artist in the timid, myopic slightly stooping figure whose afternoon consisted in being tugged from one side of the narrow room to the other by his two small boys up for the day from school? Who could have believed that here was the creator of these turgid nudes that still lived, still tempted, though conceived in tones of crimson so deep that the highest light of the cheek bone or breast held the richness of pigeon's blood: or these landscapes seen with such ferocity of ownership that one would hardly have dared walk the dark roads without the artist by one's side. Few thought of buying, and, of those few, painters predominated: Epstein, August John.[44]

Also Dick Wyndham; both Matthew Smith and Sevier were visitors to Tickerage. Smith rented the house immediately after the war. When Dick's collection was sold by Sotheby's after his death in 1948 he still owned two Matthew Smiths, also work by Severini including his enormous Futurist piece *Dynamic Hieroglyphic of the Bal Tabarin*,

115 Walking near Teffont, Wiltshire (home of David Tennant). From left to right: Arthur Tite, Dick Wyndham, Mrs Arthur Tite, Freddy Mayor, Pamela Mayor.

Plate XXVI (facing page) *Autumn Landscape* by Dick Wyndham, exhibited at Arthur Tooth and Sons, London, property of Mrs Antony Thesiger; sold Christie's March 1988.

and by Giorgio de Chirico. Tooth's put on an exhibition of De Chirico's work in 1938 but only three Englishmen bought works: Michael Sadleir, Lord Henry Cavendish Bentinck, then Chairman of the Contemporary Art Society; and Dick. His taste was impeccable and his collection included examples of Surrealism, Futurism and Cubism as well as less avant-garde work by British artists. At the Goupil Gallery, which had first showed his own paintings, he bought, between 1923 and 1926, work by John Nash, Vlaminck, Constantin Guys and Mark Gertler. The Mayor Gallery provided most of his collection, however, as well as handling sales on his behalf: Dufy, Metzinger, Rouault, Paul Nash, Cocteau, Duncan Grant, Picasso, Braque, Derain and Matisse. His last dealings with the Mayor in February 1948 included the purchase of two Eduardo Paolozzis.[45] His collection represented an excellent investment. Many of the paintings cost less than £100 each but their value has risen dramatically in comparison to the Sargent portrait of Dick's aunts (which he astutely sold at the peak of Sargent's popularity).

4

116 Tea at Tickerage: Greta and Dick Wyndham.

From 1929 onwards a regular visitor to Tickerage was Greta Wulfsberg, a Norwegian of 'piquant charm',[46] one of Dick's models. When she became pregnant in 1930, Dick

agreed to marry her; his second daughter Ingrid was born the following year. Again Dick had failed to produce an heir for Clouds as required by Perf's will. He gave Ingrid a lavish christening party at Clouds but otherwise spent little time with his baby daughter. She lived for much of her childhood with her grandfather Guy and Violet Wyndham at Parliament Piece. Meanwhile Dick and Greta agreed to remain on friendly terms, often visiting country houses together, hosting parties in London, but only occasionally cohabiting as husband and wife. With the freedom to pursue their own interests, they remained on affectionate terms. Their eventual divorce was arranged to the satisfaction of both parties. Dick wrote to Greta during the proceedings: he was recovering from influenza:

> My Sweetie
> I can't tell you how your roses helped to cheer me as well as my room. And I was so glad to get the cuff links back which, I must admit, I though I had lost.
> I am glad too to think that you are so happy with your little cottage, and long for everything to be over so I can see you again and Aubrey (whom as you know I am very fond of indeed).
> I've had a terrible temperature for a long time but I think it has gone now.
> I suppose I ought not to write to you but I can't help thanking you for the roses. And you know that whatever my behaviour has been I have always felt a deep love and devotion for you
> Dickie[47]

While the Mosselmans continued to rent Clouds House, most of the paintings acquired by Percy and Madeline remained on the walls. But at the end of 1931 Dick decided to dispose of Clouds House, the entire contents of the house and the estate. His decision was not wholly the result of his failure to provide male heirs (not to mention his failures as a husband); his investments had suffered with the Wall Street crash, and the Mosselmans' lease ended on 1 April 1932 and they decided to move on. Clouds House was in need of extensive decorations and repairs before another tenant could be found. However, the income from the estate had fallen so much that Dick could not afford to maintain the house, let alone the 15 farms and 58 cottages, while also pursuing his preferred way of life at Tickerage. The estate had been reduced to just over 3,000 acres; the rental income after deducting the outgoings (including tithe rent) of £743 and without the Mosselmans' contribution of £550, was just £1,412 5sh.11d.

Knight, Frank and Rutley drew up the particulars of the estate to be sold at auction on 28 January 1932. Clouds could still be described as a 'dignified mansion' with its suite of five principal receptions rooms and billiard room; thirteen principal bedrooms and dressing rooms; a nursery suite of two bedrooms; twelve other bedrooms; ample domestic offices in a separate wing including thirteen staff bedrooms; garaging for four cars; stabling for twenty-three horses and a model laundry. Through the summer of 1932 Knight, Frank and Rutley managed to sell only a few of the cottages to sitting tenants, and 114 acres of land, raising a total of £2,380.[48]

Meanwhile Dick began to sell off the contents of the house. Four paintings were auctioned at Sotheby's on 29 June: three Italian Renaissance paintings and a view of the Thames in London by Samuel Scott. One, at least, of the Italian paintings failed to reach its reserve and was auctioned again the following year. On 30 June Dick disposed of monumental brasses, five figures which had once hung in the hall at Clouds; also a model of a Byzantine chapel. And on Friday 1 July he sold a large selection of furniture from Clouds, including an early eighteenth-century Italian cabinet, veneered in tortoiseshell, the front door decorated with ivory panels etched with St George killing the dragon; also a seventeenth-century South German cypress wood chest carved in low relief and burnt with allegorical subjects, caryatids and escutcheons. It was supported on a stand painted by Philip Webb. The 16-feet-long Sheraton mahogany dining table was sold; several black lacquer cabinets, and five Chippendale mahogany chairs with elegantly carved backs that had once belonged to Robert Southey. Percy and Madeline had bought them in the early 1870s when the poet's furniture was sold at Keswick.

One piece included in the sale could hardly reflect better everything Dick was disposing of, everything which was anathema to him. It was a George I needlework picture in *petit point* depicting a farmer and his wife standing by a well with cows, dogs, rabbits, cock and hens; behind them is their Georgian mansion, the pinnacle of their achievements, the centre of their estates, theirs to pass on to their family generation after generation as long as they accept responsibility for its maintenance and the care of all their staff and tenants.

Dick had not been brought up as the heir to Clouds. He was emotionally scarred by the war – possibly even earlier – and never developed a sense of responsibility towards another human being: wife, lover, daughter, friend or servant. The sale of the house, its contents and the estate did not make him a millionaire: the total raised was about £45,000. However, this would give him an additional income of £2,700 a year and relieve him of the Wyndham albatross hanging round his neck.

On 11 July Dick sold a large part of the library, including the almost complete collection of books printed at the Kelmscott Press, 49 out of a total of 66. He also sold scrapbooks containing press cuttings to do with George Wyndham's literary productions, no doubt assembled by Madeline. The remaining contents of Clouds were disposed of over three days, 20–22 June 1933. Knight, Frank and Rutley handled the auction, which was conducted at Clouds itself.[49] Minnie Wyndham's grandson Peter Brooke went over to Clouds while the cataloguing was going on. He was greeted by the forlorn ex-chauffeur Smith: everything was to go, the estate would be split up, the Captain (Dick) didn't care about anything. The old butler Woods had even been allowed to die in the poorhouse in Salisbury.

Up at the house Peter began to search for his air-gun, the one he had persuaded Dick to buy for him just after the war. He tracked the gun down in a top bedroom. It was being catalogued and went under the hammer as lot 639, along with two bugles, a dagger and sheath and a pair of ice skates. The armour he used to play with made up three lots, together with flags, helmets, swords, musical instruments and carnival decorations. All the happy memories of his childhood at Clouds were being disposed of. He couldn't bring himself to bid for the gun.

In fact Dick didn't put everything up for auction. He was concerned to allow members of his family to keep items of particular sentimental value, though not any of the pictures by Burne-Jones – these he determined to sell at the market price. He wrote to Mary Wemyss: 'I am *giving* away to the Aunties & Father & Bendor anything that they feel has a "sentimental" value or belongs to them, and of course am not selling anything personal like Gan's [Madeline's] paintings – special books – or family relics', and he asked her for a list of the things she would like. The Clouds estate agent Hannam Miles collected family items together in one room for relatives to sort through at their leisure.

Dick summed up the sale in a letter to his father: 'The prices weren't too good – but not *too* bad.' Some items that went for auction were not sold: Dick gave many of these away to family and friends. Some years later Freddy and Pamela Mayor, for example, were given two panels of fighting cocks. The bust of George Wyndham by Rodin remained unsold and Dick hoped Bendor might buy it, but in the end he gave it to Aunt Mary along with five paintings of members of the Wyndham family. The Chinese paper screen painted with mountains and pagodas was acquired by Dick's cousin, Edward Scawen Wyndham.

There is no record of the total amount raised by the sale or whether most items were sold. Would anyone have bought the doormats, for example, or iron boot-scrapers or knife-cleaning machines? The surviving catalogue in the possession of the Victoria and Albert Museum only has prices against items associated with William Morris: the oak refectory dining table with an extra leaf designed by Morris went to E. Vincent and Son for 8 guineas; Morris and Company bought the 'Greenery' tapestry which hung in the hall for 150 guineas, and the hall carpet for £81.

The important paintings, tapestries and furniture collected by Percy and Madeline are lost in all the household junk, carefully catalogued page after page, bedroom after bedroom. Fifty years later, however, a similar collection of junk would in itself come to represent as significant a slice of heritage as paintings by Orpen and Burne-Jones, or the architecture of Philip Webb, as Patrick Wright noted in his commentary on the 'saving' of Calke Abbey:

> Calke had not been cleaned up. . . . The Harpur-Crewes, it was said, had not thrown anything away and Calke as a result became 'the house where time stood still' . . . Calke proved that household junk can indeed also now serve as the stuff of a national past which is valued for surviving secretly against the insidious drift of recent history.[50]

Dick lent three of the finest paintings to the Tate Gallery in July 1933: the Watts portrait of Madeline and the two Orpen portraits of Madeline and Percy. They remained at the Tate until 1935 and are now owned by descendants; presumably they were given away by Dick. The drawing-room carpet, specially made by Morris and Company for the Wyndhams, did not find a buyer at the sale. Dick exhibited it at the Victoria and Albert Museum the following year. Then, in 1936, C.E.C. Tattersall of the Department of Textiles at the V&A advised the treasurer of Cambridge University that the carpet was still for sale. On 4 May the carpet was sent off by goods train to Cambridge on approval: it has remained on the floor of the Combination Room in the Old Schools ever since.

Clouds had been emptied of everything that could fetch a price, but the house and estate were still for sale, increasingly vulnerable as they were joined by other similar properties, all in search of new owners or new uses. Wilsford, the Wiltshire home of Dick's Aunt Pamela Glenconner, was fortunate to be supported by the resources of the Tennants' fortune. When Pamela died suddenly in November 1928, it passed to her second surviving son, David. He had no desire to live in it: 'It would be like wearing your mother's old clothes.'[51] However, his younger brother Stephen inherited sufficient money of his own to be able to buy Wilsford, the contents and the surrounding estate from David for £30,000. Stephen may also have been responsible for acquiring for Wilsford the Ellis Roberts portrait of Pamela which was included in the Clouds sale. Christopher, the eldest of Pamela's sons, became the second Lord Glenconner and inherited Glen in Scotland: he may have been responsible for

117   Amisfield House.

acquiring from Morris and Company the carpet that had lain on the floor of Clouds hall. It found a new home on the floor of his library at Glen.[52]

A few years before the sale of Wilsford, another house, also belonging to Dick's relations, had been less fortunate. Amisfield was one of three country houses owned by the Earl of Wemyss. Tenants had been hard to find before the war for the elegant eighteenth-century house. Between 1907 and 1914 it was let for 10 per cent of the time and empty for the rest. When occupation by the War Office ended in December 1920 Hugo and Mary Wemyss were left with a badly knocked-about house, little possibility of finding tenants and death duties still to pay off after the death of the tenth Earl in 1914. In 1923 Amisfield was offered for sale, but for demolition only. According to the family, 'it was all done in a great hurry with insufficient care and attention.' The only person to profit from the transaction was Richard Baillie, the 'purchaser demolisher'. Descendants repeat the family legend 'that the lead statues on the roof and the (unsuspected) lead sheathing under the road surface of the carriage ramp were in themselves sufficient to recoup all he had paid for the whole building'.[53]

5

In many ways Dick's life is pure Evelyn Waugh. James had been acquainted with Percy and Madeline Wyndham and their children; Waugh knew Dick Wyndham and they had many friends in common. After the disposal of the contents of Clouds, as the world moved inexorably towards war, Dick indulged his friends at Tickerage with 'unforgettable parties, bathing parties, croquet parties [John Rayner recalls 'croquet-poquet' played after dinner by cigar light], Guy Fawkes parties and fancy-dress parties', even eel-fishing parties.[54] Freddy Mayor brought many of the artists; the Sitwells and David Tennant represented landed bohemia; Tom Driberg brought Fleet Street; Cyril Connolly and Peter Quennell represented literature; Constant Lambert and William Walton music. Occasional guests included Anthony Powell and his wife Violet; Ian Fleming and Dick's cousin Ann before her divorce from Lord Rothermere and marriage to Ian; Kit Dunn, friend of Augustus John, and Dick's cousin Robert Adeane before his marriage to Kit.

Dick woke at five every morning to drink Earl Grey tea and take pot shots at moorhens on the millpond; his guests were rarely up as early, devastated by the food and drink consumed the previous night. Menus for a special Wine and Food Society weekend held in January 1935 indicate the quality and quantity. First dinner for the guests just arrived from London:

Soupe à l'oseille/ old sherry bottled 1925
Sole au fours/ Château Filhot 1922
Selle d'agneau à la mie de pain/ Château Branaire Ducru 1919
Truffles aux xeres/ Château Haut Brion 1906
Le Vacherin/ Château Lafite 1874
Dessert/ Château Margaux 1870
Château Yquem 1924
Café
Grande Fine Champagne, De luze 1868

All the wines at this first dinner were magnificent: Château Filhot is a top Sauternes but the 1922 was probably rather dry, consequently more suitable for drinking with the

118 Dick's guests at Tickerage. Standing, from left to right: Patrick Kinross, Angela Culme-Seymour, Dick Wyndham, Tom Driberg, Cyril Connolly, Stephen Spender.

119 Angela Culme-Seymour (suffering from German measles) on the croquet lawn at Tickerage with Boswell.

sole; 1874 was a very good year, a pre-phylloxera vintage, so the Château Lafite would have been excellent drinking in 1935.

Lunch the following day was comparatively light; the German wines were all the very best vintages:

Saumon fumé/ Avelsbacher Herrenberg 1929
Moules Marinière/ Eitelsbacher Knothausen Hofberg 1921 [Ruwer]
Jambon de Virginie; Gateaux de Pommes de terres aux oignons/ Niersteiner Domtal 1921;
Rauenthaler Nonnenberg 1921 Beerenauslese; [Erbach] Marcobrunner Riesling 1921 Auslese
[Rheingan]
Pommes robes de chambres/ Schloss Johannisberg 1911 Auslese
Café/ La Grande Chartreuse

to leave space for dinner in the evening.

Soupe aux poireaux/ Chablis 1906
Rougets au fours/ Meursault 1919
Riz de veau à l'oseille/ Corton Charlemagne 1928
Perdreaux aux choix/ Grand Chambertin 1923
Pailles au fromage/ Corton 1911
Dessert/ Clos Vougeot 1904
Café
Sandeman 1868
Grande Fine Champagne, De luze 1868 [55]

Wine experts agree that Dick's selection for the final evening was again inspired: the White Burgundy Grand Cru Corton Charlemagne 1928 would have been 'sublime'[56] at the time; the three red burgundys were all excellent vintages; Sandeman's 1868 port was always judged the best that year.[57]

Though visits to Tickerage were memorable, never to be forgotten occasions for Dick's guests, Cyril Connolly detected something seriously wrong with the host:

> The mill where I sometimes stay provides another cure for Angst; the red lane through the Spanish chestnut wood, the apple trees on the lawn, the bees in the roof, the geese on the pond, the black sun-lit marsh marigolds, the wood-fire crackling in the low bedroom, the creak of the cellar-door and the recurrent monotonies of the silver-whispering weir – what could be more womb-like or reassuring? Yet always the anxious owner is flying from it as from the scene of a crime.[58]

Throughout the mid-1930s, Dick chose to devote much of his time to painting the ancestral homes of England, many occupied by his friends and relations, even though he was desperately trying to get rid of his own. Perhaps it was a sense of guilt which inspired him to record in oils and watercolour more fortunate properties? The Leicester Galleries held two exhibitions, one in 1935, the second in 1936, both called 'Paintings of Country Seats and Manor Houses'. Dick submitted paintings of Wilton House, Stanway, and Ramsbury Manor House in the village where his father lived. His friend Lord Berners submitted a painting of his house, Faringdon. Rex Whistler showed paintings of Faringdon, Wilton and Weston Hall, home of Sacheverell and Georgia Sitwell. Other country house paintings of Dick's appeared at Tooth's in 1937, including Osbert Sitwell's Renishaw Hall and Petworth, lent by Lady Leconfield. When Dick was spotted painting in the park at Petworth, his cousin Lord Leconfield was heard to enquire, 'who's that tramp sketching in my park?'

Dick's efforts are very pleasant but hardly great art: reminiscent of the paintings shown by Charles Ryder in *Brideshead Revisited*. In the novel, Anthony Blanche, based on Waugh's Oxford friends (and Dick's acquaintances) Harold Acton and Brian Howard, sums up Ryder's efforts to paint English houses: 'there was something a little *gentlemanly* about your painting . . . charm . . . too English . . . your art, my dear – is a dean's daughter in flowered muslin'. Ryder himself recalls the exhibition: 'the talk had been less of me than of the houses, anecdotes of their owners'.[59]

Ryder, not a landed gentleman, had been seduced by the world of the Flyte family and Brideshead: he was inspired and at the same time handicapped as an artist by the experience. Dick Wyndham appears to have been racked by guilt about trying to dispose of his family seat and incapable of applying to his own artistic efforts his discernment as collector and connoisseur of contemporary European art. Others who fell for the world of Sebastian Flyte included Peter Quennell, Cyril Connolly and Tom Driberg, all acquaintances of Waugh but close friends of Dick Wyndham. Dick was part Ryder and part Sebastian. He was after all the owner and defiler of Clouds, and a descendant of the Earl of Egremont. At Tickerage he continued to offer his guests something of the insouciant charm of the cultured aristocracy.

There is another link between Dick's world and that of *Brideshead Revisited*. A model for the Flyte family of Brideshead was the Lygon family (Lord Beauchamp and his children) of Madresfield. Countess Beauchamp was Lettice, stepdaughter of George Wyndham: it was her brother Bendor, Duke of Westminster, who hounded Lord Beauchamp out of the country for his homosexuality – thus providing Waugh with a model for Lord Marchmain. The chapel at Madresfield was decorated as a present from

Lettice to her husband, 'perhaps the most complete realisation of Arts and Crafts theory in Britain'.[60] On being shown the chapel by Sebastian Flyte, Charles Ryder's only response is 'Golly'.

Throughout the 1930s Ryder specialises in painting ancestral homes about to be abandoned by their hereditary owners, 'soon to be deserted or debased'. As the years passed and the Clouds estate remained on the market, Dick established a studio for himself in the housekeeper's room and also used the old windmill with its magnificent views across the countryside. He painted views of the park and of the house itself, more intensely and prolifically than at any time before: almost as if realising time was running out for Webb's house.

Peter Quennell and Cyril Connolly paid him a visit at the end of 1935. Quennell arrived first and he and Dick drove to Semley railway station to meet Connolly. Quennell remembers Connolly adjusting his bohemian beret and tie as the Bugatti purred up to the front door of the stately home: he was thrilled to be invited to stay at such a famous house. He was in for a surprise: instead of entering the Clouds of legend, filled with Pre-Raphaelite paintings, Connolly was shown into a vast but empty hall. A few large bright patches on the walls revealed where the paintings and tapestries had once hung:

> Curtains and furniture had taken flight; naked floor-boards creaked beneath the tread; and to reach Dick's refuge, originally the housekeeper's room, his guests walked through a small concealed door – behind it hung long rows of neatly labelled household bells – descended a narrow staircase and traversed a gloomy basement.[61]

Outside Quennell heard the crash of falling timber: according to Dick, ever since he had made his decision to sell the estate 'all the oaks and beeches had begun to die'.

Dick was writing as well as painting. He had been on an expedition to Sudan earlier in the year which has some similarity to the fictional flight of Tony Last in *A Handful of Dust*, published in 1934, and with Charles Ryder's trip to South America in *Brideshead Revisited* (1945). Tony Last has clung on to the no longer fashionable ancestral home of Hetton but his life is torn apart by the death of his only son and heir and the discovery of his wife's adultery. He flees to South America in search of an idealised Hetton among the Peewee Indians. Dick had no son to inherit Clouds, his two marriages had been failures, he had sold off the contents of the house but could not sell the estate: in March 1935 he made his break to join the Dinka tribe in Southern Sudan. Fact was following fiction.

Dick's journey to Sudan was rather different to his jaunts through Europe: more expensive and much less comfortable. He went out to join Jack Poole, an old friend from Sandhurst, who had been living for the last five years at Tonj. Poole had tried to pursue a career at Lloyd's after the First World War and he spent weekends at Clouds with Dick and Iris, 'hunting, shooting and indoor pastimes'.[62] but he disliked working in the City. He spent six years in Southern Rhodesia, then became Assistant District Commissioner with the Sudan Political Service, his posting Tonj, in the Bahr ed Ghazal Province, known as 'the Bog'. On every annual leave in England he described to Dick the wonderful models the Dinkas would make: Dick's photographs even more than his paintings reveal their startling beauty. The women were just to Dick's taste, tall, willowy and slim.

Once settled at Tonj Dick bought two Dinka women to be his regular models/wives. Anneege cost six cows, or approximately £4; Rafa was much cheaper, 'so cheap as to

raise a suspicion that her father had been only too glad to see what he hoped was the last of her. She was a terror.'[63] He found his models little different to the professional models of Chelsea:

120 (left)   One of Dick Wyndham's regular models in the Sudan.

121 (right)   Dinka boys study one of Dick Wyndham's paintings in the Sudan.

> If made to work late in the evening they would invariably complain, 'But what about the lions on the road?' and I found this no less tiresome than 'What about the last 'bus home'?[64]

After several weeks with Poole, Dick found himself succumbing to the beauty of the Dinkas, to their gentle companionship. On leaving after a couple of months he experienced a profound sense of loss. The antics of the London season, Chelsea parties and hunt balls were viewed with a new perspective. His eventual published description of the Dinkas, *The Gentle Savage*, reveals his abilities as a writer and the impact of his stay in Sudan:

> The drum (surely played by no hand) seemed to come from the very hearts of the dancers themselves, as it fought, first for, then against, the impoverished voices – voices that shouted triumphantly of battle, gloried over death – tortured death; or, in their lewdness, expressed the sexual desires of the whole world; voices that sang softly a love-song – a psalm, that hung like a diaphanous veil, obscuring for a moment the horror that had gone before; only to be torn by the scream of a girl. Piercing, throbbing, it focused all consciousness till the drum was no more than a pulse trembling in the soil, and the last echo of the scream left a silence that was absolute; a vacuum in sound.[65]

Dick began *The Gentle Savage* at Clouds and completed it at Tickerage, posting it off to the publishers in February 1936. Barbara Wadsworth recalls his reliance on her mother Fanny for practical criticism:

> Wyndham would stride over from Tickerage, getting someone to pick him up later by car, or relying on Edward's chauffeur to run him back home. He came generally for a late tea, tramping into the sitting-room in his shorts and brown leather boots, scattering mud and field refuse on his way with schoolboy indifference to the doormat, his manuscript tucked under his arm or in some haversack-like container; and there would be crumpets for tea, or Edward's special delight, hot buttered toast with Gentleman's Relish or Oxford marmalade. Wyndham would consume vast quantities, spreading dribbles of melted butter down his front.[66]

The book was an instant success. A second edition was planned only the second week after publication (by 1937 there were four editions). Guy Wyndham wrote to his sister Mary, who had also enjoyed *The Gentle Savage*, 'I hope [it] will have a good sale in America'. Perhaps part of its success is attributable to the numerous black-and-white photographs, almost all of naked Dinkas, dancing, or spreadeagled provocatively on the ground. The frontispiece, a painting by Dick of a Dinka tribesman, gave the model a modest loincloth which was not part of the artist's original sketches or oil paintings.

In celebration of Jack Poole's return to England in 1936, Dick hosted a Dinka dinner

122 *Dinka Herdsmen* by Dick Wyndham.

at the Savoy Hotel: the event was worthy of the fiction of Evelyn Waugh. The guests (men only) included Tom Driberg, David Tennant, Bunny Keene, Peter Quennell, Sacheverell Sitwell, Curtis Moffat, Freddy Mayor and A.J.A. Symons, also John Heygate who had been responsible for the break-up of Evelyn Waugh's first marriage.

The food was less in quantity but rather more exotic than usual. There were pawpaws, peanut soup, turtle fins which 'when cooked . . . are neither fishy nor finny, but resemble sweetbreads for texture, and calf's head for flavour. Agreeably glutinous, they formed a perfect background for the cool champagne which accompanied them and the rich madeira sauce in which they were served',[67] roast partridge, egg plant and pimentos, mango fool and corn on the cob. Mead was drunk with the corn, 'though without the live grubs which our host told us were the proper Dinka accompaniment'. A room in the Savoy had been specially decorated, the walls and ceilings shrouded in thin gauze.

> Fifteen-foot palms hid the corners. At one end of the room a camp bed, protected by mosquito nets, awaited use. The long dining table was lit by candles standing in empty wine bottles. Two impassive Africans [Dick hired two Negroes for the evening], at least six feet six high, naked save for leopard-skin loin cloths, with painted faces and huge spears, stood at the head of the table; and invisible drums sounded the tom-tom invitation to the feast.[68]

The evening ended with a showing of a film taken by Poole, 'depicting Dinka dances. . . . It was unsuitable for public release.' In his speech of thanks, A.J.A. Symons hailed Dick as one of the supreme playboys of the western world.

In April 1937 Tooth's gave Dick a one-man show called 'The Gentle Savage'. His paintings were to be as popular as the book: at the private view his images sold like hot cakes to millionaire bohemia. Shortly before the opening, in an article on the usefulness of private views, the *Bystander* commented that the most sociable one-man shows in London were those of Captain Richard Wyndham.

Tony Last, hero of *A Handful of Dust*, never returned from South America. Charles Ryder, artist-hero of *Brideshead Revisited*, made a journey to South America, like Dick to try something different, to escape from the claustrophobia of the all too familiar art world of London, and to spend time away from a wife he no longer loved. Ryder returns to produce a book of his travels and to be given a one-man show which is a triumphant success. One of the daily newspapers reports: 'Charles "Stately Homes" Ryder steps off the map. That the snakes and vampires of the jungle have nothing on Mayfair is the opinion of socialite artist Ryder, who has abandoned the houses of the great for the ruins of equatorial Africa.'[69] That the female reporter gets the continent wrong (Dick went to Africa; Charles to South America) is part of Waugh's comment on her profession and her sex.

Ryder's paintings are now found to be full of 'virility' and 'passion'; they are 'barbaric', 'forceful' and 'downright unhealthy'. A London art critic comments: 'by focussing the frankly traditional battery of his elegance and erudition on the maelstrom of barbarism, Mr Ryder has at last found himself'. Anthony Blanche, however, is unimpressed by the new Ryder, and dismisses the canvases:

> It was charm again, my dear, single, creamy English charm, playing tigers. . . . Charm is the great English blight. . . . It spots and kills anything it touches. It kills love; it kills art; I greatly fear, my dear Charles, it has killed *you*.[70]

A surfeit of charm had probably, in Dick's case, meant that his artistic ability could never mature into anything significant. All his life, even in his death, he was simply 'playing tigers'.

6

The publication of *The Gentle Savage* coincided with the sale, at last, of Clouds. Property speculators paid a total of £39,000 for the house and estate. Dick didn't completely sever his ties with East Knoyle. Slades House was not included in the 1936 sale and Dick remained its owner until 1938, when it was sold to Hubert Savory. His cousin David Tennant was renting Teffont Manor a few miles away. David's daughter Pauline remembers Dick arriving at Teffont on his motorbike, probably in the summer of 1936 just after the sale to Messrs Hucklesby and Bartlett, with an invitation to all the guests to come back to Clouds and eat the fruit before 'the barbarians move in'.[71]

Shortly before the outbreak of the Second World War, the army requisitioned Teffont, so David acquired Holloway House in East Knoyle, even closer to Clouds.[72] Dick meanwhile continued writing, completing his novel *Painter's Progress* in less than six months. He was living in Tickerage Cottage at the time; the mill house was let to his friends the architect Serge Chermayeff and his wife Barbara while their own modernist home was being built a mile or so away.

The novel is semi-autobiographical. The narrator Jack is obviously based on Dick: the owner of a country cottage and a flat in London, haunted by the mementoes and memories of his past. The painters in the novel, Patrick and Kyra, also possess Dick's characteristics. Their stormy affair explores the conflict between creative and sexual desire. Patrick compares painting to making love,

> 'Colours are bitter enemies,' he says, 'and so are all men and women.' In fact, he holds that there is no such thing in painting as a fundamental unity of colour and design – only magnificent rebellion. And there is no such thing as real love between the sexes – it is war without hope of peace. 'And that's why I paint,' he will say jokingly, 'I find it less exhausting to fight my battle on a well-primed canvas than between the sheets.'[73]

Nevertheless, Patrick rediscovers himself as an artist through his passion for Kyra and appreciation of her creative vision. She, however, loses her personal vision and can only paint in the style of her lover: she finally covers all her canvases with white paint and disappears for ever. In Dick's will, which he made in 1948, he requested his art executor Freddy Mayor to preserve only his best paintings and to give them away to friends 'who he considers would like to receive them'. The remainder were to be covered over with white paint and 'given to such Art School as he shall think fit'.[74]

At the end of 1938 the War Office raised new anti-aircraft units in the Territorial Army. Jack Poole was renting Tickerage Cottage at the time and he was asked to command the searchlight battery with headquarters in Brighton. He was gazetted Major, Royal Artillery (TA). Dick immediately joined him as second in command and from 1 November 1938 he was commissioned Captain, Royal Artillery (TA). The searchlight battery covered an area from Brighton to Newhaven and was made up of sixteen light detachments. Poole later praised Dick's abilities as second in command:

> He was quick to grasp such technicalities as the Theory of Sound for the detection of Aircraft and other scientific formulae beyond my ken. Not only was he an excellent instructor, but when clothed in his military uniform [had he reformed?] he became a strict disciplinarian and a great supporter of 'doing what the Major said'.[75]

Three of his lectures on sound location were printed, to be used in the training of the searchlight units.

The responsibility may have encouraged Dick to drink less. When he visited his father and Violet at Ramsbury in August 1939, just before mobilisation, his daughter Joan noted: 'his face is tanned and he wears a blue shirt with a red tie. He looks much better now he has stopped drinking.' He was still driving too fast: she noticed the speedometer of his Alvis touch 82 m.p.h. between Marlborough (clotted cream tea) and Ramsbury. He was also beginning to get a bald patch on the top of his head, 'like a priest's tonsure'.[76]

Freddy Mayor decided to close down the Mayor Gallery and became Poole's driver. Mobilisation was on 24 August and in November Dick was appointed Brigade Major; the following year he was promoted Temporary Major. There were light moments in the defence of southern England. Major Wyndham usually wore bedroom slippers as part of his uniform. Peter Quennell recalls that after the death of Dick's dog during a bombing raid over Dover the officers present conducted a full military funeral. All the while, however, in spite of Joan's optimism, Dick was drinking heavily. His relationships with women were as complex and unsatisfactory as ever. He was in and out of the London Clinic until finally invalided out of the army in the summer of 1942. When Joan visited him in the clinic she found him still looking distinguished, 'lying in bed wearing his major's tunic over his pyjamas',[77] but with white hair and bad teeth. His father had died in April 1941; his sister Olivia was now an American citizen. Reminders of the past were slipping away.

From the summer of 1942 onwards Dick's visits to Tickerage were less frequent. Friends rented the cottage and eventually the millhouse itself. In a short story, Francis Wyndham has given a version of Dick's life immediately after he left the army: 'things had gone badly. . . . His formerly flamboyant style cramped by money worries, he had found it hard to cash in on any one of his several remarkable gifts';[78] the epicurean wine-lover had become a drunk.

In the last years of the war Dick did manage to dry out and combined some adventurous expeditions into Persia, usually flying his own Moth, with occasional writing for the *News of the World*. Some friends are convinced he was also one of the many amateur 'spies' used by the Foreign Office to provide information on activities in the Near East. In London Dick established home base in a suite at the Hyde Park Hotel. In Cairo he stayed with his old friend Patrick Balfour, now Lord Kinross, who was press officer to the RAF. Kinross was divorced from Angela Culme-Seymour (one of Dick's girlfriends – a 'humdinger of a honeypot')[79] and shared a house with the outrageously camp Eddy Gathorne-Hardy and, slightly later, John Rayner, another Tickerage friend, who worked as a cipherer at the Embassy.

Dick's movements can only be traced through the memories of those he encountered. In 1944, for example, he was at Luxor and met up with Julian Asquith,

Earl of Oxford and Asquith. Lord Oxford found him maddeningly self-centred but still as entertaining as ever. Also in 1944 he took Joan Rayner (a 'ravishingly beautiful' guest at Tickerage when Miss Eyres-Monsell, returning as Mrs Rayner and lastly as the partner of Patrick Leigh-Fermor) on an expedition to Kurdistan. They were guarded by tribesmen armed to the teeth while Dick picked the local flowers.

At the beginning of 1946 Ian Fleming set up a foreign news service to provide stories for all the Kelmsley newspapers, including the *News of the World* and the *Sunday Times*. Dick was invited to cover the Arab-Israeli war with a series of specially commissioned articles, 'at an unusually high rate of payment'.[80]

In 1947 Dick took off on a solo expedition into Afghanistan. His aeroplane was wrecked but he survived by living off sunflowers and managed to walk through the mountains of Iran to safety, though badly crippled by frostbite. The following year he was not so fortunate. He went out to Palestine in the spring to report for Ian Fleming's foreign news service. But when he incautiously stood without cover to photograph a skirmish between Israeli troops and the Arab Legion he was shot dead by a Jewish sniper. Some reports claimed he was wearing Arab dress. It was 19 May 1948: he was fifty-two.

He had been working continuously on a study of the Marsh Arabs. They made a strong appeal to his aesthetic sense; 'he found in the wearing of loose robes a comfortable liberation from buttons, braces, collar studs and sock suspenders; and there was nothing in the subjection of women at odds with his own erotic tastes'.[81] The manuscript was stolen when all his belongings were rifled through immediately after his death.[82]

When Dick's will was read, Cyril Connolly and Freddy Mayor learnt that they had half-shares in the wine cellar at Tickerage. There was much debate as to which fine wines might still be in the house. Matthew Smith and Bunny Keene had been renting Tickerage when they heard the news of Dick's death. Bunny wrote in the visitors' book:

> Today, as the last tenants of Tickerage, we learnt the tragic news of Dick's death in Jerusalem. To us, who knew him well, this means not only the passing of a beloved friend, but also the end of an epoch, of twenty years of Tickerage, and the closing of this so familiar book.

Cyril Connolly, Dick's literary executor, took care of the book. He added the final entry:

> Sunday May 30 . . . 'Because man goeth to his long home and the mourners go about the streets'.[83]

11 From Home to Institution

It is so easy to judge the past; it is so frightfully difficult to risk your money on the present.[1]

I

On 21 July 1936 Dick Wyndham and the two remaining trustees of Perf's estate, Edward Scawen Wyndham and George Henry Drummond, sold Clouds House and 2,982 acres to Frank Reginald Hucklesby of Broad Street Place, London and Ernest William Smith Bartlett of Farnham, Surrey. Dick received £670 for three particular fields; the trustees received £38,330 for the rest, to be invested on Dick's behalf.[2]

Messrs Hucklesby and Bartlett had no intention of either living in Clouds House or maintaining the estate. They had only bought the estate to make a quick profit. They were property speculators and almost immediately they put the estate back on the market. The particulars drawn up by Messrs Senior & Godwin and John D. Wood & Company in 1936 differed considerably from the 1932 particulars of Knight, Frank and Rutley, drawn up for Dick. The entire estate was cut up piecemeal into potential building sites:

> The Auctioneers are prepared to sell privately sites of practically any area and will vary boundaries to suit prospective purchasers' requirements. The Auctioneers, therefore, suggest that prospective purchasers should look over the Estate and pick sites for themselves, suiting their own tastes.

Clouds House came with only 26 acres of land. This 'important well-built mansion' was for sale 'at a sacrificial price or will be sold later for demolition'. At least the 1932 particulars had suggested it might be suitable for a school or club, if not a home. The domestic offices were treated as a separate dwelling, ideal to form 'a desirable small country residence ... nicely situated in its own grounds, of just over one acre'. Whoever bought the house and the offices would be required to block up the passages which once connected the properties. The stables were similarly described as a complete unit in themselves, with seven acres of grounds; the former electric light and battery house would make an 'attractive cottage'; the bathing lake, with three acres of woodland and orchard, provided 'a very attractive site for a small residence'. Sites alongside the main roads around and through East Knoyle suggested commercial use. The one acre of lot 68, for example, could be a 'fine site for a Tea-House or Petrol Station. . . . This site can be seen for a long distance on both roads and will command the attention of the large amount of traffic passing on those roads.'

Estates had been divided up in similar ways all over Britain since the slump after the First World War; the practice continues to this day. Ernest Bartlett was, in his own small way, responsible for quite a number of such transactions. Others like him, so far under-researched by historians, were steadily dismantling one surviving element of 'old England': responsible for the movement of land from ownership by a few to ownership

239

123 Mr and Mrs Bartlett, Farnham, *c.*1935.

by many. Bartlett was so successful at buying and disposing of estates that he was able to buy each of his five daughters a house of her own, provide each with a reasonable private income, and educate all his grandchildren at private schools.[3]

Bartlett was born in 1863 at Hatherleigh, Devon and after a short period as a civil servant in London he joined the family timber business in Devon. By the beginning of the First World War he was successful enough to buy part of Lord Portsmouth's estate at Eggesford for the timber contained in the Eggesford Forest. The demand for timber during the First World War assured him of financial success. After the war he continued to buy up estates throughout Devon and north Cornwall, primarily for their timber.

In 1933 Bartlett was bankrupted by the failure of the family sawmill at Hatherleigh; the cause was mismanagement by the salaried manager, 'something to do with miscalculation of the length of railway sleepers',[4] and the poor state of the trade in general. Bartlett moved to Farnham in Surrey and, probably through Freemason connections, was able to restart buying up estates then dividing them up and reselling, first in partnership and then alone. By the beginning of the Second World War he had paid off his creditors. His energy and resilience contrasts with the dilettantish lifestyle of Dick and his friends, indulging in the 'good life' at Tickerage. However, they could not be accused of being environmental vandals in search of a quick profit.

Peper Harrow, near Godalming, home of William St John Brodrick, first Earl of Midleton (and brother-in-law of Hugo, Earl of Wemyss) was one of the estates Bartlett purchased, also the Waverley Abbey Estate just outside Farnham; with a consortium he bought up Margam near Port Talbot. The houses survived on these estates – Peper Harrow is now a centre for the rehabilitation of young offenders. By chance Clouds House also survived, though not before articles in the national newspapers forewarned of its imminent destruction. *The Times*, on 22 October 1936, called for 'one of the most remarkable mansions in England' to be saved. But as Lawrence Stone and J.C. Fawtier Stone have suggested, Webb's architectural style was not popular in the 1930s:

> Not architecturally interesting enough or old enough to be worth preserving for their own sake, not modest enough to be habitable in an age of servant shortage, depressed rents, and high taxes, huge Victorian houses and house expansions were among the first victims of the social upheavals of the twentieth century.[5]

Bartlett received a bid from a demolition firm and it looked as if Clouds would go the way of dozens of other country houses – thirteen were demolished every year between 1920 and 1955. However, an imaginative young designer called Geoffrey Houghton-Brown – who had been at the Slade with Oliver Messel, his chief friend, and with Rex Whistler; another student at the time was Stephen Tennant – persuaded his parents to take a look at the house. Throughout the 1930s Geoffrey Houghton-Brown had acquired 'unwanted' country houses, carrying out restoration and demolition work as appropriate before selling off the properties. In 1934, for example, he bought and remodelled Waresley Hall near Cambridge. The large eighteenth-century mansion had been entirely 'modernised' by the Duncomb family in 1830 but later part-demolished. Geoffrey Houghton-Brown transformed the remainder into an attractive residence, selling off the walled garden, stable block, dairy and gardener's cottage. In 1937 he bought Culham House near Abingdon, a beautiful Queen Anne building. The kitchen quarters were demolished, then the house itself was decorated, furnished and lived in for a time by Geoffrey Houghton-Brown before he sold it in 1939.

Percy Houghton-Brown had retired from the Bar and planned to settle near his brother, who lived close to East Knoyle. He first rented Sedgehill Manor near Shaftesbury, then bought land on which to build his retirement home; the first plot close to Clouds Park, then another on Windmill Hill. His son Geoffrey suggested they should scrap the idea of building a new house and buy Clouds itself. Percy Houghton-Brown was dubious about the entire scheme: he and his wife Elizabeth were no longer young, and turning the vast mansion into a reasonably sized house (of some ten bedrooms) would be a considerable undertaking. Geoffrey and his mother persuaded him otherwise. Clouds was too good a bargain to lose, and the stables would be more than adequate for the use of all the Houghton-Brown children. Their previous house in London had been built by Elizabeth Houghton-Brown's father James Malcolm in 1914 on land that had been part of the former park of Wimbledon House. Their own grounds consisted of 24 acres of gardens, a lake and considerable stables.[6]

On 29 April 1937 Messrs Hucklesby and Bartlett conveyed, to Elizabeth Houghton-Brown, Clouds House, along with the domestic offices, the stables and 50 acres of land. The price paid was £3,300, approximately £76,700 less than it had cost to build. The house was still sited in a park of reasonable size – the plot bought by the Houghton-Browns had been intended by Messrs Hucklesby and Bartlett for at least two building sites. The buildings themselves were all of a piece apart from the head gardener's cottage, just between the offices and the stables, which, together with one acre of land, had been bought by its tenant Mrs Ruperta Shand on 22 August of the previous year.

2

Though Clouds was still to be used as a private home, the Houghton-Browns decided they had to reduce it in size. The architect Charles Biddulph Pinchard was commissioned to 'rationalise' the house. Ironically, one of his important commissions in London was the London Clinic which Dick came to know well while he was being dried out; he also had a successful practice working on alterations to country houses. He came up with plans which involved the demolition of about one-third of the main house. The north side, including the main entrance and dining room, was sliced off; the top floor with George Wyndham's library was reduced to attic space only (the windows were removed and the library fittings sold to Exeter University); the entrance was moved from the north to the west side; two bays were removed on the west side, and part of the offices were demolished.

The most dramatic undertaking was the blowing up of Webb's tower, which contained the lift and water tanks. Geoffrey Houghton-Brown recalled trying to persuade his parents to keep the tower; however, they wanted Clouds to look 'modest', and thought the tower made the house look pretentious. The army had to be brought in to carry out the demolition. Major Spottiswood and a detachment of the Royal Engineers first tried to blow up the tower on 11 May 1938, but 'so strongly built was the tower that efforts to raze it were only partially successful'.

> It was decided to make a further attempt [the following day] and during the morning men were busily engaged in inserting high explosives in the tower walls. By three o'clock all was in readiness and spectators gathered at a discreet distance to watch the noble edifice topple to the ground. At a word from Major Spottiswood a corporal touched off the charge. There was a deafening roar, followed by huge clouds of smoke and dust. Onlookers anxiously awaited for the clouds to clear. Engineers were confident that this time their efforts had been successful, but when the smoke had cleared it was found that although the outer walls had been brought down the central lift shaft remained. Another attempt to demolish this was made later in the afternoon.[7]

Alterations to Clouds cost about £7,000, including the addition of six bathrooms, making a total of around £10,000 with the purchase price. The biggest change to the interior (after the demolition of the north side) was in the great hall. This was reduced in size by 'filling in' between Webb's pillars, creating an inner courtyard or 'winter garden' in which a pond was constructed. The mantelpieces from the south drawing room and the dining room were turned into plant containers.

The Houghton-Browns' decision to knock down part of Clouds was made purely because they wanted a manageable size of house to live in, with about ten bedrooms. Webb's devotees naturally regard their action as desecration. If, however, the Houghton-Browns had not taken on such an undertaking, Clouds would undoubtedly have been totally demolished. As Geoffrey Houghton-Brown commented, his parents were very courageous, though perhaps foolish, to struggle to save Clouds from demolition at such a time, as the world awaited the outbreak of war.

The Houghton-Browns were not destined to stay long at Clouds. The declaration of war forced them to abandon the house as it was too expensive to run: they rented Cleeve in East Knoyle and let Clouds to Miss E. Chynoweth (she paid £300 a year

124 (facing page, above) Demolition of the north side of Clouds House, 1938.

125 (facing page, below) Demolition of the tower.

126   The pond in the
winter garden, 1992.

including water), who ran it as a secretarial college. The army requisitioned part of the
basement of Clouds from November 1940.[8] Hilary Houghton-Brown married in 1940
and moved to the Wincanton area to take up farming; her brother Alastair was serving
overseas so the stables were no longer of use.

Then, in 1941, Elizabeth Houghton-Brown died at Cleeve and the same year Alastair
was killed in North Africa. His name was added to the village war memorial alongside
the names of the young Wyndham soldiers from Clouds, Perf and George Hereman,
who had lost their lives in an earlier world war. In memory of his son, 'who spent so
many happy days at Clouds House', Percy Houghton-Brown gave £1,000 to the village
hall in East Knoyle to build a stage. In 1943 he died: the Houghton-Browns had owned
Clouds for six years and lived there less than two.

Since Percy Wyndham's death in 1911 the record for the occupation of Clouds –
seven years – was held by the Mosselman family. George Wyndham had owned the
estate for two years, his son Perf for just over a year. Dick owned it for twenty-two
years, from 1914 until 1936 but occupied the house only during his brief marriage to Iris
and very occasionally between the end of the Mosselmans' tenancy and the sale of the
house to Messrs Hucklesby and Bartlett. Clouds was still not demolished. After Percy
Houghton-Brown's death it entered its last phase, the only alternative to demolition: it
became an institution.

3

While the fate of Clouds was being decided in south Wiltshire, other country houses belonging to the grandchildren (and great-grandchildren) of Percy and Madeline Wyndham, also to the descendants of their closest friends, were undergoing transformations. Babraham, the home of the Wyndhams' second daughter Madeline from 1888, remained the property of the Adeanes until 1948. Madeline died in 1941, her husband Charles in 1943.

Their only son and heir Robert had graduated from Trinity College, Cambridge in 1927 with a degree in economics, and married Joyce Burnett two years later. Even before they were married, Joyce had suggested her uncle, Lord St Davids, find Robert work in his investment group. Lord St Davids was an enormously successful railway tycoon: in the 1880s he had been responsible for the building of railways throughout Central and South America. Both of his sons by his first marriage were killed in the First World War; Harley Drayton became his business 'heir' and Robert Adeane was taken under his wing. The Adeanes' first posting was to Buenos Aires and the A1 Pacifico Railway; for the rest of his life Robert Adeane pursued a successful career as a financier and businessman. He was chairman and director of dozens of companies ranging from steel to tropical agriculture, and his involvement in railways took him chiefly to Latin America – he was chairman of the Costa Rica Railway – and to Turkey.[9]

Robert and Joyce paid regular visits to Babraham with their family, and his children recall being spoilt by their grandmother Madeline Adeane. They called her Gan-Gan,

127 (left) Charles Adeane at Babraham holding his only son Robert.

128 (right) Robert Adeane at Babraham holding his eldest son Philip. A photograph of Orpen's portrait of Madeline Wyndham is on the table.

just as her own mother Madeline Wyndham had been called by her grandchildren. There was Dundee cake for tea; ginger beer was made in the basement; the bedrooms were named after the months of the year and along the top landing, where the children slept, hung large Hollyer photographs of the paintings of Burne-Jones. The Adeanes had also acquired Burne-Jones's cartoons 'Poesis' and 'Musica', presumably at Dick Wyndham's sale of the contents of Clouds.

Robert joined the Royal Artillery in 1938 and was promoted Lieutenant-Colonel in 1941, Colonel in 1943. He spent much of the war in Africa and the Middle East and in 1943 was awarded the military OBE, the year he inherited Babraham. The house and park were knocked about by the military during the war: soldiers camped in the park and tanks ploughed up the ground. When peace was declared Robert was faced with an estimate of £17,000 just to repair the roof. He made the difficult decision to sell Babraham House but keep most of the estate. All his life he maintained the profession of 'farmer' in his passport. Though the major part of his working life was devoted to business ventures, he was no 'gentleman farmer'; he ran an estate of 3–4,000 acres as effectively as he pursued his activities in the City.

The contents of Babraham were sold in 1946; two years later the house together with 450 acres of farm and woodland and 46 cottages – the greater part of the village – were sold to the Agricultural Research Council. Just after the sale, Robert Adeane made a very large amount of money in the City: it was too late, however, to buy back the family home. Babraham became the Institute of Animal Physiology, where basic research is conducted on the physiology and biochemistry of farm animals as a foundation for improved animal production.

Meanwhile Robert was divorced by Joyce and married Kit Dunn, the wealthy daughter of the Canadian financier, Sir James Dunn (whose own second wife was Irene, Marchioness of Queensberry, previously the girlfriend of Dick Wyndham and co-respondent in his first divorce). Dunn was a patron of both Augustus John and Sickert and Kit virtually grew up with the John family. Robert had become interested in modern art through his older cousin Dick Wyndham who introduced him, at the end of the war, to Freddy Mayor. Robert's first purchase, in 1946, was a Matthew Smith. Kit further encouraged him so that for the next thirty years he devoted himself to collecting and to supporting public collections. His own collection contained some outstanding paintings and, with Kit's money as well as his own, it easily surpassed Dick's. Yet he denied the term collection,

> for such a word is not applicable to the relatively unconnected assembling of works ... acquisitions made by an individual untrained in Art, with an ambivalent taste and inclinations towards Surrealism and the 'off beat' ... I bought what I liked, what I was advised was good and what, at the time, I could afford.[10]

This included works by Matisse, Picasso, Edward Burra, Henri Gaudier-Brzeska, Max Ernst, Kandinsky, Giorgio de Chirico, Joe Tilson, Robert Rauschenberg and Andy Warhol; examples of French and English contemporary art but also modern American, Australian and Spanish painting; portraits, abstract compositions and constructional works. Robert was helped by the Mayor Gallery in particular, and he bought several paintings by Dick Wyndham.

As a collector he was passionate about colour, and in the business world he was an eccentric and colourful character. He combined business trips abroad with other pleasures, in Paris, after the war, for example, visiting galleries and gambling with

Freddy Mayor. His favourite niece Penny Allen often accompanied him on trips to Central America and Australia (Kit preferred to stay behind in England) where he frequently surprised his hosts by appearing in informal, sometimes eccentric clothes. As one of his children recalls, his appearance fitted into the world of Cork Street rather than the City. But he was also a landowner: in the 1950s he acquired Quendon Hall near Stansted after Kit inherited £1 million from her father. Later he acquired Loudham Hall near Wickham Market; he tried, unsuccessfully, to buy Glen in Peebleshire from the Tennant family. He continued to be a Justice of the Peace in Cambridgeshire until 1956, and paid for the erection of the memorial east window and restoration of the parish church at Babraham. John Piper was commissioned to design the stained glass. He was Trustee of the Tate Gallery from 1955 to 1962 and in 1958 founded the Friends of the Tate Gallery. He was knighted in 1961 for his services to the arts and in 1969, after the death of Kit, he donated £100,000 to the Fitzwilliam Museum towards the cost of building the Adeane Gallery. After his death in 1979, his wife Jane gave one of his paintings by Graham Sutherland to the Fitzwilliam in his memory. At her death in 1993, many more of his paintings have been left to a public collection, the Tate in East Anglia Foundation.

Babraham no longer belongs to the Adeanes but through Robert Adeane's art collecting their name is permanently associated with public art. Robert's father Charles, agriculturalist and President of the Royal Agricultural Society of England, would no doubt have been pleased that his former home is now the leading international centre for livestock research and production.

Hewell Grange, like Babraham, was granted a new lease of life as a public institution immediately after the war. It had been built by Robert Windsor-Clive, Lord Windsor (whose wife Gay was the intimate friend of George Wyndham), between 1884 and 1891, at the cost of £250,000 (three times the cost of Clouds) and was supposed to look genuinely Elizabethan, a virtual copy, on the outside, of Montacute House in Somerset. Lord Windsor also owned St Fagan's Castle in Glamorgan and Oakly Court in Shropshire. His decision to rebuild the damp, crumbling eighteenth-century mansion at Hewell coincided with the payment of large royalties from the family's investments in the South Wales coal industry and the development of docks on their land at Penarth. A descendant has commented that his decision was something of a folly: he was only in his early twenties, 'clearly not very experienced at the time', and undoubtedly wanted to impress.[11]

Lord Windsor became the first Earl of Plymouth in 1905. His son Ivor inherited the family estates in 1923, two years after his marriage to Irene Charteris, youngest child of Hugo and Mary Wemyss (hence a granddaughter of Madeline and Percy Wyndham). Ivor sold off much of the Worcestershire estates to defray death duties and lived at St Fagan's and Oakly Court – Hewell was too expensive to run. He pursued a career in government until the outbreak of the Second World War, as MP for Ludlow, Chief Whip in the House of Lords, Under-Secretary of State for the Dominions and the Colonies and finally Parliamentary Under-Secretary of State at the Foreign Office. During the Second World War, Hewell was occupied by the army, then Ivor died suddenly in 1943. Irene carried on running the estates until Other, the new earl, returned from war service.

Almost at once the decision was made to retain only one country residence, Oakly Court. Hewell Grange was sold for £35,000 to the government and on 14 August 1947 transferred to the Home Office for use as a Borstal. Nothing was demolished. The real

129 Hewell Grange Young Offender Institution.

tennis court was converted into a gymnasium; the stable block became the works unit for maintenance of the property; Detmar Blow's chapel, the ceiling reputedly carved with the heads of III individual children from the estate, remained in use. A small Home Farm of 200 acres was established on the estate with a herd of Jersey cows providing milk, and there is a pig unit for bacon. Vegetables are grown for the house, also flowers – used for displays in Hewell and sold to other prisons all over the Midlands.

The term Borstal is no longer used; Hewell is now a Young Offenders Institution. It accommodates between 140 and 190 young offenders, all boys, who work on the farm, in the gardens and the house. The vast hall which once contained the magnificent paintings and tapestries of the Plymouths is used as the dining room; it is scrubbed and polished twice a day. A bronze statue remains, and magnificent chimneypieces and ceilings; the walls of the 'garden vestibule' are still covered with painted tapestries executed by the scene painter at the Burg Theatre in Vienna, who copied tapestries in the possession of the Emperor at Schönbrunn. The relatively good behaviour of the residents of Hewell may partly be explained by the impact of their surroundings.

Ivor Plymouth sold the rest of his property in Worcestershire at the same time as Hewell; he also disposed of St Fagan's Castle in Glamorgan, though not for any profit. The castle, gardens and surrounding grounds, 18 acres, together with a further 80 acres from the park, were offered to the National Museum of Wales as the centre of a new folk museum. Following a national appeal for funds, the Welsh Folk Museum opened to the public in July 1948. For a modest entrance fee, anyone can now enjoy the romantic setting which brought together George Wyndham and Gay Windsor-Clive and inspired Wilfrid Blunt. At Hewell there is no entrance fee, and the visitors stay for as long as Her Majesty's government pleases.

Wortley Hall near Sheffield was frequently visited by Percy and Madeline Wyndham. It was the seat of Edward Montagu-Stuart-Wortley-Mackenzie, first Earl of Wharncliffe and the patron of Edward Poynter. Members of the Stuart-Wortley family were close friends of the Wyndhams, George and Rosalind Howard and the Grosvenors.

Wortley was part-occupied by the army during the Second World War, then left to fall semi-derelict, the gardens overgrown with weeds. The contents were sold in 1948 but entailments on the property meant that the house could only be sold leasehold. There were few enquiries until the Wharncliffe Estates was approached by a group consisting of members of the Trade Union, Socialist, Co-operative and Labour movements; their intention was to turn Wortley into an educational holiday centre for the Labour Movement. After lengthy negotiations, the Wharncliffe Estate sold a 14-year lease on Wortley: the rent for the first year was £50; £500 thereafter. In 1954 the Earl of Wharncliffe died and the entailment conditions became null and void. To avoid death duties, the estate sold Wortley to the sitting tenants: £10,000 for the freehold of the hall, six cottages and 28 acres of land.

Wortley Hall is now part of a limited company – Labour's Educational Recreational Holiday Homes Limited. The former domestic offices, including the dairy, bakery, wash-house, laundry and estate office, have been converted into a ballroom and concert lounge. There are 56 bedrooms, offering dormitory accommodation for 160. From April to October the hall is a holiday centre; during the winter season it is used for conferences, weekly and weekend schools and dinner dances. The Victorian painted ceilings, ornamental friezes and wood carvings have been restored, including the magnificent ceiling of the salon, now called the Foundry dining-hall, originally the work of the Sheffield artist Geoffrey Sykes but completed by Poynter. According to the brochure produced for its twenty-fifth anniversary, Wortley is now 'a little oasis of socialism that is owned and controlled by its own independent rank and file organisation'.

> The Wharncliffes – the previous owners of Wortley Hall, derived much of their wealth out of the coal mines of South Yorkshire. With this wealth they built Wortley Hall. All the fine carvings, painting and stonemasonry that were put into the building of Wortley Hall were only there for a privileged few.
>
> Now, in the course of a year, the beauties and amenities of Wortley Hall are used in some form or other, by thousands of ordinary people.
>
> It can now be said that in the last 25 years, there is one place in Britain – Wortley Hall – where the wheel of social change has made a full turn.[12]

Robert Wyndham Ketton-Cremer, a distant relation of the Wyndham family, and owner of Felbrigg in Norfolk from 1933 until his own death in 1969, described how his home fortunately avoided army occupation during the Second World War:

> Felbrigg survived the war, shaken now and then by bombs, a few windows broken, a few additional cracks in the ceilings, nothing worse. Since it was then still without electricity, it could not be adapted for any military or civilian purpose whatever. In

Gosford House,
immediately after the
Second World War.

contrast to its neighbours, occupied from cellar to attic and ringed round with
camps and hutments, it remained undisturbed.[13]

Gosford, the principal seat of the Earls of Wemyss, was, like Babraham, Hewell Grange
and Wortley, occupied by the army. It was the least fortunate of all: in 1940, the
soldiers managed to set fire to the central Adam block during a cinema show. The
damage was so severe that the whole block was rendered uninhabitable. Hugo and
Mary Wemyss had both died in 1937; their grandson David Charteris (great-grandson
of Percy and Madeline Wyndham) became the twelfth Earl of Wemyss. Apart from one
visit home in 1938, he was serving the government in Africa from 1937 until 1944. On
his return Gosford presented a sorry site, the centre burnt out and the north wing,
added on by the tenth Earl for Hugo and Mary, riddled with dry rot.[14]

However, Gosford was neither sold nor demolished: 'family ambition' kept it 'alive'.
Most of the roof was removed from the north wing, the central block was temporarily
patched up and the south wing, including the marble gallery, was made into a
comfortable home for the summer months; during the winter, Lord and Lady Wemyss
removed themselves to the warmer stable block. In 1987 the roof over the burnt
portion was renewed; there are further plans to safeguard the house and its immediate
grounds, including the possible development of a golf course on the estate and the
selling of some land for building houses.

The tenth Earl had always been willing to make Gosford and its collection available
to any members of the public interested in being shown around. The irony must be
that now his palace is an enormous tax loss against which profits from the surrounding
estates can be set; it is open to the public to save taxation. The family hopes that the
present fiscal policy of the government and the partial restoration of the house will

prevent any further dispersal of the contents. It was a fate the tenth Earl constantly feared for his own and other 'art collections brought together through the art-love, good taste, and wise expenditure of one generation, to be, in due time, scattered through extravagance, or want of taste, of successors'.[15] Neither Dick Wyndham nor Robert Adeane can be accused of lacking taste; they did not, however, share any ambition to keep their family homes 'alive'.

4

On 10 February 1944 Clouds House, the domestic offices and 20 acres of land were conveyed to the Church of England Incorporated Society for Providing Homes for Waifs and Strays, known now as the Children's Society. The surviving Houghton-Browns received £8,000: Clouds became a nursery for unwanted babies.[16]

The stable block, together with about 30 acres, which made up the rest of the Houghton-Brown purchase of 1937, was inherited by Geoffrey Houghton-Brown and part was converted by him into an attractive 'gentleman's residence'; the other part

131 Clouds House from the south with prams. The 'Waifs and Strays' put back the attic windows which had been removed for the Houghton-Browns by Charles Biddulph Pinchard.

Part of the stables, converted by Geoffrey Houghton-Brown into a 'gentleman's residence'.

remains in use as a livery stable with Webb's fittings intact. The block was sold in the late 1940s to Colonel Stephen Scammell who eventually became the owner of Clouds House.

Stephen Scammell first came to live in the area when invalided out of the army in 1946 after service in Burma. He married Susan McLaren, who had settled with her young family in Milton during the war, her husband being posted overseas where he was killed on active service – again in Burma.

Scammells have been traced back in Wiltshire to the beginning of the eleventh century, when a Walter Cammel (De Cammel, Descammel) owned land in Somerset.[17] Over the centuries, Scammells continued to farm land around the Somerset, Dorset and Wiltshire border. Some enterprising branches have moved away to seek their fortunes in North America and New Zealand; some were banished to Australia.[18] The less enterprising remained, content to farm their land within the same score of parishes in southern England. Scammells can still be found in local telephone directories, all no doubt related if their forebears could be traced back far enough.

Colonel Scammell began to acquire land offered for sale around East Knoyle and he established his estate office in part of Clouds' stable block: it was once home to the lawnmower pony (Peter Brooke's Alice?). He was not attempting to rebuild the estates of the Seymours and the Wyndhams but, in his own words, to 'safeguard the village'.

Meanwhile, the nursery planned for Clouds could not open in the house until 1946, when Miss Chynoweth and the army moved out. A smaller version did begin, at the end of 1943, even before the negotiations with the Waifs and Strays Society had been completed, on the first floor of Knoyle House, still the home of Beatrix, Dowager

Countess of Pembroke. Though elderly, the Countess was an active supporter of the Waifs and Strays Society. She had first become associated with the Society in 1887 when she and her husband began regular visits to two of the children's homes outside London.

The society was founded in 1881 by two brothers, Edward and Robert de Montjoie Rudolf.[19] The Rudolfs were canny in engaging the support of a network of aristocratic wives and professional men of independent means to raise money and support. The interest of the Earl and Countess of Pembroke was extended to their children, who were founder members of the Children's Union, established in 1889, 'for the enrolment of children in happier circumstances to help unfortunate children'. Their daughter Beatrix became honorary secretary of the Wilton House branch of the Children's Union, and in 1904 President of the Children's Union. By 1911 she had helped to establish 569 branches of the union with 26,000 members. Annual sales at Wilton to raise money attracted a cluster of the rich and titled, including, in 1904, the Prince and Princess of Wales.

Beatrix married Major Sir Nevile Wilkinson in 1903. He used his talents as an amateur artist and craftsman to make the extraordinary miniature palace which became known as Titania's Palace for his daughter Guendolen. The palace was seen by the family as an effective means for raising money and after it was officially opened by Queen Mary in 1922 it travelled all over the world in aid of children's charities. Meanwhile Guendolen made her home at Knoyle with her grandmother, in the 1920s regularly visiting Clouds House to see her friends Iris Wyndham and then Nancy Mosselman.

During the war Guendolen worked as a VAD in the children's ward of Salisbury Infirmary where she trained under Ada Blake. The two women became firm friends and decided to set up their own baby and toddler nursery. The interest of Guendolen's grandmother, the Countess of Pembroke, was easily engaged. The Waifs and Strays Society negotiated the purchase of Clouds with the understanding that Guendolen Wilkinson and Ada Blake would run the nursery as sister and matron. The nursery was named Beatrix after both Guendolen's grandmother, who died in 1944, and her mother who later became Countess of Wicklow.

It is an ironic twist of fate that the Chairman of the Waifs and Strays Executive Committee when Clouds was purchased was none other than the Hon. Edward Scawen Wyndham, the son of Henry Leconfield of Petworth, nephew of Percy Wyndham and one of Perf Wyndham's trustees. The Petworth Wyndhams, like the Wilton and Knoyle Pembrokes, were active supporters of the society. Their London house in Chesterfield Gardens was a regular venue for fund-raising. Both Edward Scawen Wyndham and his younger brother Everard paid considerable annual amounts towards the maintenance of children in society homes. Edward became Chairman of the Executive Committee in 1933. Three years later he was involved, as trustee of the Clouds estate, with the sale by Dick Wyndham to Messrs Hucklesby and Bartlett. When the Waifs and Strays began negotiations for Clouds in 1943 he must have taken an interest, though his son can recall no mention of the coincidence. His final act as ex-trustee of Clouds was to give back to the house much of the joy and happiness it had enjoyed during its occupation by Percy and Madeline, for the Beatrix Nursery turned out to be an exceptional institution.

It remained open for twenty years, with Ada and Guendolen in charge for the entire period. The total number of children admitted between 1 November 1943 and 1 July 1964 was 534. Of these, 376 were found adoptive parents, 63 were transferred elsewhere, 93 returned home and there were 2 deaths. About 42 children could be accommodated at one time. The youngest, from a few days old up to nine months, occupied the Snowdrop Nursery which was situated in the drawingroom. A bathroom containing four basins big enough for bathing babies was constructed at one end of the room. Among the babies who entered Snowdrop were occasional seriously ill cases sent from the local maternity hospitals. Snowdrop offered a sort of intensive-care unit. One of the sick babies whose life was saved there was a daughter of Winifred Stevens, nanny in the 1920s to Nancy Mosselman's children, who was now married for the second time, to Cyril Hyde of Milton Farm.

Many of the fifteen babies in Snowdrop were adopted. The next nursery Primrose, was situated on the first floor. It took only five babies from 9 months to about 13 months. Pinks took about six babies from 13 months to 2 years; Daffodils took eight toddlers from 2 years up to 3 or 4 years; Tulips took eight children from 4 years up to 7. Most had moved on by the age of 5 but a few stayed, attending the village school. Each nursery was run by a staff nurse and one or two juniors. There was also a nursery nurse training school in the house. Students came at the age of sixteen and spent two years studying for the National Nursery Nurses Examination Board.

The house and grounds were alive with movement, noise and colour. Ada Blake bred budgerigars in a specially constructed aviary, and the children loved to go inside the cages to see the birds building their nests. There was great rejoicing when a missing

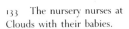

133   The nursery nurses at Clouds with their babies.

yellow bird was brought back safe and sound. It had landed on the engine of a car travelling down Shaftesbury Hill and the surprised driver, being local, knew where it belonged. Madeline Wyndham would have appreciated the birds; even more so the daily activity and the presence everywhere of children. On fine days dozens of prams were parked out on the lawns and hundreds of nappies fluttered from the washing lines. Traditional children's teaparties took place inside and outside the house. When the Bishop of Salisbury dedicated the 'Princess Anne' cot in 1958 to mark the 70th anniversary of the foundation of the Children's Society, he summed up the spirit of the Beatrix Nursery at Clouds:

> There were those who regretted the passing of old homes of England owing to social changes, but if they were no longer to be homes for families then at least they could be put to good use. The home at East Knoyle was *still* a Home – for little ones who, through no fault of their own, had no other one. He was glad they lived there surrounded by beauty and by love.[20]

The Beatrix Nursery was particularly fortunate with its Pembroke connection. When the Dowager Countess died in 1944 Knoyle House was let out to a Mr Russell as an old people's home. Much of the furniture was moved up to Clouds, so the staff and children enjoyed rather different surroundings from most institutions. Sir Nevile Wilkinson's interest in the society was commemorated with the gift of a playground. Titania's Palace also played a part in the life of the nursery: some of the miniature chairs, clocks and other furnishings were used in the annual Christmas display created by the staff.

For a month every year, from Christmas through January, the public were invited to visit Clouds to enjoy the tableaux, which were usually inspired by children's fairy stories. The first decorations, for Christmas 1948, were relatively simple: a giant snowman looked over the Italian winter garden, the pond was filled with paper swans. At Christmas 1951, the year of 'Cinderella', the staff staged twenty-five nursery rhymes in miniature tableaux all over Clouds House. Prince Charming stood at the foot of the main staircase, Cinderella was hurrying down the stairs, one shoe already off, as the grandfather clock struck midnight. All the clothes for the dolls, over 200, were made out of coloured paper by the staff. An East Knoyle gardener, Victor Gerald Hull, painted the sets.

'Cinderella' was so popular that it was repeated in 1955. Three thousand visitors passed through the house, some leaving donations for the Waifs and Strays (admission was free). It is impossible to imagine what Philip Webb would have made of it all.

> Then in the alcoves of the architecture of the house the visitor meets some of the most popular songs and nursery rhymes depicted with figures in perfect detail. Among them being: 'Singin' in the Rain', 'How much is that Doggie in the Window'. . . . Then comes 'The King's Breakfast', with the poor King just asking for 'A little bit of butter for my bread'.
>
> Coloured chandeliers hang from the top of the garden with their coloured candles, and below, in the spacious garden, with its indoor lily pond and flower beds, the great 'centrepiece' . . . is staged. There is the castle, the gaily decorated ballroom with Cinders entering from a doorway beneath a flower-decked balcony.

Artificial flowers covered Webb's massive oak staircase, butterflies and dragonflies

134 'Cinderella' at Clouds.

hovering above. And on the landing stood a large fairy, 'guard over all who come in with her wand outstretched'.[21]

The Christmas before, children's fairy stories had been abandoned in favour of a complete staging of the coronation itself in Westminster Abbey. Every last detail was included, even a tiny figure representing Prince Charles, Duke of Cornwall, watching the ceremony. In 1961–2, 4,600 visitors came to Clouds. The following Christmas was the great snowstorm and only 400 struggled through the winter landscape. The display was called 'Blue Bird, or the story of the search for happiness'. It was repeated the following Christmas, 1963–4, a fitting subject for the last time: the Beatrix Nursery closed on 1 July 1964.

While the house was occupied as a nursery, the Church of England Children's Society (Waifs and Strays was dropped in 1946–7) began to change its policy towards homeless children. By the beginning of the 1960s the society considered that more suitable accommodation could be provided in smaller units; large homes such as Clouds were no longer ideal. The need to dispose of Clouds was first raised by the society in February 1959. The annual allowance paid to the nursery had reached £12,000; central heating alone used up over £1,500 a year. Bank overdrafts had been taken out to cover extra costs, and interest charges were mounting. At the same time there was no money set aside for essential decorations and maintenance. On 25 February the Executive Committee agreed: 'there is no doubt that this vast house is a constant drain on the Society's resources'.[22]

Nothing further was done until the House Committee met on 14 May 1963. It was then decided that the retirement of Miss Blake and Miss Wilkinson in June the following year would be 'an excellent opportunity of getting rid of East Knoyle'. The nursery would close on 1 June 1964. Colonel Birnie, secretary of the society, explained the problems to a committee member, Lady Clutterbuck. The costs of the upkeep of Clouds were only part of the difficulty. 'Its remote situation creates quite a number of staffing problems, and it is also very difficult for such people as Moral Welfare Workers to reach the children and [for] prospective adopters to visit'.[23]

Demolition was an option for the society, as it had been for Messrs Hucklesby and Bartlett. A large number of villas could be built on Clouds site. However, Mr Cane, representing the sale for the society, gave this advice: 'I feel we should endeavour to find a purchaser for the house as it stands in that it would be sacrilege to consider its destruction'.[24]

Once more Clouds was up for sale, the price £27,500 for the house, 20 acres of parkland, and the remains of the domestic offices. The particulars drawn up by Rawlence and Squarey still described the drawingroom as 'elegant', with a 'most attractive embossed ceiling by Webb. Fireplace with carved surround.' The institutional use of the house was stressed: it could be 'adapted for various uses including nursing home, summer home, school, institution and other like purposes'.[25]

Though Mr Cane realised the significance of Webb's mansion, the Victorian revival was not yet under way. The society would be fortunate to find a purchaser for Clouds. In East Knoyle itself there had been an example of the treatment regularly meted out to unfashionable, unwieldy Victorian country houses. The use of Knoyle House as a home for elderly women was only temporary. No member of the Seymour family wanted to take it on (Alfred's only child Jeannie Seymour had died in Bournemouth in 1943) so Knoyle was demolished. One newspaper account revealed the lack of interest in Alfred Seymour's creation: 'Knoyle House is in no sense one of the historic homes of the West Country. It was built as recently as the early 1870s.'[26] It did not match the country house taste of the 1950s, so was condemned. The older residents of East Knoyle were most distressed. They shared fond memories of its occupancy by the Dowager Countess of Pembroke: now the centre of their village was ripped out. The new Fonthill Abbey, built by the Marquess of Westminster in the first half of the nineteenth century and occupied by his daughter Octavia Shaw-Stewart, was also demolished in 1955, the year after Knoyle, though descendants still farm the land and occupy the converted stable block.[27]

Clouds was to be more fortunate. The society was successful in finding a purchaser, Colonel Stephen Scammell, who was already owner of the stable block and the adjoining section of the park. He first wrote to Sir Keith Officer, Chairman of the society, on 21 October:

> On returning from a rather hectic week laying up the boat I hear – being always the last person in the village to hear of anything – that Clouds is closing down next June. . . . Perhaps you may remember that I once mentioned that if ever the Society sold Clouds House I would be a prospective purchaser – not because I want it, heaven knows, but in order to insure that I have a good neighbour, and the village a suitable inhabitant. . . . If I could find no tenant there is a Charitable Foundation that I am interested in which would I think take the house as a gift leaving me with a piece of Park.[28]

Five days later he made an offer, £15,000, on behalf of the McLaren Foundation, a family trust he had set up with his wife.

On 12 November he raised his offer for Clouds to £23,000 subject to contract, though he made it quite clear to Sir Keith Officer that he regarded the offer as generous:

> I consider that in doing so we are making a charitable contribution of about £7000–£8000 – certainly the greatest of our lifetime – and although I do not expect anyone else to see it in that light (your Committee or Messrs. Rawlence and Squarey for instance), it is the only way in which we can justify such a price to ourselves.[29]

Messrs Rawlence and Squarey advised Colonel Birnie, as secretary of the society, to try for an increase to £25,000. At the end of November the deal was finally struck: Clouds House was sold for £24,000.

The transfer of Clouds to the McLaren Foundation was, for some, a painful occasion. Ada and Guendolen had devoted their lives to the care of children: for over twenty years Clouds had been their home. In an interview with the *Daily Sketch* Guendolen revealed her deep regret: her own life's work would not continue.

> Nowadays people don't dedicate their lives to things. That is what the joy here means – giving your life to children. . . . We had hoped someone would take over from us, but it is not to be. It is such a pity.[30]

She and Ada retired to Cleeve House in Holloway (the house the Houghton-Browns had rented from 1941 to 1943), then next door to Guenada, the name of the cottage commemorating their long friendship. Photographs of their 'kiddies' covered the walls; many of their waifs and strays regularly visited Guenada bringing, as they grew up, photographs of husbands and their own babies.

When the nursery closed, two pieces of property dating from the Wyndhams' occupation of Clouds were removed by the society: the altar table and a marble plaque which hung above it in the chapel. The table, which went to the society's offices, was over six feet long, with legs and frame of carved oak. The plaque, of the Madonna and Child, was 40″ × 49″ and extremely heavy. It remained in the offices of Rawlence and Squarey while a valuation was sought: the society hoped it might prove to be valuable.

Sotheby's response was discouraging. The plaque was a nineteenth century copy of the *Madonna and Child* by Mino da Fiesole, in the Bargello, Florence, 'of small commercial value and . . . not worth sending to London for sale'.[31] Guendolen Wilkinson was unconvinced by the Sotheby's verdict: 'Mrs Percy Wyndham was not a person to deal with things that were not genuine'. When the *Madonna* was included in the contents sale of June 1932 it was described simply as an Italian marble alto-relievo. Whether it was indeed a nineteenth century copy can never be proven. Three years after the society disposed of Clouds House, the plaque was broken up.

The McLaren Foundation had completed the necessary repairs and decorations at Clouds by 1965. Separate accesses were created to the house and the stable block. A bank (planted with hornbeam) was constructed across the original driveway which had passed the stables and offices. The McLaren Foundation decided to let Clouds to a registered charity, so Colonel Scammell approached various organisations including the Cheshire Homes in search of a suitable tenant. From 1965 the house provided a home and school to fifty maladjusted boys and their teachers but it was badly knocked about. Since 1983 Clouds has been tenanted by the Life Anew Trust, and is run as an 'alcohol and drug dependency treatment centre', with facilities for up to fifty-seven

135 (facing page, above) Clouds drawing room, c.1910. Burne-Jones's *Annunciation* (whereabouts unknown) is placed between Watts's portraits of George and Guy Wyndham; below are Burne-Jones's *Caritas, If Hope were not, Heart should break*, and *Justitia*. Both *Caritas* and *Justitia* were included in the sale of Clouds' contents, 1933. The portrait of Guy Wyndham is in a private collection. *The Annunciation* is a preliminary study in watercolour and gold for the oil painting bought by George Howard and now in the Lady Lever Gallery. All four Burne-Joneses were lent by the Wyndhams to the Burlington Fine Arts Club, 1899.

136 (facing page, below) Clouds drawing room 1992.

patients.[32] The Trust, in the words of their landlord, Colonel Scammell, 'fortunately maintains Clouds to a very high standard indeed'.

Patients at Clouds come from all walks of life: a few have been media celebrities, and some are descendants of the guests entertained at countryhouse weekends by Percy and Madeline Wyndham. Philip Webb's mansion, designed for the height of late Victorian aristocratic living, now serves as a retreat from the excesses of late twentieth-century living – for a century nearly all its inmates (Captain Wyndham excepted) have found that Clouds lives up to its name. The therapeutic effects of the house and its setting are, by general consent, profound.

Note on Sources

Individual note references are not given for material in the following two archives.

Webb Papers, London (in the possession of John Brandon-Jones). This contains the bulk of the correspondence between Philip Webb, Percy and Madeline Wyndham; photographs of Webb's houses; Webb's notebooks; letters between Webb and his assistants, builders, workmen.

Stanway Papers, Stanway House, Gloucestershire (in the possession of Lord Neidpath). This archive contains most of the material relating to Madeline and Percy Wyndham, including the diary kept by Mary Wyndham (later Lady Elcho, Countess of Wemyss); letters between Mary and her mother Madeline Wyndham; letters to Mary from her father Percy, her sister Madeline Adeane and her brother Guy Wyndham; single letters from Percy Wyndham to his sister Fanny Montgomery, the Duke of Westminster to Mary Wyndham, George Wyndham to his mother Madeline Wyndham; letters from Perf Wyndham to his grandmother Madeline Wyndham and his mother Sibell Countess Grosvenor; letters from Perf's widow Diana to Madeline Wyndham and Sibell Countess Grosvenor; letters from Dick Wyndham to his grandmother Madeline Wyndham and his aunt Mary Countess of Wemyss; letters from Sibell Grosvenor to her sister-in-law Mary Wemyss; letters from Edwina Wyndham to her sister-in-law Mary Wemyss.

There are also letters to Mary from artists and writers whom she knew as a child and who stayed at Stanway, including Francis Brett Young, Edward, Georgiana and Philip Burne-Jones, L.P. Hartley, Maurice Hewlett, Edward Poynter, William Rothenstein and Angela Thirkell.

Letters between Mary and Arthur Balfour are also at Stanway House.

Primary sources in public collections or collections open to public queries
Wilfrid Blunt Papers, Fitzwilliam Museum, Cambridge
Castle Howard Papers, Castle Howard, Yorkshire
Children's Society Papers, London
Gosford Papers, Gosford House, East Lothian
Grosvenor Estate Papers, London and Eaton, Cheshire
Knight, Frank and Rutley sale catalogues (selection), National Art Library, Victoria and Albert Museum
Wyndham Lewis Letters, Cornell University Library, New York
Edward Marsh Letter Collection, Berg Collection, New York Public Library
Petworth Papers, West Sussex County Record Office
Royal Literary Fund Archive, British Library, London
Society for the Preservation of Ancient Buildings (SPAB) archives, 37 Spital Square, London E1

Sotheby's sale catalogues (selection), National Art Library, Victoria and Albert Museum
Stanway Papers, Stanway House, Gloucestershire
Sun Insurance records, Guildhall Library, London
Watts Papers, Watts Gallery, Compton, Surrey
Philip Webb's designs for Clouds House, Royal Institute of British Architects Drawings Collection, Portman Square and Victoria and Albert Museum
Dick Wyndham's exhibition catalogues (selection), National Art Library, Victoria and Albert Museum

Private Collection. Some material is identified as 'private collection' to respect the wishes of the owners and to indicate that this material is neither at Stanway nor in the collection of John Brandon-Jones. The owners of such private collections may be contacted through the author.

The owners of other collections identified by name but not location, for example *Adeane Papers* (James Adeane), *Mells Papers* (the Earl of Oxford and Asquith), *Clouds Papers* (the executors of the estate of the late Geoffrey Houghton-Brown), may also be contacted through the author.

Notes

Introduction

1 Stanway Papers, Stanway House, Gloucestershire.
2 Walburga, Lady Paget, *In My Tower* (London, 1924), 2 vols, vol.2, p.5.
3 Mark Girouard, *The Victorian Country House* (New Haven, 1979), p. 82.
4 Nancy Waters Ellenberger, 'The Souls: High Society and Politics in Late Victorian England', PhD thesis, University of Oregon, 1982.
5 Francis Wyndham, 'Ursula', *Mrs Henderson and other stories* (London, 1985), p. 121.
6 Private collection.
7 W.R. Lethaby, *Philip Webb and His Work* (London, 1979); first published in book form 1935.
8 Girouard, *The Victorian Country House*; Jill Franklin, *The Gentleman's Country House* (London, 1981); Roderick Gradidge, *Dream Houses: The Edwardian Ideal* (London, 1980); Mark Swenarton, *Artisans and Architects: The Ruskinian Tradition in Architectural Thought* (London, 1989).
9 Sheila Kirk, 'Philip Webb 1831–1915: Domestic Architecture', PhD thesis, University of Newcastle–upon–Tyne, 1990.
10 F.M.L. Thompson, *English Landed Society in the Nineteenth Century* (London, 1980); Martin Wiener, *English Culture and the Decline of the Industrial Spirit, 1850–1980* (Cambridge, 1981); Pamela Horn, *Labouring Life in the Victorian Countryside* (Dublin, 1976); Pamela Horn, *The Rise and Fall of the Victorian Servant* (Stroud, 1990); David Cannadine, *The Decline and Fall of the British Aristocracy* (New Haven, 1990); J.V. Beckett, *The Aristocracy in England 1660–1914* (Oxford, 1986); L. and J.C.F. Stone, *An Open Elite? England 1540–1880* (Oxford, 1984).
11 Wilfrid Blunt, *My Diaries* (London, 1919), 2 vols; Mary, Countess of Wemyss, *A Family Record* (London, 1932); Cynthia Asquith, *Haply I May Remember* (London, 1950); J.W. Mackail and Guy Wyndham, *The Life and Letters of George Wyndham* (London, 1926), 2 vols; Jane Ridley and Clayre Percy, *The Letters of Arthur Balfour and Lady Elcho 1885–1917* (London, 1992).
12 Nicola Beauman, *Cynthia Asquith* (London, 1987); Max Egremont, *The Cousins* (London, 1977); Elizabeth Longford, *A Pilgrimage of Passion: The Life of Wilfrid Scawen Blunt* (New York, 1980); Kenneth Young, *Arthur James Balfour* (London, 1963); Nancy Crathorne, *Tennant's Stalk: The Story of the Tennants of the Glen* (London, 1973); Simon Blow, *Broken Blood* (London, 1987); Michael Luke, *David Tennant and the Gargoyle Years* (London, 1991); Philip Hoare, *Serious Pleasures: The Life of Stephen Tennant* (London, 1990); Francis Wheen, *Tom Driberg: his life and idiosyncrasies* (London, 1990); John Pearson, *Facades, Edith, Osbert and Sacheverell Sitwell* (London, 1978); Jeffrey Meyers, *The Enemy: A Biography of Wyndham Lewis* (London, 1980); Barbara Wadsworth, *Edward Wadsworth: A Painter's Life* (Wilton, 1989).
13 East Knoyle Women's Institute Scrapbooks, East Knoyle, Wiltshire.
14 Edith Young, *The History of East Knoyle School* (Salisbury, 1984); Violet Bradby, *A Family Chronicle* (Plymouth, 1942); Colonel Stephen Scammell's typescript of his history of East Knoyle parish.
15 Wemyss, *A Family Record*: Max Egremont, *The Cousins*.

1 Percy Wyndham and Madeline Campbell

1 Henry James, *The Spoils of Poynton* (Harmondsworth, 1964), pp. 11–12; first published 1897.
2 Ibid., p. 11.
3 Various histories of Petworth and the Wyndhams: Hugh Wyndham, *A Family History 1410–1688 The Wyndhams of Norfolk and Somerset* (London, 1939); Hugh Wyndham, *A Family History 1688–1837 The Wyndhams of Somerset, Sussex and Wiltshire* (London, 1950); Rev. Francis M. Wyndham, *Genealogy of the Family of Wyndham in the elder male line* (London, 1917); Lord Egremont (John Wyndham), *Wyndham and Children First* (London, 1968); Constance Leconfield, *Random Papers* (Southwick, 1938); Gervase Jackson-Stops, *Petworth House*, National Trust (London, 1983). Also Petworth Papers.
4 A.M.W. Stirling, *Life's Little Day* (London, 1925), p. 138.
5 Jackson-Stops, *Petworth House*, p. 45.
6 L. Strachey and R. Fulford (eds.), *The Greville Memoirs 1814–1860* (London, 1938), 8 vols, vol. 2, pp. 335–6.
7 Egremont, *Wyndham and Children First*, p. 33. See also David Cecil, *The Young Melbourne* (London, 1939).
8 Leconfield, *Random Papers*, p. 51.
9 Letters from Percy Wyndham to Madeline Campbell (1860), private collection.
10 Egremont, *Wyndham and Children First*, pp. 29–30.
11 Leconfield, *Random Papers*, p. 51.
12 General Henry Wyndham had a distinguished career in the Coldstream Guards, serving in the Peninsular War and at Waterloo. He married in 1812 a daughter of Lord Charles Somerset but in 1826 he eloped with Letitia de la Becke who had separated from her husband Sir Henry de la Becke, the previous year. True to form, the Earl of Egremont was not particularly concerned by his son's behaviour and he apparently gave Letitia £27,000 as some sort of security shortly before he died. Henry promptly put most of the money into buying a house near Hyde Park and settling his debts. See note 13 below for sources.

13 See Egremont, *Wyndham and Children First*; also *Copies of the Statements of Col. Wyndham and Gen. Wyndham [as to their hunting rights over the Petworth country]* and the *Correspondence Relating Thereto* (Godalming, 1839).

Henry's mistress was never accepted by the local gentry in the Lake District and in 1841 she was asked to leave. Henry accused her of stealing the household linen and plate, he refused to make any settlement on her and denied that Lord Egremont's gift of money was ever intended for her. See Anne Auriol, *Statement and Correspondence consequent upon the Ill-treatment of Lady De La Becke by Major-General Henry Wyndham* (London, 1843), in which Letitia writes, 'Have I not, for him, lost rank, caste and character?'

Though George Leconfield did not countenance his children visiting their uncle, Percy kept a bust of Henry in a prominent position in the hall of his London house. It later inspired Percy's grandson Edward Wyndham Tennant (Bim) who referred to it in his last letter to his mother from the western front, 20 September 1916: 'pray that I may be worthy of my fighting ancestors. The one I know best is Sir Henry Wyndham' (Anne Powell, *Bim: A Tribute to the Honourable Edward Wyndham Tennant, Lieutenant 4th Battalion Grenadier Guards 1897–1916* (Salisbury, 1990).

14 Private collection.

15 Examples at Petworth House.

16 [Fanny Montgomery], *Early Influences* (London, 1845), p. 120.

17 See Egremont, *Wyndham and Children First*; also the Petworth Papers (West Sussex County Record Office). Helen appears to have suffered severely from the Wyndham temper, unbecoming in an aristocratic woman. Surviving letters from her mother Mary to Helen convey a sort of mental cruelty in the relationship. Whenever Helen expressed anger she received deeply unsympathetic responses from her mother.

> I shall pray that God may be merciful to you and help you to endeavour to make all those around you happy. This I think is the duty which the Lord more especially calls upon you to fulfil and therefore in the great Judgement Day when we shall all appear before Him to give an account of our works, and of how we fulfilled the duties he apportioned to each – you will be called upon to answer for this (Petworth Papers).

18 Stirling, *Life's Little Day*, p. 134.

19 Petworth Papers.

20 Ibid.

21 Ibid.

22 See John Wyatt, *History of the First Battalion Coldstream Guards during the Eastern Campaign* (London, 1858); Lt.-Col. Ross of Bladensburg, *A History of the Coldstream Guards from 1815 to 1895* (London, 1896); a Regimental Officer, *Our Veterans of 1854* (London, 1854).

23 A Regimental Officer, *Our Veterans of 1854*, pp. 8–9.

24 Ibid., p. 19.

25 Ross of Bladensburg, *A History of the Coldstream Guards*, p. 145.

26 A Regimental Officer, *Our Veterans of 1854*, p. 47.

27 Ibid., p. 67.

28 Ibid., p. 93.

29 See Ross of Bladensburg, *A History of the Coldstream Guards*.

30 Elizabeth Longford, *A Pilgrimage of Passion: The Life of Wilfrid Scawen Blunt* (New York, 1980), Chapter 1.

Many of Percy's friends at this time were fellow officers in the Coldstream Guards, their relationships sometimes intersected with his own family. Henry Armytage, for example, had been a lieutenant in Percy's company during the Crimean campaign. He was older than Percy, remaining in the Coldstream Guards to become Lieutenant-Colonel, and had married in 1851. His first child, born in 1853, was given the name of Percy. In 1857 Armytage's brother-in-law Lord Fitzhardinge of Berkeley married Georgiana Holme Sumner. In 1860 Georgiana's brother Arthur Sumner married another Georgiana, who was also stepsister of Percy's own brother-in-law Colonel Kingscote. Berkeley Castle became a regular place for Percy and Madeline (also married in 1860) to visit; the Fitzhardinges were cousins of Madeline's; Mrs Arthur Sumner became a particularly close friend of Madeline's and one of Wilfrid Scawen Blunt's 'conquests' (she called their illegitimate child Berkeley after the place he was born).

William Wellesley, son of Lord Cowley, was another fellow officer of Percy's; his younger brother Arthur Wellesley also joined the Coldstream Guards. Lady Cowley was a Fitzgerald, so the Wellesley children were cousins of Madeline's.

31 Petworth Papers.

32 Surviving material in the Stanway Papers (Stanway House), Petworth Papers and some in private collections.

33 Petworth Papers.

34 Visiting Dublin in August 1859, Greville made a note in his diary: 'then to my old friend Lady Campbell whose beautiful daughters are as well worth seeing as anything in Ireland', Strachey and Fulford, *The Greville Memoirs*, vol. 7, p. 436.

35 Violet Dickinson (ed.), *Miss Eden's Letters* (London, 1919), pp. 250–1.

36 His remains were interred in the cemetery at the rear of the Royal Barracks, Dublin.

37 Stanway Papers.

38 Emily Eden, *The Semi-Attached Couple* (London, 1927), p. 281; first published 1860.

39 Debate on her illegitimacy in (among others) Gerald Campbell, *Edward and Pamela Fitzgerald* (London, 1904); Violet Wyndham, *Madame de Genlis* (London, 1958); Jane Abdy and Charlotte Gere, *The Souls* (London, 1984). Violet Wyndham, p. 286, quotes a letter from Pamela, Lady Campbell to her mother written on 3 February 1831 at the death of Madame de Genlis: 'Dear mama, I suffered with you. I know how much you would feel the loss of Madame de Genlis. Your mother in short, for was not that the tie?'

40 See Dr Richard Madden, *The United Irishmen, Their Lives and Times* (Dublin, 1858); Roy Foster, *Modern Ireland 1600–1972* (Harmondsworth, 1989), Chapter 12.

41 Katharine Tynan, *Lord Edward: A Study in Romance* (London, 1916), p. 302.

42 Thomas Moore, *The Life and Death of Lord Edward Fitzgerald* (London, 1831).

43 Her son Edward remained with his grandmother, the Duchess of Leinster; baby Lucy went to an aunt, Lady Sophia Fitzgerald (see Moore).

44 Violet Wyndham, *Madame de Genlis* (London, 1958), p. 225.

45 Moore, p. 252.

46 See Brian Fitzgerald (ed.), *The Correspondence of Emily, Duchess of Leinster 1731–1841* (Dublin, 1949, 1953, 1957).

47 Campbell, *Edward and Pamela Fitzgerald*, pp. 248–9.
48 Dickinson, *Miss Eden's Letters*, p. 60.
49 See Napier's *History of the Peninsular War* (London, 1828–40), 6 vols, for details of exploits of Sir Guy Campbell and his father Colin (Book X, Chapter 5; Book XV, Chapter 5; Book XXI, Chapter 5); also see their individual entries in the *Dictionary of National Biography*.
50 Dickinson, *Miss Eden's Letters*, p. 61.
51 Ibid., pp. 125–6.
52 Ibid., p. 127.
53 Ibid., p. 162.
54 Lady Campbell's three sons all pursued military careers: Edward joined the 60th Rifles after Sandhurst, then went out to India as ADC to his cousin Sir Charles Napier and married the daughter of the Governor of Bengal; Guy joined the navy and died aged twenty-nine in Singapore; Frederick joined the 60th Rifles and fought in the China War. Lady Campbell wrote a characteristic letter to Emily Eden on 27 September 1840 (Dickinson, *Miss Eden's Letters*, pp. 328–31) describing her children's progress:

> Yes, Sir Guy's Fanny is married and very happy Captain [Henry Boys] Harvey is a very handsome, nice person; they have not much money at present, but that cannot be helped. Pam [to marry the Rev. C. Stanford in 1841] has been with her for the last month at Carlisle, where Fanny is quartered. Pam was very ill with ague, so I sent her to the Napiers. She comes back to me next week. I long to show her to you – not for the beauty, for she is no beauty, tho' nice looking. But, Emmy, she is quite, quite one of us – I need not explain how pleasant, how good, how full of sense and fun. She is such a comfort to me.
>
> The next, Georgina, is very pretty and very dear, but not so gentle and patient as Pam [she was to marry Thomas Preston in 1847].
>
> I had my sailor boy for two blessed months. This boy, Guy, came home so improved, so gentle and affectionate, and delightful, from sea. I felt so thankful, as I rather feared the sea. It is a dreadful life to be the mother of a sailor; so hard to bear. Wind always to me was a sad sound, but now I can hardly help crying. All the rest are good little nice things, and I have no governess, so I have a good deal of their company more or less . . . I have got a nice two-year-old baby just pour me desennuyer; such a nice duck! [Frederick] The youngest after six girls. Pam says he is doomed to wear all the old bent bonnets out, and accordingly I found him in the hay with a bonnet on.

55 Wilfrid Blunt Papers, Fitzwilliam Museum, Cambridge.
56 Walburga, Lady Paget, *Embassies of Other Days* (London, 1923), p. 295.
57 Adeane Papers (James Adeane).
58 Private collection.
59 Ibid.
60 Ibid.
61 J.W. Mackail and Guy Wyndham (eds), *The Life and Letters of George Wyndham* (London, 1926), 2 vols, vol. 1, p. 17.
62 Ibid.
63 See Pat Jalland, *Women, Marriage and Politics 1860–1914* (Oxford, 1988), Chapter 2: 'Money and Marriage'.
64 Petworth Papers.
65 Private collection.
66 Ibid.

2 Early Married Life and Patronage, 1860–76

1   Grosvenor Estate Papers, Grosvenor Estate Office, London. The leaseholder who sold to Percy Wyndham was Mrs Clarissa Miles. The original lease was drawn up between Earl Grosvenor and George Haldimand.
2   Petworth Papers, West Sussex County Record Office.
3   At Petworth, Percy and Madeline occupied the Cambridge rooms. The Chapel rooms provided day and night nurseries for the children, their nurse Mrs Horsenail and nursemaid. Madeline's personal maid Thomas, or 'Tompy', fell in love and married Lord Leconfield's valet, Mr Owen (Petworth Papers).
4   Petworth Papers.
5   Constance's sister Caroline was married to Madeline's cousin Charles Fitzgerald, who became the seventh Duke of Leinster in 1874. Constance and Caroline Leveson-Gower's uncle was the seventh Earl of Carlisle, Lord-Lieutenant of Ireland and Madeline's host when she first met Percy in Ireland.
6   There were several marriages between these families in the 1860s and 1870s, brought about during the London season and at country house weekends. As couples married, the circle of country houses regularly visited by the friends gradually enlarged. Lady Alice Kerr's sister-in-law Constance (Marchioness of Lothian) was the daughter of Henry Talbot, eighteenth Earl of Shrewsbury. Constance's sister Adelaide married the third Earl of Brownlow in 1868 (Belton and Ashridge); her brother Walter married Amabel Cowper in 1873 (Panshanger and Wrest Park); her sister Gertrude married the twelfth Earl of Pembroke in 1874 (Wilton); her brother Reginald married Margaret Stuart-Wortley in 1877 (Wortley).
7   See Mrs Russell Barrington, *The Life, Letters and Works of Frederic Leighton* (London, 1906), 2 vols; Leonee and Richard Ormond, *Lord Leighton* (New Haven, 1975).
8   See A.M.W. Stirling, *A Painter of Dreams* (London, 1916).
9   Virginia Surtees, *The Artist and the Autocrat: George and Rosalind Howard, Earl and Countess of Carlisle* (Wilton, 1988), p. 30.
10 See M.S. Watts, *George Frederic Watts: The Annals of an Artist's Life* (London, 1912), 2 vols; Dorothy Henley, *Rosalind Howard Countess of Carlisle* (London, 1958); Charles Roberts, *The Radical Countess: The History of the Life of Rosalind Countess of Carlisle* (Carlisle, 1962); Surtees, *The Artist and the Autocrat*.
11 See *The Volunteer Rifleman's Magazine, A Monthly Journal, being a complete record of the Volunteer Movement*, No. 1, August 1860; B. A. Young, *The Artists and the S.A.S.* (London, 1960).
12 Private collection.
13 Watts Papers, Watts Gallery, Compton, Surrey.
14 Airlie Papers (Earl and Countess of Airlie).
15 Ibid.
16 Watts Papers.
17 George Leconfield's illness during the winter months of 1866 to 1867 may have been a contributory factor.
18 Private collection.
19 See Jeremy Maas, *Gambart, Prince of the Victorian Art World* (London, 1975) and *The Victorian Art World in Photographs* (London, 1984).
20 Surtess, *The Artist and the Autocrat*.

---

21 Earl of Wemyss and March, *Memories 1898–1912* (Edinburgh, 1912); further information on the tenth Earl of Wemyss from the Gosford Papers, Gosford House, East Lothian, Scotland.
22 Wemyss and March, *Memories*.
23 Petworth Papers.
24 Ibid.
25 Pat Jalland, *Women, Marriage and Politics, 1860–1914* (Oxford, 1988), pp. 66–7.
26 See Ormond and Ormond, *Lord Leighton*.
27 Information on the Prinseps and Pattles from M. S. Watts, *George Frederic Watts; A Victorian Album, Julia Margaret Cameron and her Circle* (London, 1975); Colin Ford (ed.), *The Cameron Collection: An Album of Photographs by Julia Margaret Cameron presented to Sir John Herschel* (Rugby, 1975); Nagham Jarrah, 'Valentine Cameron Prinsep', MA thesis, Courtauld Institute, 1983. Virginia Pattle married the third Earl Somers; Julia Margaret married Charles Cameron.
28 Thoby's sister Sophie married George Haldimand, the first leaseholder of 44 Belgave Square.
29 Watts, *George Frederic Watts*, p. 128.
30 Georgiana Burne-Jones, *Memorials of Edward Burne-Jones* (London, 1904), 2 vols, vol. 1, p. 186.
31 Alice Buchan, *A Scrap Screen* (London, 1979), p. 92.
32 Stirling, *A Painter of Dreams*, pp. 298–9.
33 A.M.W. Stirling, *The Letter-Bag of Lady Elizabeth Spencer-Stanhope* (London, 1913), 2 vols, vol. 2, p. 259.
34 Deborah Cherry, 'The Hogarth Club', *Burlington Magazine*, April 1980, pp. 237–44.
35 See W.R. Lethaby, *Philip Webb and His Work* (London, 1979); first published 1935; John Brandon-Jones, 'Philip Webb', in *Victorian Architecture* (London, 1963); Mark Swenarton, *Artisans and Architects: The Ruskinian Tradition in Architectural Thought* (London, 1989).
36 Holland Park was close to the London residences of 'society', the Red House was not. Walburga, Lady Paget records the trip she and Madeline Wyndham finally made, late in the century, to the Red House, 'a thing which we both had wished to accomplish for twenty years. . . . After miles of horrible, omnibus-infested roads through the southern suburbs of London we suddenly emerged into a perfectly rural country with distant views over the Weald of Kent. We found the Red House, not without some trouble, set down in the middle of Bexley Heath' (*In My Tower*, London, 1924, 2 vols, vol. 2, pp. 422–3).
37 Surtees, *The Artist and the Autocrat*, p. 50.
38 See 'Artists Homes no. 8', *Building News*, 29 October 1880; *The Architect*, 16 November 1894 and 21 December 1894; Mark Girouard, 'The Victorian Artist at Home', *Country Life*, 16 November 1972.
39 Webb Papers (John Brandon-Jones).
40 Girouard, 'The Victorian Artist at Home'.
41 Barrington, *The Life, Letters and Works of Frederic Leighton*, p. 6.
42 Benjamin Disraeli, *Lothair* (London, 1870), vol. 1, p. 273.
43 See Ormond and Ormond, *Lord Leighton*; also papers in the Stanway Collection.
44 Private collection.
45 *Illustrated London News*, 30 May 1868.
46 Christopher Newall, *The Etruscans: Painters of the Italian Landscape 1850–1900*, Stoke on Trent Museum and Art Gallery exhibition catalogue, 1989, p. 35. Newall quotes Julia Cartwright on Costa (1883).
47 Ibid. Newall quotes George Fleming on Costa (1882).
48 Ibid., p. 40.
49 Evidence from private letters and visitor's books.
50 Airlie Papers.
51 Watts Papers.
52 Ibid.
53 Penelope Fitzgerald, *Edward Burne-Jones: A Biography* (London, 1975), p. 176.
54 G. Burne-Jones, *Memorials*, vol. 2, p. 91.
55 Jarrah, 'Valentine Cameron Prinsep'. See also entry in Dictionary of National Biography.
56 Private collection.
57 Lord Egremont (John Wyndham), *Wyndham and Children First* (London, 1968), p. 65.
58 Petworth Papers.
59 Ibid.
60 Private collection.
61 RIBA Drawings Collection, Portman Square, London.
62 Moncure Daniel Conway, *Travels in South Kensington with notes on Decorative Art and Architecture in England* (London, 1882), p. 164.
63 Three of the five sold at Christie's on 22 June 1990, apparently remaining in the house until 1940.
64 Stanway House, no date. Percy looks around thirty-five years old.
65 Private collection.
66 Watts Papers.
67 Private collection.
68 Mark Bence-Jones, *The Viceroys of India* (London, 1982), p. 64.
69 Egremont, *Wyndham and Children First*, p. 54.
70 The aims of the society, quoted by Barbara Morris, *Victorian Embroidery* (London, 1962). See also Winifride Jackson and Elizabeth Pettifer, *The Royal School of Needlework Yesterday and to-day* (Leicester, 1986).
71 Anthea Callen, *Angel in the Studio: Women in the Arts and Crafts Movement 1870–1914* (London, 1979).
72 From the 1870s onwards Madeline's social diary is interspersed with school engagements. If she isn't attending committee meetings, she is helping with monthly and annual fund-raising activities, often with her daughter Mary. The Christmas bazaar of 1879 is described by Mary: 'the tea was at four and all the ladies came trooping in, each brought a friend, mother, sister, daughter, brother or cousin etc. which naturally made it much better fun . . . The tea-room looked very nice hung with embroidery & coloured silks; Princess Christian sat in the middle at one of the tables, so every [one] might see her, a great attraction' (Stanway Papers).
73 Martin Harrison and Bill Waters, *Burne-Jones* (London, 1979), p. 89.
74 W. Graham Robertson, *Time Was* (London, 1945) pp. 73–7; first pubblished 1931.
75 See Fitzgerald, *Edward Burne-Jones*; also Jan Marsh, *Pre-Raphaelite Sisterhood* (London, 1985).
76 Castle Howard Papers, Castle Howard, Yorkshire.
77 Lethaby, *Philip Webb and His Work*, p. 88.
78 Surtees, *The Artist and the Autocrat*, p. 52.
79 Ibid., p. 53.

80 Ibid., pp. 55–6

81 *The Studio*, Vol. 15, October 1898.

82 Surtees, *The Artist and the Autocrat*, p. 89.

83 Messrs Driver, Particulars of a valuable and highly important Freehold Residential Investment and Sporting Domain, situate at East Knoyle, Wiltshire (London, 1876).

84 Christopher Hussey, 'Wilbury', *Country Life*, 3 December 1959.

85 Nikolaus Pevsner, *Wiltshire* (Harmondsworth, 1975).

86 H. Avray Tipping, 'Wilbury Park', *Country Life*, 23 June 1932, pp. 96–102.

87 When a granddaughter was born to the Malets, they came to Wilbury to enter her name in their family Bible, kept locked in a cupboard in a room occupied by Percy (Stanway Papers).

88 Lethaby, *Philip Webb and His Work*, p. 112.

89 Ibid., p. 188.

90 Brandon-Jones, 'Philip Webb', p. 262.

3 Philip Webb: The Design and Building of Clouds, 1876–85

1 See Mark Swenarton, *Artisans and Architects: The Ruskinian Tradition in Architectural Thought* (London, 1989), Chapter 2.

2 W. R. Lethaby, *Philip Webb and His Work* (London, 1979); first published 1935, p. iii.

3 Sheila Kirk, 'Philip Webb 1831–1915: Domestic Architecture', PhD thesis, University of Newcastle–upon–Tyne, 1990.

4 Lethaby, *Philip Webb and His Work*, p. 111.

5 John Brandon-Jones, 'Philip Webb', in *Victorian Architecture* (London, 1963), pp. 260–1.

6 Lethaby, *Philip Webb and His Work*, p. 128.

7 See Brandon-Jones, 'Philip Webb'.

8 Details from the Victoria County History (1980), also Colonel Stephen Scammell's (the present owner of Clouds) typescript of the history of East Knoyle parish.

9 Lethaby, *Philip Webb and His Work*, p. 129.

10 Virginia Surtees, *The Artist and the Autocrat: George and Rosalind Howard, Earl and Countess of Carlisle* (Wilton, 1988), p. 146. Mary was known as Maisie Stanley, Surtees suggests her last child, Venetia, intimate friend of H.H. Asquith, may have been George Howard's.

11 Lethaby, *Philip Webb and His Work*, pp. 94–5.

12 Ibid., p. 95.

13 Petworth Papers, West Sussex County Record Office; RIBA.

14 Wilfrid Blunt, *My Diaries* (London, 1919), 2 vols, vol. 1, p. 193, quoted by Mark Girouard, *The Victorian Country House* (New Haven, 1979), p. 86.

15 Wilfried Blunt Papers, Fitzwilliam Museum, Cambridge.

16 Ibid.

17 SPAB archives, 37 Spital Square, London, E1

18 Ibid., Manifesto of the SPAB, founded 1877.

19 See Martin Harrison and Bill Waters, *Burne-Jones* (London, 1979); additional information from Charlotte Gere.

20 Harrison and Waters, *Burne-Jones*, p. 124.

21 W. Graham Robertson, *Time Was* (London, 1945), p. 47; first published 1931.

22 Watts Papers, Watts Gallery, Compton, Surrey.

23 Ibid.

24 A. Young, M. MacDonald, R. Spencer, *The Paintings of James McNeill Whistler* (New Haven, 1980), 2 vols, vol. 2, pp. 88–9.

25 John Ruskin, 'On Whistler's Nocturne in Black and Gold',

letter lxxix, 18 June 1877 in *Fors Clavigera* (London 1871–84).

26 Henry James, 'The Picture Season in London', *Galaxy*, August 1877.

27 Watts Papers.

28 Georgiana Burne-Jones, *Memorials of Edward Burne-Jones* (London, 1904), 2 vols. vol. 2, pp. 77–8.

29 Brandon-Jones, 'Philip Webb', pp. 262–3.

30 Private collection.

31 Lethaby, *Philip Webb and His Work*, p. 100.

32 Private collection.

33 William Graham to Edward Burne-Jones, 22 November 1877: see Oliver Garnett, 'William Graham', Mellon Centre Lecture, 21 March 1985; also Caroline Dakers, 'Patronage and the Country House', MA thesis, Royal College of Art, 1988. Letters between Graham and Burne-Jones are in the Mells Papers (Earl of Oxford and Asquith).

34 Frances Horner, *Time Remembered* (London, 1933), p. 5.

35 Wilfrid Scawen Blunt, 'Clouds', *Country Life*, 19 November 1904, pp. 744–8.

36 Lethaby, *Philip Webb and His Work*, p. 115.

37 Ibid.

38 See Clive Aslet, *The Last Country Houses* (New Haven, 1982), p. 259.

39 Clouds Papers (the executors of the estate of the late Geoffrey Houghton-Brown).

40 Wilfrid Blunt Papers.

4 At Home

1 W.R. Lethaby, *Philip Webb and His Work* (London, 1979), p. 99.

2 John Brandon-Jones, 'Philip Webb', in *Victorian Architecture* (London, 1963), pp. 255–6.

3 Mark Girouard, *The Victorian Country House* (New Haven, 1979), pp. 80–1.

4 Georgiana Burne-Jones, *Memorials of Edward Burne-Jones* (London, 1904), 2 vols, vol. 2, p. 109.

5 Adeane Papers (James Adeane).

6 Ibid.

7 Edith Olivier, *Four Victorian Ladies of Wiltshire* (London, 1945), pp. 95–6.

8 Ibid., pp. 99–100.

9 Wilfrid Blunt Papers, Fitzwilliam Museum, Cambridge.

10 Walburga, Lady Paget, *In My Tower* (London, 1924), 2 vols, vol. 2, p. 5.

11 Wilfrid Blunt Papers.

12 Adeane Papers.

13 Scrapbook of Madeline Wyndham, from the collection of Christopher Gibb. Acquired by Madeline's daughter Pamela, Lady Glenconner, sold at the Sotheby's sale of the contents of Wilsford House (home of Stephen Tennant).

14 For details of gardens see East Knoyle Women's Institute scrapbooks, including an interview with Harry Brown.

15 Ibid., interview with Mr Brown, 9 June 1906.

16 Wilfrid Blunt Papers.

17 Linda Parry, *William Morris Textiles* (London, 1983), p. 140.

18 Sold by Dick Wyndham out of the family, brought back by the Tennant branch for Glen House; sold by Lord Glenconner at Sotheby's for £50,600, 19 December 1986.

19 Clouds Papers (the executors of the estate of the late Geoffrey Houghton-Brown).

20 Private collection.

21 Adeane Papers.

22 Olivier, *Four Victorian Ladies of Wiltshire*, p. 94.

23 Adeane Papers.

24 Clouds Papers.

25 See Parry, *William Morris Textiles*; further information about textiles in general from Linda Parry and Mary Schoeser.

26 Clouds Papers. Clouds drawing-room carpet now at Cambridge in the Old Combination Room. See exhibition catalogue: *Morris and Company in Cambridge*, Duncan Robinson and Stephen Wildman, Fitzwilliam Museum, Cambridge, 1980.

27 Fiona Clark, *William Morris Wallpapers and Chintzes* (New York, 1973), p. 8.

28 Olivier, *Four Victorian Ladies of Wiltshire*, p. 92.

29 Ibid.

30 Parry, *William Morris Textiles*, pp. 83–4.

31 Evan Charteris, *John Sargent* (London, 1927), p. 174.

32 Adeane Papers.

33 Ibid.

34 Olivier, *Four Victorian Ladies of Wiltshire*, p. 91.

35 Adeane Papers.

36 Stanway Papers, Stanway House, Gloucestershire.

37 Pamela Horn, *The Rise and Fall of the Victorian Servant* (Stroud, 1990), p. 25.

38 Elspeth Huxley, *Nellie's Letters from Africa* (London, 1980), pp. 26–7.

39 F.M.L. Thompson, *English Landed Society in the Nineteenth Century* (London, 1980), p. 187.

40 Horn, *Rise and Fall of the Victorian Servant*, Appendix A: 'Domestic Servant Wage Rates', pp. 211–15; also pp. 145–51. Also see Frank E. Huggett, *Life Below Stairs* (London, 1977), Chapters 1 and 2.

41 See Philip Webb drawings for Clouds House at the Dept of Prints and Drawings, Victoria and Albert Museum.

42 Local information.

43 See Horn, *Rise and Fall of the Victorian Servant*, pp. 100–101, who quotes Mrs S. Beeton, *Book of Household Management* (London, 1861), repr. 1888 and 1906, p. 21.

44 Stanway Papers.

45 Ibid.

46 Horn, *Rise and Fall of the Victorian Servant*, p. 81.

47 Ibid., p. 99.

48 Stanway Papers.

49 Ibid.

50 Adeane Papers.

51 Stanway Papers.

52 Ibid.

53 Adeane Papers.

54 Horn, *Rise and Fall of the Victorian Servant*, pp. 100–1, quoting Lady Violet Greville, 'Men-Servants in England', *National Review*, February 1892, pp. 816–17.

55 Adeane Papers.

56 Ibid.

57 Local information.

58 Information from Mrs Hall, granddaughter of William Mallett.

59 Henry James, *English Hours* (London, 1905), p. 260.

5   The Clouds Estate and the Agricultural Community

1 See F.M.L. Thompson, *English Landed Society in the Nineteenth Century* (London, 1980), Chapter II.

2 Ibid., p. 308; and see David Cannadine, *The Decline and Fall of the British Aristocracy* (New Haven, 1990), pp. 91–2.

3 Thompson, *English Landed Society in the Nineteenth Century*, p. 310.

4 Ibid., pp. 312–13.

5 Frances Horner, *Time Remembered* (London, 1933), p. 85.

6 Ibid., p. 198.

7 Ibid., p. 187. See also Caroline Dakers, *The Countryside at War 1914–1918* (London, 1987).

8 Thompson, *English Landed Society in the Nineteenth Century*, p. 314.

9 East Knoyle Women's Institute scrapbooks, East Knoyle, Wiltshire.

10 Messrs Driver, *Particulars of a valuable and highly important Freehold Residential Investment and Sporting Domain, situate at East Knoyle, Wiltshire* (London, 1876).

11 Stanway Papers, Stanway House, Gloucestershire.

12 Violet Bradby, *A Family Chronicle* (Plymouth, 1942), pp. 44–5.

13 See Nikolaus Pevsner, *Wiltshire* (Harmondsworth, 1975); Victoria County History for Wiltshire (London, 1980), vol. II; Colonel Stephen Scammell's typescript of his history of East Knoyle parish.

14 Rory Spence, 'Theory and Practice in the Early Work of the Society for the Protection of Ancient Buildings', in *A School of Rational Builders*, Heinz Gallery exhibition catalogue 10 March–1 May 1982, p. 9.

15 Neville Lytton, *The English Country Gentleman* (London, 1925), p. 25.

16 Edith Young, *The History of East Knoyle School* (Salisbury, 1984).

17 Canon Milford, East Knoyle parish magazine, quoted by Young, *History of East Knoyle School*.

18 Adeane Papers (James Adeane).

19 Young, *History of East Knoyle School*.

20 Stanway Papers.

21 Ibid.

22 Ibid.

23 Cannadine, *Decline and Fall of the British Aristocracy*, p. 148, quoting Lord Willoughby de Broke.

24 Private collection.

25 Cannadine, *Decline and Fall of the British Aristocracy*, p. 142.

26 Thompson, *English Landed Society in the Nineteenth Century*, p. 95.

27 Bradby, *A Family Chronicle*, p. 36.

28 Nancy Waters Ellenberger, 'The Souls: High Society and Politics in Late Victorian England', PhD thesis, University of Oregon, 1982, p. 150.

6   Clouds Rises

1 Henry James, *The Portrait of a Lady* (Harmondsworth, 1979), pp. 5–7; first published 1881.

2 Wilfrid Blunt Papers, Fitzwilliam Museum, Cambridge.

3 Ibid.

4 Lord Drumlanrig shot himself, possibly because of the threat of blackmail over his relationship with Lord Rosebery; Bosie was besotted with Oscar Wilde and contributed to his downfall.

5 Wilfrid Blunt Papers.

6 Ibid.

7 Henry James, 'The Private Life', *Atlantic Monthly*, April 1892, repr. in *The Figure in the Carpet* (Harmondsworth, 1986), p.212.

8 J.W. Mackail and Guy Wyndham (eds) *The Life and Letters of George Wyndham* (London, 1926), 2 vols, vol.1, p.39. Also Wilfrid Blunt Papers.

9 Mackail and Wyndham, *Life and Letters of George Wyndham*, vol.1, p.213.

10 Henry James, *The Tragic Muse* (Harmondsworth, 1982), Chapter 9; first published 1890.

11 Wilfrid Blunt Papers. Also see Max Egremont, *The Cousins* p.88 – letter from Duke of Westminster to George giving his consent:

> I hope that all will go well, tho' you cannot expect that I give my 'consent' – all that I can do is to say that I will not stand in the way of Sibell's and your happiness any longer.
>
> It will be for you to do all you can, in the coming year, to remove all the objections that we all see and feel to exist.

12 Mackail and Wyndham, *Life and Letters of George Wyndham*, vol.1, p.188.

13 See Jane Ridley and Clayre Percy, *The Letters of Arthur Balfour and Lady Elcho 1885–1917* (London, 1992), pp.34–5.

14 Wilfrid Blunt Papers.

15 Ibid.

16 Ibid.

17 See Ridley and Percy, *Letters of Arthur Balfour and Lady Elcho*, p.77. Mary Elcho comments on the elaborate grounds of Wrest, the home of the Wyndhams' friends Lord and Lady de Grey: 'Shady alleys, delicious yew thickets, ponds, summer houses, and gardens make it perfect for all conversational purposes.'

18 Wilfrid Blunt Papers.

19 Stanway Papers, Stanway House, Gloucestershire.

20 Henry James, *The Spoils of Poynton*, (Harmondsworth, 1964), p.7; first published 1897.

21 See Jane Abdy and Charlotte Gere, *The Souls* (London, 1984).

22 James, *The Spoils of Poynton*, pp.11–12.

23 Ibid., pp.18–19.

24 Ibid., pp.179–80.

25 Ibid., p.11.

26 Nicola Beauman, *Cynthia Asquith* (London, 1987), p.3.

27 Wyndham Papers (Joan Wyndham).

28 Ibid.

29 Edith Oliver, *Four Victorian Ladies of Wiltshire* (London, 1945), p.89.

30 Ibid., pp.88–9.

31 Mary, Countess of Wemyss, *A Family Record* (London, 1932), pp.22–3.

32 Violet Bradby, *A Family Chronicle* (Plymouth, 1942), p.46.

33 Victoria County History, also Elspeth Huxley, *Nellie's Letters from Africa* (London, 1980), p.1.

34 Huxley, *Nellie's Letters from Africa*, p.9.

35 Ibid.

36 W.R. Lethaby, *Philip Webb and His Work* (London, 1979), p.98.

37 Mackail and Wyndham, *Life and Letters of George Wyndham*, vol.1, p.231.

38 Egremont, *The Cousins*, pp.144–5.

39 Ridley and Percy, *Letters of Arthur Balfour and Mary Elcho*, pp.54–5.

40 Though much of the Sun Insurance Company records are in the Guildhall library, there are no papers which provide details regarding the claim on Clouds. It is interesting to note, however, that Norman Grosvenor, a close friend of the Wyndhams, was a director. No records survive from the Royal Insurance Company. The *two* claims would suggest Percy had insured the building with one company, the contents with the other.

41 Webb Papers; Lethaby, *Philip Webb and His Work*, p.99.

42 Private collection.

43 Mells Papers, (the Earl of Oxford and Asquith).

44 Private collection.

45 Information from William Mallett's granddaughter Mrs Hall.

46 Jill Franklin, *The Gentleman's Country House* (London, 1981), pp.148–9.

47 Adeane Papers (James Adeane).

48 Mary, Countess of Wemyss, *A Family Record*, p.11.

49 Earl of Wemyss and March, *Memories 1898–1912* (Edinburgh, 1912).

50 Clayre Percy and Jane Ridley, *The Letters of Edwin Lutyens to his wife Lady Emily* (London, 1985), p.96.

51 Walburga, Lady Paget, *In My Tower* (London, 1924), 2 vols. vol.1, p.104.

52 Cynthia Asquith, *Haply I May Remember* (London, 1950), p.63.

53 Mark Girouard, *The Victorian Country House* (New Haven, 1979).

54 Wemyss, *Memories 1898–1912*

55 Clouds Papers (the executors of the estate of the late Geoffrey Houghton-Brown).

56 Ibid.

57 G.W. [George Wyndham], *The Ballad of Mr Rook* (London, 1901), with pictures by the Hon. Mrs Percy Wyndham.

58 Mark Girouard, *The Return to Camelot: Chivalry and the English Gentleman* (New Haven, 1981), p.274.

7 The Wyndham Circle: Country House Patronage at Clouds, Stanway and Wilsford

1 See Nancy Waters Ellenberger, 'The Souls: High Society and Politics in Late Victorian England', PhD thesis University of Oregon, 1982; also Nancy W. Ellenberger, 'The Souls and London Society at the End of the 19th Century', *Victorian Studies*, 1981–2, pp.133–60; Jane Abdy and Charlotte Gere, *The Souls* (London, 1984); Angela Lambert, *Unquiet Souls* (London, 1984); Caroline Dakers, 'Patronage and the Country House 1880–1940', MA thesis, Royal College of Art, 1988.

2 J.W. Mackail and Guy Wyndham (eds), *The Life and Letters of George Wyndham* (London, 1926), 2 vols, vol.2, p.356.

3 Mells Papers, (The Earl of Oxford and Asquith).

4 Ibid.

5 Ibid.

6 Ibid.

7 Walter Crane, *An Artist's Reminiscences* (London, 1907), p.171.

8 Alexander Fisher, *The Art of Enamelling upon Metal with a Short Appendix Concerning Miniature Painting on Enamel* (London, 1906).

9 Ibid., p.36.

10 Wilfrid Blunt Papers, Fitzwilliam Museum, Cambridge.

11 Private collection.

12 Ibid.

13 Ibid.

14 Charlotte Gere and Geoffrey C. Munn, *Artists' Jewllery* (Woodbridge, 1989), p.238.

15 Wilfrid Blunt Papers.

16 Sold with Whittingehame contents after the death of Arthur Balfour. Exhibited by the Fine Art Society, October 1973: see catalogue entry no M29 in *The Arts and Crafts Movement, Artists Craftsmen and Designers 1890–1930* (Eastbourne, 1973).

17 At Gosford House, East Lothian, Scotland.

18 Nicholas Harris collection, London.

19 Collection of Percy and Madeline Wyndham's great-granddaughter.

20 Private collection, New York.

21 Information from Anne Cecile Lansing.

22 Nancy Ellenberger in her PhD thesis on the Souls (p.160) identifies such a response to art as being particular to the Souls: 'the feelings they expected to encounter were ones of reverence, or possibly poignancy, or melancholy, not those of anger, cynicism, or despair'.

23 Private collection, and Christopher Gibb collection, London.

24 Mary, Countess of Wemyss, *A Family Record* (London, 1932), pp.30–7.

25 Ibid., p.36.

26 Jane Ridley and Clayre Percy, *The Letters of Arthur Balfour and Lady Elcho 1885–1917* (London, 1992), pp.140–1.

27 Nigel Cross, *The Common Writer* (Cambridge, 1985), p.88.

28 Norman and Jeanne Mackenzie (eds), *The Diary of Beatrice Webb* (London, 1983), 2 vols, vol.2, p.255.

29 Ibid., pp.262–3.

30 David Cecil, *Max* (London, 1983), p.206.

31 Royal Literary Fund Archive, British Library, London.

32 Stanway Papers, Stanway House, Gloucestershire; Denis Mackail, *The Story of J.M.B. A Biography* (London 1941), and Janet Dunbar, *J.M. Barrie. The Man behind the Image* (London, 1970); Nicola Beauman, *Cynthia Asquith* (London, 1987).

33 Ann Thwaite, *Edmund Gosse: a Literary Landscape 1849–1928* (London, 1984), p.451.

34 The Edward Marsh Letters are in the Berg Collection, New York Public Library; see also Christopher Hassall, *Edward Marsh, Patron of the Arts: A Biography* (London, 1959).

35 Edith Wharton, *The Buccaneers* (London, 1938), p.135.

36 Ibid., p.272; see also Stanway Papers; Edith Wharton, *A Backward Glance* (New York, 1934); R.W. Lewis, *Edith Wharton: A Biography* (New York, 1977).

37 'Stanway House', *Country Life*, 1 July 1899.

38 'Stanway House', *Country Life*, 25 November 1916.

39 Ellenberger 'The Souls', PhD thesis, p.91.

40 Ibid., p.216.

41 Constance, Lady Battersea, *Reminiscences* (London, 1922), p.122.

42 Elinor Glyn, *Romantic Adventure* (London, 1936), pp.78–9.

43 Wilfrid Blunt Papers.

44 Walburga, Lady Paget, *In My Tower* (London, 1924), 2 vols, vol.1, p.151.

45 Abdy and Gere, *The Souls*, p.124.

46 Ibid., p.73.

47 Stanway Papers.

48 Paget, *In My Tower*, vol.2, p.309.

49 The Elchos' version remains at Stanway House.

50 Lambert, *Unquiet Souls*, p.80.

51 Mells Papers.

52 Margot Asquith, *More Memories* (London, 1933), p.111 on Harry Cust: 'if he had not had a fatal fascination for every woman that he met, [he] might have gone far in life. But he was self-indulgent, and in spite of a charming nature and perfect temper, he had not got a strong character.'

53 Simon Blow, *Broken Blood: The Rise and Fall of the Tennant Family* (London, 1987), p.115.

54 Margot Asquith, *The Autobiography of Margot Asquith* (London, 1920), p.7.

55 Glen Papers, (Lord Glenconner).

56 Blow, *Broken Blood*, p.121.

57 Ridley and Percy, *The Letters of Arthur Balfour and Lady Elcho*, p.123.

58 Paget, *In My Tower*, p.138.

59 Clouds Papers, (the executors of the estate of the late Mr Houghton-Brown).

60 Mells Papers.

61 See Stanley Olson, *John Singer Sargent: His Portrait* (London, 1986), Chapter 8.

62 Wilfrid Blunt Papers.

63 Clouds Papers, (the executors of the estate of the late Geoffrey Houghton-Brown).

64 Ibid.

65 Blow, *Broken Blood*, p.90.

66 Now at Gosford House, East Lothian, Scotland.

67 Wyndham Papers (Joan Wyndham).

68 Private collection.

69 Blow, *Broken Blood*, p.117.

70 Ibid., pp.115–16.

71 Private collection.

72 Clive Aslet, *The Last Country Houses* (New Haven, 1982), p.247.

73 Gervase Jackson-Stops, 'From Craft to Art. Detmar Blow's Wiltshire Houses', *Country Life*, 3 July 1986.

74 Mackail and Wyndham, *Life and Letters of George Wyndham*, vol.2, p.544.

75 Ibid., p.551.

76 Aslet, *The Last Country Houses*, p.249.

77 Blow, *Broken Blood*, p.122.

78 *The Contents of Wilsford Manor*, catalogue of Sotheby's Sale, 9–12 October 1987, p.7.

79 Philip Hoare, *Serious Pleasures* (London, 1990), p.9.

80 Blow, *Broken Blood*, p.139.

81 Lord Glenconner in conversation, 1992.

82 Blow, *Broken Blood*, p.140.$

83 See Keith Robbins, *Sir Edward Grey* (London, 1971).

84 See Hoare, *Serious Pleasures*, p.27. Professor Tonks of the Slade was a close friend of the Asquiths.

85 Laurence Whistler, *The Laughter and the Urn – The Life of Rex Whistler* (London, 1985), p.81.

86 Countess of Wemyss, *A Family Record*, p.37.

87 Ibid., p.175.

88 Aslet, *The Last Country Houses*, p.249.

89 Simon Blow, in the *Spectator*, 25 June 1986, reviewing George Ridley's biography, *Bend'Or, Duke of Westminster* (London, 1986), and quoting the *Survey of London*.

90 Aslet, *The Last Country Houses*, p.249.
91 Blow, *Spectator* review.
92 Hoare, *Serious Pleasures*, pp.384–5.
93 V.S. Naipaul, *The Enigma of Arrival* (London, 1987), p.175.

8 Death Comes to Clouds, 1910–14

1 Bruce Arnold, *Orpen: Mirror to an Age* (London, 1981), p.159.
2 At Stanway House and at Petworth House.
3 Wyndham Papers (Joan Wyndham).
4 See Elizabeth Longford, *A Pilgrimage of Passion: The Life of Wilfrid Scawen Blunt* (New York, 1980), p.368 and onwards. At his death Blunt left Dorothy Newbuildings.
5 J.W. Mackail and Guy Wyndham (eds) *The Life and Letters of George Wyndham* (London, 1926), 2 vols, vol.2, p.557.
6 Ibid., p.704.
7 Ibid., p.706.
8 Ibid., vol.1, p.71.
9 Ibid.
10 Ibid., p.72.
11 See R.F. Foster, *Modern Ireland 1600–1972* (Harmondsworth, 1989); Mark Bence-Jones, *Twilight of the Ascendancy* (London, 1987) and Max Egremont, *The Cousins* (London, 1977).
12 Walburga, Lady Paget, *In My Tower* (London, 1924), 2 vols, vol.2, p.423.
13 Mackail and Wyndham, *Life and Letters of George Wyndham*, vol.1, p.91.
14 Egremont, *The Cousins*, p.286.
15 Mackail and Wyndham, *Life and Letters of George Wyndham*, vol.2, p.543.
16 Ibid., p.551.
17 Ibid., p.638–9.
18 Ibid., p.640.
19 John Gross, *The Rise and Fall of the Man of Letters: Aspects of English Literary Life since 1800* (Harmondsworth, 1969), pp.174–5.
20 Mackail and Wyndham, *Life and Letters of George Wyndham*, vol.2, p.498.
21 See Nancy Waters Ellenberger 'The Souls: High Society and Politics in Late Victorian England', PhD thesis University of Oregon, 1982; also Nancy W. Ellenberger, 'The Souls and London Society at the End of the 19th Century', *Victorian Studies*, 1981–2.
22 Angela Thirkell, *Three Houses* (Oxford, 1931), p.39.
23 Adeane Papers (James Adeane).
24 Opinions expressed in correspondence with the art historians Raymond Lister and Simon Reynolds, 1992.
25 A.M.W. Stirling, *The Richmond Papers* (London, 1926), pp.370–1.
26 Mackail and Wyndham, *Life and Letters of George Wyndham*, vol.1, p.227.
27 Frederic V. Grunfeld, *Rodin* (Oxford, 1989), p.435.
28 Mackail and Wyndham, *Life and Letters of George Wyndham*, vol.2, pp.479–80.
29 Ibid., p.415.
30 Ibid., pp.747–8.
31 Ibid., pp.710–11.
32 Ibid., p.712.
33 Ibid., vol.1, p.122.

34 Ibid., vol.2, p.712.
35 Ibid., vol.1, p.124.
36 Ibid., vol.2, p.729.
37 Ibid., p.741; fuller version in Petworth Papers, West Sussex County Record Office.
38 Ibid., pp.713–14. Anti-Semitic remarks are fairly common among letters of the Souls. Harry Cust, for example, writes to Mary Elcho after spending an evening at Aston Clinton with members of the Rothschild and Sassoon families: 'organs were going by waterwork & orchids growing by electricity and ones nostrils grew thick with gold at every breath and we eat for two hours & forty minutes without a check, & of such are the kingdom of Israel'. (Stanway Papers).
39 Local information: interviews with East Knoyle and Milton residents, 1990–92.
40 Mackail and Wyndham, *Life and Letters of George Wyndham*, vol.2, p.729.
41 Ibid., vol.1, p.123.
42 Wyndham Papers (Joan Wyndham).
43 Mackail and Wyndham, *Life and Letters of George Wyndham*, vol.2, p.735.
44 Ibid., vol.1, p.123.
45 Ibid., vol.2, p.731.
46 Jane Ridley and Clayre Percy, *The Letters of Arthur Balfour and Lady Elcho 1885–1917* (London, 1992), p.294.
47 Mackail and Wyndham, *Life and Letters of George Wyndham*, vol.1, p.124.
48 Ibid., vol.2, p.748.
49 Mary, Countess of Wemyss, *A Family Record* (London, 1932), p.23.
50 Jane Abdy and Charlotte Gere, *The Souls* (London, 1984), p.124.
51 Ibid., p.125.
52 Longford, *Pilgrimage of Passion*, p.391.
53 Mackail and Wyndham, *Life and Letters of George Wyndham*, vol.1, p.126.
54 Egremont, *The Cousins*, p.286.
55 Ibid., pp.177–8.
56 Herbert Asquith, *Moments of Memory: Recollections and Impressions* (London, 1937), p.168.
57 Mackail and Wyndham, *Life and Letters of George Wyndham*, vol.2, p.740.
58 Egremont, *The Cousins*, p.294.
59 Mackail and Wyndham, *Life and Letters of George Wyndham*, vol.1, p.127.
60 Wilfrid Blunt Papers, Fitzwilliam Museum, Cambridge.
61 See Caroline Dakers, *The Countryside at War 1914–18* (London, 1987).

9 The Impact of the First World War on Clouds: Dick Wyndham Inherits, 1914–20

1 Adeane Papers (James Adeane) and see Caroline Dakers, *The Countryside at War 1914–18* (London, 1987), Chapter 3.
2 For details of the action of the King's Royal Rifle Corps in the First World War, see Major-General Sir Stewart Hare, *The Annals of the King's Royal Rifle Corps* (London, 1932), vol.5, *The Great War*; also *The King's Royal Rifle Corps Chronicle 1915, 1916, 1917, 1918,* (Winchester 1916, 1917; London 1920; Winchester 1919).

3   Mary, Countess of Wemyss, *A Family Record* (London, 1932), pp.281–2.
4   Richard Wyndham to Edward Marsh, Marsh Letter Collection, Berg Collection, New York Public Library.
5   Richard Wyndham, *The Gentle Savage* (London, 1936), pp.89–90.
6   Richard Wyndham, *Painter's Progress* (London, 1938), p.148.
7   Col. W.J. Long, *The King's Royal Rifle Corps Chronicle 1917* (London, 1920), p.69.
8   Anne Powell, *Bim: A Tribute to the Honourable Edward Wyndham Tennant, Lieutenant 4th Battalion Grenadier Guards 1897–1916* (Salisbury, 1990).
9   Private collection.
10 Lord Ribblesdale, *Charles Lister: Letters and Recollections with a Memoir by His Father* (London, 1917), p.16.
11 Adeane Papers.
12 Conversation with Letitia Fowler, 1986.
13 Conversation with the late Major Peter Brooke, 1991.
14 Jane Ridley and Clayre Percy (eds), *The Letters of Edwin Lutyens to his Wife Lady Emily* (London, 1985), p.372. See also Dakers, *The Countryside at War*.
15 See F.M.L. Thompson, *English Landed Society in the Nineteenth Century* (London, 1980).
16 Dakers, *The Countryside at War*.
17 See Roy Foster, *Modern Ireland 1600–1972* (Harmondsworth, 1989), Chapter 20; also Mark Bence-Jones, *Twilight of the Ascendancy* (London, 1987).
18 Conversation with the Duke of Leinster, 1991.
19 Bence-Jones, *Twilight of the Ascendancy*, p.193.

10   **Clouds Abandoned**

1   Conversation with the late Major Peter Brooke, 1991.
2   Wyndham Papers (Joan Wyndham).
3   Ibid.
4   Ibid.
5   Conversation with Mary Hall, 1991.
6   Richard Wyndham, *Painter's Progress* (London, 1938), p.21.
7   Peter Quennell, *The Marble Fount* (London, 1976), p.127.
8   Wyndham, *Painter's Progress*, p.169.
9   Stanway Papers, Stanway House and information from Wellington College.
10 Major Jack Poole, *Undiscovered Ends* (London, 1957), p.8.
11 See, for example, John Pearson, *Facades: Edith, Osbert and Sacheverell Sitwell* (London, 1978); Barbara Wadsworth, *Edward Wadsworth: A Painter's Life* (Wilton, 1989); Francis Wheen, *Tom Driberg: His Life and Indiscretions* (London, 1990); Julian Symons, *A.J.A. Symons, His Life and Speculations* (Oxford, 1986); Michael Luke, *David Tennant and the Gargoyle Years* (London, 1991); Cyril Connolly *The Unquiet Grave: A Word Cycle* (London, 1951) and Peter Quennell, *The Marble Fount*.
12 Francis Wyndham, 'The Half Brother', in *Mrs Henderson and Other Stories* (London, 1985), p.38.
13 Wyndham, *Painter's Progress*, p.96.
14 Local information: conversations with residents of East Knoyle and Milton, 1991–2.
15 Wyndham Papers (Joan Wyndham).
16 Wyndham Lewis, *Blasting and Bombardiering* (London, 1937), pp.236–7.
17 Ibid.
18 See Christopher Hassall, *Edward Marsh, Patron of the Arts: A Biography* (London, 1959).
19 Edward Marsh Letter Collection, Berg Collection, New York Public Library.
20 Wyndham Lewis Letters, Cornell University Library. Selection published in W.K. Rose (ed.), *The Letters of Wyndham Lewis* (London, 1963).
21 Ibid.
22 Pearson, *Facades*, p.188.
23 Information from East Knoyle Women's Institute scrapbooks and Edith Young, *The History of East Knoyle School*, (Salisbury, 1984).
24 Local information; information from descendants of Mosselman's family.
25 Correspondence and conversation with Peter Quennell, 1989–91.
26 See Symons, *A.J.A. Symons: His Life and Speculations.*
27 Richard Wyndham, *South-Eastern Survey* (London, 1940), p.2.
28 Osbert Sitwell, *Left Hand Right Hand* (London, 1952), p.225. Much later, Dick's first cousin Robert Adeane, a discerning art collector and very successful businessman, tried to buy back *The Wyndham Sisters*. The Metropolitan Museum would not be persuaded to sell.
29 See Francis Wyndham, 'Ursula', in *Mrs Henderson and Other Stories*, pp.53–123.
30 Tickerage visitors' book, private collection.
31 Jeffrey Meyers, *The Enemy: A Biography of Wyndham Lewis* (London, 1980), p.113.
32 Wadsworth, *Edward Wadsworth*, p.134.
33 Wyndham Lewis Letters.
34 Meyers, *The Enemy*, p.112.
35 Richard Wyndham, *A Book of Towers and other Buildings of Southern Europe: A Series of Dry-Points Engraved by Richard Wyndham and with an Introduction and Brief Description by Sacheverell Sitwell* (London, 1928).
36 Edward Marsh Letter Collection.
37 Wyndham Lewis Letters.
38 Ibid.
39 Ibid.
40 Wyndham Lewis, *The Apes of God* (London, 1930), pp.178, 189, 191.
41 Meyers, *The Enemy*, p.176.
42 Ibid., pp.178–9.
43 Mayor Gallery archive, London. The early history of the Mayor Gallery is unclear. Information here comes from *The Times*, 10.1.25 and 19.10.25.
44 Included in Cyril Connolly, 'Matthew Smith: Job and Prospero', in *Matthew Smith*, exhibition catalogue, Barbican Art Gallery, 1962, pp.50–1.
45 Mayor Gallery archive.
46 Private information.
47 Private collection.
48 Knight, Frank and Rutley, *Illustrated Particulars, Plan and Conditions of Sale of the Freehold Residential, Agricultural and Sporting Clouds Estate*, 28 January 1932.
49 This sales catalogue and Sotheby's sales catalogues for individual pieces, furniture and library are in the National Art Library, Victoria and Albert Museum. Some of the items (in particular Morris and Company) in the Knight, Frank and

Rutley catalogue are marked with indications of prices obtained and names of buyers.

50 Patrick Wright, *On Living in an Old Country: The National Past in Contemporary Britain* (London, 1991), pp.40–1.

51 Luke, *David Tennant and the Gargoyle Years*, p.66.

52 Sold at Sotheby's, 19 December 1985 by Lord Glenconner, for £50,600 (*Applied Arts from 1880*, No.381 19 December 1985).

53 Caroline Dakers, *The Countryside at War 1914–18* (London, 1987), pp.203–4.

54 Wadsworth, *Edward Wadsworth*, p.353.

55 Tickerage visitors' book, entries by A.J.A. Symons, private collection.

56 Editing and commentary on wines by Serena Sutcliffe head of Sotheby's Wine Department.

57 Wine expert Serena Sutcliffe has also pointed out differences in taste: nowadays, we would not match dessert with a top Red Burgundy such as Clos Vougeot. She confirms that every wine selected was of very good if not excellent vintage.

58 Palinurus [Cyril Connolly], *The Unquiet Grave: A Word Cycle* (London, 1951), p.96.

59 Evelyn Waugh, *Brideshead Revisited* (Harmondsworth, 1973), pp.258–9, 255.

60 Clive Aslet, *The Last Country Houses* (New Haven, 1982), p.250.

61 Quennell, *The Marble Fount*, p.127.

62 Poole, *Undiscovered Ends*, p.69.

63 Richard Wyndham, *The Gentle Savage* (London, 1936), p.131.

64 Ibid., p.138

65 Ibid., p.34.

66 Wadsworth, *Edward Wadsworth*, pp.237–8.

67 A full-length description of the meal was written up by A.J.A. Symons for the *Wine and Food* journal and included in Symons's *A.J.A. Symons: His Life and Speculations*, pp.206–8.

68 Ibid.

69 Waugh, *Brideshead Revisited*, p.254.

70 Ibid., pp.253, 260.

71 Conversations with Pauline, Lady Rumbold, 1990–92.

72 Luke, *David Tennant and the Gargoyle Years*.

73 Wyndham, *Painter's Progress*, p.75.

74 Somerset House.

75 Poole, *Undiscovered Ends*, p.115.

76 Joan Wyndham, *Love Lessons: A Wartime Diary* (London, 1985), pp.6–7.

77 Joan Wyndham, *Love is Blue: A Wartime Diary* (London, 1986), p.31.

78 Francis Wyndham, 'The Half Brother', pp.45–6.

79 Private information.

80 Wyndham, 'The Half Brother', p.48. See also Mark Amory (ed.), *The Letters of Ann Fleming* (London, 1985), pp.50–3.

81 Ibid., p.48.

82 Information from Joan Leigh-Fermor, 1990–91.

83 Tickerage visitors' book, private collection.

11 From Home to Institution

1 Neville Lytton, *The English Country Gentleman* (London, 1925), p.167.

2 Information from documents of solicitors, Anstey, Sargent and Probert.

3 Correspondence with the descendants of Ernest Bartlett.

4 Ibid.

5 Lawrence and J.C. Fawtier Stone, *An Open Elite? England 1540–1880* (Oxford, 1984), p.375.

6 Information from Hilary Fitzgerald (Houghton-Brown) and the late Geoffrey Houghton-Brown.

7 Clouds papers (the executors of the estate of the late Geoffrey Houghton-Brown).

8 East Knoyle Women's Institution scrapbooks and Edith Young, *The History of East Knoyle School* (Salisbury, 1984).

9 Information about Charles Adeane from members of the Adeane family (his children Philip Adeane, Christine Page-Blair, Rose Adeane, James Adeane; his niece Penny Allen). See also Tom Jackson in conjunction with MIM Ltd, *The Origin and History of the Drayton Group* (Charles Knight, 1991).

10 Whitworth Art Gallery, *Modern Pictures from the Adeane Collection* (Manchester, 1962).

11 Information about Hewell Grange from the Earl of Plymouth and the staff of the Young Offenders' Institution at Hewell; also see Jill Franklin, *The Gentleman's Country House and its plan 1835–1914* (London, 1981), p.30; Margaret Mabey, *The Windsors of Hewell* (Birmingham, 1981); [Gay, Countess Plymouth], *Robert George Earl of Plymouth 1857–1923* (Cambridge, 1932).

12 From the publicity material for Wortley: *Labour's Education, Recreational Holiday Homes Ltd* (Manchester, n.d.).

13 R.W. Ketton-Cremer, *Felbrigg: The Story of a House* (Glasgow, 1982), p.349.

14 Correspondence and conversations with the twelfth Earl of Wemyss and March, 1985–90.

15 Earl of Wemyss and March, *Memories 1898–1912* (Edinburgh, 1912).

16 Children's Society Papers, London.

17 Correspondence with Colonel Scammell, 1991–3.

18 Ibid. One Scammell who sailed to North America became George Washington's Chief of Staff; another, probably reaching Australia 'at Her Majesty's expense', was the first of the Snowy Mountain settlers who opened up a drift way for his stock through the thick bush climbing 7,000 feet to the alpine pasture of Mount Kosciusko.

19 See Prebendary Edward Rudolf, *The First Forty Years A Chronicle of the Church of England Waifs and Strays Society 1881–1920* (London, 1922) and Mildred de M. Rudolf, *Everybody's Children. The Story of the Church of England Children's Society 1921–48* (Oxford, 1950).

20 Waifs and Strays Papers (Miss Ada Blake).

21 Ibid.

22 Children's Society Papers.

23 Ibid.

24 Ibid.

25 Ibid.

26 *Western Gazette*, 2 July 1954.

27 During the Second World War, Fonthill Abbey housed volunteer harvest workers of the Wiltshire Agricultural Executive Committee; American forces erected Nissen huts on the foundations of the old Fonthill which provided homes after the war for sixteen tenants of the Rural District Council.

28 Children's Society Papers.

29 Children's Society Papers.

30 Waifs and Strays Papers (Miss Ada Blake).

31 Children's Society Papers.

32 Information from Director of Life Anew Trust.

Index